RACE RELATIONS
IN AMERICA

Recent Titles in
Major Issues in American History

RACE RELATIONS IN AMERICA

A Reference Guide with Primary Documents

Thomas J. Davis

Major Issues in American History
Randall M. Miller, Series Editor

GREENWOOD PRESS
Westport, Connecticut • London

Library of Congress Cataloging-in-Publication Data

Davis, Thomas J.
    Race relations in America : a reference guide with primary documents / Thomas J. Davis.
        p.   cm.—(Major issues in American history, ISSN 1535–3192)
    Includes bibliographical references and index.
    ISBN 0–313–31115–3 (alk. paper)
    1. United States—Race relations.   2. United States—Race relations—Sources.   3. Racism—United States—History.   4. Racism—United States—History—Sources.   I. Title.   II. Series.
    E184.A1D283   2006
    305.800973—dc22   2005025450

British Library Cataloguing in Publication Data is available.

This book is included in the African American Experience database from Greenwood Electronic
Media. For more information, visit www.africanamericanexperience.com.

Library of Congress Catalog Card Number: 2005025450
ISBN: 0–313–31115–3
ISSN: 1535–3192

First published in 2006

Greenwood Press, 88 Post Road West, Westport, CT 06881
An imprint of Greenwood Publishing Group, Inc.
www.greenwood.com

Printed in the United States of America

∞™

The paper used in this book complies with the
Permanent Paper Standard issued by the National
Information Standards Organization (Z39.48–1984).

10 9 8 7 6 5 4 3 2 1

ADVISORY BOARD

Dedicated to
All those who toiled from can't see to can't see, for whom life
was "no crystal stair," but who labored on pursuing democracy in
America,
and especially to
Thomas Richard Davis and Mollie McDougal Davis
and
Thomas Balfour McKenzie and Margaret Whiting McKenzie

Contents

Series Foreword

This series of books presents major issues in American history as they have developed since the republic's inception to their present incarnation. The issues range across the spectrum of American experience and encompass political, economic, social, and cultural concerns. By focusing on the "major issues" in American history, the series emphasizes the importance of an issues-centered approach to teaching and thinking about America's past. *Major Issues in American History* thus reframes historical inquiry in terms of themes and problems rather than as mere chronology. In so doing, the series addresses the current, pressing need among educators and policymakers for case studies charting the development of major issues over time, so as to make it possible to approach such issues intelligently in our time.

The series is premised on the belief that understanding America demands grasping the contentious nature of its past and applying that understanding to current issues in politics, law, government, society, and culture. If "America" was born, and remains, as an idea and an experiment, as so many thinkers and observers have argued, issues inevitably have shaped whatever that America was and is. In 1801, in his presidential inaugural, Thomas Jefferson reminded Americans that the great strength of the new nation resided in the broad consensus citizens shared as to the rightness and necessity of republican government and the Constitution. That consensus, Jefferson continued, made dissent possible and tolerable, and, we might add, encouraged dissent and debate about critical issues thereafter. Every generation of Americans has wrestled with such issues as defining and defending freedom(s), determining America's place in the world, waging war and making peace, receiving and assimilating new peoples, balancing church and state, forming a "more perfect union," and pursuing "happiness." American identity(ies) and interest(s) are not fixed. A nation of many peoples on the move across space and up and down the so-cioeconomic ladder cannot have it so. A nation charged with ensuring that, in Lincoln's words, "government of the people, by the people, and for the people shall not perish from the earth" cannot have it so. A nation whose heroes are not only soldiers and statesmen but also ex-slaves, women reformers, inventors, thinkers, and cowboys and Indians cannot have it so. Americans have never rested content locked into set molds in thinking and doing—not so long as dissent and difference are built into the character of a people that dates its birth to an American Revolution and annually celebrates that lineage. As such, Americans have been, and are, by heritage and habit an issues-oriented people.

We are also a political people. Issues as varied as race relations, labor organizing, women's place in the work force, the practice of religious beliefs, immigration, westward movement, and environmental protection have been, and remain, matters of public concern and debate and readily intrude into politics. A people committed to "rights" invariably argues for them, low voter turnout in recent elections notwithstanding. All the major issues in American history have involved political controversies as to their meaning and application. But the extent to which issues assume a political cast varies.

As the public interest spread to virtually every aspect of life during the twentieth century—into boardrooms, ballparks, and even bedrooms—the political compass enlarged with it. In time, every economic, social, and cultural issue of consequence in the United States has entered the public realm of debate and political engagement. Questions of rights—for example, to free speech, to freedom of religion, to equality before the law—and authority are political by nature. So, too, are questions about war and society, foreign policy, law and order, the delivery of public services, the control of the nation's borders, and access to and the uses of public land and resources. The books in *Major Issues in American History* take up just those issues. Thus, all the books in this series build political and public policy concerns into their basic framework.

The format for the series speaks directly to the issues-oriented character of the American people and the democratic polity and to the teaching of issues-centered history. The issues-centered approach to history views the past thematically. Such a history respects chronology but does not attempt to recite a single narrative or simple historical chronology of "facts." Rather, issues-centered history is problem-solving history. It organizes historical inquiry around a series of questions central to understanding the character and functions of American life, culture, ideas, politics, and institutions. Such questions invariably derive from current concerns that demand historical perspective. Whether determining the role of women and minorities and shaping public policy, or considering the "proper" relationship between church and state, or thinking about U.S. military obligations in the global context, to name several persistent issues, the teacher and student—indeed, responsible citizens everywhere—must ask such questions as, "How and why did the present circumstance and interests come to be as they are?" and "What other choices as to a policy and practice have there been?" so as to measure the dimensions and point the direction of the issue. History matters in that regard.

Each book in the series focuses on a particular issue, with an eye to encouraging readers and users to consider how Americans at different times engaged

the issue based on the particular values, interests, and political and social structures of the day. As such, each book is also necessarily events-based in that the
key event that triggered public concern and debate about a major issue at a
particular moment serves as the case study for the issue as it was understood
and presented during that historical period. Each book offers a historical narrative overview of a major issue as it evolved; the narrative provides both the
context for understanding the issue's place in the larger American experience
and the touchstone for considering the ways Americans encountered and engaged the issue at different times. A timeline further establishes the chronology and place of the issue in American history. The core of each book is the
series of between ten to fifteen case studies of watershed events that defined
the issue, arranged chronologically to make it possible to track the development of the issue closely over time. Each case study stands as a separate chapter. Each case study opens with a historical overview of the event and a
discussion of the significant contemporary opposing views of the issue as occasioned by the event. A selection of four to nine critical primary documents
(printed whole or in excerpts and introduced with brief headnotes) from the
period under review presents differing points of view on the issue. In some
volumes, each chapter also includes an annotated research guide of print and
non-print sources to guide further research and reflection on the event and the
issue. Each volume in the series concludes with a general bibliography that
provides ready reference to the key works on the subject at issue.

Such an arrangement ensures that readers and users—students and teachers
alike—will approach the major issues within a problem-solving framework. Indeed, the design of the series and each book in it demands that students and
teachers understand that the crucial issues of American history have histories
and that the significance of those issues might best be discovered and recov-
ered by understanding how Americans at different times addressed them,
shaped them, and bequeathed them to the next generation. Such a dialectic for
each issue encourages a comparative perspective not only in seeing America's
past but also, and perhaps even more so, in thinking about its present. Individually and collectively, the books in *Major Issues in American History* thereby
demonstrate anew William Faulkner's dictum that the past is never past.

Randall M. Miller
Series Editor

Preface and Acknowledgments

Race relations have been a major issue in American history, for they have continually colored every aspect of American life. At every turn as the United States has looked to define and develop its image and reality, it has confronted race as an essential element of its popular perceptions and public practices.

This work outlines and illustrates something of the broad structure and sweep of race relations as they have ebbed and flowed to flood and drain the landscape of U.S. history. It attends to both the particular and the pattern to understand various historical moments. It suggests no neat line tracing origins and consequences from one moment to another. The course of history has rarely run so certain. The fact of history has been that things were exactly as they were only for the moment, for while similar to things at other moments, things never repeat exactly from one moment to the next. The patterns illustrated here show similarities, continuities, and connections; and they show dissimilarities, discontinuities, and disconnections. They show also the continuing social choices that have rendered historical results as they were as people acted out the fundamental human behaviors of identifying self and others.

U.S. race relations have been no story of fateful consequences from so-called unthinking decisions. Historical consequences have had no cast of immutable inevitability. History has overflowed with chance and coincidence. Yet choice always has been key, and it has formed the central theme here. People chose to perceive, believe, and act in selected ways to achieve selected ends. Race relations in the United States have been purposeful, not accidental. The conscious decision of choice produced them.

Concentrating on race may disturb readers who prefer alternative descriptions or who say simply race does not exist as an objective fact. The rejoinder is that the work here is not about scientific fact; it is about historical fact. And, simply put, race has persisted as a historical fact, constructed with cultural and social norms. Race has also been a historical judgment. It has been an expression and reflection of cultural and social assignment of values.

This work treats race as what scholars and commentators have come to call a "social construction." Race and racial identities have been conventions, ways of organizing perception and understanding that communities have created, imposed, and projected. The conventions of U.S. race relations have not been inherent. They did not arise by themselves. Rather, they have been extrinsic, arising externally as put-ons, as creations placed on persons. They have arisen and operated to excuse as reasonable and right the fact of different treatment of groups because of their perceived differences—differences often cast as irreconcilable. They have existed to exert and extend power.

Race relations describes patterns of social behavior and systemic social functioning based on group differences giving rise to advantage and disadvantage. Race relations thus have not been merely an aspect of intergroup relations but a distinct feature of power relations. Operating in a common environment of domination and subordination, race relations have marked interaction between dominant and subordinate groups given a racial cast. The terms *majority* and *minority* have sometimes replaced *dominant* and *subordinate*. But numbers have been less the issue than power. What has counted has not necessarily been how many but how much. What has counted has been power—the power to coerce, to have others do your will, to establish the standards that direct self and others to their position (their racial roles) within the society. Thus, race relations have been structured historically to foster and maintain power. Race relations have privileged racial roles above other roles; and the political structure of race has positioned other roles so as to privilege racial roles and in that way to privilege the dominant race.

The work here aims to illustrate, rather than to document fully, the history of U.S. race relations. It is suggestive, not comprehensive. It necessarily condenses the complexities and contradictions of a complicated reality. At best it can but hint at the voluminous detail of lived experiences that have made U.S. race relations individual, personal, and private. Its focus falls on policies and practices of public interaction with selected groups historically considered as races—primarily African Americans, American Indians, Asian Americans, Mexican Americans, and most recently Arab Americans—all with European Americans called whites.

It offers a limited set of examples that leaves much untouched. For example, the work does not treat how whiteness was created and maintained as a dominant racial category. It does not treat American anti-Semitism. Nor does it treat relations between and among subordinated groups. Rather, it focuses on dominant whites' relations with differing peoples of color. It does not treat the filtered effects of race relations, understanding that events have not affected all members of any group in the same way at the same moment. Individuals have not occupied the same space and time. They have not had the same experiences. Their experiences have differed not merely from group to group but also within every group. Nothing in this work seeks to suggest any homogeneity of experience among groups. Yet even when personal acquaintance or attributes such as gender, education, employment, income, or residence have tempered reach to any individual, U.S. race relations have nevertheless signaled structural limits in American life. They have reflected a commonality of policy and purpose: The short handle of that commonality has been white supremacy and determined nonwhite resistance.

To be sure, race relations in America have not been simply what whites have done to nonwhites. While the white/nonwhite dynamic has dominated U.S. race relations, it has hardly captured the entirety. Race relations in America have reflected continuing struggles for power among, between, and within groups. The multiplicity of encounters and the multiple intersections of groups with shifting positions and divergent perspectives have given U.S. race relations almost innumerable aspects and facets. The focus here has been on the powerful, historical core. Other foci offer points for other works.

This work presents fifteen extended historical moments that have indicated and influenced the course and content of U.S. race relations as public policy or popular practice. An essay introduces each moment to suggest its character and course. Then follow usually four to eight documents to supply varying perspectives from persons who lived the moment. An annotated research guide to print and nonprint sources—including audiovisual and electronic materials—closes the reflection on the moment. Overlapping time among the moments reinforces their commonalities and strengthens understanding of race relations as integral and shared history rather than isolated events confined in any false dichotomy of simple pairings such as black-white, red-white, Asian-American, or Latino-Anglo.

Race relations have not been aberrations in U.S. development. Rather, they have expressed realities at the core of America's life and development as a national community and as constituent state and local communities. They have conditioned how the nation and its people have perceived themselves and others and ordered their lives. Whether or how the persistent patterns of American race relations will continue time will tell. As in all the past, the substance of the historical moment depends on how people choose to see and treat themselves and others.

I thank the many who made this work a reality. Special thanks go to series editor Randall M. Miller for inviting me to do the book and for persevering with good humor through the too-long process. Similarly, I thank my editors at Greenwood Press, Barbara Rader and Michael Hermann, for their patience, and copyeditor Susan E. Badger and project editor John Donohue for their work. My thanks for support from the Arizona State University College of Law and particularly to my colleague Robert N. Clinton for sharing with me his immense expertise on U.S. federal Indian law and history; to Sonja Quinones and Sharon Kavanaugh, who supplied expert secretarial assistance; and to Victoria K. Trotta's able staff at the John J. Ross-William C. Blakley Law Library, especially Marianne Alcorn, Connie Strittmatter, and Jennifer Murray, who tracked, traced, and found documents and references.

My thanks also to Special Collections, Department of Archives and Manuscripts, University Libraries, Arizona State University, Tempe; to the Labriola National American Indian Data Center, University Libraries, Arizona State

University, Tempe; to the Library, Brigham Young University, Provo, Utah; to the Alabama Department of Archives and History; to the Lyndon Baines Johnson Library and Museum in Austin, Texas; and to the John Fitzgerald Kennedy Library and Museum, Boston, Massachusetts.

I thank my students who over the years have taught me so much about history, law, and life. For general and specific advice, aid, counsel, and friendship that helped sustain me and thus this project, I thank Diane Avery, Mary Frances Berry, Lula Johnson Davis, Alfred S. Konefsky, Asunción A. Lavrin, Daniel C. Littlefield, Moses N. Moore, Wilson Jeremiah Moses, and Mary Magdalene Mendoza Staten. Most of all, for reminding me of the most important thing of all—love—I thank beyond any measure of adequate expression Brenda M. Brock.

Chronology of Events

1619	Virginia settlers buy Africans as slaves from Dutch.
1622–1644	Powhatan Indian wars in Virginia.
1637	Pequot Indian War in New England.
1675–1676	King Philip's Indian War in New England.
1754–1763	French and Indian War.
1763	Royal Proclamation Line demarcates Indian "Reserves."
1775	Continental Congress creates the Committee on Indian Affairs—predecessor to the Bureau of Indian Affairs created in 1824.
1775–1783	U.S. War for Independence.
1780–1804	First emancipations in North.
1784	Second Treaty of Fort Stanwix with Iroquois Confederation.
1787	Northwest Ordinance; Constitutional Convention.
1790	Iroquois protests; First Naturalization Act.
1793	Fugitive Slave Act.
1793–1804	Black-led revolution creates Haiti.
1800	Gabriel's slave revolt in Virginia.
1807	United States outlaws importation of slaves beginning in 1808.
1812–1815	United States at war against Great Britain and its Indian allies.

1816	American Colonization Society (ACS) formed to settle free blacks from the United States to Africa.
1817–1818	First Seminole War.
1823	*Johnson v. M'Intosh.*
1829	President Andrew Jackson calls for Indian removal; David Walker's *Appeal* published.
1830	Indian Removal Act; Choctaw emigration begins.
1831	Nat's Rebellion in Virginia; *Cherokee Nation v. Georgia.*
1832	Sauk and Fox Black Hawk War; *Worcester v. Georgia.*
1834	Congress creates "Indian country."
1835–1836	Texas Revolution.
1835–1842	Second Seminole War.
1838–1839	Cherokee "Trail of Tears."
1845	United States annexes Texas as a state; journalist John L. O'Sullivan coins the phrase "Manifest Destiny."
1846–1847	Wilmot Proviso seeks to ban slavery from territory that may be acquired in the war with Mexico.
1846–1848	U.S. War with Mexico.
1847	American Colonization Society (ACS) colony in Africa becomes independent nation of Liberia.
1849	*Roberts v. City of Boston*; Bureau of Indian Affairs transferred from the War Department to the Department of the Interior; California Gold Rush draws Chinese immigrants.
1850	Congress stiffens the Fugitive Slave Act, outlaws the slave trade in the District of Columbia, and admits California as a nonslave state as part of the so-called Compromise of 1850.
1851	Treaty of Fort Laramie shifts U.S. Indian policy to reservation system; Federal California Land Settlement Act of 1851.
1854	Kansas-Nebraska Act.
1855–1858	Third Seminole War.
1857	*Scott v. Sanford* (the Dred Scott case).
1858	Coeur d'Alene War or Spokane War.
1860	Paiute War.
1861–1863	Cochise and Mangas Colorado Apache Uprisings.
1861–1865	U.S. Civil War.

1862   Congressional acts provide for rebels to forfeit slaves and allow for blacks to enlist in U.S. Armed Forces.

1862–1863   Santee Sioux uprising.

1863   Emancipation Proclamation; New York City Draft Riots; Shoshone War.

1863–1866   Navajo, or Dïné, War and "Long Walk" to reservations.

1864   Sand Creek massacre in Cheyenne-Arapaho War (1864–1865).

1865   Thirteenth Amendment ratified.

1865–1867   Ex-Confederate states enact Black Codes.

1866   First federal Civil Rights Act; riots against blacks in Memphis and New Orleans; Ku Klux Klan organizes in aftermath of Memphis riot.

1868   Fourteenth Amendment ratified; heavy Chinese immigration follows U.S.-China Treaty; Fort Laramie Treaty.

1868–1869   Southern Plains Wars.

1869–1877   President Ulysses S. Grant pursues Indian Peace Policy.

1870   Fifteenth Amendment ratified.

1871   Indian Appropriations Act; anti-Chinese riots in Los Angeles, California.

1872–1873   Modoc Indian War along the Oregon-California border.

1874   Gold discovery in South Dakota's Black Hills.

1875   Civil Rights Act.

1876   Battle of Little Big Horn.

1877   Anti-Chinese riots in San Francisco, California.

1877–1880   Victorio Apache resistance.

1878   *In re Ah Yup.*

1879   California's new constitution has anti-Chinese provisions; *Standing Bear v. Crook.*

1881–1886   Geronimo Apache resistance.

1882   Chinese Exclusion Act bars immigration.

1883   *The Civil Rights Cases.*

1884   *Elk v. Wilkins.*

1886   *Yick Wo v. Hopkins*; Geronimo surrenders.

1887   Dawes General Allotment Act.

1890   Congress reduces Indian territory to Oklahoma; Wounded Knee massacre at the South Dakota Oglala Sioux Pine Ridge reservation ending Ghost Dance Movement.

1893   *Fong Yue Ting.*

1895   Frederick Douglass dies; Booker T. Washington elevated in press as the national black leader following his Atlanta Exposition Address.

1896   *Plessy v. Ferguson.*

1898   U.S. war with Spain.

1898–1908   Rioting spreads fear of "Race War" and gives rise to the National Association for the Advancement of Colored People (NAACP), which organizes in 1909–1910.

1907–1908   Gentlemen's Agreement closes U.S. entry to Japanese.

1913   California enacts Alien Land Laws; ten western states follow suit.

1914–1919   World War I; Great Black Migration accelerates the south-to-north movement, which sparks antiblack riots that include East St. Louis, Illinois, in 1917 and Chicago in 1919.

1916   Marcus Garvey arrives in New York City and organizes a branch of his Universal Negro Improvement Association (UNIA), rallying black mass support.

1918–1921   Palmer Raids.

1921   Tulsa, Oklahoma, Race Riot.

1923   U.S. Supreme Court upholds anti-Japanese Alien Land Laws.

1924   Indian Citizenship Act; Immigration Act, establishing the national origins quota system.

1925   *The New Negro* anthology published.

1929   Oscar DePriest elected to Congress.

1934   Indian Reorganization (or Indian Self-Government) Act.

1939   NAACP organizes independent Legal Defense and Educational Fund (LDEF).

1939–1945   World War II; Nazi racial atrocities; U.S.-Mexico *braceros* guest workers programs.

1941   Blacks threaten March on Washington; Fair Employment Practices Committee (FEPC) created; Pearl Harbor attacked.

1942–1946   Japanese American internment.

1943   Race riots rock New York City; Beaumont, Texas; Detroit, Michigan; Mobile, Alabama; and Los Angeles, California.

1943–1944   *Hirabayashi v. United States* (1943) and *Korematsu v. United States* (1944) uphold U.S. internment of Japanese Americans.

1944   National Congress of American Indians founded.

1946   U.S. grants Philippine Islands independence; Indian Claims Commission Act of 1946 authorizes Indian tribes to sue U.S. government for recovery of land and other property.

1947   *"To Secure These Rights"* published; Jackie Robinson and Larry Doby break Major League Baseball's color barrier.

1948   Dixiecrats oppose federal civil rights initiatives.

1953   Baton Rouge Bus Boycott.

1954   *Hernandez v. Texas* outlaws racial discrimination against Mexican Americans; two weeks later *Brown v. Board of Education of Topeka* outlaws racial segregation against blacks in public schools.

1955–1956   Montgomery Bus Boycott leads to *Browder v. Gayle*, outlawing racial discrimination in public transportation.

1957   Rev. Martin Luther King Jr. and others form Southern Christian Leadership Conference (SCLC).

1960   Sit-in protest movement spreads through the South; Student Nonviolent (later National) Coordinating Committee (SNCC) organized.

1961   Twenty-third Amendment ratified; President John F. Kennedy's initiates "affirmative action"; University of Georgia enrolls two black students.

1962   University of Mississippi enrolls black students.

1963   March on Washington for "Jobs and Freedom."

1964   Twenty-fourth Amendment ratified; Civil Rights Act of 1964; Cassius Clay becomes heavyweight boxing champion as Muhammad Ali.

1965   Watts riots in Los Angeles, California; Malcolm X (El-Hajj Malik El-Shabazz) assassinated; President Lyndon B. Johnson promotes affirmative action as part of the Great Society and War on Poverty; Voting Rights Act and Immigration and Nationality Act of 1965.

1967   *Loving v. Virginia*; black rioting erupts in major cities; National Advisory Commission on Civil Disorders created.

1968   American Indian Movement (AIM) founded; Indian Civil Rights Act of 1968 (ICRA); Martin Luther King Jr. assassinated.

1969   President Richard M. Nixon advances affirmative action.

1969–1971   AIM seizes and occupies Alcatraz Island.

1970   Native American Rights Fund (NARF) organized.

1971   National Tribal Chairman's Association (NTCA) organized; *Griggs v. Duke Power Co.*

1973   AIM leads seventy-one-day siege at Pine Ridge reservation, site of the 1890 Wounded Knee massacre.

1975   Shoot-out at Pine Ridge reservation.

1978   *Regents of the University of California v. Bakke.*

1979   *United Steelworkers of America v. Weber.*

1986   Immigration Reform and Control Act (IRCA) of 1986.

1988   Apologies and reparations to interned Japanese Americans; Indian Gaming Regulatory Act.

1989   *Richmond v. J. A. Croson Co.*

1992   Haitian refugee influx.

1993   World Trade Center bombing in New York City.

1994   California voters pass Proposition 187.

1994–1995   "O. J." Simpson double murder trial.

1995   *Adarand Constructors, Inc. v. Peña;* Million Man March in Washington, D.C.

1996   *Seminole Tribe v. Florida;* California voters pass Proposition 209.

1997   President Bill Clinton announces a national initiative on race.

1998   Washington state prohibits using race and gender as factors in state action.

1999   Florida bans race as a factor in state employment, contracting, or public school admissions.

2001   Terrorists attack United States on September 11, 2001; President George W. Bush declares "War on Terrorism"; USA Patriot Act passes.

2002   United States invades Afghanistan; Homeland Security Act passes.

2003   United States invades Iraq; *Grutter v. Bollinger; Gratz v. Bollinger;* California voters reject Proposition 54.

2004   Arizona voters pass Proposition 200.

RACE RELATIONS
IN AMERICA

Introduction

Race was fundamental in the construction of the United States. The universal tones opening the nation's founding Declaration of Independence in 1776 muted the divides, but harsh distinctions vibrated beneath the soaring words. The document denounced "merciless Indian Savages." It dubbed Africans "a distant people," in its draft, although the final version shrank from mentioning slavery or the slave trade. Clashing with racial realities, the resounding phrase "all men are created equal" rang hollow, and its echoes would ever haunt the American nation.

Like the Declaration of 1776, the Constitution of 1787 shied from direct mention of race. Yet it embodied the concept without specifying terms. It distinguished "free Persons," "Indians not taxed," and "other Persons." Some have insisted such distinctions reflected no racial discrimination nor really anything untoward but merely acknowledged political realities. In such a view, the Constitution simply recognized the relative position of three commonly recognized major divisions among the peoples who occupied the new nation's geography. That very divergence of opinion has represented a basic and persistent problem in treating U.S. race relations—a lack of agreement about what race was and about its reach as a fact or force in American life and development.

Distinguishing differences among humanity was neither new nor peculiar to the fledgling United States of America. Such practices and principles stretched far back. Cave paintings in the age before writing depicted discrimination. Ancient Egyptians and ancient Greeks did also. So, too, did medieval Europeans. All distinguished who belonged, who shared origins, who were related, and who were connected in what degree. Little counted more than "blood," denoting a lineage of physical characteristics. Appearances were compelling. And few features cast so deep a shadow as color in marking boundaries long be-

fore the relatively recent term *race* first emerged in English usage in the 1500s
to mean a group "connected by common descent or origin." In the 1700s race
came to mean "one of the great divisions of mankind, having certain physical
peculiarities in common."[1] Whatever the language, race was never fixed as a
scientific fact. It has always been a culturally constructed prism serving political and social purposes.

From the outset, race and consequent race relations dominated the history
of what Europeans in the 1500s labeled the "New World." Indeed, the New
World developed as a series of encounters in race relations as tens of millions
from Africa, Europe, and Asia joined earlier inhabitants of the place called the
Americas. Perhaps nowhere were New World group encounters more extensive than in what became the United States.

Colonial encounters projected the reality of race relations as first and foremost power relations. Quaint tales have sometimes personalized the contacts.
The romance of the Powhatan chieftain's daughter Matoaka, more commonly
known in history as Pocahontas, and the English Captain John Smith at the initial Virginia colony settlement at Jamestown in 1607 has excited more than a
little sentiment, with her saving him from death and later becoming the wife
of the pioneer Virginia tobacco magnate John Rolfe. Similarly, the story of the
Patuxent Indian Squanto's befriending the Pilgrims soon after their arrival
aboard the ship *Mayflower* at the settlement they called Plymouth has warmed
many hearts. Squanto's teaching the Pilgrims how to survive and their 1621
harvest celebration have become the stuff of lore as the first Thanksgiving.
Often lost has been the fact that neither Pocahontas nor Squanto fared well
from the encounters. Both became English captives. Indeed, Squanto was enslaved. During that encounter, he apparently learned English ways and words
that facilitated the part he played with the Pilgrims. The Christianized Pocahontas, baptized with the name Lady Rebecca, died of smallpox in England.
Her story, like Squanto's, may have signaled happy events for English settlers,
but they were hardly happy for the Indians. And in many ways Indian-white
relations only worsened. Skirmishes and deadly struggles such as the
Powhatan wars (1622–1644) in Virginia and the Pequot War (1637) and King
Philip's War (1675–1676) in New England more directly revealed the predominant character of the Indian encounters with settlers.

The nation's first century and a quarter of Indian-white relations revealed
race as a strong but unhealthful proxy for power and position. Race relations
were extensions of political economies that projected the management and
maintenance of power. Race relations were status relations that represented relative positioning between and among groups. They were about group positioning for competitive advantage and disadvantage. They were about
controlling land, labor, and other resources as part of group self-aggran-
dizement and self-enhancement. The other side was group dispossession and
disinvestment. Race relations were about peoples' being "put in their place,"
to use once fashionable terminology. They were also about peoples resisting
others to decide their own place.

While race relations in American history have consistently been about power,
whatever race has been as a social reality has been less immutable. Race has
varied, shifted, and changed. While flexible and, indeed, permeable at its

edges, race nevertheless has been stiff at its core. Race in America traditionally has fixed four clusters that have conflated biology, geography, and much more. The clusters have demarcated aboriginal Americans, African Americans, Asian Americans, and European Americans. Membership and meaning have shifted on the margin over time, but purpose has remained constant. The clusters created a continuing context for social interaction. They formed the framework for political place and social space.

Clumsily formed, the clusters represented a lumping effect that increasingly elevated Europeans as whites and distinguished others as nonwhites, often fusing internal differences to mask individuality and other distinctions. The lumping effect cast aboriginal Americans into a simple cluster. They became popularly interchangeable, except perhaps when friends or foes during war or when negotiating treaties. Rather than Algonquin, Apache, Cherokee, Iroquois, Navajo, or Sioux, for example, the cluster became simply Indian. African Americans suffered even more complete loss of distinguishable identity, separated as they were without communal continuity or connection to ancestral homelands, which many Indians retained. The lumping effect cast blacks as a simple clump.

From the nation's beginning onward, many whites felt ill at ease with either blacks or Indians. Some felt shame at how their community or their fellows treated Indians and blacks. For others, Indians and blacks stood as frustrations of what in time was called America's Manifest Destiny as "a white man's land." The vision of such a future appeared clearly in the nation's first naturalization act in 1790, which made only "free whites" eligible to become U.S. citizens.[2] Such a vision made Indian and black removal a common aim of early U.S. race relations, for each appeared embarrassing for the American nation at its beginning—and as it matured.

American Negro slavery, which would grow into the antebellum South's "Peculiar Institution," was at the inauguration of government under the Constitution in 1789 nearly everywhere present in the original states. New York in 1790 had 21,193 slaves, only a few thousand fewer than Georgia. By then *Negro* and *slave* had become synonyms. And by whatever terms, the American norm settled black as the social bottom. Indians were not at the bottom but altogether outside the developing American social scheme. They had no immediate position within the nation. The federal census of 1790 provided no category for them. They stood as outsiders. They marked the border of settlement or what some thought of as civilization. Thus, the nation began. It accounted blacks to be within the American body politic and yet not to be part of that body. They were the internal other. Indians were the external other. Many white Americans feared both and wished to be rid of both. That was the basic reality of early American race relations.

Hope flared in the young nation that the United States could and would soon rid itself of blacks. Consensus fixed the Constitution to stop bringing blacks into the nation. The predominant thinking was that ending the slave trade would end any black influx. The constitutional framers allowed a twenty-year window for importing slaves, and Congress closed the trade by statute effective in 1808.

Banning blacks from entry was a start. It did not, of course, do anything about blacks already in the nation. There the early thinking among many was that ending slavery would end the troublesome black presence. The so-called First Emancipation in northern states during and after the War for Independence (1775–1783) animated hopes that slavery's end lay within one or two generations. Some southern slaveholders, such as future president Thomas Jefferson, in the 1780s and 1790s said they saw and wanted a not-too-distant end to slavery.

What to do with blacks after slavery raised difficult questions. The predominant sentiment seemed sure that there was no place for blacks in the United States except as slaves. A continuing majority of whites agreed that once released from slavery, the place for blacks was somewhere else. Due to "unconquerable prejudice resulting from their color, they never could amalgamate with the free whites of this country," argued Kentucky's Henry Clay, the Speaker of the U.S. House of Representatives who would be a major national antebellum political figure.[3]

Early talk of what then was called "gradual abolition" included talk of colonizing blacks somewhere. Sending them back to Africa was a prominent idea that gave rise to the American Colonization Society (ACS) in 1816 and its African outpost that would in 1847 become the independent nation of Liberia. ACS founders included Henry Clay and such other prominent public figures as future presidents James Monroe and Andrew Jackson and U.S. Supreme Court Justice Bushrod Washington—the first president's nephew.

The bloody Caribbean slave revolt from 1793 to 1804 that gave rise to Haiti as the second independent republic in the Americas and Gabriel's aborted slave revolt in Virginia in 1800 made black removal more urgent in many minds. Anxious whites fixed on the need to hold blacks tightly in bondage or to see them settled at a safe distance. Few abided the notion of living with blacks except under tight control.

Proponents of an emancipation-colonization combination lacked the means and will to defeat blacks' natural increase. Nor could they keep pace with rapidly rising slave prices and profits after Eli Whitney's 1793 cotton gin led to rapidly expanding production. Blacks continued then to be relegated as slaves and shunted aside as social outcasts. When not enslaved, they were especially unpopular. When they proved useful as artisans or in other economic positions, their supplying services, usually to upper-class whites, provoked envy and anger among other whites. Competing with black labor, whether slave or unenslaved, was nothing white working people wished to do. They preferred no blacks around. And they made that sentiment clear in new states formed from the Northwest Territory. Beginning with Ohio in 1804 and followed by Illinois (1819), Michigan (1827), and Indiana (1831), territories that became new states in the old Northwest not only rejected slavery; they banned blacks. The trend followed the frontier westward. Iowa (1839) would also ban blacks. So, too, would Oregon (1849). Exclusion, either in slavery or distant separation, was the clear white preference in black-white race relations. Both public policy and popular practice endorsed it in the early American Republic.

While whites worked to keep blacks where they were until they could be removed, they consistently fixed on removing Indians from where they were, as immediately as possible. That drive set the early and persistent pattern of

Indian-white relations. It alternated war and peace but never wavered from pressing toward almost ineluctable removal of Indians from the path of white development.

Getting rid of Indians altogether was one means of removal. At times it approached genocide. By the end of the first century under the Constitution in 1890, relentless wars had reduced the American Indian population to less than 250,000. Pushing Indians from place to place without directly killing them was another way to advance white settlement. Using diplomacy rather than war produced treaties that seldom assured Indians a permanent place. Traders, settlers, and miners repeatedly encroached on lands U.S. officials set aside for Indians.

The treaties transferring Indian lands from the perspective of U.S. law reached back to a basic principle of European colonization. The principle was called "discovery." U.S. Chief Justice John Marshall explained it in *Johnson v. M'Intosh* (1823). In short, it reduced Indian claims to lands to those of virtual tenants. They were no longer lords of their ancestral domains in U.S. law that recognized their right of occupancy but not their ownership. The law vested ownership in the U.S. government. It also diminished Indians' sovereignty as independent nations. It reduced Indians to being "domestic dependent nations" that were "in a state of pupilage," as Chief Justice Marshall elaborated in *Cherokee Nation v. Georgia* (1831). "Their relation to the United States resembles that of a ward to his guardian," he succinctly summarized in stating what became a fundamental principle of federal Indian law.[4]

Shifting Indians' locations became an intermediate way to advance white settlement. It failed to solve the problem of where to put Indians so they would be out of the way altogether. Such a solution early and often proved elusive. President Andrew Jackson called for such a solution in his December 1829 annual message to Congress. He hoped to settle forever the national problem with Indians, whom he described as a "much-injured race." Congress responded with the Indian Removal Act of 1830. It provided for removing Indian tribes east of the Mississippi to unsettled lands dubbed "Indian country," west of the river. The Cherokee "Trail of Tears" in the 1830s illustrated the process. They and others of the so-called Civilized Tribes were not alone in their westward exile. Some resisted more than others. The Seminoles were perhaps the most resistant.

Moving Indians beyond the frontier never proved an answer. It had not during British colonial administration, as the failed Royal Proclamation Line of 1763 showed. Settlers respected no boundaries. They flowed hard after the Indians, impatient to bear any inconvenience or restriction arising from any Indian occupancy. So friction and fighting persisted. Shrinking the vast stretches allotted to Indians to more limited reservations increasingly became U.S. policy in the 1840s. Even that failed to slake white greed for what Indians had. It was as if everything valuable belonged in the hands of whites and, if not there already, should flow in that direction.

National values and visions underlay the framework of race relations. Contested as they were, constant tensions strained the balance and interplay of elements. Debate and dispute marked every apparent or announced shift in policy or practice. President Jackson's Indian removal proposal, for example,

set off unprecedented popular and political opposition. More than Indians resisted. Many whites worried about the meaning of the plan for the nation.
What would America be, what would America become, if it followed the proposed line and adopted the proposed methods? Such questions nagged the nation from its start. The U.S. Constitution's compromises over slavery, for
instance, readily revealed hostilities and suspicions clouding the present and
future of blacks.

Indian removal in the 1830s released more profound argument about the
character and complexion of America's national community. At issue was the
degree to which the nation was open. Was it to be closed from contact with Indians? Could Indians exist within the nation? President Jackson said no. Indians could stay as individuals but not as tribes. If Indians became and behaved
like others abiding by local and national law, then Indians had a future in
America. Otherwise, Indians could only face exile on the frontier, existing on
the nation's edge.

Jackson's view contrasted competing prospects for Indians. One relegated
them to external segregation. Cut off from regular contact, they would remain
within their own communities separate from other Americans. That was one
means of getting rid of them. Another means was to mix Indians within white-
dominated communities. That prospect suggested assimilation, which appealed to many as a solution. Not everyone believed, however, that Indians
could be made to stop being Indians or acting like Indians. Others believed Indians could be changed. If converted to Christianity, stripped of their communal ways and tribal living, and taught English and so-called civilizing arts, such
as farming, Indians could become indistinguishable Americans, advocates of
assimilation insisted. Others questioned whether and why Indians should stop
being Indians or acting like Indians. U.S. policy weaved unsteadily among the
prospects, seldom fully abandoning or embracing a course to simply isolate,
exterminate, or assimilate Indians.

As Indian removal plunged the nation into heated argument in the 1830s,
the continuing quarrel over slavery amplified. A slave named Nat, once held
by Benjamin Turner, along with several dozen others in Virginia's Southampton County killed more than fifty whites in August 1831. Nearly 200 blacks
died in reprisal. Opponents of slavery invoked what people called "Nat's Rebellion" as signaling the urgent need to end slavery immediately. Proponents
of slavery said the slaughter showed the need to suppress blacks more force-
fully. The clash increasingly pushed slavery from being a matter of troublesome property to illustrating race relations' function as a wedge. In that
historical moment, it separated the nation's northern and southern sections.

Slavery's divisive politics reflected how race relations permeated the full
range of American life and politics. It was not simply about black-white relations. Few whites in any section disagreed about blacks' position. Their dispute was not about doing more or less for blacks. They argued about what was
happening to whites. The dispute was about whites' vision of the nation's future. It was about distribution of power and position. The oppressed condition
of blacks figured at most as a tangent, as almost always true in U.S. history.

The focus of dispute fell not on slaves but on slavery as a system of political economy. The national concern was not slavery as an economic or racial

condition. Blacks were central on few agendas other than their own. The sectional competition to claim new territory in the nation's westward expansion exposed the internecine rhetoric. From debate about the status of Missouri in the Compromise of 1820 to the status of California in the Compromise of 1850, the conflict centered on the balance of power in Congress. That, too, was the essence of the so-called Texas Question that delayed the Lone Star Republic's being annexed into the Union from its Declaration of Independence from Mexico in 1836 until 1845.

The Texas Question led the nation into expanded dimensions of race relations. It introduced Mexican Americans as coordinates in the nation's social space. It incorporated territory that fulfilled the nation's self-professed Manifest Destiny to stretch from the Atlantic to the Pacific. With the Mexican Cession Territory that would become the states of Arizona, California, Colorado, Nevada, New Mexico, and Utah came an array of peoples whose presence and mobility along a porous 2,000-mile border posed problems. Peoples designated Indians within the area magnified the nation's Indian problem. The Apache and Navajo, for example, proved formidable in resisting the encroachment of white settlement. Questions raised in dealing with the near 80,000 non-Indian former Mexican citizens presented further difficulties. The U.S. policy of Indian exclusion put the tribes at arm's length. Treating recognized former Mexican citizens raised matters of law, both domestic and international.

In the Treaty of Guadalupe Hildago ending the War with Mexico in 1848, the United States pledged to provide Mexican citizens who remained in the cession territory "enjoyment of all the rights of citizens of the United States."[5] Like the war itself, whether the United States ever lived up to its treaty promises long lingered as a sore spot between Mexico and the United States as well as for people of Mexican heritage in the United States. In the postwar period, U.S. treatment of Mexican Americans seldom satisfied the nation's highest legal standards. And that remained true for generations afterward. Dispossession proved the American rule with Mexico's former citizens, as it did in Indian-white relations. Most lost their claims to lands, and more than a few lost their lives in resistance. Their Latino heritage put many Mexican Americans, particularly those with non-European physical features, among disfavored U.S. inhabitants. Whether officially designated a race or not, Mexican Americans became a group treated much like Indians and blacks.

Not only Mexican Americans entered the U.S. race relations matrix after the War with Mexico. Thousands of Chinese did also, drawn to California in the 1849 Gold Rush. An almost immediate and ugly backlash met them. U.S. law offered them little comfort. Whites assaulted and even murdered them with apparent impunity. The California Supreme Court in 1854 released one convicted white murderer, for example, ruling that Chinese testimony against him was legally inadmissible. Circumstances worsened with new waves of Chinese immigration after the U.S. Civil War (1861–1865).

After the Civil War, the United States dropped all pretense of making a place for Indians. It reduced any image of the noble savage to that of simply savage. With its frontier rapidly closing as European immigrants marched west from their Atlantic crossing, the nation saw few places for Indians. It directed an end to tribal roaming. It wanted Indians confined to reservations, out of the way of developing settlement. More, it wanted Indians out of the way altogether. Thus did assimilation reassert itself as a solution to the Indian problem.

President Ulysses S. Grant's 1869 Indian Peace Policy aimed "to promote civilization among said Indians."[6] It hoped to pacify by conversion. Missionaries went forth to do the work. When they failed, the cavalry followed. From the Great Plains to the Southwest's deserts and mountains, the U.S. Army ultimately settled the issue with Indians. It sealed federal reservation policy. It hunted to death any Indians not on their designated reservation.

Notably, those whom Indians tagged as "Buffalo soldiers" stood in the first ranks of postbellum U.S. Indian fighters. Formally they were the Ninth and Tenth U.S. Cavalry and the Twenty-fourth and Twenty-fifth U.S. Infantry regiments. Recruited from Civil War U.S. Colored Troops, these grizzled veterans earned their foes' respect. But there was jeering, too, for one set of men of color set by whites to subdue another set of men of color. With the Apache chieftain Geronimo's surrender in 1886, the U.S. Indian wars finally ended.

The reservation policy was fully in place. Assimilation became the order of the day, as evidenced in the General Allotment Act of 1887. Also called the Dawes Severalty Act, the statute provided for treating Indians as individuals rather than as tribes. It aimed to destroy tribes by destroying tribal relations. It signaled an ultimate assault. Traditional Indian culture sat as the primary target. Federal agents sought to suppress all resistance, as illustrated in the so-called Ghost Dance Uprising with its tragic end in the massacre at Wounded Knee, South Dakota, in December 1890. Cultural amalgamation appeared to be the Indians' future. Their race relations with whites appeared to depend on the degree to which they became no longer identifiably Indian.

The Civil War wrought fundamental changes in race relations. In abolishing slavery the nation changed blacks' legal position. It provided blacks with civil rights and with citizenship itself, as it shifted U.S. citizenship from state to federal control. It further restricted state power to deny any person due process or equal protection of law. It outlawed "race, color, or previous condition of servitude" as grounds for denying the right to vote. The nation etched those changes into its fundamental charter with its three Reconstruction amendments—the Thirteenth (1865), Fourteenth (1868), and Fifteenth (1870). The principles marked a change in the customary conception and configuration of U.S. law and in race relations dependent on that law.

Old practices hardly fled in the face of new principles. Slavery ended as a legal form but not as a practical function. During and after the Civil War, most whites, regardless of section, resisted accepting blacks as full and equal members of the local and national community. For many whites the war's result represented the victory of their vision of America as a white man's land. And that proved true at home and abroad. For as the nation settled into its postwar recovery called Reconstruction (1865–1877), new waves of immigrants crossed from Europe to enjoy the bounty of what President Abraham Lincoln at Gettysburg in 1863 had called "a new birth of freedom."

The war's aftermath opened new vistas. It promised profound changes in race relations. Blacks' dreams of freedom clearly expanded American images of "life, liberty, and the pursuit of happiness." Many of those images disgusted whites. For them, full black freedom recurred as a nightmare. It terrified them. The prospect of unrestrained blacks ruined what many whites viewed as the proper and prosperous life to which they were entitled.

A central postbellum question fixed on labor. Who would do the work blacks had done, work that most whites refused to do, at least under the conditions that blacks labored? Working as blacks had was slavery, and whites refused to be reduced to that. Indeed, for many whites, working *with* blacks was to be reduced to slavery, and that they also rejected. They wanted no contact with blacks. They shrank from working with blacks except as their clear superiors. They recoiled from living near blacks who were not in service to them. In short, most whites detested any contact with blacks; and where contact occurred, they preferred clear lines of separation.

So while the law of slavery died, the lines of black-white racial separation brightened and broadened. Law no longer excluded blacks from being recognized as persons. They ceased being property as slaves. They had rights by law. Popular attitudes did not, however, allow blacks to practice all the law allowed. Further, the apparent promises of postbellum legal change proved soon shallow. Possibilities and permissions receded with Reconstruction.

Ending slavery returned thinking to black removal. And not by whites alone. Former slaves saw freedom as a chance to move. For many, their first steps were to cities that had served as havens for antebellum free blacks. But their retreats seldom proved safe. White residents resented black inflow. Major and minor violence resulted. The Memphis riot of May 1866 represented the worst. Its backwash spawned the Ku Klux Klan. Similar self-appointed groups determined to maintain local white domination and black subordination by any means necessary.

Many blacks increasingly fled the vehemence and violence of that racial subjugation. The results spread the old, sectional "slave problem" into a national "Negro problem." The South—defined as the fifteen states that in 1860 maintained slavery—held 95 of every 100 blacks in the United States when the Civil War ended. The number dwindled from there. Within a half century it was only 89. Within a century, it was a mere 45. Blacks surrendering hope of change in the South reached for opportunities in other regions. They flowed west. Some stopped on the Plains, like the Exodusters from the 1870s to 1890s in Kansas. Others went as far as they could, ending in California. Most went north.

The expanded black presence merged with a peaking flow of immigrants from abroad. The combination proved volatile. Black competition with whites for jobs, housing, political place, and social space strained relations. Both native-born whites and foreign-born whites, who suffered their own resentments with each other, joined in common cause with their shared whiteness to exclude blacks from living and working spaces.

Blacks were not alone as objects of exclusion. Even more virulent revulsion greeted tens of thousands of Chinese immigrants. Entering mostly through California, as they had earlier in the Gold Rush, postwar Chinese immigrants spread along the Pacific Coast. Some went east, particularly to the booming port of New York City. On both coasts they crowded with other immigrants. Competing with them for jobs and space produced much the same response blacks experienced.

Chinese found themselves victims of riots. Their large presence in California made them particular targets there. White workingmen pushed statewide legal bans against Chinese workers. Political pressure mounted nationally to ban Chinese immigration altogether in 1882. The ban was virtually absolute until the 1940s and only slightly less stringent until the 1960s. So Chinese were unwelcome to come, and they were unwelcome to stay. They could not become citizens. Their rights were insecure. Like blacks, Chinese and other Asian children found themselves in segregated public schools.

Hundreds of long-term residents were deported in anti-Chinese hysteria in the 1890s. The turbulence also seized the smaller but growing number of Japanese immigrants. They, too, were excluded. An unofficial but effective ban followed the so-called Gentlemen's Agreement of 1907. Full, statutory exclusion came in the Immigration Act of 1924, which established a national origins quota system. Official U.S. rejection of Japanese entry festered with other ill will and clashing national interests, leading to Pearl Harbor in 1941.

U.S. treatment of Chinese and Japanese immigrants extended the old exclusionary lines developed in black-white and Indian-white relations. While never fully articulated nor acted out invariably in preset forms, U.S. domestic and foreign policy accepted the superiority of whites as a race, Europe as a place of origin and culture, Protestant Christianity as the holiest religion, and economic development as the highest human aspiration. Rejecting Asian immigrants showed the international dimensions of domestic race relations, as had the handling of Mexicans in ceded territories following the 1848 Treaty of Guadalupe Hidalgo.

Spanning the 1880s to the 1900s, Chinese and Japanese exclusion occurred as the United States grappled for a place as a leading world power. The 1898 War with Spain gave the nation an overseas presence. It made America a colonial power primarily in the Pacific and also in the Caribbean. It put America in position to bear the so-called white man's burden of enlightening the darker peoples of the world at home and abroad with blacks, Indians, Asians, Pacific Islanders, and people of Hispanic descent. Race relations thus became both domestic policy and foreign policy.

Other nations studied U.S. conduct. They scoffed at U.S. self-contradiction. The land where "all men are created equal" seemed no such thing. It purported to be a "new Colossus," boasting of exceptional importance not only in world affairs but in human history. Its Statue of Liberty, erected in 1886, proclaimed that its beacon shown on a golden door of worldwide welcome. Yet many stood unwelcome, debased as undesirables in America's vaunted liberality.

The outbreak of World War I (1914–1919) in Europe moved many Americans to cradle their nation's distinctiveness against dreaded millions of recently arrived, foreign born who had not yet become American. The issue was more than the oath of citizenship. It was a matter of identity. It was a matter of ancestry, appearance, heritage, and history. It was a matter of culture. It was a matter of race. Again, race reached broadly to ethnicity, national origin, and religion. Always present in different degrees, the elements complemented the traditional American distinction of color as race extended to its core as power-laden identity.

At the opening of the twentieth century, Americans obsessed over identity. They argued over answers to early and perennial questions: What did it mean to be an American? Who was an American? Who could be an American? Some answers were immediate and obvious to most Americans.

Blacks remained excluded. The infamous Dred Scott doctrine no longer held as official law. The Fourteenth Amendment nullified Chief Justice Roger B. Taney's 1857 ruling that persons of African descent had never been and could never be part of "We, the People," whom the Constitution recognized as Americans. Yet the separate-but-equal doctrine confirmed in *Plessy v. Ferguson* (1896) testified that U.S. law had not fully embraced blacks as Americans. Popular treatment left no question about blacks' lesser status.

So, too, with Indians. While born in America and, indeed, being the longest inhabitants, they were not deemed Americans. After 1868, law at least acknowledged blacks as U.S. citizens. Indians generally could not claim that right until the Indian Citizenship Act of 1924.

Chinese, Japanese, other Asians, and Arabs as immigrants had no right to U.S. citizenship. Law banned their being naturalized. It also effectively banned their even entering America. Political and popular pressure pushed Congress to extend the principles of the Chinese Exclusion Act of 1882 into the Immigration Act of 1924. It effectively closed America to most of the world's peoples outside of Europe. It reiterated the image projected in America's first naturalization act in 1790: To be American began with being white.

Granted, contention aplenty fell on the question of who was white. The Irish and a succession of polyglot Europeans had to *become* white. Transforming processes of shifting sentiment and standards of social acceptability constructed common white people from Germans, Greeks, Irish, Italians, Poles, and Russians. Being white for many was a process of becoming that was political, social, and cultural. It brought with it privilege. It came with ideology. It was not static. It was never scientific or strictly biological. It existed as part of a divide. It turned on contrast. It was a separator. It was the unvarying standard for who belonged. Those on the edge desperately defended their position within the white race. They violently rejected any association or contact with peoples of color, particularly blacks. Race riots in the first quarter of the century repeatedly confirmed the point. They bloodied the U.S. landscape from Atlanta to Springfield, Illinois, to East St. Louis, to Chicago, to the District of Columbia, to Tulsa. White violence sought to put blacks in their place. The Ku Klux Klan revived and thrived in the 1920s.

Many with only a tenuous hold on being white not merely accepted segregation; they advocated American-style apartheid in seeking to elevate themselves. It confirmed their identity. For some it was a rite of assimilation, a rite of becoming fully American. As U.S. policy directed Indians to stop being identifiably Indian, immigrants also were directed to stop being identifiably other and become indistinguishably American. Speaking English was a start. Calls arose with English-only campaigns to make English the nation's official language. Some states and locales banned foreign-language instruction in public schools. Assigning identity through attributes such as appearance and accent ran to the core of U.S. race relations. It put everyone into an ascribed position descending from white preference.

It was systemic. It colored every aspect of American life. It was overtly political and intensely ideological. Under the banner of protecting America, zealots reached from foreign tongues to also attack what they viewed as foreign thinking. The so-called Red Scare of 1919 and the Palmer Raids of 1918–1921 illustrated the reach. In the name of defending America and Americanness, U.S. Attorney General A. Mitchell Palmer, with his special assistant J. Edgar Hoover, arrested and deported thousands without notice or hearing.

From one view, Palmer targeted radical enemies who had infiltrated America. He removed those who did not belong. What he did had nothing to do with race. Yet from another view, what Palmer and his conservative cohort did was essentially, if not entirely, about race. It was about a view of the American race. Color was not its chief fetish. It focused on other physical characteristics. Primarily it fingered culture. It fixed public attention on vilified ideas and habits. It declared certain behavior un-American. Cleaving such primary distinctions cut to the quick of the thinking and treatment that lumped peoples in clusters, segregating them from common contacts. Its imitation ideals dismissed difference. It classed peoples as problems, stripping their individuality and, indeed, their humanity. It talked of the Indian problem, the Negro problem, the Chinese problem, or the immigrant problem. Many of those problems converged in the contentious 1920s. The initial result was a conservative triumph.

Ever-present resistance nevertheless scratched out a fresh basis for race relations. As the most visible minority, blacks led the movement against white supremacist exclusion and segregation. Having shouldered arms answering President Woodrow Wilson's World War I call "to make the world safe for democracy," black veterans returned home insisting on democracy at home. The emerging New Negro character of the 1920s exuded firm self-assurance in the face of segregationist debasement. Black masses rallied to black organizer Marcus A. Garvey's call for prideful racial identity and universal self-improvement. Indians likewise rallied in rejecting assimilationist models and insisting on tribal development, to which Congress acceded in part in the Indian Self-Government Act of 1934.

The collapsing national and world economies in the Great Depression of the 1930s shifted governmental positions, particularly that of the federal government, to allow blacks, Indians, and others to advance as part of the national general welfare. World War II (1939–1945) opened the floodgates of change, however. Active white hostility to living and working with blacks hardly abated. The national emergency nevertheless advanced mobility, housing, and jobs. It reaccelerated the Great Migration of blacks from south to north. Black populations in northern industrial cities multiplied almost exponentially. Riots in Detroit and New York in 1943 showed the persisting and rising racial tensions.

America's two-front war exposed its hypocrisy. In Europe it fought Adolf Hitler's Germany as a monster vilified for its racist asserted superiority and extermination. Yet in the Pacific, America fought an enemy it racially vilified. At home it used race to create its own concentration camps, interning Japanese Americans by the tens of thousands. It imprisoned Germans and Italians, too, but nowhere on the same scale. It strictly segregated its servicemen. Indeed, German prisoners of war (POWs) enjoyed privileges denied black GIs.

Victory in Europe and Victory over Japan raised expectations of changing relations. Peoples long held as European colonies in Africa and Asia seized the momentum for their independence. The United States was not immune as a colonial power. After long delay, on July 4, 1946, it proclaimed the Philippine Islands independent. At home, it reorganized to answer demands to desegregate. On the world stage, it faced an audience applauding "recognition of the inherent dignity and of the equal and inalienable rights of all members of the human family," as the United Nations' Universal Declaration of Human Rights put it in 1948.[7]

People everywhere looked hard at how the United States handled its race relations. In the intensifying Cold War with its strategic posturing among Third World nations, how the United States treated peoples of color came under the spotlight. A candid world had long clamored against U.S. treatment of blacks and Indians. America's opening the atomic age with two devastating bombs on Japan raised further questions. The United States stood self-conscious then, as it scrambled for the moral high ground against the Union of the Soviet Socialist Republics.

Insistent blacks quickened their confrontations to expose America's segregationist standards as corrupt and unconstitutional. The campaign commonly called the Civil Rights Movement swelled as it orchestrated national and international attention to the unacceptable conditions and conduct blacks faced, particularly in the South. Its theater featured simple right and wrong. The innovation of television in the 1950s allowed the campaign to conduct its drama for all the world to see. The American nation watched itself, most enthralled and appalled at the violent repression of black protest.

The scene reduced white supremacist to sad, appalling caricatures. As worldwide ridicule had scorned American Negro slavery in the 1850s, so in the 1950s worldwide ridicule scorned American apartheid. Airing the extremes of segregation gained public sympathy for black grievances. Exposing its legal inconsistencies earned segregation's condemnation as unconstitutional. The 1954 U.S. Supreme Court decision in *Brown v. Board of Education*, outlawing racial segregation in public schools, signaled the legal shift.

Law flowed as it had in the 1860s and 1870s with the Reconstruction amendments and the major Civil Rights Acts of 1866 and 1875. The Twenty-third Amendment (1961) provided for the mostly black District of Columbia to vote for president. The Twenty-fourth Amendment (1964) barred poll taxes in federal elections, eliminating that long-used device of black disfranchisement. The Civil Rights Act of 1964 and the Voting Rights Act of 1965 capped changes long hoped, prayed, and worked for. The figure of the day was a young, Southern Baptist minister, the Rev. Dr. Martin Luther King Jr., recipient of the 1964 Nobel Peace Prize.

Long-deferred dreams loomed. As white resistance to public school desegregation demonstrated, if law had shifted the structure or style of race relations, its substance remained stuck in many minds. As during the 1860s and

1870s, in the 1960s and 1970s even whites who agreed that law should not dictate any lesser status for blacks still resisted any personal contact with blacks outside of service roles. Most whites preferred not to live, work, or socialize with blacks. They fled to suburbs to avoid contact, by that fact segregating blacks in urban ghettos.

The cold reality of continued rejection clashed with blacks' rising expectations. The six-day Watts riots in Los Angeles in August 1965 exhibited the violent result. Sadly it was only an opening spectacle in a horrifying series of long hot summers with too-common cries of "Burn, baby, burn!" The five-day Detroit riot of 1967 further exposed black anger over police brutality, substandard housing, job discrimination, debilitating unemployment, and general public indifference.

The assassination of Martin Luther King Jr. in April 1968 triggered riots in more than 100 U.S. cities. President Lyndon B. Johnson's National Advisory Commission on Civil Disorders, directed to probe the causes of the 1967 riots, uncovered what most blacks and other people of color saw as obvious: America lay polarized. "Discrimination and segregation have long permeated much of American life," the commission noted. Deploring "deepening racial division," it urged "quick and visible progress. It is time to make good the promises of American democracy to all citizens—urban and rural, white and black, Spanish-surnamed, American Indian, and every minority group," the commission concluded.[8]

The rioting alarmed all America. Shock, fear, disgust, and dismay followed the violence. Yet it did not move everyone in the same direction. Removing legal barriers was the most blacks could reasonably require in the views of many whites. They merited no special treatment. The problems blacks faced were no different from the problems of others. If legal segregation had blocked blacks from solving their problems, outlawing segregation released them to solve their problems like everyone else. That was the view of many whites. Many fretted, too, that focusing on blacks, or more broadly on race, diminished attention they deserved for their own needs and desires.

The Civil Rights Movement stirred strong action and reaction in race relations. It stretched far beyond black and white. Indian cries of "Red Power" echoed in the 1960s and 1970s alongside those of "Black Power." From less than 250,000 in 1900, the American Indian, Eskimo, and Aleut populations more than tripled to over 825,000 by 1970. Having escaped annihilation, the tribes mobilized to fight another day. They appeared to face the same old foes that attacked their cultural identity and communal integrity. Their being American yet remaining apart as tribal sovereigns continued to rankle many. Their traditional and treaty rights to resources and exclusive rights also annoyed many.

The bitterness was hardly fresh. Nor were the continuing near catastrophes Indians faced from centuries-long dispossession and disinvestment. Groups such as the militant American Indian Movement (AIM), the Native American Rights Fund (NARF), and the National Tribal Chairman's Association (NATC) advanced Indian agendas. Their efforts represented intertribal alliances that many had urged since Ottawa Chief Pontiac and Shawnee Chief Tecumseh in the 1700s and early 1800s.

Political forces opposed to special treatment of groups attacked Indian sovereignty. They decried the new Indian militancy. AIM's 1969 seizing of Alcatraz Island in California's San Francisco Bay for nineteen months signaled the escalating confrontation. The 1973 siege at the South Dakota Oglala Sioux Pine Ridge reservation, site of the 1890 Wounded Knee massacre, and the subsequent 1975 shoot-out between Indians and state and federal officers compelled grave concerns.

State economies suffering shortfalls begrudged Indian tribes with burgeoning reservation gaming revenues. They resented the Indians' advantage and the renewed self-assertion it supported. Contention returned as ever to tribal sovereignty. Tribal independence from the states in which reservations sat was a sore spot that stretched back to the 1820s and 1830s, as illustrated in the U.S. Supreme Court cases of *Cherokee Nation v. Georgia* (1831) and *Worcester v. Georgia* (1832). States that outlawed gambling took exception to Indian tribes' operating casinos on reservations within the state's borders. At the very least, such states demanded to share the revenues. Similarly, states took exception to Indian tribal immunity from state taxing power. On commodities such as gasoline and tobacco, some states lost significant revenue to reservation enterprises.

Whether the United States had a special duty to Indians was at issue. Also at issue was whether Indians, blacks, and other peoples of color continued to be subjected to unfair treatment. After an intense campaign over a generation, Japanese Americans interned during World War II received an apology and reparations from Congress in 1988. Which, if any, other groups were entitled to an apology or reparations? Was prejudice all past? Were barriers, systemic discrimination, and deliberately inflicted damage simply bygone in race relations? Or were there, in fact, no longer any race relations? Had America reached the point of treating every person as an individual evaluated on her or his own abilities and achievements?

The issues of relative positioning that marked race relations from the beginning of U.S. history thus resurfaced in heated outcry, particularly as the federal government moved to do more in the 1960s and 1970s for those designated as "blacks and other minorities." The phrase "affirmative action" became a rallying cry. Indeed, it became a war cry. To some, such as President Lyndon B. Johnson, affirmative action meant advancing to achieve "equality as a fact and equality as a result."[9] To others, it meant "reverse discrimination."

If the antisegregation campaign had been legally and morally correct in rejecting law directing different treatment of persons based on race, then what, if anything, could justify such treatment after the outlawing of de jure racial segregation? That was the question affirmative action foes often posed. It was a question the nation's courts repeatedly heard in a line of cases beginning in the 1970s. Lower courts split in their answers. The U.S. Supreme Court itself wobbled. Few bright lines emerged as the Court ruled on what the Constitution permitted private persons and entities, or localities, states, and the federal government itself, to do in regard to race.

High stakes intensified contention in and out of court. Jobs, housing, schooling, and every other element of advantage and exclusion were in the offing—as they had been since the nation's start. Race served from the beginning to position peoples. Was that history at an end? "Almost, but not completely," the

Supreme Court seemed to say in *Adarand Constructors v. Peña* (1995). The 5–4 majority held that "government may treat people differently because of their race only for the most compelling reasons."[10] Clearly a compromise and inconclusive, the ruling nevertheless signaled a policy shift against affirmative action. Popular attitudes appeared also to have yielded to intense campaigning that railed against affirmative action as a program of "preferential treatment." California voters in 1996 and Washington voters in 1998 evidenced the tide in banning their state's use of race- or gender-based affirmative action.

A majority of voters with a consistent white core had appeared fed up with race matters as Ronald Reagan rose to the presidency in 1980. They rallied to calls for a color-blind America. Yet anxieties continued to ride race as a whipping boy. Pros and cons trotted it out to show it explained either everything or nothing. It became the center of many misfortunes. It fed a large part of the nation's obsession with celebrity, former pro football star O. J. Simpson's 1994–1995 double murder trial. It fed fears and hopes surrounding the October 1995 black Million Man March called by Nation of Islam Minister Louis Farrakhan. President Bill Clinton saw the need for a national conversation on race and in June 1997 announced an initiative to advance toward "One America in the 21st Century." Opponents such as Republican Speaker of the U.S. House of Representatives Newt Gingrich of Georgia countered that "racism will not disappear by focusing on race."[11]

The polarity that the National Advisory Commission on Civil Disorders noted in the 1960s yawned ever wider in the 1990s. Anxieties over where the nation was and where it was going gripped many. Tightening economies and domestic and international unrest left many Americans uneasy about their present and future. Insecurity fortified conservative retrenchment based on America's need to refocus on so-called traditional values that thinly veiled a return to the old white standard.

Diversity and multiculturalism became anathema for many, just as affirmative action was. Calls of "America for Americans" and for "100% Americanness" reechoed in a fresh phase of centuries-old American culture wars. Campaigns for English-only and English as the official language gained popularity. Aimed especially at rapidly expanding numbers of Spanish speakers, the campaigns also carried nativist, antiimmigrant messages. Proponents denied that such were their themes. Instead, they insisted their topic was law and order. They were not against immigration. They were against illegal immigrants. Their focus fell, nevertheless, on darker complexioned peoples crossing the Mexico-U.S. border. And, in fact, hundreds of thousands, if not millions, of undocumented persons swelled the waves of new immigrants that flowed after the Immigration and Nationality Act of 1965 scrapped the overt racial bars to gaining U.S. residence.

The new immigrants were primarily people of color. Many were from formerly excluded areas. China, India, and the Pacific Islands topped the new waves. The Caribbean and Central and South America also rose rapidly in the flow. Their impact on communities and labor markets was much disputed. In the context of America's being a nation of immigrants, few public commentators openly attacked immigration itself. They used *illegal* immigration as their front.

The traditional American practice of lumping compacted not only new immigrants but often the freshly arrived with longtime citizens. Dragnets for so-called illegals targeted people by physical profiles. Appearance, not behavior, served as the distinctive characteristic for law enforcement. Similarly, talk of "Hispanics" and "Latinos" often obscured individuality and divergent backgrounds. Old-line racial views awkwardly clustered Spanish-speaking, Spanish-surnamed, Hispanic, and Latino. Except among the peoples themselves, distinguishing Cubans, Dominicans, Colombians, Guatemalans, Mexicans, and Puerto Ricans, for instance, was often lost.

The same often was so among Asians. The episodic makeup of Asian immigration altered little of the singular set of Chinese features lumped as inscrutable. The wave of Japanese immigrants in the 1890s and early 1900s changed few impressions. Nor did the U.S. encounter with Filipinos following the 1898 War with Spain and U.S. colonial administration of the Philippine Islands until 1946. The Cold War arrival of new waves of Chinese in the 1950s and 1960s and the wave of Koreans that arrived at the same time altered few perceptions. The 1970s added Vietnamese and other Indochinese. Yet the distinctive peoples became indistinguishable layers within America's popularly perceived Asian cluster. Even the arrival of Indians from the subcontinent shifted few features of the fixed Asian cluster.

Worries about the face of America, about its character and culture, disturbed many of the nation's generations-old citizens. From many perspectives a battle brewed for America's heart and soul. Skirmishers engaged in California's 1986 ballot proposition to declare English the state's official language. The state's 1994 Proposition 187 ballot initiative to declare "illegal aliens" ineligible for state services revealed hostilities across a broad front. A sharp racial edge marked the battle lines.

The announced "War on Terrorism" following the attacks on the United States on September 11, 2001, whetted the cutting force of racial division. Arabs and Muslims became targets of opportunity as U.S. political and popular reactions appeared to retrace centuries of American history in referencing enemies by race and objectifying them abroad and at home. The retold story replayed the clash of power and privilege against democratic and humanitarian principles that has consistently constituted U.S. race relations.

NOTES

1. *The Shorter Oxford English Dictionary on Historical Principles*, 3rd ed. (Oxford: Clarendon Press, 1973), 1735–1736.

2. Naturalization Act of March 26, 1790, 1 Stat. 103.

3. Richard L. Troutman, "Emancipation of Slaves by Henry Clay," *Journal of Negro History* 40 (1955): 179–181; Robert V. Remini, *Henry Clay: Statesmen for the Union* (New York: Norton, 1991), 174.

4. *Cherokee Nation v. Georgia*, 30 U.S. (5 Pet.) 1, 17 (1831).

5. Treaty of Guadalupe Hildago, February 2, 1848, in Henry Miller, ed., *Treaties and Other International Acts of the United States*, 8 vols. (Washington, DC: GPO, 1931–1948), 5:219–222.

6. See 16 Stat. 13, 40 (April 10, 1869).

7. G.A. Res. 217 A (III) (December 10, 1948).

8. *Report of the National Advisory Commission on Civil Disorders* (Washington, DC: GPO, 1968), 2.

9. President Lyndon B. Johnson, Commencement Address at Howard University, "To Fulfill These Rights," June 4, 1965, in *Public Papers of the Presidents of the United States: Lyndon B. Johnson, 1965* (Washington, DC: GPO, 1966), 2:635–640.

10. *Adarand Constructors v. Peña*, 515 U.S. 200, 227 (1995).

11. See *One America in the 21st Century: Forging a New Future—the President's Initiative on Race, the Advisory Board's Report to the President* (Washington, DC: GPO, 1998); and Craig Hines, "Gingrich Predicts Failure of 'Traditional' Panel on Race," *Houston Chronicle*, June 14, 1997, A5.

1

Constituting the Republic: Who Counted as What?

By definition, the Constitution of the United States of America is the fundamental document of the nation as a federal republic. It designates the basic relations and underlying structures that make up the nation.

Written in Philadelphia during a convention that met in the Pennsylvania
State House (later renamed Independence Hall) from May 25 to September 17,
1787, the original Constitution exhibited the prevailing state of race relations.
In declaring who would count as persons to determine national policy, it fixed
an apportionment formula calculated on the basis of "the whole number of
free Persons, including those bound to service for a term of years, and excluding Indians not taxed, [and] three fifths of all other Persons."[1] The formula faintly coded three groups. The phrases "free Persons" and "other
Persons" thinly veiled direct references to whites and enslaved blacks. The
meaning was hardly secret. Readers at the time readily understood the em-
bedded signals and symbols. Some in later generations could argue that the
phrasing appeared a denial of a racial standard or an acceptance of what might
be called a color-blind standard. Earlier phrasing in fact explicitly contained
the word *white*, but delegates eliminated the word in shifting to what appeared
a basis of civil status rather than color. The code allowed an ambiguity that
relieved the document from a blatant embrace of racial division in regard to
blacks and whites but not in regard to Indians, who were explicitly excluded—
although again on what appeared as civil status attached to the paying of
taxes, rather than merely race.

The phrasing acknowledged the historical fact that white was the national
standard in the Constitution's opening words: "We, the People." To be white
was the basic qualification to be free and to count fully as a person without
any further prerequisite or stipulation. The first Congress under the Constitu-

tion made the standard for citizenship clear when it provided in March 1790 that only "free whites" were eligible to become naturalized U.S. citizens.

To be an Indian was to be wholly excluded, depending on your tax status. That implicated where and how the Indian lived—whether with his tribe or separate from it in a state that accepted Indians as residents and taxpayers. The phrase "excluding Indians not taxed" encouraged an inference that Indians taxed were included fully in "the whole number of free Persons." But such an inference depended on interpretation, not plain language; and the result was more than arbitrary.

The first federal census begun in August 1790 included no categories for Indians. As a group they were considered to be outside the nation. They marked the border of settlement or what some thought of as civilization. They were the external other, even though to the east of the Appalachians—the 1,500-mile mountain system from Canada to Alabama segmenting the seaboard and the hinterland—settlements entirely surrounded remnants of tribes such as the Six Nations of the Iroquois Confederacy (the Mohawk, Oneida, Onondaga, Cayuga, Seneca, and Tuscarora) in New York or the Penobscot and the Passamaquoddy in what became Maine. Indians thus occupied an anomalous status. They were separate polities sometimes treated as autonomous and independent units capable of entering and maintaining treaties. But what sovereignty Indians had was increasingly conditional in the view of U.S. law. Chief Justice John Marshall reflected the wavering view in *Cherokee Nation v. Georgia* (1831). Rather than sovereign nations, Indians were "domestic, dependent nation[s]," he declared.[2] Their members were not part of the U.S. population included in "We, the People." (Indians generally were not deemed U.S. citizens until 1924.)

As Indians stood as an external "other," blacks stood as an internal "other." Counted only partially, depending on condition and state of residence, blacks were not fully among "We, the People." Chief Justice Roger Brooke Taney made blacks' separate status legendary in his notorious opinion in the Dred Scott case in 1857. "The words 'people of the United States' and 'citizens' are synonymous terms, and mean the same thing. They both describe the political body who . . . form the sovereignty, and who hold the power and conduct the Government through their representatives," he explained. On that basis, "people of African ancestry" did not and could not "compose a portion of this people" or be "constituent members of this sovereignty."[3]

Elaborating on the status of "people of African ancestry," Taney declared that

> they are not included, and were not intended to be included, under the word "citizens" in the Constitution, and can therefore claim none of the rights and privileges which that instrument provides for and secures to citizens of the United States. On the contrary, they were at that time considered as a subordinate and inferior class of beings, who had been subjugated by the dominant race, and, whether emancipated or not, yet remained subject to their authority, and had no rights or privileges but such as those who held the power and the Government might choose to grant them.[4]

From such a vision of the original U.S. Constitution, blacks' status would follow its own peculiar set of rules in U.S. law and society.

A more extensive code than that used in the formula to calculate "We, the People" sought to conceal the blunt structure of race relations in the fledgling nation. The original Constitution nowhere used the words *slave* or *slavery* or the phrase *slave trade*. New Jersey's William Paterson, later the state's governor and a U.S. Supreme Court justice, noted that the framers of the nation's first constitution—the Articles of Confederation—"had been ashamed to use the term 'Slaves'" and that framers of the Constitution of 1787 felt similarly.[5]

Despite the absence of the terms, the topics appeared repeatedly in key sections of the Constitution. The slavery issue appeared first in the apportionment formula (Article 1, sec. 2, para. 3) with its three-race division. The provision became known as the "Three-fifths Compromise" because counting slaves as "three fifths of all other Persons" proved crucial to securing agreement. It reflected not merely division over whether slaves were to count as persons or property; it revealed the twist of race in the politics to control national power.

To increase their representation in Congress, southern states with their growing slave populations insisted on counting slaves fully as persons and not at all as property. They wanted their representation high but their taxes low. Northern states insisted on counting slaves fully as property and not at all as persons. Adopting the Three-fifths Rule that the Confederation Congress had created in 1783 for apportioning taxes, the compromise Virginia's James Madison proposed and South Carolina's John Rutledge and Pennsylvania's James Wilson supported allowed sufficient measure to soothe delegates from the South and North. Each got some, but not all, of what they originally proposed.

The slavery issue's second appearance came in the Suppression Clause (Article 1, sec. 8, para. 15) that directed Congress to use federal power in the states and territories to suppress insurrections. Fear of slave revolts conjured the need for national, crushing power. Fear of slave revolts figured also in the third appearance of the slavery issue in the Constitution: the promise of federal protection offered in the Domestic Violence Clause (Article 4, sec. 4). The fourth appearance occurred in protecting the slave trade from federal interference until 1808 (Article 1, sec. 9, para. 1). The fifth appearance was in the Rendition Clause (Article 4, sec. 2, para. 3). Also called the Fugitive Slave Clause, it sought to secure property rights to reclaim slaves who escaped beyond state lines. The sixth, and final, appearance of the slavery issue in the original Constitution arose in restricting the amending process in Article 5 to further protect the slave trade from federal action until 1808.

How the Constitution treated the slavery issue, which included slaves and the slave trade, was crucial to its being accepted. Abraham Baldwin, one of Georgia's delegates to the Philadelphia Convention in 1787 and a member of the House of Representatives in the first Congress under the Constitution, explained the "delicate nature" of the Constitutional Convention's discussion of the slavery issue. "Gentlemen who had been present at the formation of this Constitution could not avoid the recollection of the pain and difficulty which the subject caused in that body," Baldwin told his House colleagues in February 1790. "The members from the Southern States were so tender upon this point, that they had well nigh broken up without coming to any determination; however, from the extreme desire of preserving the Union, and obtaining an efficient Government, they were induced mutually to concede, and the Constitution jealously guarded what they agreed to."[6] Baldwin rose in Congress on more than that occasion to caution his colleagues against any reconsideration of the issues. "If gentlemen look over the footsteps of that body," Baldwin warned with reference to the Constitutional Convention, "they will find the greatest degree of caution used to imprint them, so as not to be easily eradicated; but the moment we go to jostle on that ground, I fear we shall feel it tremble under our feet."[7]

The ground did tremble as Baldwin feared, for slavery persisted as an insidious issue in the nation's development under the Constitution. Just as it menaced the creation of the Constitution, it threatened to sunder the Union in the Civil War (1861–1865). Even at the moment of its Declaration of Independence, the emerging United States groped with the issue of slavery's place in a polity announcing itself as "dedicated to the proposition that all Men are created equal."

In drafting the Declaration of Independence, Virginia's Thomas Jefferson, himself a slaveholder, denounced the African slave trade as "piratical warfare." He branded it a "cruel war against human nature," one that violated the "most sacred rights of life and liberty." He blamed Britain's King George III for maintaining "this assemblage of horrors" and suggested the king somehow forced African slaves on American colonists.

George III had hardly begun the trans-Atlantic slave trade. He came to the throne in 1760, almost a century and a half after English colonists first bought Africans as slaves in Virginia. Jefferson indicted the king for being "[d]etermined to keep open a market where MEN should be bought and sold." George III blocked suppression of the trade and thwarted American attempts to end it, Jefferson charged. Referring to the king, Jefferson declared "he has prostituted his negative for suppressing every legislative attempt to prohibit or to restrain this execrable commerce." King George III, in fact, no more made American colonists transport and trade African slaves than he made American colonists keep African slaves.

Jefferson's invective against the slave trade did not survive scrutiny in the Continental Congress, which received his litany of condemnation in June 1776. His harsh words rankled many, but not because the words misrepresented King George's role. Some of Jefferson's fellow southerners, who along with their forebears received the bulk of slaves landed in North America, cringed at the censure. So did northerners who owned slaves. New York State held about as many slaves in 1790 as Georgia. Jefferson's language disturbed some New England delegates whose states, such as Rhode Island, supplied the bulk of slaves in the Atlantic trade to North America.

Massachusetts's John Adams later hailed Jefferson's failed attack. Referring to Jefferson's draft, Adams wrote: "I was delighted with its high tone and the flights of oratory with which it abounded, especially that concerning negro slavery." Jefferson's words, after all, suggested Africans had claims to "sacred rights of life and liberty," which made not only the slave trade but slavery itself both unwarranted and un-Christian. Strong feelings on the touchy topic kept Jefferson's rhetoric from being adopted as an official statement. "I knew his Southern brethren would never suffer [it] to pass in Congress," Adams explained.[8]

Like many Americans, Adams shifted support for slavery and the slave trade wholly to the South. But at neither the time of the Declaration of Independence in 1776 nor at the time of the drafting of the Constitution in 1787 was slavery peculiarly southern. Slaves existed in all of the thirteen colonies before the be-

ginning of the War for Independence. Granted, slaves were increasingly concentrated in the South, and the gap in proportion between North and South
grew as European immigrants hurried to the North almost immediately after
the war ended in 1783 and the northern states by law renounced slavery. In
1750 the six southern colonies (Virginia, Maryland, North Carolina, South Carolina, Delaware, and Georgia) held 87.2 percent of 236,420 blacks in the thirteen colonies; as states in 1790 the six held 92.4 percent.

The slavery issue then developed increasingly as a North-South conflict, but
it was not so simple. Slavery masked multifarious matters that made up race
relations. Power was the core. That was clear in the debate about who would
count in apportioning representatives in Congress. No delegate embraced
counting slaves as a matter of equity or justice to blacks. The focus fell exclusively on whites. The debate was about proportioning power among whites.
Slaves were mere pawns maneuvered for the advantage of one or another
group of whites. The issue was who would have power.

Virginia's George Mason declared philosophically, "From the nature of man
we may be sure, that those who have power in their hands will not give it up
while they can retain it. On the contrary we know they will always when they
can rather increase it."[9] Mason understood that counting slaves meant more
power for Virginia and less for Massachusetts. So did the Massachusetts delegates.

Elbridge Gerry of Massachusetts, later a U.S. vice president (1813–1814), argued against enslaved blacks' counting in any way as persons in apportioning
congressional representatives under the Constitution. Turning slaveholders' arguments on the sanctity of slave property against them, he insisted that slaves
were property, and property was the basis—or what he called the "rule"—for
setting taxes, not for setting representation. Equating blacks with mules, Gerry
asked rhetorically, "Why, then sh[oul]d the blacks, who were property in the
South, be in the rule of representation more than the cattle & horses of the
North?" He insisted, "Slaves [were] not to be put upon the Footing of freemen."
And he was adamant that the "Freemen of Mass[achuset]ts [were] not to be
put upon a Footing with the Slaves of other States."[10]

New Jersey's William Paterson agreed with Gerry's objection to counting
blacks. He declared that he "could regard negroes slaves in no light but as
property. They are no free agents, have no personal liberty, no faculty of ac-
quiring property, but on the contrary are themselves property, & like other
property entirely at the will of the Master." Pointing both to blacks' exclusion
from politics within the states and to an apparent double standard in seeking
to have slaves count in apportioning representatives, Paterson asked, "[I]f Negroes are not represented in the States to which they belong, why should they
be represented in the Gen[era]l Gov[ernmen]t?"[11]

Paterson further elaborated on popular sentiment and basic political principles as he saw them. "What is the true principle of Representation? It is an expedient by which an assembly of certain individ[ua]ls chosen by the people is
substituted in place of the inconvenient meeting of the people themselves," he
explained. "If such a meeting of the people was actually to take place, would
the slaves vote? They would not," he was sure. So, he concluded, "Why then
sh[oul]d they be represented?"[12]

The arguing at the constitutional convention over counting slaves advanced the delegates' unquestioned central conception of the United States as a white man's land. Even some southern slaveholders announced a wish that slavery had never become so intertwined in the body of their new nation. At the time of the Constitution's framing, some such slaveholders willingly considered plans to remove slaves gradually. Their emancipation plans almost always included colonization plans to remove blacks. They hoped to whiten America, to remove from it the other that had become attached to the nation's innards.

NOTES

1. U.S. Const., Art. I, sec. 2, para. 3.
2. *Cherokee Nation v. Georgia*, 30 U.S. (5 Pet.) 1, 17 (1831).
3. *Scott v. Sanford*, 60 U.S. (19 How.) 393, 403 (1857).
4. Ibid.
5. Max Farrand, ed., *The Records of the Federal Convention of 1787*, 3 vols. (New Haven, CT: Yale University Press, 1911), 1:561 (remarks of Paterson, July 6, 1787).
6. 1 *Annals of Cong.*, 1200–1201 (Joseph Gales, ed., 1790).
7. Ibid. See also Baldwin's comments in debates of June 16–20, 1798, 5th Cong., 2nd sess., 2 *Annals of Cong.*, 1968–2005.
8. Charles Francis Adams, ed., *The Works of John Adams*, 10 vols. (Boston: Little and Brown, 1850), 2:514.
9. Farrand, *Records*, 1:580 (remarks of George Mason, July 11, 1787).
10. Ibid., 1:201 (taken from Yates).
11. Ibid., 1:561 (Paterson).
12. Ibid.

DOCUMENTS

1.1.   "There is room for everybody in America," 1785

One of the foremost persistent themes in U.S. race relations has arisen from the recurrent question basic in considering who counted in the new American nation: "Who is an American?" In his 1782 essays titled Letters from an American Farmer, *French-born American author J. Hector St. John de Crèvecoeur (1735–1813), who became a New Yorker in 1765, offered a view of "the American." It presented a view later labeled the "melting pot," but the mixture envisioned when the framers of the U.S. Constitution gathered in 1787 countenanced only European stock. And males at that. It excluded both Africans and Native American Indians from being what Crèvecoeur described as the "New Man," "the American," who rid himself of old society and old politics to enter "a new race of men" marked by their deeds, not by their descent.*

[W]hence came all these people? They are a mixture of English, Scotch, Irish, French, Dutch, Germans, and Swedes. From this promiscuous breed, that race, now called Americans, have arisen. . . .

Urged by a variety of motives, here they came. Everything has tended to regenerate them: new laws, a new mode of living, a new social system. Here they are become men. . . . [H]ere they rank as citizens. . . .

His country is now that which gives him land, bread, protection, and consequence. . . . He is either a European, or the descendant of a European, hence, that strange mixture of blood, which you will find in no other country. . . .

He is an American, who, leaving behind him all his ancient prejudices and manners, receives new ones from the new mode of life he has embraced, the new government he obeys, and the new rank he holds. . . . Here individuals of all nations are melted into a new race of men, whose labors and posterity will one day cause great changes in the world.

Americans are the western pilgrims, who are carrying along with them that great mass of arts, sciences, vigor, and industry, which began long since in the east. They will finish the great circle. . . .

There is room for everybody in America. . . . Thus Europeans become Americans.

Source: J. Hector St. John de Crèvecoeur, *Letters from an American farmer: describing certain provincial situations, manners, and customs . . . and conveying some idea of the late and present interior circumstances of the British colonies in North America, Written for the information of a friend in England* (London: Printed for T. Davies, 1782).

1.2.   "Deep rooted prejudices," 1788

*The primary author of the U.S. Declaration of Independence illus-
trated fundamental views on race relations at the time of the Constitution of 1787. In his* Notes on the State of Virginia, *penned and
published in the 1780s, Thomas Jefferson (1743–1826) elaborated on
his view that blacks were inferior to whites and would remain so. The
black-white divide was unbridgable in his view. It began with color
and showed in physical and mental differences. He favored emanci-
pating enslaved blacks after a period of service and then removing
them from the United States. Blacks and whites if "equally free, cannot live in the same government. Nature, habit, opinion has drawn
indelible lines of distinction between them," he later summarized in
his 1821* Autobiography. *By then, perhaps from personal qualms from
his relations with his slave mistress, Sally Hemming, who bore him
children, Jefferson worried especially over what would come to be
called miscegenation—sexual relations between blacks and whites
that produced mixed-race children.*

Deep rooted prejudices entertained by the whites; ten thousand recollections,
by the blacks, of the injuries they have sustained; new provocations; the real
distinctions which nature has made; and many other circumstances, will divide us into parties, and produce convulsions which will probably never end
but in the extermination of the one or the other race.

—To these objections, which are political, may be added others, which are
physical and moral.

The first difference which strikes us is that of colour. . . .

And is this difference of no importance? Is it not the foundation of a greater
or less share of beauty in the two races? . . .

Besides those of colour, figure, and hair, there are other physical distinctions
proving a difference of race. They have less hair on the face and body. They
secrete less by the kidneys, and more by the glands of the skin, which gives
them a very strong and disagreeable odour. This greater degree of transpira-
tion renders them more tolerant of heat, and less so of cold, than the whites. . . .
They seem to require less sleep. A black, after hard labour through the day, will
be induced by the slightest amusements to sit up till midnight, or later, though
knowing he must be out with the first dawn of the morning.

They are at least as brave, and more adventuresome. But this may perhaps
proceed from a want of forethought, which prevents their seeing a danger till
it be present. When present, they do not go through it with more coolness or
steadiness than the whites.

They are more ardent after their female: but love seems with them to be more
an eager desire, than a tender delicate mixture of sentiment and sensation.
Their griefs are transient. Those numberless afflictions, which render it doubtful whether heaven has given life to us in mercy or in wrath, are less felt, and
sooner forgotten with them.

In general, their existence appears to participate more of sensation than reflection. To this must be ascribed their disposition to sleep when abstracted from their diversions, and unemployed in labour. An animal whose body is at rest, and who does not reflect, must be disposed to sleep of course.

Comparing them by their faculties of memory, reason, and imagination, it appears to me, that in memory they are equal to the whites; in reason much inferior, as I think one could scarcely be found capable of tracing and comprehending the investigations of Euclid; and that in imagination they are dull, tasteless, and anomalous. . . .

The Indians . . . will often carve figures on their pipes not destitute of design and merit. They will crayon out an animal, a plant, or a country, so as to prove the existence of a germ in their minds which only wants cultivation. They astonish you with strokes of the most sublime oratory; such as prove their reason and sentiment strong, their imagination glowing and elevated.

But never yet could I find that a black had uttered a thought above the level of plain narration; never see even an elementary trait of painting or sculpture. In music they are more generally gifted than the whites with accurate ears for tune and time, and they have been found capable of imagining a small catch. Whether they will be equal to the composition of a more extensive run of melody, or of complicated harmony, is yet to be proved. . . .

The improvement of the blacks in body and mind, in the first instance of their mixture with the whites, has been observed by every one, and proves that their inferiority is not the effect merely of their condition of life. . . .

The opinion, that they are inferior in the faculties of reason and imagination, must be hazarded with great diffidence. . . . I advance it therefore as a suspicion only, that the blacks, whether originally a distinct race, or made distinct by time and circumstances, are inferior to the whites in the endowments both of body and mind.

This unfortunate difference of colour, and perhaps of faculty, is a powerful obstacle to the emancipation of these people. Many of their advocates, while they wish to vindicate the liberty of human nature, are anxious also to preserve its dignity and beauty. Some of these, embarrassed by the question "What further is to be done with them?" join themselves in opposition with those who are actuated by sordid avarice only. Among the Romans emancipation required but one effort. The slave, when made free, might mix with, without staining the blood of his master. But with us a second is necessary, unknown to history. When freed, he is to be removed beyond the reach of mixture.

Source: Thomas Jefferson, *Notes on the State of Virginia* (Philadelphia: Printed and sold by Prichard and Hall, 1788).

1.3.   "To eradicate that train of absurd and false ideas and opinions," 1791

Benjamin Banneker (1731–1806), a mostly self-educated black scientist, famous for his astronomical calculations and almanacs, coun-

tered Thomas Jefferson's dim view of blacks and the cast of race re-
lations in the United States. "[T]o eradicate that train of absurd and
false ideas and opinions, which so generally prevails with respect to
us," in 1791 Banneker sent then U.S. Secretary of State Jefferson a
manuscript copy of his first almanac, along with pointed commen-
tary. Banneker challenged Jefferson as a scientist, as a believer in "one
universal Father," and as an adherent to the self-evident truths he
penned in the Declaration of Independence. Banneker's essential
question of hypocrisy resounded throughout the history of U.S. race
relations.

To Thomas Jefferson,

I am fully sensible of that freedom, which I take with you in the present occasion; a liberty which seemed to me scarcely allowable, when I reflected on that
distinguished and dignified station in which you stand, and the almost general prejudice and prepossession, which is so prevalent in the world against
those of my complexion.

I suppose it is a truth too well attested to you, to need a proof here, that we
are a race of beings, who have long labored under the abuse and censure of
the world; that we have long been looked upon with an eye of contempt; and
that we have long been considered rather as brutish than human, and scarcely
capable of mental endowments. . . .

Now Sir, [I hope] . . . your sentiments are concurrent with mine, which are,
that one universal Father hath given being to us all; and that he hath not only
made us all of one flesh, but that he hath also, without partiality, afforded us
all the same sensations and endowed us all with the same faculties; and that
however variable we may be in society or religion, however diversified in situation or color, we are all in the same family and stand in the same relation to
him.

Sir, if these are sentiments of which you are fully persuaded, I hope you cannot but acknowledge, that it is the indispensable duty of those, who maintain
for themselves the rights of human nature, and who possess the obligations of
Christianity, to extend their power and influence to the relief of every part of
the human race, from whatever burden or oppression they may unjustly labor
under. . . .

Sir, I freely and cheerfully acknowledge, that I am of the African race, and
in that color which is natural to them of the deepest dye; and it is under a sense
of the most profound gratitude to the Supreme Ruler of the Universe, that I
now confess to you, that I am not under that state of tyrannical thraldom, and
inhuman captivity, to which too many of my brethren are doomed, but that I
have abundantly tasted of the fruition of those blessings, which proceed from
that free and unequalled liberty with which you are favored. . . .

Sir, [there] was a time when you clearly saw into the injustice of a state of
slavery, and in which you had just apprehensions of the horror of its condition. It was now that your abhorrence thereof was so excited, that you publicly
held forth this true and invaluable doctrine, which is worthy to be recorded
and remembered in all succeeding ages: "We hold these truths to be self-
evident, that all men are created equal; that they are endowed by their Creator

with certain unalienable rights, and that among these are, life, liberty, and the pursuit of happiness."

Here was a time, in which your tender feelings for yourselves had engaged you thus to declare, you were then impressed with proper ideas of the great violation of liberty, and the free possession of those blessings, to which you were entitled by nature; but, Sir, how pitiable is it to reflect, that although you were so fully convinced of the benevolence of the Father of Mankind, and of his equal and impartial distribution of these rights and privileges, which he hath conferred upon them, that you should at the same time counteract his mercies, in detaining by fraud and violence so numerous a part of my brethren, under groaning captivity, and cruel oppression, that you should at the same time be found guilty of that most criminal act, which you professedly detested in others, with respect to yourselves.

I suppose that your knowledge of the situation of my brethren, is too extensive to need a recital here; neither shall I presume to prescribe methods by which they may be relieved, otherwise than by recommending to you and all others, to wean yourselves from those narrow prejudices which you have imbibed with respect to them, and as Job proposed to his friends, "put your soul in their souls stead"; thus shall your hearts be enlarged with kindness and benevolence towards them; and thus shall you need neither the direction of myself or others, in what manner to proceed herein.

Source: Benjamin Banneker, *Copy of a Letter from Benjamin Banneker to the Secretary of State, with His Answer* (Philadelphia: Printed and sold by Daniel Lawrence, 1792).

1.4. "The utmost good faith shall always be observed towards the Indians," 1787

The Congress under the Articles of Confederation announced the basic U.S. policy of "maintaining a good correspondence between [U.S.] citizens and the several nations of Indians, in amity with them," in its August 1786 Ordinance for Regulation and Management of Indian Affairs. Its most noted announcement of the nation's formal Indian policy appeared in the Northwest Ordinance of July 1787. The first Congress under the Constitution fully endorsed the policy respecting Indian nations as separate sovereigns—a policy that changed with a shifting balance of power.

The utmost good faith shall always be observed towards the Indians; their lands and property shall never be taken from them without their consent; and in their property, rights and liberty, they never shall be invaded or disturbed, unless in just and lawful wars authorised by Congress; but laws founded in justice and humanity shall from time to time be made, for preventing wrongs being done to them, and for preserving peace and friendship with them.

Source: "An Ordinance for the government of the territory of the United States North West of the river Ohio," July 13, 1787, in *Journals of the Continental Congress, 1774–1789*, 34 vols. (Washington, DC: GPO, 1904–1937), 32:334, 340–341.

1.5.   "As if our want of strength had destroyed our rights," 1790

In 1790 the Seneca of the Six Nations Iroquois League sent a delegation to President George Washington and the first Congress at the new American nation's capital in New York City to protest their territorial dispossession and general treatment. Throughout the colonial era the Iroquois—including the Seneca, Mohawk, Oneida, Onondaga, Cayuga, and the Tuscarora after 1722—had dominated the area north of Albany, New York, up to the Great Lakes and westward. Splintered but siding mostly with the British in the U.S. War for Independence (1775–1783), the Iroquois were humbled at the second Treaty of Fort Stanwix in 1784, where they ceded lands to the United States in return for living undisturbed in other lands. Here Corn Planter, whose native name was Gyantwaia, through an interpreter, described the Seneca view of their relations with the United States and raised what would be perennial issues of Americans' continually changing to suit themselves the terms and conditions of their agreements with Indians. Corn Planter asked two ringing questions: Would the United States honor its word as given in its treaties? Would Americans treat Indians as their brothers, as they had promised?

Father: The voice of the Seneca nations speaks to you; the great counsellor, in whose heart the wise men of all the *thirteen fires* [states] have placed their wisdom. It may be very small in your ears, and we, therefore, entreat you to hearken with attention; for we are able to speak of things which are to us very great.

When your army entered the country of the Six Nations, we called you the *town destroyers*; to this day, when your name is heard, our women look behind them and turn pale, and our children cling close to the necks of their mothers.

When our chiefs returned from Fort Stanwix, and laid before our council what had been done there, our nation was surprised to hear how great a country you had compelled them to give up to you, without your paying to us any thing for it. Every one said, that your hearts were yet swelled with resentment against us for what had happened during the war, but that one day you would consider it with more kindness. We asked each other, *What have we done to deserve such severe chastisement?*

Father: when you kindled your 13 fires separately, the wise men assembled at them told us that you were all brothers; the children of one great father, who regarded the red people as his children. They called us brothers, and invited us to his protection. They told us that he resided beyond the great water where the sun first rises; and that he was a king whose power no people could resist, and that his goodness was as bright as the sun. What they said went to our hearts. We accepted the invitation, and promised to obey him.

What the Seneca nation promises, they faithfully perform. When you refused obedience to that king, he commanded us to assist his beloved men in making you sober. In obeying him, we did no more than yourselves had led us to promise. We were deceived; but your people teaching us to confide in that king, had helped to deceive us; and we now appeal to your breast. *Is all the blame ours?*

Father: when we saw that we had been deceived, and heard the invitation which you gave us to draw near to the fire you had kindled and talk with you concerning peace, we made haste towards it. You told us you could crush us to nothing; and you demanded from us a great country, as the price of that peace which you had offered to us: *as if our want of strength had destroyed our rights.*

Our chiefs had felt your power, and were unable to contend against you, and they therefore gave up that country. What they agreed to has bound our nation, but your anger against us must by this time be cooled, and although our strength is not increased, nor your power become less, we ask you to consider calmly— Were the terms dictated to us by your commissioners reasonable and just? . . .

Father: you have said that we were in your hand, and that by closing it you could crush us to nothing. Are you determined to crush us? If you are, tell us so; that those of our nation who have become your children, and have determined to die so, may know what to do. In this case, one chief has said, he would ask you to put him out of his pain. Another, who will not think of dying by the hand of his father, or his brother, has said he will retire to the Chataughque, eat of the fatal root, and sleep with his father in peace.

All the land we have been speaking of belonged to the Six Nations. No part of it ever belonged to the king of England, and he could not give it to you.

Hear us once more. At Fort Stanwix we agreed to deliver up those of our people who should do you any wrong, and that you might try them and punish them according to your law. We delivered up two men accordingly. But instead of trying them according to your law, the lowest of your people took them from your magistrate, and put them immediately to death. It is just to punish the murder with death; but the Senecas will not deliver up their people to men who disregard the treaties of their own nation.

Source: Samuel G. Drake, *Book of the Indians of North America* (Boston: Antiquarian Institute, 1837), Book 5:113–115. My thanks to Special Collections, Department of Archives and Manuscripts, University Libraries, Arizona State University, Tempe.

ANNOTATED RESEARCH GUIDE

Books

Allison, Robert J. *The Founding Fathers and Slavery*. Washington, DC: National Endowment for the Humanities, 1986. Examines the views on race and slavery of representative leaders at the Constitutional Convention of 1787.

Cerami, Charles A. *Benjamin Banneker: Surveyor, Astronomer, Publisher, Patriot*. New York: John Wiley, 2002. Discusses the achievements of an authentic genius confined by race and time but who shouldered his lot fighting against slavery and refuting the derogatory racial ideas of the likes of Thomas Jefferson.

Debo, Angie. *A History of the Indians of the United States*. Norman: University of Oklahoma Press, 1970. Remains a splendid read for a sympathetic introduction to the Indians' view of their relations with those who would come to call themselves Americans.

Farrand, Max, ed. *The Records of the Federal Convention of 1787*. Rev. ed. 4 vols. New Haven, CT: Yale University Press, 1966. With index and supplement, these notes and documents form the most commonly accepted basis of insight to the meaning and manner of the construction of the U.S. Constitution.

Finkelman, Paul. *Slavery and the Founders: Race and Liberty in the Age of Jefferson*. 2nd ed. Armonk, NY: M. E. Sharpe, 2001. Places slavery squarely as a central contentious issue in the nation's founding, pointing up calamitous contradictions between pronounced ideology and persistent racial beliefs.

Joshi, S. T., ed. *Documents of American Prejudice: An Anthology of Writings on Race from Thomas Jefferson to David Duke*. New York: Basic Books, 1999. A collection of more than 100 excerpts, valuable more for the documents than for explanation or interpretation.

Mellon, Matthew Taylor. *Early American Views on Negro Slavery from the Letters and Papers of the Founders of the Republic*. Boston: Meador Publishing Company, 1934. New ed. New York: Bergman Publishers, 1969. Documents the views of Benjamin Franklin and the first four U.S. presidents.

Nash, Gary B. *Race and Revolution*. Madison, WI: Madison House, 1990. Focuses on the revolutionary generation's compromises with, and protection of, slavery as a contradiction to the new nation's spirit, recognizing racial hypocrisy as not merely southern but national.

———. *Race, Class, and Politics: Essays on American Colonial and Revolutionary Society*. Urbana: University of Illinois Press, 1986. Explores developing race relations in polygot early America as the distribution of power and wealth fixed the meaning and uses of race and rights.

Richter, Daniel K. *Facing East from Indian Country: A Narrative History of Early America*. Cambridge, MA: Harvard University Press, 2001. Examines from the perspective of Indian country Europeans' westward movement from first contact in the 1500s to the early 1800s.

Robinson, Donald L. *Slavery in the Structure of American Politics, 1765–1820*. New York: Harcourt Brace Jovanovich, 1970. Reveals the racial animosity and sectional divide over slavery with its black presence during the American Revolutionary and early national eras.

Sheehan, Bernard W. *Seeds of Extinction: Jeffersonian Philanthropy and the American Indian*. Chapel Hill: University of North Carolina Press, 1973. Focuses on how early white American self-concepts shaped perceptions of Indians and resulted in federal policies that sometimes held goodwill but ended in rending Indian cultures.

Wallace, Anthony F. C. *Jefferson and the Indians: The Tragic Fate of the First Americans*. Cambridge, MA: Harvard University Press, 1999. Probes Jefferson's complex attitudes about race with a focus on his paradoxical observations on, dealings with, and policies toward Indians.

Web Sites

http://memory.loc.gov/ammem/amlaw/lwfr.html—provides Max Farrand's *The Records of the Federal Convention of 1787*, along with other documentary records on the creation of the Constitution.

http://www.usconstitution.net/consttime2.html—provides a helpful timeline of events surrounding the constitutional convention in 1787, with links discussing the ratification process and the working of the Constitution.

http://www.yale.edu/lawweb/avalon/debates/debcont.htm—provides James Madison's notes on the debates at the federal convention.

2

A Trail of Tears: Indian Removal from East to West

In December 1829, President Andrew Jackson sent Congress his first annual message, expressing his view of the "State of the Nation." Identifying national problems and needs, he announced his program to advance the population of 12 million in twenty-four states toward his vision of what the nation should be. About one-seventh of his message treated race relations with Indians, a subject on which Jackson had definite views.

While he won enduring historical notice for defeating British forces in January 1815, outside New Orleans in the last major battle of the War of 1812, much of Jackson's popularity came from his exploits as an Indian-fighter on the southern frontier. In a six-month campaign known as the Creek War (1813–1814), General Jackson led southern militia against Creek warriors called "Red Sticks." Allied with the British, the Red Sticks had responded to the Shawnee leader Tecumseh's call for a transcontinental confederation among Indians along the frontier to repel ever-encroaching white settlers. Directing a take-no-prisoners drive, Jackson led 5,000 militiamen and Indian allies, including Cherokee under Chief Junaluska, to annihilate Creek communities at Tallasahatchee and Talladega. His forces eliminated any further Creek threat in the Battle of Tohopeka (later Horseshoe Bend) in Alabama. He dictated elements of the Treaty of Ft. Jackson, signed in August 1814, that forced Indians, both foes and friends, to cede 23 million acres—part of southern Georgia and more than half of Alabama, which in 1819 became the twenty-second state.

Jackson embellished his reputation as an Indian-fighter in the First Seminole War (1817–1818) when he invaded Spanish-held Florida to attack Seminoles harboring fugitive slaves. (Coincidentally, the tribal name *Seminole* itself appeared to derive from *simanó-li*, Creek for "runaway" or "separatist.") Jackson directed a scorched-earth policy that razed Indian settlements and boosted U.S.

leverage in negotiating the Transcontinental Treaty of 1819 in which Spain ceded Florida to the United States.

Jackson stood then not only as the hero of New Orleans but as the "Hero of the West" because of his exploits against Indians. Also, while born in South Carolina in 1762, he was a Tennessean by long residence. With an estate called the Hermitage, near Nashville, he was the first president to reside west of the Appalachian Mountains. He represented frontier interests bent on furthering settlement, and that meant further displacing Indians. Thus, the president whose name would become synonymous with expanding the rights and reach of the average white man would also become synonymous with brutal repression of the rights and reach of Indians.

Jackson entered the presidency in March 1829 with Indian issues on his mind. With what sounded like a diplomatic tone in his inaugural address, he announced,

> It will be my sincere and constant desire to observe toward the Indian tribes within our limits a just and liberal policy, and to give that humane and considerate attention to their rights and their wants which is consistent with the habits of our Government and the feelings of our people.[1]

Jackson sought again to sound a judicious tone in his annual message in December 1829. Yet he left no doubt about his view that the continuing presence of Indian tribes within Georgia and Alabama was a major national problem. As he phrased it with an attempted benign twist: The "interesting question [was] whether something can not be done, consistently with the rights of the States to preserve this much-injured race."[2]

Jackson's answer to his own question was emigration. He proposed that the tribes whom he identified as the Choctaw, Cherokee, and Creek "abandon the graves of their fathers and seek a home in a distant land" by removing from their remaining 5 million acres in the Southeast—an area originally among the most densely populated by Indians in North America—to west of the Mississippi River. Individual Indians could stay, if they "submit to the laws of those States," Jackson said, but the tribes had to go.[3]

Jackson's proposal triggered alarms. Americans concerned about their nation's character and increasingly troubled by its treatment of Indians and blacks protested. Many, moved with the religious fervor of the so-called Second Great Awakening that swept particularly the Northeast and Midwest in the 1820s and 1830s with evangelical revivalism, questioned whether Indian removal fit with Christian principles. A burgeoning American reform movement based on benevolence especially attracted white churchwomen to stand against Jackson's proposal. With a sense of preserving and promoting public virtue, such women organized a national campaign that deluged Congress with antiremoval petitions. They excoriated removal as a sheer act of brutal robbery. It was not an issue of state's rights, as the president suggested, but merely avaricious whites seeking to steal Indian property, opponents charged.

The Cherokee garnered most attention from foes and friends of removal. Even while reduced from being on the losing side during the War for U.S. Independence (1775–1783), the tribe still stretched from eastern Tennessee and western North and South Carolina to Georgia. The Cherokee thereafter allied themselves with the fledgling Americans, notably during the War of 1812. More than allies in war, many Cherokees adopted white ways. Abandoning their traditional windowless, bark-roofed log cabins with a single entry and smoke hole (not unlike the longhouses of their more northern Iroquoian family), the Cherokee began building homes on whites' models and reconfigured their communities into towns. They took to farming and weaving. They modeled their government on the U.S. Constitution. They became literate after 1821 when Sequoyah (ca. 1770–1843) devised an eighty-six-character alphabet and a system in which characters represented a syllable in the Cherokee language. They adopted a written constitution and a flourishing literature, including the first Indian newspaper, the *Cherokee Phoenix*, which began publishing in February 1828.

By the late 1820s, the Cherokee appeared to be not only thriving but rapidly assimilating. Intermarriage with whites produced a significant class called "mixed bloods," who emulated almost invariably their white fathers. They converted to Christianity, and they accelerated the tribe's Americanization by abandoning other Indian ways. They rose to lead the Cherokee in literacy and wealth. Many became slaveholders and pushed the Cherokee to adopt black codes like those of their white southern neighbors: They banned marrying blacks; they restricted manumitting slaves; and they excluded blacks from any official role in Cherokee public life. The 1827 Cherokee Constitution declared simply, "No person who is of negro or mulatto parentage . . . shall be eligible to hold any office or trust under this government."[4]

The Cherokee stood as a model of what was best and worst in the developing position of Indians in American life. They stood as symbols of success or failure, as objects of respect or resentment—depending on the viewer's perspective. For those who wanted Indians absorbed and integrated into American life, the Cherokee served as prime examples of what could be. For those who wanted Indians gone and forgotten and who cringed at even a hint of race mixing, the Cherokee served as prime examples of what should not be. From either perspective, the Cherokee showed the sun had set on the so-called noble savage in America. If noble, the Indian could no longer be savage. If savage, the Indian could no longer be noble. Either perspective projected the Indian as ceasing to be Indian. Either the Indian would assimilate to become simply American, or the Indian would simply decease.

Proposing to remove the Cherokee then engaged visions of the present and future of American Indians. President Jackson cast removal as telling for the nation's character. It was, he said, merely voluntary on the Indians' part but a benevolent endeavor on America's part "to preserve this much-injured race."[5] Opponents agreed with Jackson that removal told much about America's character. They cast it, however, as contrary to conscience and morality and as the antithesis of benevolence. They charged that it basely surrendered to the gold fever a discovery on Cherokee lands in northwestern Georgia spread at the end of the 1820s. They mourned further that removal targeted the material success of Indians, such as the Cherokee, whom Jackson described as "having mingled much with the whites and made some progress in the arts of civilized life."[6]

Removal was wrong in itself, it aimed at the wrong Indians, and it put America on the wrong course, one not destined to make Indians integral parts of the nation but to separate them forever, critics charged. And they made their voices heard. Extensive, organized, public protests against removal slowed the president's plan in Congress, but he prevailed. The Senate passed removal 28 to 19 in April 1830. A month later the House begrudgingly voted 102 to 97. So Indian removal became law.

Both those for and against the Indian Removal Act of 1830 marked it as a major shift in U.S. relations with Indians. It committed the United States no longer simply to segregating Indians within states but to moving Indians beyond the frontier—to pushing them from sight. It replaced figurative separation with significant physical distance. It marked coexistence as impossible with Indian tribes. As individuals, Indians could exist within the settled United States only if they assimilated to become indistinguishable Americans. The process, in President Jackson's words, called for Indians simply to become "like other citizens," for them to "become merged in the mass of our population." If Indians insisted on continuing their tribal traditions, including their sense of sovereign self-rule, then they had to go. And to implement the Indians' going, the act provided the president with a $500,000 appropriation and authority to remove "the Indians residing in any of the states or territories" to lands west of the Mississippi River.[7] The act reflected the U.S. sense that it now had the upper hand and no longer depended on the goodwill of Indian tribes.

Since the War for Independence, the United States had treated Indian tribes formally as independent peoples, as nations possessing and exercising political sovereignty. Congress under the Articles of Confederation featured treaty making with Indians as a major part of what it accomplished. It entreated for peace with Indians with compacts such as the October 1784 Treaty of Fort Stanwix signed with the Cayuga, Mohawks, Oneidas, and Onondagas near what became Rome, New York. The pact, known also as the Treaty with the Six Nations, ceded to the United States title to thousands of acres in western New York. The coup, however, was cession of more than 7 million acres in western Pennsylvania. The ceded land amounted to about one-quarter of Pennsylvania's total 45,308 square miles (117,348 square kilometers).

The Confederation Congress announced the basic U.S. policy of "preserving peace and friendship" and of "maintaining a good correspondence between [U.S.] citizens and the several nations of Indians." The first Congress under the Constitution fully endorsed the policy, which colonial settlers had practiced almost from the founding of England's first permanent settlement in North America—Jamestown, Virginia, founded in May 1607.

Early settlers' survival not infrequently had depended on gaining sufferance from local Indians. Members of the six-tribe Powhatan Confederacy saved Jamestown from starvation, for instance, after thirteen-year-old Powhatan princess Pocahontas reportedly interceded for the life of settlement leader John Smith, when he faced execution in December 1607 at the direction of her father, Chief Wahunsonacock (whom settlers merely called Powhatan).

Kindly treatment from Indians also spared the Pilgrim settlement at Plymouth in 1620. Indeed, in his *History of Plimouth Plantation*, Governor William

Bradford described what appeared to be the first peace treaty between English settlers and Indians in North America. Made in March 1621 with Wampanoag Chief Massasoit through the negotiations of the Pawtuxet Squanto, who had earlier traveled to England and other parts of Europe and spoke English, the treaty illustrated that when settlers were few and Indians many, the settlers eagerly sought peace.

The Powhatan wars (1622–1644) in Virginia and the Pequot War (1637) and King Philip's War (1675–1676) in New England further illustrated the turn of events. Whites relentlessly pushed against Indians. Trappers, hunters, then settlers depleted forests, draining and diverting the resources on which the tribes depended. Growing settlement changed not only the ecology but the balance of power. From central and indispensable, Indians became increasingly peripheral and nuisances to settlers. Thus began a continual push to the frontier's margins. The northeastern coastal tribes, for example, were pushed north into Canada or west beyond settlement. Only a relative few individual Indians who forsook their tribal ties to adopt white ways lingered on as settlements engulfed old tribal homelands.

Working their own balance of power, tribes in the mid-1700s forestalled being immediately swept back by colonial settlement. Allying on one side or another to play the colonial powers—mostly the British, French, and Spanish—against themselves, northeastern and southeastern tribes blocked advancing settlement. Indeed, they appeared to succeed in a stalemate after the pivotal French and Indian War (1754–1763), when the British issued the Royal Proclamation of 1763. Acknowledging Indian presence and power, the proclamation announced a policy of leaving Indians in peace on the lands they then possessed. The means of achieving that end was to segregate Indians from whites. The 1763 proclamation demarcated what it called Indian "Reserves." Indians were to be west of the proclamation line and whites to the east.

British authorities barred whites from moving west of the proclamation line and ordered their own removal program that directed whites then west of the line "forthwith to remove themselves."[8] Settlers refused to obey. They were determined to push west, notwithstanding the king or the Indians. That determination featured as a major issue in the coming of the American Revolution.

With the close of the War for Independence and then the War of 1812, the Indians lost the British as a major ally against the fledgling Americans. Various tribes succumbed, either moving further west or becoming surrounded by settlement. Pressure mounted against tribes who did not move, as President Jackson noted in 1829. That was the problem the Removal Act aimed to solve. It adopted the old aim of separating Indians from whites. Instead of the 1763 proclamation line, Congress demarcated the Mississippi River, which in 1830 loomed in most Americans' view as the distant West. Only two of the nation's twenty-four states—Louisiana admitted in 1812 and Missouri in 1821—then sat west of the Mississippi. The problem was that unlike in 1763 the Indians were not already west of the line. They would have to move.

Jackson proposed that "emigration should be voluntary, for it would be as cruel as unjust to compel the aborigines to abandon the graves of their fathers and seek a home in a distant land."[9] But the reality proved otherwise. Emigration became forced removal. The process exposed the menacing undertow of U.S. race relations with Indians that was eddying not merely toward their continued exclusion from the developing U.S. society but toward their physical extermination. Rather than treating Indians as independent nations and recognizing their sovereignty, the removal process virtually abrogated Indians' independent legal and political rights.

The Choctaw in Mississippi were the first to acquiesce to removal among those later to call themselves the Five Civilized Tribes—the Cherokee, Chickasaw, Choctaw, Creek, and Seminole—that predominated among Indians in the southeastern United States. In September 1830, Choctaw representatives signed the Treaty of Dancing Rabbit Creek. Surrendering earlier treaty rights, they "determined to sell their lands east of the Mississippi." In exchange they accepted "a tract of country west of the Mississippi River," near Fort Smith on the Arkansas River. They agreed to the terms with the expressed hope "that [they] may live under their own laws in peace with the United States and the State of Mississippi."[10] And so what came to be known as the Trail of Tears began in 1831 and 1832, as the Choctaw took up their possessions (including their slaves) and trudged to what the U.S. government then declared "the Indian country."

The Cherokee refused to acquiesce as the Choctaw had. They sued to sustain their rights. They found cold comfort at best. They found no ally in the federal government. They found individual states, such as Georgia and Mississippi, to be implacable enemies who refused to recognize the Indian sovereignty that the United States guaranteed. The Cherokee asserted their sovereignty as assured in a series of U.S. treaties from 1785 to 1819.

Until Andrew Jackson, successive presidents had reaffirmed the U.S. commitment to Cherokee sovereignty. Georgia adhered, however, to the opinion Jackson expressed in his 1829 annual message: Neither the Cherokee nor any other Indian tribe could exist as a sovereign within a state. Referring to Georgia and its neighbor Alabama, Jackson had noted, "These States, claiming to be the only sovereigns within their territories extended their laws over the Indians."[11] The Choctaw accepted such as extension as fact. The Cherokee sought to rely on U.S. law in rejecting any such fact. They took their argument to the U.S. Supreme Court in *Cherokee Nation v. Georgia* (1831) and *Worcester v. Georgia* (1832), sometimes referred to collectively as *The Cherokee Cases*.

Were Indian tribes holding lands within states such as Georgia to be sovereign over their lands, or must the tribes yield to state law? That was the central question, and it would persist as such in Indians' relations with other Americans. In *Cherokee Nation v. Georgia* (1831), the Supreme Court ducked the question. Chief Justice John Marshall repeated some of the political nimbleness he showed early in his tenure. Understanding that the Court had no physical means to force any president to act, Marshall sought to avoid confronting Jackson's opinion on whether an Indian tribe could exist as a sovereign within a state. As an exit, the chief justice found the Cherokee lacked standing to sue in the Supreme Court. The Cherokee fit none of the categories over which the Court had jurisdiction, Marshall ruled. In the process, he stripped Indian tribes within the United States of independence and sovereignty. He dubbed them "domestic dependent nations" and declared Indians were "in a state of pupilage. Their relation to the United States resembles that of a ward to his guardian."[12]

The Supreme Court dismissed the Cherokee's 1831 case. The president had already refused to protect them. So the Cherokee then stood naked in Georgia's face as the state pushed harder, not simply to strip them of tribal sovereignty but to segregate them completely. It required whites to get a Georgia license to live or work in Cherokee country. And to illustrate how serious it was, Georgia prosecuted eleven white missionaries for "residing within the limits of the Cherokee nation without a license."[13] Sentenced to four years at hard labor in the Georgia penitentiary, Samuel A. Worcester challenged his conviction. A Congregationalist minister from Vermont, Worcester united with the Cherokee defending their sovereign rights. He argued that the U.S. Constitution barred Georgia from extending its jurisdiction over the Cherokee Nation. The appeal worked its way to the U.S. Supreme Court.

In *Worcester v. Georgia* (1832), Chief Justice Marshall backtracked to his words in *Cherokee Nation v. Georgia*. He had dubbed Indian tribes "domestic dependent nations" and wards of the United States. That being so, he ruled in *Worcester* that the Cherokee were "under the protection of the United States, and of no other power."[14] The sovereignty of tribes such as the Cherokee yielded to the United States but not to individual states such as Georgia. "The Cherokee nation, then, is a distinct community occupying its own territory . . . in which the laws of Georgia can have no force," the chief justice concluded.[15] Holding Georgia's law "void, as being repugnant to the constitution, treaties, and laws of the United States," the Court reversed Worcester's conviction.[16] The minister and the Cherokee had won, as the Court upheld at least a portion of Indian tribal sovereignty.

If law had turned to the Cherokee's favor, the facts had not. Georgia pointedly ignored the *Worcester* ruling. It kept the missionary in prison at the state capital in Milledgeville. Holding to his view that state sovereignty should prevail over tribal sovereignty, President Jackson refused to enforce the Supreme Court's ruling in *Worcester*.

Pressed on every side and divided within, the Cherokee acquiesced at last. Their exodus west followed the Choctaw. A handful of federally selected Cherokee leaders signed a treaty at the Cherokee capital of New Echota in December 1835, ceding tribal lands east of the Mississippi River for $5 million— a price of about $1 per acre. Much of the ceded acreage was improved land cleared for farming and containing buildings, which raised the market value far beyond the government's paltry price that stood below the $1.25 it sold an unimproved acre under its Public Lands Act of 1820. The sellout enraged most Cherokees, and the rage spilled over to the murder of three of the four Cherokee signers of the treaty.

President Jackson ordered the U.S. Army to direct Indian removal. The assignment fell to Virginia-born U.S. Army General Winfield Scott—a hero of the War of 1812 and later of the War with Mexico (1846–1848), nicknamed "Old Fuss and Feathers." Commanding 7,000 troops, Scott supervised the internment of about 15,000 Cherokees in holding camps for a march westward in groups of a thousand. The army's schedule allowed the Cherokee little opportunity to arrange their own affairs. No orderly disposition of Cherokee property occurred. So-called voluntary emigration became virtual eviction. With troops ushering Indians out, local whites burst in to loot and ransack what the Indians could not carry with them.

The army's logistics for the thousand-mile trek west during the fall and winter of 1838–1839 proved poor. The military provided virtually no transportation. Almost all the Cherokee walked, regardless of age or condition, or were carried by their kith and kin. Nor did the pace take conditions into account. The mounted infantry escort sometimes proceeded as if alone on maneuvers, refusing to slow or stop for the trudging mass of exiles. Exhaustion and hunger exacted a deadly toll. More than 1 in 4 (about 4,000 in all) of the 15,000 Cherokee who set out on the journey of more than 100 days perished. Cherokee lore remembered the trek as the "Trail of Tears."

The army removed in all about 100,000 Indians westward. The Seminole went least quietly. Indeed, some went not at all, as removal precipitated the Second Seminole War (1835–1842). Defiant in their demand to remain on their reservation north of Lake Okeechobee in south central Florida, most Seminoles refused to move west, as called for in the 1832 Treaty of Payne's Landing. Using as cover the 4,000 square miles (10,000 square kilometers) of marshy land and swamps of the Everglades, which they called *Pa-May-Okee* or "Grassy Water," Seminole warriors under Osceola—whom whites earlier had forced from Georgia—waged resolute guerilla combat. They killed more than 2,000 U.S. Army troops and cost the federal government about $50 million—ten times more than the United States paid for the Cherokee land. Only duplicity in dishonoring a flag of truce to seize Osceola while he attended supposed peace talks at St. Augustine, Florida, squelched the main resistance and got the bulk of the Seminole to move to the Indian territory. Osceola never went west. He died in 1842 imprisoned at Ft. Moultrie in Charleston, South Carolina. A stubborn remnant also refused to go west until after the Third Seminole War (1855–1858).

The "Indian country" Congress created in 1834 in what many at the time considered the remote west quickly proved to be not so distant from, nor undesirable to, land-hungry settlers after all. The Texas Revolution (1835–1836), the War with Mexico (1846–1848), and the California Gold Rush that began in 1848 all attracted white interest in Indian lands. Fresh skirmishes began, followed by negotiations for new treaties to have Indians again cede lands. In 1854 Congress carved the Kansas and Nebraska territories out of Indian country, and in 1866 Congress further reclaimed the western half of what was then called "Indian Territory." Increased white movement west excited a new round of battles that became the last Indian wars.

In 1890 Congress organized a more reduced Indian territory of about 70,000 square miles (180,000 square kilometers) and, using the Choctaw words *okla* (people) and *humma* (red), named it Oklahoma. In 1907 it became the forty-sixth state. By then the reality of Indian removal shown clearly. Confined to reservations, the once independent and numerous tribes mostly sat as impoverished remnants isolated from the mainstreams of American life. That boded continuing problems for U.S. race relations.

NOTES

1. President Andrew Jackson, First Annual Message to Congress, December 8, 1829, in *A Compilation of the Messages and Papers of the Presidents, 1789–1897* (New York: Bureau of National Literature, 1897), 999–1001.

2. Ibid.

3. Ibid.

4. *Constitution of the Cherokee Nation, made and established at a general convention of delegates, duly authorized for that purpose, at New Echota, 26 July 1827* (New Echota, GA: Printed for the Cherokee Nation, at the Office of the Statesman and Patriot, 1827).

5. Jackson, First Annual Message, 1011.

6. Ibid.

7. 4 Stat. 411 (May 28, 1830).

8. Royal Proclamation of 1763, 3 Geo. 3 (October 7, 1763), in *British Royal Proclamations Relating to America*, ed. Clarence S. Brigham, *Transactions and Collections of the American Antiquarian Society*, 12 vols. (Worcester, MA: American Antiquarian Society, 1911), 12:212–218.

9. Jackson, First Annual Message, 1011.

10. Treaty of Dancing Rabbit Creek with the Choctaw Nation of Red People, 7 Stat. 333 (September 27, 1830).

11. Ibid.

12. *Cherokee Nation v. Georgia*, 30 U.S. (5 Pet.) 1, 17 (1831).

13. *Worcester v. Georgia*, 31 U.S. (6 Pet.) 515, 537 (1832).

14. Ibid., at 555.

15. Ibid., at 561.

16. Ibid., at 562.

DOCUMENTS

2.1. "By persuasion and force they have been made to retire," 1829

In December 1829, President Andrew Jackson (1767–1845) announced to Congress his view that Indian tribal sovereignty was incompatible with state's rights and development. Jackson proposed removing Indians from inside states east of the Mississippi to unsettled lands west of the river. His proposal focused particularly on the most numerous and wealthy of the tribes of the southeastern United States—the Cherokee, Chickasaw, Choctaw, Creek, and Seminole. The tensions between tribes and states proved persistent, but removing Indians westward proved no solution as relentless settlement followed them and continued to reduce their lands and attack their way of life.

The condition and ulterior destiny of the Indian tribes within the limits of some of our States have become objects of much interest and importance. It has long been the policy of Government to introduce among them the arts of civilization, in the hope of gradually reclaiming them from a wandering life. This policy has, however, been coupled with another wholly incompatible with its success.

Professing a desire to civilize and settle them, we have at the same time lost no opportunity to purchase their lands and thrust them farther into the wilderness. By this means they have not only been kept in a wandering state, but been led to look upon us as unjust and indifferent to their fate. Thus, though lavish in its expenditures upon the subject, Government has constantly defeated its own policy, and the Indians in general, receding farther and farther to the west, have retained their savage habits.

A portion, however, of the Southern tribes, having mingled much with the whites and made some progress in the arts of civilized life, have lately attempted to erect an independent government within the limits of Georgia and Alabama. These States, claiming to be the only sovereigns within their territories extended their laws over the Indians, which induced the latter to call upon the United States for protection.

Under these circumstances the question presented was whether the General Government had a right to sustain those people in their pretensions. The Constitution declares that "no new State shall be formed or erected within the jurisdiction of any other State" without the consent of its legislature. If the General Government is not permitted to tolerate the erection of a confederate State within the territory of one of the members of this Union against her consent, much less could it allow a foreign and independent government to establish itself there. . . .

Actuated by this view of the subject, I informed the Indians inhabiting part of Georgia and Alabama that their attempt to establish an independent government would not be countenanced by the Executive of the United States, and advised them to emigrate beyond the Mississippi or submit to the laws of those States.

Our conduct toward these people is deeply interesting to our national character. Their present condition, contrasted with what they once were, makes a most powerful appeal to our sympathies. Our ancestors found them the uncontrolled possessors of these vast regions. By persuasion and force they have been made to retire from river to river and from mountain to mountain, until some of the tribes have become extinct and others have left but remnants to preserve for a while their once terrible names.

Surrounded by the whites with their arts of civilization, which by destroying the resources of the savage doom him to weakness and decay, the fate of the Mohegan, the Narragansett, and the Delaware is fast over-taking the Choctaw, the Cherokee, and the Creek. That this fate surely awaits them if they remain within the limits of the States does not admit of a doubt.

Humanity and national honor demand that every effort should be made to avert so great a calamity. It is too late to inquire whether it was just in the United States to include them and their territory within the bounds of the new States, whose limits they could control. That step can not be retraced. . . . But the people of those States and of every State, actuated by feelings of justice and a regard for our national honor, submit to you the interesting question whether something can not be done, consistently with the rights of the States to preserve this much-injured race.

As a means of effecting this end I suggest for your consideration the propriety of setting apart an ample district west of the Mississippi, and without the limits of any State or Territory now formed, to be guaranteed to the Indian tribes as long as they shall occupy it, each tribe having a distinct control over the portion designated for its use. There they may be secured in the enjoyment of governments of their own choice, subject to no other control from the United States than such as may be necessary to preserve peace on the frontier and between the several tribes. There the benevolent may endeavor to teach them the arts of civilization, and, by promoting union and harmony among them, to raise up an interesting commonwealth, destined to perpetuate the race and to attest the humanity and justice of this Government.

This emigration should be voluntary, for it would be as cruel as unjust to compel the aborigines to abandon the graves of their fathers and seek a home in a distant land. But they should be distinctly informed that if they remain within the limits of the States they must be subject to their laws. In return for their obedience as individuals they will without doubt be protected in the enjoyment of those possessions which they have improved by their industry. But it seems to me visionary to suppose that in this state of things claims can be allowed on tracts of country on which they have neither dwelt nor made improvements, merely because they have seen them from the mountain or passed them in the chase. Submitting to the laws of the States, and receiving, like other citizens, protection in their persons and property, they will ere long become merged in the mass of our population.

Source: President Andrew Jackson, First Annual Message to Congress, December 8, 1829, in *A Compilation of the Messages and Papers of the Presidents, 1789–1897* (New York: Bureau of National Literature, 1897), 1005–1025.

2.2.   "Arguments in favor of the bill," 1830

> *In July 1829, the Vermont-born Yale College graduate and lawyer Jeremiah Evarts (1781–1831) emerged as a leading opponent of Indian removal when his "William Penn" Essays—demonstrating the southeastern Indians' legal title to, and rightful possession of, their remaining lands—became the most widely read American political pamphlet since Tom Paine's* Common Sense *(1776). As part of his opposition, Evarts later outlined the other side's arguments in Congress in support of the Removal Act of 1830. He raised questions about what rights Indians had, about what justice required, and about the future of race relations between Indians and whites.*

On the question, whether the Indians had any right to their country or not, it was alleged, by the advocates of the bill . . . [:]

That the Cherokees are a conquered people, having been the allies of Great Britain in the revolutionary war, and

That, being a conquered people, they have no claim to territory or self-government.

It is not unjust, or oppressive, therefore, in Georgia to assert her claims to the land of the Cherokees.

In answer to the plea for protection, which the Cherokees offer, it was urged,

That, although many compacts had been made between the United States and Indians, which had been called treaties, and which had been sent to the Senate and ratified as treaties, yet, when made with tribes residing in any State, they were not in fact treaties, within the meaning of the Constitution:

That these compacts, which are called treaties, were submitted to by the several States, because the States acquired lands in this manner; but when the States were limited in their jurisdiction, and restrained in their rights, by these compacts, it could not be expected that they would submit any longer.

That compacts with Indians not within the limits of States are treaties, according to the Constitution; because, in these cases, the national government alone can treat with them. . . .

That it is very absurd to suppose, that independent States will suffer their limits to be curtailed by tribes of savages. . . .

As to the conflicting claims of Georgia and the Cherokees, while some advocates of the bill considered all existing treaties with Indians as mere nullities, others held, that the treaties would be binding on the United States, were it not for pre-existing obligations, incompatible with these treaties. . . . [I]t was argued, that the United States had guaranteed the integrity of all the separate States, and therefore could not guaranty the possession of the Indians residing upon any part of the chartered territory of States. The general government must therefore do the best it can. When it cannot fulfil an obligation, it must indemnify for the failure to fulfil. . . .

It was stated, also, that the removal of the Indians would be greatly to their advantage, and, on this account, should receive the support of all their real friends. The country to which they were invited to remove, was represented as very fertile, and abundantly large for a residence of all the tribes. . . .

In carrying on the business of removal, all the advocates of the bill disclaimed a resort to force. The subject is to be fairly proposed to the Indians; and, if they are willing to remove, the government will kindly aid them in doing so. If they prefer to stay, they must come under State laws, and, of course, be subject to all the laws which the States shall see fit to enact hereafter. From the operation of these laws the United States cannot protect them.

The present condition of the Indians was represented as being exceedingly wretched. They were said to be, generally, in a more hopeless state than at any previous period of their history. The chiefs were charged with ruling the common people with severity. It was said, that the chiefs appropriate all the annuities to their own benefit.

The sympathy professed, in different parts of the United States, for the Cherokees, was described as the work of fanatics, and pretended philanthropists, who had their own purposes to answer, and who were well paid for their services from the Cherokee treasury. This allegation is so gross a slander, that it would be wrong to repeat it without saying, that it is totally destitute of foundation; and that there is not, and never was, a particle of evidence in support of it.

The foregoing summary embraces, it is believed, all the arguments in favor of the bill. Some of its advocates expressed a strong belief that the removal of the Indians would be for their benefit. But others boldly declared, that this was not their *object*, and that the Indians would not be improved in their condition, whether they should remove or remain.

Source: Speeches on the Passage of the Bill for the Removal of the Indians, Delivered in the Congress of the United States, April and May, 1830 (Boston: Perkins and Martin; New York: Jonathan Leavitt, 1830).

2.3.   "We are not willing to remove," 1830

The Committee and Council of the Cherokee Nation offered an official response to President Andrew Jackson's removal policy and to the Removal Act of May 1830 in an "Address . . . to the People of the United States," published in the official tribal newspaper, the Cherokee Phoenix and Indians' Advocate in July 1830. The Cherokee message was clear: "We are not willing to remove," and the United States guaranteed our rights by treaty to stay in "the pleasant land," "the land of our fathers." Snubbed by federal officials, the Cherokee found the U.S. government no friend in fending off incursions on Indians lands

*and rights. They raised fundamental issues: What was the basis of re-
lations between Indians and whites? What, if any, duty did the United
States have in regard to Indians? Would the United States honor its
treaty promises? And they noted that Indians were not all one and the
same, simply to be lumped together in one place.*

Some months ago a delegation was appointed by the constituted authorities
of the Cherokee nation . . . to lay before the government of the United States
such representations, as should seem most likely to secure to us, as a people,
that protection, aid, and good neighborhood, which had been so often promised to us, and of which we stand in great need. . . .

During four long months our delegation waited at the doors of the National
Legislature of the United States, and the people at home, in the most painful
suspense, to learn in what manner our application would be answered; and,
now that Congress has adjourned, on the very day before the date fixed by
Georgia for the extension of her oppressive laws over the greater part of our
country, the distressing intelligence has been received, that we have received
no answer at all; and no department of the government has assured us that we
are to receive the desired protection. But just at the close of the session, an act
was passed, by which half a million of dollars was appropriated towards effecting a removal of Indians; and we have great reason to fear that the influence of this act will be brought to bear most injuriously upon us. . . .

Thus have we realized, with heavy hearts, that our supplication has not been
heard; that the protection heretofore experienced is now to be withheld; that
the guaranty, in consequence of which our fathers laid aside their arms and
ceded the best portions of their country, means nothing; and that we must either emigrate to an unknown region and leave the pleasant land to which we
have the strongest attachments, or submit to the legislation of a State which
has already made our people outlaws, and enacted that any Cherokee, who
shall endeavor to prevent the selling of his country, shall be imprisoned. . . .

The Cherokees have always fulfilled their engagements. . . . Is the duty of fulfilling engagements on the other side less binding than it would be, if the
Cherokees had the power of enforcing their just claims?

The people of the United States will have the fairness to reflect, that all the
treaties between them and the Cherokees were made at the solicitation, and for
the benefit, of the whites. . . . [O]ur people have trusted their country to the
guaranty of the United States. If this guaranty fails them, in what can they
trust? [A]nd where can they look for protection?

We are aware that some persons suppose it will be for our advantage to remove beyond the Mississippi. We think otherwise. Our people universally
think otherwise. . . . We are not willing to remove; and if we could be brought
to this extremity, it would be not by argument; not because our judgment was
satisfied; not because our condition will be improved—but only because we
cannot endure to be deprived of our national and individual rights, and subjected to a process of intolerable oppression.

We wish to remain on the land of our fathers. We have a perfect and original right to claim this, without interruption or molestation. The treaties with
us, and laws of the United States made in pursuance of treaties, guaranty our

residence, and our privileges, and secure us against intruders. Our only request is, that these treaties may be fulfilled, and these laws executed.

But if we are compelled to leave our country, we see nothing but ruin before us.

The country west of the Arkansas territory is unknown to us. From what we can learn of it, we have no prepossessions of its favor. All the inviting parts of it, as we believe, are pre-occupied by various Indian nations, to which it has been assigned. They would regard us as intruders, and look upon us with an evil eye. The far greater part of that region is, beyond all controversy, badly supplied with wood and water; and no Indian tribe can live as agriculturists without these articles. All our neighbors, in case of our removal, though crowded into our near vicinity, would speak a language totally different from ours, and practise different customs. The original possessors of that region are now wandering savages, lurking for prey in the neighborhood. They have always been at war, and would be easily tempted to turn their arms against peaceful emigrants.

Were the country to which we are urged much better than it is represented to be, and were it free from the objection which we have made to it, still it is not the land of our birth, nor of our affections. It contains neither the scenes of our childhood, nor the graves of our fathers. The removal of families to a new country, even under the most favorable auspices, and when the spirits are sustained by pleasing visions of the future, is attended with much depression of mind and sinking of heart. . . .

[A]ll will agree only in this, that they have been cruelly robbed of their country, in violation of the most solemn compacts which it is possible for communities to form with each other; and that, if, they should make themselves comfortable in their residence, they have nothing to expect hereafter but to be the victims of a future legalized robbery! . . .

We appeal to the judge of all the earth, who will finally award us justice, and to the good sense of the American people. . . . On the soil which contains the ashes of our beloved men, we wish to live, on this soil we wish to die.

We entreat those to whom the foregoing paragraphs are addressed, to remember the great law of love, "Do to others as ye would that others should do to you." Let them remember that of all nations on the earth, they are under the greatest obligation to obey this law.

Source: "Appeal to the People of the United States," *Cherokee Phoenix and Indians' Advocate*, July 24, 1830.

2.4.   "A great many talks from our great father," 1830

In contrast to the Cherokee Nation's appeal to the people of the United States, the Cherokee Speckled Snake ridiculed removal policies. He highlighted the incongruities of U.S. policy to show his fellow Cherokee the devastating pattern of their relations with whites' continually taking what Indians had and pushing them to the margin. Using irony, Speckled Snake mocked not only President Andrew Jack-

son but any Indians who refused to see and stand against the repeated assaults on Indian life.

Brothers! We have heard the talk of our great father. It is very kind. He says he loves his red children.

Brothers! When the white man first came to these shores, the Muscogees gave him land, and kindled him a fire to make him comfortable. And when the pale faces of the south made war on him, their young men drew the tomahawk, and protected his head from the scalping knife.

But when the white man had warmed himself before the Indian's fire, and filled himself with the Indian's hominy, he became very large. He stopped not for the mountain tops, and his feet covered the plains and the valleys. His hands grasped the eastern and the western sea.

Then he became our great father. He loved his red children; but said, "You must move a little farther, lest I should, by accident, tread on you." With one foot he pushed the red man over the Oconee [river in northeastern and central Georgia], and with the other he trampled down the graves of his fathers. But our great father still loved his red children, and he soon made them another talk. He said much; but it all meant nothing, but "move a little farther; you are too near me."

I heard a great many talks from our great father, and they all began and ended the same, *Brothers!*

When he made us a talk on a former occasion, he said, "Get a little farther; go beyond the Oconee and the Oakmulgee [in west central Alabama]. There is a pleasant country." He also said, "It shall be yours forever."

Now he says, "The land you live on is not yours; go beyond the Mississippi; there is game; there you may remain while the grass grows or the water runs."

Brothers! Will not our great father come there also? He loves his red children, and his tongue is not forked.

Source: Samuel G. Drake, *The Book of the Indians*, 8th ed. (Boston: Antiquarian Bookstore, 1841), 450. My thanks to my former colleague, Professor Albert L. Hurtado, for help with locating this source. Also, my thanks to Special Collections, Department of Archives and Manuscripts, University Libraries, Arizona State University, Tempe.

2.5.   "That the Choctaw may live under their own laws in peace," 1830

The Choctaw were the first of the major tribes in the southeastern United States to accede to removal. The Treaty of Dancing Rabbit Creek with the Choctaw Nation of Red People in September 1830 expressed the terms of their agreement to undergo removal. It was not what the Choctaw wanted to do; it was what they felt they had no other choice but to do.

A treaty of perpetual friendship, cession and limits. . . .

WHEREAS the General Assembly of the State of Mississippi has extended the laws of said State to persons and property within the chartered limits of the same, and the President of the United States has said that he cannot protect the Choctaw people from the operation of these laws;

Now therefore that the Choctaw may live under their own laws in peace with the United States and the State of Mississippi they have determined to sell their lands east of the Mississippi and have accordingly agreed to the following articles of treaty: [The U.S. Senate refused to ratify the foregoing paragraph.]

ARTICLE 1. Perpetual peace and friendship is pledged and agreed upon by and between the United States and . . . the Choctaw Nation of Red People. . . .

ARTICLE 2. The United States under a grant specially to be made by the President of the U.S. shall cause to be conveyed to the Choctaw Nation a tract of country west of the Mississippi River, in fee simple to them and their descendants, to inure to them while they shall exist as a nation and live on it. . . .

ARTICLE 3. In consideration of the provisions contained in the several articles of this Treaty, the Choctaw nation of Indians consent and hereby cede to the United States, the entire country they own and possess, east of the Mississippi River; and they agree to move beyond the Mississippi River, early as practicable, and will so arrange their removal, that as many as possible of their people not exceeding one half of the whole number, shall depart during the falls of 1831 and 1832; the residue to follow during the succeeding fall of 1833; a better opportunity in this manner will be afforded the Government, to extend to them the facilities and comforts which it is desirable should be extended in conveying them to their new homes.

ARTICLE 4. The Government and people of the United States are hereby obliged to secure to the said Choctaw Nation of Red People the jurisdiction and government of all the persons and property that may be within their limits west, so that no Territory or State shall ever have a right to pass laws for the government of the Choctaw Nation of Red People and their descendants; and that no part of the land granted them shall ever be embraced in any Territory or State; but the U.S. shall forever secure said Choctaw Nation from, and against, all laws except such as from time to time may be enacted in their own National Councils, not inconsistent with the Constitution, Treaties, and Laws of the United States; and except such as may, and which have been enacted by Congress, to the extent that Congress under the Constitution are required to exercise a legislation over Indian Affairs. But the Choctaws, should this treaty be ratified, express a wish that Congress may grant to the Choctaws the right of punishing by their own laws, any white man who shall come into their nation, and infringe any of their national regulations.

Source: Treaty of Dancing Rabbit Creek with the Choctaw Nation of Red People, 7 Stat. 333 (September 27, 1830); proclaimed ratified February 24, 1831.

ANNOTATED RESEARCH GUIDE

Books

De Rosier, Arthur H., Jr. *The Removal of the Choctaw Indians*. Knoxville: University of Tennessee Press, 1970. Succinctly describes the removal experience of the eastern tribe that set the pattern for the forced Indian trek from the southeast to west of the Mississippi.

McLoughlin, William G. *After the Trail of Tears: The Cherokees' Struggle for Sovereignty 1839–1880*. Chapel Hill: University of North Carolina Press, 1993. Picks up the story after the trek to follow the tribe's cultural, social, and political development.

Norgren, Jill. *The Cherokee Cases*. New York: McGraw-Hill, 1996. Treats the historical context and consequences of Chief Justice John Marshall's opinions in *Johnson v. McIntosh* (1823), *Cherokee Nation v. Georgia* (1831), and *Worcester v. Georgia* (1832), which form the so-called Marshall trilogy as the bedrock of federal Indian law.

Perdue, Theda, and Michael D. Green. *The Cherokee Removal: A Brief History with Documents*. Boston: Bedford/St. Martin's Press, 2004. Neatly sets the Cherokee Trail of Tears with the tribe's expulsion from the eastern United States in an outline of early national racial attitudes and expansionism.

Remini, Robert V. *Andrew Jackson & His Indian Wars*. New York: Viking, 2001. Views Jackson's policy of forced Indian removal and relocation west of the Mississippi through a sympathetic lens that casts Jackson as a man of justice who insisted on enforcing rights guaranteed Indians by U.S. treaties.

———. *The Legacy of Andrew Jackson: Essays on Democracy, Indian Removal, and Slavery*. Baton Rouge: Louisiana State University Press, 1988. Exposes the "awful legacy" for Indians and blacks of the whites-only essence of Jackson's push for national integrity and security.

Rogin, Michael Paul. *Fathers and Children: Andrew Jackson and the Subjugation of the American Indian*. New York: Vintage Books, 1976. Mixes biography, history, and psychohistory to explain Jackson's stance against Indians in the War of 1812, in the Creek and Seminole Indian Wars, and later in his presidency.

Wallace, Anthony F. C. *The Long, Bitter Trail: Andrew Jackson and the Indians*. New York: Hill and Wang, 1993. Treats Indian relocation broadly but focuses especially on the Cherokees, Creeks, Choctaws, Chickasaws, and Seminoles and on the continuing effects of their removal from their eastern homelands to west of the Mississippi.

Williams, David. *The Georgia Gold Rush: Twenty-Niners, Cherokees, and Gold Fever*. Columbia: University of South Carolina Press, 1993. Describes the impact on relations of the thousands of white prospectors who worked the southern Appalachians mountains and valleys in search of gold from the late 1820s through the early 1840s.

Web Sites

http://www.nationaltota.org—the Trail of Tears Association Web site provides general information, trail maps, stories, and databases illustrating the trek and its impact on the Indian tribes.

http://www.nhc.rtp.nc.us/tserve/nattrans/ntecoindian/ecolinksindianrem.htm—offers links to online resources including essays on the effects of the removal on American Indian tribes and official Web sites of the five tribes, in addition to bibliographies.

http://www.pbs.org/wgbh/aia/part4/4p2959.html—overviews policies and practices focused on expanding white settlement and dispossession of the Indians east of the Mississippi from 1814 to 1858, with links to related documents, a resource bank, and a teacher's guide.

http://www.rosecity.net/tears/trail/tearsnht.html—treats the National Historic Trail—1838–1839 Cherokee Trail of Tears, providing documents and links to other Web sites treating Indian removal.

http://www.synaptic.bc.ca/ejournal/IndianRemovalAct.htm—a resource page on Andrew Jackson, his Indian removal policy, and the Trail of Tears in the track of U.S. westward expansion.

http://www.tampabayhistorycenter.org/semwars.htm—provides a timeline of the Seminole Wars and links to broad history of removal of the eastern Indians.

3

Nat's Rebellion: Slaves and America's Future

In August 1831, blacks in Virginia's Southampton County acted out a perennial nightmare of American slaveholders. Arming themselves according to plan, several gathered on Sunday, August 21, to make good their vision of a better life. In the dark, early before sunrise on Monday, August 22, they started at Joseph Travis's home.

A thirty-year-old named Nat led the planning. A slave Benjamin Turner once owned but whom Travis had bought twenty months earlier, Nat struck the first blow. Killing Travis and then his wife and three children in their sleep, the group marched into Southampton's countryside and headed toward Jerusalem, where the district armory held guns, powder, shot, and other munitions. Less than 100 miles southeast of the state capital at Richmond, the town was the site of local power. It was the county seat and population center for Southampton's 16,000, in which blacks outnumbered whites about six to four.[1]

The number of black rebels ebbed and flowed as they progressed over two days, reaching at least forty and perhaps as many as seventy-five. Along their way, they killed at least sixty whites—slaughtering all they found, regardless of age, sex, or infirmity.

Their route headed toward the Dismal Swamp 30 miles (48 kilometers) to the east. Its densely forested marshlands, stretched about 2,000 square miles (5,200 square kilometers) on the Atlantic coast from southeastern Virginia to northeastern North Carolina. It promised refuge. It offered an escape to the ocean, too, through the connections to the Chesapeake Bay. The fugitives needed, however, to bypass the traffic on the Dismal Swamp Canal, constructed between 1790 and 1828 as an intracoastal waterway.

The uprising alarmed whites near and far. Locals immediately rallied, and Virginia Governor John Floyd dispatched state militia. More than 3,000 white men mustered to hunt the insurgents, responding from Virginia and neighboring North Carolina.

A mounted posse discovered part of the rebel band on August 22 about three miles outside Jerusalem and the next day routed the remainder after it attacked another home. Nat, whom some reports had taken to calling "General Nat," escaped along with others.

Pursuing the remnant and bitter at the white blood blacks had shed, vengeful whites slaughtered unspoken-for black men they laid hands on, regardless of whether the blacks had been part of Nat's band. They decapitated perhaps a dozen and posted the heads on pikes as terrible signs to show who held ultimate power. A correspondent, whose account appeared in Richmond's semi-weekly *Constitutional Whig* newspaper on September 3, described the retaliation as a clear threat that "another insurrection will be followed by putting the whole race to the sword."[2]

Nat eluded capture for nearly nine weeks, until October 30. An object of intense curiosity, while in the Southampton County jail Nat entertained inquiries from the enterprising Thomas R. Gray, who saw profit in "the gratification of public curiosity."[3] Many whites craved an account of what they called a "mystery." How had this atrocity happened? What caused it? How was it carried out? Who was involved?

Nat's statement to Gray, given on November 1 and 3, was labeled a "confession"—*The Confessions of Nat Turner, the Leader of the Late Insurrection in Southampton, Va.* Detailing his actions and visions, Nat explained his role by way of autobiography. He cast his life as one of destiny from his birth to an African-born mother and a runaway-slave father on a small, Virginia plantation Benjamin Turner owned (thus accounting for many calling him Nat Turner, as slaves often carried their holder's family name). Nat noted that he had learned to read and write and that he had religious visions that prompted some of his fellow blacks to call him "the Prophet." He further described himself, like Moses, as called by God to set his people free.

When Nat stood trial in Southampton County Court on Saturday, November 5, 1831, for "feloniously counselling, advising and conspiring with . . . divers slaves to rebel and make insurrection and making insurrection and taking the lives of divers free white persons of the Commonwealth," the outcome was a foregone conclusion.[4] The court declared him guilty and sentenced him to hang by the neck until dead on November 11.

The rampage Nat led spread infectiously into the American popular psyche. Questions attached to both the cause and career of "ole Nat's fray" and his seventy days at large after the insurgents' rout added to concerns. Was the episode merely a foolish "fray" a fanatic had directed, or was it a flare-up signaling more profound danger?

Hawking his own product, Thomas R. Gray labeled the episode "the first instance in our history of an open rebellion of the slaves."[5] But the plot Nat led was not unprecedented. It occurred almost exactly thirty-one years after hurricanelike rainstorms and floods in August 1800 aborted a three-pronged attack on Richmond by about 1,000 blacks that Thomas H. Prosser's slave Gabriel planned.

Like Nat, Gabriel also claimed to have had religious visions. His mother also was born in Africa. And he, too, suffered Nat's fate. Gabriel and more than thirty of his fellow plotters hanged to death as a result of the investigation and prosecution that followed Virginia Governor James Monroe's being informed of the plot.

Nat's plan appeared much less grand than Gabriel's, who was perhaps inspired by Toussaint-Louverture—the slave born François Dominique Toussaint, who amid the French Revolution (1789–1799) led what became the most vast and victorious slave rebellion in history. The Haitian Revolution began in 1791 in France's Caribbean island colony then called Saint-Domingue. It ended in 1804 with Haiti's declaration of independence as the second new nation of the Americas.

Nat had other examples to follow. One was Denmark Vesey, an artisan who had purchased his freedom from slavery in South Carolina in 1800 and had studied Toussaint's feats. Chafing at the chains on blacks inside and outside of slavery, Vesey built a network of perhaps as many as 9,000 blacks in and around South Carolina's leading city, Charleston. Vesey planned a massive uprising to raze the Atlantic port city and its environs; but word leaked in June 1822, and state authorities arrested at least 130 blacks, including the leader.

Vesey hanged along with thirty-six others convicted of plotting insurrection. Harsh reaction from South Carolina's ruling whites reflected their fear of concerted action among the 258,497 blacks who composed the majority (52.7 percent) of the state's 1820 population. The response also reflected memory of the Stono Rebellion of 1739 when a band of slaves, not unlike those who gathered with Nat in 1831, rampaged about twenty miles outside of Charleston and set out on a path to promised freedom in Spanish Florida, killing twenty to twenty-five whites along the way.

Wherever Nat and his band's action fit with slave resistance or whatever it was labeled—a first, a rebellion, an insurrection, a revolt—the deadly action in the nation's largest slaveholding state in 1830 spotlighted slavery as a national worry. With the number of slaves in the nation multiplying, not only local safety but the prevailing vision of the United States as a white man's country appeared increasingly imperiled.

The nearly 2 million slaves in the United States in 1830 were spreading farther into the new territories slated to become the nation's future states. Of the eleven states admitted to the Union after the thirteen original states and before 1830, six were slave states—Kentucky (1792), Tennessee (1796), Louisiana (1812), Mississippi (1817), Alabama (1819), and Missouri (1821). By 1830 those six states held 624,708 slaves, almost one-third—31.4 percent, to be exact—of the nation's 1,987,428 slaves.

Such a spread of slaves to new states undermined the vision of the United States as a land of opportunity for whites. Because black slave labor limited the market for local white labor, many whites objected to slavery. They objected to competing with slaves. They wanted slavery *and* slaves banished from the

United States, much as Virginia slaveholder Thomas Jefferson had suggested in the 1780s in his *Notes on the State of Virginia*, when he advocated emancipation and colonization.[6]

The American Colonization Society (ACS) organized in 1817 for the express purpose of transporting blacks from the United States to Africa. Congress endorsed the removal idea. So did such prominent persons as future presidents James Monroe and Andrew Jackson, Speaker of the House Henry Clay, and Bushrod Washington, an associate justice of the U.S. Supreme Court and nephew of the first president. In the 1820s the ACS made headway for a settlement in the Cape Mesurado area of West Africa, south of the large natural harbor named Freetown, where Great Britain established its colony of Sierra Leone as a haven for Africans the Royal Navy rescued from the outlawed trans-Atlantic slave trade. The ACS named its primary settlement Monrovia in honor of President James Monroe. From it developed Liberia, which declared itself an independent nation in 1847.

Ridding the United States of all blacks, beginning with the unenslaved called "free negroes," appealed to many. Indeed, new states and territories eschewed blacks unless they were slaves. And a movement to end slavery itself was growing. Even within southern slaveholding areas, antislavery had continued to flicker from interest between 1777 and 1804. The South had watched with attention as all of the states north of Maryland adopted policies to end slavery.

Nat's actions in August 1831 excited all sides on the slavery issue. The Southampton episode especially widened the growing sectional split between the southern states that maintained slavery and those states, commonly called the North, that prohibited it. Southern slaveholders viewed Nat as a creature spawned by northern antislavery agitators. Indeed, the radical David Walker in 1829 had urged slaves to do what Nat and his band had done—take up arms.

In a fiery pamphlet titled *Walker's Appeal, in Four Articles; Together with a Preamble, to the Coloured Citizens of the World, but in Particular, and Very Expressly, to Those of the United States of America*, Walker outlined a race war in which it was "kill or be killed."[7] Referring to whites, Walker told his fellow blacks that "they want us for their slaves, and think nothing of murdering us." In that context, the North Carolina–born black then living in Boston, Massachusetts, counseled his fellows that "it is no more harm for you to kill a man who is trying to kill you, than it is for you to take a drink of water when thirsty."[8] Such language enraged many whites, especially slaveholders who discovered copies in Georgia, Louisiana, and Virginia within weeks of the *Appeal*'s publication in Boston.

Walker stood virtually alone as a public advocate of slave violence. A growing number joined him, however, in rejecting blacks' removal in schemes such as the ACS's emigration program. A small number joined also in Walker's uncompromising moral opposition to slavery. Some joined with spilled-over indignation from the U.S. treatment of Indians in the Removal Act of 1830. Many took heart from antislavery successes in Europe. Activity in Great Britain particularly encouraged antislavery thinking and organizing in the United States. In 1833 agitation in Britain would push Parliament to enact an emancipation plan to end slavery in its West Indian colonies. Antislavery appeared on the move, and its advocates in the United States were becoming increasingly shrill.

Walker's *Appeal* and increasing outside agitation against slavery moved many white southerners to recalcitrance. Nat's actions solidified that stance. The Southampton episode reconfirmed for many whites the need for an ever-present iron heel to suppress blacks. Stricter laws immediately resulted. States stiffened both their slave code and their black code governing the unenslaved. Nat's revelations that he was literate and that he had shared his religious visions with other blacks provoked particularly forbidding reaction. Not only in Virginia but throughout the slave states, focus fell on prohibiting and punishing slaves' preaching or congregating or learning to read. To defend slavery further, proponents resorted to increasingly elaborate arguments. They used the Bible, church teaching, economic necessity, and social conditions to nurture the germ of so-called scientific racism and white supremacy.

Thus the "great Bandit," as some called Nat, stirred highly flammable personal passions and national politics. Without exaggerating the action as "Old Nat's War," the more than sixty whites dead at Nat and his fellows' hands frightened people far and wide. The fetching white southern myth that portrayed slaves as contented, servile Sambos incapable of posing any real danger on their own at least flickered, if not faded, in the light of Nat's torches. His deeds also polarized positions for and against slavery.

In symbol and substance, Nat became an exhibit to sway people. Not only on slavery but on the proper structure of race relations, at least in regard to blacks and whites, Nat's doings served to show the U.S. public much of what it feared and did not want to hear. Nat became a figure in the national white man's country theme with its motif that blacks were the enemies within. His actions aggravated tensions in what Abraham Lincoln, an Illinois candidate for the U.S. Senate in 1858, would describe as a "house divided against itself."[9]

Nat stood then in a long line reaching back before the Constitution of 1787. It resurrected colonial slave uprisings such as that at Stono in 1739. It hearkened also to persistent sectional tensions over slavery and what later became known as "the Negro problem." Congress under the Articles of Confederation had responded to the tensions in 1787. Its Northwest Ordinance adopted a policy to section national territory: It prohibited slavery north of the Ohio River, while allowing slavery to the south. The so-called Missouri Compromise of 1820, treating the Louisiana Territory acquired in 1803, continued the policy. It set a line at 36° 30', allowing only Missouri north of the line to maintain slavery.

Nat emerged as a deadly symbol that loomed larger as old compromises on slavery faded. The Compromise of 1850, treating the territory the United States took in the War with Mexico (1846–1848), seemed a last gasp. Spreading violence erupted in "Bloody" or "Bleeding" Kansas after the Kansas-Nebraska Act of 1854 threw the two territories open to "popular sovereignty" that allowed settlers alone to decide the slavery question. The slave insurrection John Brown planned in his 1859 raid on the arsenal in Harpers Ferry in northwest Virginia seemed then not far removed at all from the slave insurrection of Nat and his Southampton fellows in southeast Virginia in 1831. Both hastened the Civil War (1861–1865) and major changes in race relations in the United States.

NOTES

1. Jerusalem later changed its name to Courtland and has continued to serve as the county's seat, as it has since 1749.

2. *Constitutional Whig* (Richmond, VA), September 3, 1830.

3. *The Confession, Trial, and Execution of Nat Turner, the Negro Insurrectionist: Also, a List of Persons Murdered in the Insurrection in Southampton County, Virginia, on the 21st and 22nd of August, 1831, with Introductory Remarks by T. R. Gray*, 1881 ed. (Petersburg, VA: Published by J. B. Ege, 1881; reprint, New York: AMS Press, 1975).

4. Ibid.

5. Ibid.

6. Thomas Jefferson, *Notes on the State of Virginia* (London: J. Stockdale, 1787).

7. David Walker, *Walker's Appeal, in Four Articles; Together with a Preamble, to the Coloured Citizens of the World, but in Particular, and Very Expressly, to Those of the United States of America, Written in Boston, State of Massachusetts, September 28, 1829*, 3rd and last ed. (Boston: D. Walker, 1830), 29.

8. Ibid., 29–30.

9. Abraham Lincoln, "A House Divided Against Itself Cannot Stand," speech at Springfield accepting the Republican nomination for U.S. Senate from Illinois, June 17, 1858, in *The Writings of Abraham Lincoln*, ed. Arthur Brooks Lapsley, 8 vols. (New York: G. P. Putnam's Sons, 1906), 3:1–13.

DOCUMENTS

3.1. "Rather be killed than to be a slave," 1829

David Walker (1785–1830) was born of a free black mother and an enslaved father in North Carolina. He removed to Boston, Massachusetts, where he owned and operated a used clothing store on the waterfront and contributed frequently to Freedom's Journal, *a weekly that began publishing in New York City in March 1827 as the first newspaper blacks owned and operated in the United States. His* Appeal, *published in Boston in September 1829, was one of the most radical antislavery documents ever circulated in the United States. It was a black nationalist and Pan-Africanist document long before the terms were coined. It offered a dark view of race relations rarely glimpsed in public in the United States or elsewhere; and it limned the setting for Nat's Rebellion. Walker preached defiant, aggressive black self-defense to change the basic conditions of race relations.*

I will ask one question here.—Can our condition be any worse?—Can it be more mean and abject? . . .

This question, my brethren, I leave for you to digest; and may God Almighty force it home to your hearts. . . .

Never make an attempt to gain our freedom or natural right, from under our cruel oppressors and murderers, until you see your way clear.

It is not to be understood here, that I mean for us to wait until God shall take us by the hair of our heads and drag us out of abject wretchedness and slavery. . . . God has been pleased to give us two eyes, two hands, two feet, and some sense in our heads. . . .

[Whites] have no more right to hold us in slavery than we have to hold them; we have just as much right, in the sight of God, to hold them and their children in slavery and wretchedness, as they have to hold us, and no more. . . .

When that hour arrives and you move, be not afraid or dismayed. . . . [I]f you commence, make sure work—do not trifle, for they will not trifle with you—they want us for their slaves, and think nothing of murdering us in order to subject us to that wretched condition—therefore, if there is an attempt made by us, kill or be killed.

Now I ask you, had you not rather be killed than to be a slave to a tyrant, who takes the life of your mother, wife, and dear little children? Look upon your mother, wife, and children, and answer God Almighty; and believe this, that it is no more harm for you to kill a man, who is trying to kill you, than it is for you to take a drink of water when thirsty; in fact, the man who will stand still and let another murder him, is worse than an infidel, and, if he has common sense, ought not to be pitied.

Source: *Walker's Appeal, in Four Articles; Together with a Preamble, to the Coloured Citizens of the World, but in Particular, and Very Expressly, to Those of the United States of America, Written in Boston, State of Massachusetts, September 28, 1829*, 3rd and last ed. (Boston: D. Walker, 1830).

3.2.   "That insurrection reads some salutary lessons," 1831

The Constitutional Whig, a leading semiweekly newspaper published in Richmond, Virginia, in its issue dated September 3, 1831, provided an overview and commentary on the Southampton episode, along with an impression of its impact on local race relations and of the then-still-elusive Nat. It downplayed the actual damage black rebels could inflict on whites and cautioned blacks not to think they could win anything lasting by violence. It cautioned whites also not to show fear and so encourage blacks to think or act foolishly. Throughout, the newspaper emphasized its view of the natural order of race relations—that blacks existed by whites' sufferance and needed to bow to white supremacy or be slaughtered.

Editors seem to have applied themselves to the task of alarming the public mind as much as possible by persuading the slaves to entertain a high opinion of their strength and consequences. While truth is always the best policy, and best remedy, the exaggeration to which we have alluded are calculated to give the slaves false conceptions of their numbers and capacity, by exhibiting the terror and confusion of the whites, and to induce them to think that practicable, which they see is so much feared by their superiors. . . .

The universal opinion in that part of the country is that Nat, a slave, a preacher, and a pretended prophet was the first mover, the actual leader, and the most remorseless of the executioners. . . . He is represented as a shrewd fellow, reads, writes, and preaches; and by various artifices had acquired great influence over the minds of the wretched beings whom he has led into destruction. . . .

We therefore incline to the belief that he acted upon no higher principle than the impulse of revenge against the whites, as the enslavers of himself and his race; that, being a fanatic, he possibly persuaded himself that Heaven would interfere. . . .

We suspect the truth will turn out to be that the conspiracy was confined to Southampton, and that the idea of its extensiveness originated in the panic which seized upon the South East of Virginia.

Such we believe to be a summary outline of the Southampton insurrection!—that insurrection reads some salutary lessons; to the whites the propriety of incessant vigilance; to the blacks, the madness of all attempts such as that in Southampton. A few lives they may indeed sacrifice, but possession of the country, even for a week, is the most chimerical of notions. We assert confidently that 20 armed whites would put to the route the whole negro population of Southampton, and we repeat our persuasion, that another insurrection will be followed by putting the whole race to the sword.

Source: Constitutional Whig (Richmond, VA), September 3, 1831.

3.3.   "The calamity will fall upon the whites," 1831

> *The* Daily Advertiser, *a newspaper in New York City, took issue with the Richmond, Virginia,* Constitutional Whig's *September 3 "summary outline of the Southampton insurrection." The "salutary lessons" of the episode in the* Advertiser's *view lay in recognizing the brutality of slavery. Much as the* Whig's *editor had admonished other southerners for "alarming the public mind," the* Advertiser *in an issue published between September 3 and 17, 1831, admonished the* Whig *for endangering public safety with wholesale racial threats in writing "that another insurrection will be followed by putting the whole race to the sword." The* Advertiser *suggested more discretion was in order so as to calm race relations and not foment deadlier black-white violence.*

The Richmond *Whig* contains an account, drawn by the editor of that paper, of the events and circumstances which occurred in the late negro insurrection in that State. . . .

The butcheries on both sides were dreadful. On the part of the insurgents, the indiscriminate slaughter of families—men, women, and children—were heartbreaking to the feelings, and affords a melancholy and most distressing, as well as natural result of the state of things in a large portion of our country. It is one of the necessary consequences of slavery; and it is perfectly idle to attempt to conceal it. . . .

After speaking of the atrocities committed by the blacks, [the *Whig*] says: "It is with pain that we speak of another feature of the Southampton rebellion; for we have been most unwilling to have our sympathies for the sufferers diminished or affected by their misconduct. We allude to the slaughter of many blacks without trial and under circumstances of great barbarity. How many have been thus put to death (generally by decapitation or shooting) reports vary; probably, however, some five and twenty, and from that to forty; possibly a yet larger number." . . .

The editor, however, acknowledges that his feelings were changed afterwards, and induced him in some measure to apologize for these people, and he adds, "Let the fact not be doubted by those whom it most concerns *that another such insurrection will be the signal for the extirpation of the whole black population,* in the quarter of the State where it occurs" and he afterwards repeats his persuasion "that another insurrection will be followed by putting *the whole race to the sword.*"

This language, and the ideas and feelings which it naturally and even necessarily excites, are shocking to the mind. It is obviously intended to be understood as a threat to the blacks, to deter them from the commission of such outrages in the future. But the consequences of it, if it is understood by that description of persons, may be as terrible to the whole as to the blacks. Miserably ignorant and degraded as the latter are, a sense of their own situation, and the oppressions under which they consider themselves as suffering, whenever they become so far excited by any cause, as to make an effort for their own emancipation, it is to be expected that they will be aroused to madness; and, in such bosoms, vengeance is the most natural feeling of the heart. Convince them that, if subdued, they will be subjected to promiscuous and indiscriminate slaughter, and the evils to be apprehended are of the most terrible and appalling character. All the whites who may fall within their power, must expect to be butchered without mercy. And as they will have the first opportunity to give vent to their feelings, the calamity will fall upon the whites, before there will be the least possible chance for interference from abroad to save them.

Whatever feelings, then, the editor of the *Whig* might have imbibed from the distressing scenes which he had so recently witnessed, we cannot but think it would have been more discreet in him to have withheld them from the public, lest the consequences of their promulgation might, in some possible emergency, have proved fatal to those whose security he was desirous of promoting.

Source: (New York City) *Daily Advertiser*, September 1831; reprinted in the *Liberator* (Boston, MA), September 17, 1831.

3.4.   "Woe to this guilty land," 1831

Founded and edited by abolitionist crusader William Lloyd Garrison (1805–1879), the weekly newspaper titled Liberator *began in Boston, Massachusetts, in January 1831 and grew into the most influential and reviled antislavery periodical in the antebellum United States. Its issue dated September 3, 1831, cast the Southampton episode in the context of heightened tensions over U.S. slavery and antislavery. While defending itself against charges of fomenting slave insurrection, the weekly described the episode as an inescapable consequence of slavery to which the nation should accustom itself unless and until it abolished the so-called Peculiar Institution and reoriented its race relations toward the true equality of liberty.*

What we have long predicted,—at the peril of being stigmatized as an alarmist and declaimer,—has commenced its fulfillment. . . .

In the first number of the *Liberator*, we alluded to the hour of vengeance. . . .

Read the account of the insurrection in Virginia, and say whether our prophecy be not fulfilled. . . . Turn again to the record of slaughter! Whole families have been cut off—not a mother, not a daughter, not a babe left. Dreadful retaliation! "The dead bodies of white and black lying just as they were slain, unburied"—the oppressor and the oppressed equal at last in death—what a spectacle!

Ye accuse the pacific friends of emancipation of instigating the slaves to re-volt. . . . The slaves need no incentive at our hands. They will find in their stripes—in their emaciated bodies—in their ceaseless toil—in their ignorant minds—in every field, in every valley, on every hill top and mountain, wher-ever you and your fathers have fought for liberty—in your speeches and con-versations, your celebrations, your pamphlets, your newspapers—voices in the air, sounds from across the ocean, invitations to resistance above, below, around them! What more do they need? Surrounded by such influences, and smarting under the newly made wounds, is it wonderful that they should rise to contend—as other "heroes" have contended—for their lost rights? It is *not* wonderful.

For ourselves, we are horror-struck at the late tidings. We have exerted our utmost efforts to avert the calamity. We have warned our countrymen of the danger of persisting in their unrighteous conduct. We have preached to the slaves the pacific precepts of Jesus Christ. We have appealed to Christians, phi-lanthropists and patriots, for their assistance to accomplish the great work of national redemption through the agency of moral power—of public opinion—of individual duty. How have we been received? We have been threatened, pro-scribed, vilified and imprisoned—a laughing stock and a reproach. . . .

If we have been hitherto urgent, and bold, and denunciatory in our efforts—hereafter we shall grow vehement and active with the increase of danger. We shall cry, in trumpet tones, night and day,—Woe to this guilty land, unless she speedily repents of her evil doings! The blood of millions of her sons cries aloud for redress! IMMEDIATE EMANCIPATION can alone save her from the vengeance of Heaven, and cancel the debt of ages!

Source: *Liberator*, September 3, 1831.

3.5.   "Warn the southern people of their danger," 1831

> A letter to the editor published in the Liberator on September 17, 1831, further emphasized the inescapable bloodshed slavery would let in the United States unless abolition occurred. But it went further to place the slaves' cause in the context of a worldwide freedom movement of which Fourth of July celebrations in the United States were themselves paradoxical evidence. The state of race relations in the United States between blacks and whites exposed the nation's per-sisting hypocrisy, the writer suggested.

Sir—I have sometimes heard people say that if it had not been for the *Liberator*, the slaves in Virginia would have been quiet. Opinions of this kind are uttered with the greatest gravity and confidence by persons who have never seen the *Liberator*, and in the absence of all evidence that any of the persons concerned in the late sanguinary proceedings in Virginia had ever read the paper.

The Truth is that men are too ready to ascribe sudden and violent eruptions of evil to the operation of temporary causes. Everyone is more ready to charge any sickness under which he may be suffering to some accident, rather than to a decaying constitution; he is willing to flatter himself that his malady is not deeply rooted in his frame.

There would, perhaps, be some show of justice in charging the recent insurrection to the *Liberator*, if no other obvious and sufficient causes of such rising could be pointed out, or if this were the first occasion on which slaves had risen against their masters. But, sir, the causes of negro insurrections may be discovered without any deep research,—they obtrude themselves upon our observation.

Negroes, like other men, have a spirit which rebels against tyranny and oppression. It is their wrongs and sufferings which have driven them to the unjustifiable measures which we now observe. Let any unprejudiced person read the law, which serve the practice of slavery in the Southern States, and he will see sufficient causes of insurrection, and will only wonder that they are not more frequent. . . .

Other obvious causes of insurrection might easily be pointed out; but I shall only advert to one.—This is a land of freedom. Nothing can prevent the slaves from hearing conversation and declamations of liberty and the rights of man. They perceive our annual celebration on the fourth of July. Can they fail to learn something of its causes? Do not our boastings of our resistance to British oppression sometimes reach their ears? Are they deaf to the sympathizing applause which the accounts of the noble resistance of Poland to Russian despotism, have been received in America? It cannot be. Even if they had less of a human nature than the whites, even if they were not keenly sensible of their wrongs, they would soon learn from their masters how to prize freedom.

But sir, everyone who is at all familiar with history, ancient or modern, must be aware that conspiracies and insurrections have always been frequent among slaves. They are the natural fruit of oppression. . . .

For slaveholders then to ascribe the recent disturbance in Virginia to the *Liberator*, seems very much like the charge of the wolf against the lamb of muddying the stream from which he was drinking, when she was standing at a point below him. It is unreasonable to call the *Liberator* the author of the outrages of the blacks, because it has endeavoured to warn the southern people of their danger, as it would be to charge a man with having set fire to your house, because he woke you and told you that it was in flames.

Source: *Liberator*, September 17, 1831.

3.6. "About this time I had a vision," 1831

> Nat's capture almost exactly ten weeks after his "insurrection"
> quickened demands for answers about him and the episode. His "confession," recorded and certified in Thomas R. Gray's fast-selling
> twenty-four-page pamphlet, hardly ended questions. Rather, it stirred
> continuing controversy. Many were unsure what to believe: Were the

words really Nat's? Were they a transcript or a translation? Could a slave have thought and talked as the language suggested? How had a slave got so out of hand? Did religion, misguided or not, trigger the violence? Were there others like Nat, other slaves who if they learned to read and write would follow the same course to take up arms to slay what Nat called the "serpent" of slavery's racial oppression? Suspicions about blacks' character, capacities, and intentions toward whites reflected the foundation of fears on which race relations lay in slavery and afterward. Below are excerpts from Nat's "Confessions."

You have asked me to give a history of the motives which induced me to undertake the late insurrection, as you call it. To do so I must go back to the days of my infancy. . . .

To a mind like mine, restless, inquisitive, and observant of everything that was passing, it is easy to suppose that religion was the subject to which it would be directed, and although this subject principally occupied my thoughts, there was nothing that I saw or heard of to which my attention was not directed.

The manner in which I learned to read and write, not only had great influence on my own mind. . . . This was a source of wonder to all in the neighborhood, particularly the blacks, and this learning was constantly improved at all opportunities. . . .

I was not addicted to stealing in my youth, nor have ever been, yet such was the confidence of the negroes in the neighborhood even at this early period of my life, in my superior judgment, that they would often carry me with them when they were going on any roguery, to plan for them. . . .

By this time, having arrived to man's estate and hearing the scriptures commented on at meetings, I was struck with that particular passage which says: "Seek ye the kingdom of heaven and all things shall be added unto you." . . .

Now, finding I had arrived to man's estate, and was a slave, and these revelations being made known to me, I began to direct my attention to this great object, to fulfil the purpose for which, by this time, I felt assured I was intended.

Knowing the influence I had obtained over the minds of my fellow-servants, (not by the means of conjuring and such like tricks, for to them I always spoke of such things with contempt,) but by the communion of the Spirit, whose revelations I often communicated to them, and they believed and said my wisdom came from God.

I now began to prepare them for my purpose by telling them something was about to happen that would terminate in fulfilling the great promise that had been made to me.

About this time I was placed under an overseer, from whom I ran away, and after remaining in the woods thirty days I returned, to the astonishment of the negroes on the plantation, who thought I had made my escape to some other part of the country, as my father had done before.

But the reason of my return was, that the Spirit appeared to me and said I had my wishes directed to the things of this world, and not to the kingdom of heaven, and that I should return to the service of my earthly master—"For he who knoweth his Master's will, and doeth it not, shall be beaten with many stripes, and thus have I chastened you."

And the negroes found fault and murmured against me, saying that if they had my sense they would not serve any master in the world.

And about this time I had a vision—and I saw white spirits and black spirits engaged in battle, and the sun was darkened—the thunder rolled in the heavens, and blood flowed in streams—and I heard a voice saying, "Such is your luck, such you are called to see, and let it come rough or smooth, you must surely bear it." . . .

And on the 12th of May, 1828, I heard a loud noise in the heavens, and the Spirit instantly appeared to me and said the Serpent was loosened, and Christ had laid down the yoke he had borne for the sins of men, and that I should take it on and fight against the Serpent, for the time was fast approaching when the first should be last and the last should be first. . . .

And by signs in the heavens that it would make known to me when I should commence the great work, and until the first sign appeared I should conceal it from the knowledge of men; and on the appearance of the sign (the eclipse of the sun last February,) I should arise and prepare myself and slay my enemies with their own weapons.

And immediately on the sign appearing in the heavens the seal was removed from my lips, and I communicated the great work laid out for me to do, to four, in whom I had the greatest confidence, (Henry, Hark, Nelson, and Sam.)

It was intended by us to have begun the work of death on the 4th of July last. Many were the plans formed and rejected by us, and it affected my mind to such a degree that I fell sick, and the time passed without our coming to any determination how to commence. Still forming new schemes and rejecting them, when the sign appeared again, which determined me not to wait longer. . . .

On Saturday evening, the 20th of August, it was agreed between Henry, Hark, and myself to prepare. . . .

[I] asked Will how came he there. He answered, his life was worth no more than others, and his liberty was dear to him. I asked him if he thought to obtain it. He said he would, or lose his life. This was enough. . . .

It was quickly agreed we should commence at home (Mr. J. Travis') on that night, and until we had armed and equipped ourselves, and gathered sufficient force, neither age nor sex was to be spared. . . .

A general destruction of property and search for money and ammunition, always succeeded the murders.

Source: The Confession, Trial, and Execution of Nat Turner, the Negro Insurrectionist: Also, a List of Persons Murdered in the Insurrection in Southampton County, Virginia, on the 21st and 22nd of August, 1831, with Introductory Remarks by T. R. Gray, 1881 ed. (Petersburg, VA: Published by J. B. Ege, 1881).

ANNOTATED RESEARCH GUIDE

Books

Aptheker, Herbert. *American Negro Slave Revolts*. New York: Columbia University Press, 1943. The classic catalog of slave resistance and white reaction, offering a historical sweep in which to place Nat Turner.

———. *Nat Turner's Slave Rebellion. Together with the Full Text of the So-called "Confessions" of Nat Turner Made in Prison in 1831*. New York: Published for AIMS by Humanities Press, 1966. Remains an insightful source to context and meaning, while supplying the historical text.

Egerton, Douglas R. *Gabriel's Rebellion: The Virginia Slave Conspiracies of 1800 and 1802.* Chapel Hill: University of North Carolina Press, 1993. Cuts to the core of blacksmith Gabriel's much-mythologized 1800 plot and reaches Sancho's 1802 slave plot to detail the racial hostility, economics, and class conflict that incited slave rebellion.

———. *He Shall Go out Free: The Lives of Denmark Vesey.* Rev. and updated ed. Lanham, MD: Rowman & Littlefield, 2004. Places Vesey and his fellow 1820s South Carolina plotters in the context of Charleston society to explain the experiences and expectations that fed black resistance.

Freehling, Alison Goodyear. *Drift Toward Dissolution: The Virginia Slavery Debate of 1831–1832.* Baton Rouge: Louisiana State University Press, 1982. Probes deep, continuing, and irrepressible divisions among white Virginians over slavery, as class and geography joined with racial views in reaction to Nat's Rebellion.

French, Scot. *The Rebellious Slave: Nat Turner in American Memory.* Boston: Houghton Mifflin, 2004. Fits Nat into a broad framework of developing perspectives on U.S. history and thinking about blacks and race relations.

Greenberg, Kenneth S., ed. *The Confessions of Nat Turner, and Related Documents.* Boston: Bedford/St. Martin's Press, 1996. Excerpts from the historical document along with other documents illustrate the time, place, and event.

———, ed. *Nat Turner: A Slave Rebellion in History and Memory.* New York: Oxford University Press, 2003. Essays reflecting fresh work on slave life and rebellion use multiple perspectives ranging from psychobiography to folklore to explain what Nat and his fellows did and what their actions meant.

Hinks, Peter P. *To Awaken My Afflicted Brethren: David Walker and the Problem of Antebellum Slave Resistance.* University Park: Pennsylvania State University Press, 1997. Reveals Walker as no lone voice crying in a wilderness but as resounding frustrations from a chorus of black leaders resisting growing antiblack proscriptions.

Tragle, Henry Irving, ed. *The Southampton Slave Revolt of 1831: A Compilation of Source Material.* Amherst: University of Massachusetts Press, 1971. Remains the single most comprehensive collection of documents and discussion of Nat's episode.

Web Sites

http://www.nathanielturner.com/nattunertroublesomeproperty.htm—provides details and links to and from the independent sixty-minute film *Nat Turner: A Troublesome Property* (San Francisco, CA: subpix LLC, 2002).

http://www.pbs.org/wgbh/aia/part3/3p1518.html—treats Nat Turner's Rebellion in Part Three of the PBS special *Africans in America* and links to a resource bank, a timeline on slave rebellions, and a discussion of the independent sixty-minute film *Nat Turner: A Troublesome Property* (2002).

4

War with Mexico: Race, Borders, and Manifest Destiny

The War with Mexico (1846–1848) stood at a confluence of developing race relations in the United States and profoundly influenced their history. It introduced on an unprecedented scale a new group in U.S. race relations—Mexican
Americans—and it shaped the basis for subsequent race relations, particularly
in the Southwest. The war also carved a path of fresh collisions over the place
of Indians in the United States, with racial overtones already clear from the
"Trail of Tears" removal of the 1830s and 1840s. Further, it directly impacted
the place of blacks with antislavery issues that cut along the sectional divide
that produced the Civil War and its monumental influence on race relations
throughout the United States.

The War with Mexico was the last cut of continental expansion westward
from Atlantic coastal settlements that laid the basis for race relations from even
before the United States established its independence. The initial settlements
that grew into the original United States involved encounters between European colonists and their descendants and North American Indians and then
also imported Africans and their descendants. Race accompanied expansion at
every step. Under the varying banner of culture, religion, or merely civilization, a kindred sense of entitled white, Protestant Christian community animated American settlers' self-extension and served as excuse for their
encroachment. Journalist John L. O'Sullivan in 1845 coined the phrase "Manifest Destiny" to explain the sense of just duty that required America to expand.
"Providence" directed the United States to "the fulfillment of our manifest destiny to overspread the continent," O'Sullivan declared.[1] In 1846 Mexico felt the
sharp edge of that destiny as its territory sat as the final barrier to the United
States' stretching from Atlantic to Pacific.

In confronting Mexico, the United States faced what it might have seen as a darker version of itself. It faced another new American nation that had thrown off European colonial rule and established independence. It also faced another multicultural society composed like itself mostly of Indians, Europeans, and Africans—although with very different proportions and policies of treating the various groups.

Like the United States, Mexico stretched across an area of broad cultural diversity. It included the remnants of great Indian civilizations such as the Maya and the Aztecs. It also included hundreds of thousands of Africans and their descendants Spain introduced as slaves in the colonial expanse called Nueva España (New Spain). The revolution for independence in what became Mexico exposed the racial hierarchy and discrimination of Spain's colonial regime. In 1810 when the creole Catholic priest Father Miguel Hidalgo y Costilla sounded his rebel cry in the village of Dolores, at least 60 percent of the population of 6.2 million in New Spain were Indians. Perhaps 20 percent were mestizos or mixed bloods. About 10 percent were of African descent. Less than 10 percent were Spaniards born in Spain. Tens of thousands of Indians, mestizos, and blacks rallied to the banner of national independence with hopes of racial equality and land redistribution. The revolution succeeded in giving birth in 1821 to Los Estados Unidos Mexicanos (the United Mexican States).

Unlike the United States of America, the United Mexican States formally incorporated its Indians and its Africans into its body politic. Indians were not excluded by definition as a group. Nor were blacks. Nevertheless, European lineage marked the core of Mexico's leadership. Its common borders with the United States added elements of white preference, particularly as the new Mexican nation competed along with its northeastern frontier with the neighboring United States.

The contest came to center in Mexico's province of Tejas, where settlers moved from the United States. By 1825, settlers, mostly from Louisiana and Mississippi, numbered 1,347 whites and 443 enslaved blacks. By 1831 the total numbered 5,665 persons spread across several settlements. Others from the United States joined the flow, increasing what was called the Anglo-American population to about 20,000 by 1835.[2]

Some settlers chafed against Mexican law, which among other things prohibited trafficking in slaves. More than a few settlers envisioned developing Texas's vast lands with enslaved blacks. Others opposed introducing any slaves. Indeed, Virginia-born emigrant leader Stephen F. Austin long opposed introducing slaves into Texas. "The idea of seeing such a country as this overrun by a slave population almost makes we weep," Austin confided to an acquaintance in June 1830.[3] But the demands of settlers, particularly from Louisiana and Mississippi, made slavery a reality in Texas—first contrary to, and then as a concession from, the Mexican government.

By 1835, disgruntled Texas emigrants were skirmishing with Mexican troops and forming a provisional government. The celebrated twelve-day siege, and eventual slaughter, at San Antonio's old Franciscan mission called the Alamo rallied the rebels. Six weeks later their victory over Mexican leader Antonio López de Santa Anna at the San Jacinto River in April 1836 signaled the success of the revolution and the start of the Republic of Texas.

Texans voted almost immediately in 1836 in favor of U.S. annexation. But the prospect of admitting another slave state to the Union, and one as vast as Texas, provoked deep political discord in the United States. New slave states meant new representatives and senators in Congress supporting slavery. That also meant more proslavery votes in determining who became president and vice president and more influence on whom the president appointed to public offices and projects. Most important to many, slavery's spread to new territories meant the spread of blacks where their presence might retard the growth of white population and thus further thwart the United States' becoming a "white man's country," which many argued was the nation's true Manifest Destiny. Not until December 1845 did Congress accept Texas as the twenty-eighth state.

Annexing Texas severed the already tenuous relations between Mexico and the United States. It also aggravated deep domestic divides over America's character and content. When war erupted in May 1846, its prospect and prosecution provoked widespread protest in the United States. Many saw the war as a plot to extend slavery. They viewed it as a land grab to add slave states to enhance slaveholders' power in local and national politics. For such reasons, they had opposed annexing Texas, and for such reasons, they abhorred going to war with Mexico. They viewed both as mistaken. To many such opponents, America's true Manifest Destiny existed in a vigorous and virtuous racial community, an expanding nation of white, Protestant Christians. War with Mexico threatened to spread slavery's stain on America's character. It threatened to extend competition between blacks and whites in territories whites preferred to reserve exclusively for themselves. It threatened also to push America to embrace new hordes of nonwhites and non-Protestants.

The onset of war pushed America to consider its limits. While some early suggested seizing all of Mexico, Congress shrank from the central, populous areas below the Rio Grande. It fixed on California and Mexico's less populated territories north and west of the river. No one appeared to want the people of Mexico. They wanted land, and that was where the slavery question stuck. Within three months of the U.S. declaration of war in May 1846, U.S. Representative David Wilmot, a Democrat from western Pennsylvania, moved to ban slavery from any territory acquired from Mexico. The so-called Wilmot Proviso declared,

> That, as an express and fundamental condition to the acquisition of any territory from the Republic of Mexico by the United States . . . neither slavery nor involuntary servitude shall ever exist in any part of said territory, except for crime, whereof the party shall first be duly convicted.[4]

The House twice passed the measure (in August 1846 and February 1847), but it twice failed in the Senate—although not without acrimonious debate.

The fighting in which the United States took the territory called the Mexican Cession proved mostly anticlimactic and one-sided. The Treaty of Guadalupe Hidalgo evidenced the overpowering fact. Signed in February 1848 at a villa in northern Mexico City, the treaty transformed perspectives and politics on a vast landscape. The United States gained, and Mexico lost, about 530,000 square miles (1,372,700 square kilometers). The transfer included all or part of what became the states of Arizona, California, Colorado, Nevada, New Mexico, and Utah. It shrank Mexico by about 40 percent and enlarged the United States by about 20 percent. And that did not include Texas, once Mexican territory that itself stretched 390,000 square miles (1,010,100 square kilometers). To compensate in part for Mexico's losses, the United States paid Mexico $15 million and assumed liability for any U.S. citizens' war-related claims against Mexico.

Dealing with more than territory, the treaty provided for shifting the status of a significant population. Article IX of the treaty provided that Mexicans who remained in the ceded territory "shall be incorporated into the Union of the United States and be admitted at the proper time (to be judged of by the Congress of the United States) to the enjoyment of all the rights of citizens of the United States."[5] The degree to which former Mexican citizens entered "enjoyment of all the rights of citizens of the United States," as promised in the treaty, became a persistent issue in U.S. race relations and in relations between the United States and Mexico. To begin with, the United States recognized the eligibility of only a portion of the Mexican citizens who stayed in the cession territory. It wholly ignored tens of thousands of other Mexican citizens and refused to acknowledge Indians. Importing its Indian exclusion doctrine, the United States distinguished Indians in the Mexican Cession territory not as citizens of Mexico. Rather, it treated them as "wild Indians" or as "domestic dependent[s]," in the terms U.S. Chief Justice John Marshall used in the 1831 case of *Cherokee Nation v. Georgia*. Marshall there described Indians as "in a state of pupilage. Their relation to the United States resembles that of a ward to his guardian," the chief justice had ruled.[6]

The firmly fixed image of Indians and the U.S. policy of treating them, long in place before 1848, made improbable recognizing as citizens Indians in the Cession territory. The U.S. pattern of unyielding dispossession shaped both the past and immediate future in relations with the Indians. The Cherokee Trail of Tears prefigured the westward path to the continuing Indian wars that in the end yielded the Chiricahua Apache leader Goyathlay ("One Who Yawns"), known in U.S. history as Geronimo. His surrender at Skeleton Canyon in the Sonora Mountains of southwestern Arizona in 1886 would mark the end of the last major U.S. Indian wars and move the United States in 1890 to declare that a frontier line no longer existed.

The treatment of Indians in the Southwest developed over time as a significant issue. More immediate, however, was U.S. treatment of the approximately 80,000 non-Indian, Mexican citizens who remained in the Cession territory and to whom a promise of U.S. citizenship attached. The Treaty of Guadalupe Hidalgo's provisions for "enjoyment of all the rights of citizens of the United States" proved to be only a promise, however. And one more breached than honored, it proved to have no force of its own or to be what U.S. law termed "self-executing." To be effective and binding, the treaty provision required Congress to act. The result stripped the newly coined Mexican Americans of their lands. By force and fraud, the former Mexicans who remained on their lands after U.S. accession often found themselves without formal recourse to protect their property or their persons.

Even the appearance of law failed to stop dispossession. William McKendree

Gwin, a physician who became one of California's first U.S. senators, pushed to secure fair treatment for Mexican land claims in his new state. The federal California Land Settlement Act of 1851 that Gwin sponsored proved in practice, however, to be a disaster for persons holding claims from Mexico or its parent Spain. The Land Settlement Act empowered the U.S. president to appoint a three-man tribunal to decide claims. It allowed also for federal courts to hear appeals of tribunal decisions. The process was formal, lengthy, and costly. It appeared fair in theory. In fact, it proved rigged. Trying to vindicate their title bankrupted the middling. The poorest holders got short shrift. Only the wealthiest of holders survived. In sum, the formal claims process dispossessed most former Mexicans who entered it.[7]

Many Mexican claims succumbed to hordes of squatters. The swarms started with the California Gold Rush that followed gold finds in January 1848 at John A. Sutter's sawmill on the American River at what became Sacramento. More than 80,000 persons raced into the area in 1849 alone—giving rise to the term *forty-niner*. Squatters swamped the settlement the Swiss immigrant Sutter had developed on his Mexican land grant. Signaling the fate to befall others holding Mexican claims, Sutter lost title to his lands in the U.S. courts and went bankrupt.

Newcomers from the United States moved also to displace Mexicans from gold mining. They pushed the new state legislature in 1850 to pass the Foreign Miners Act to give themselves preference to mining claims and work and to exclude others. The move to exclude others and prefer whites showed itself throughout the legislature's actions. In 1850 it also prohibited anyone other than whites from testifying in criminal trials of whites.

Many former Mexicans fought their dispossession and became outlaws or bandits in the eyes of U.S. officials. This marked only a start to struggles that would encompass not merely those who came to be called "Anglos" and "Mexicanos" or the initially derogatory truncation "Chicanos." It came to touch others deemed nonwhites.

Mexican Americans proved a further challenge in U.S. racial classification. What race were they in the race-conscious United States? *Mexican*, like *American*, represented a nationality. Yet *Mexican American* became no ordinary compounded or hyphenated nationality within the United States. It became a racialized ethnic group. Pushed into a political and social construct, Mexican Americans shared being outcasts like Indians and blacks. Dominant American practices segregated them. Even while calling Mexican Americans white and conceiving of whiteness as integral to U.S. citizenship and identity, actual American practices discriminated against Mexican Americans. It marked them as perhaps nominally white but nevertheless inferior.

Mexican American over time came to serve as something of a catchall label that revealed race in the United States as an arbitrary category. Little formally distinguished the deep mixture among Mexican Americans. They became another cluster, lumped together. The 1930 U.S. Census illustrated the catchall usage, counting as Mexican Americans all persons in the United States born in Mexico but also all persons born in the United States of parents who were not in other census categories—Caucasian, Chinese, Japanese, Indian, or Negro. The 1940 census substituted "Spanish-speaking" as the category label. The 1950 and 1960 censuses switched to "Spanish surname." The U.S. Census Bureau would in time come to explain that persons in the expanding group "may belong to any race."[8]

Absorbing hundreds of thousands of former Mexican citizens into the United States as a result of the War with Mexico foreshadowed a similar result from the 1898 War with Spain. It clearly laid the misshapen basis for confusing the individual identities of Spanish-speaking peoples in the United States, lumping them together regardless of personal characteristics or country of origin. The consequences and remote repercussions would reach far into the future of the United States.

A repeating pattern persisted. Wreathed in visions of its own virtues, the United States continued to pursue a Manifest Destiny that moved its borders to include more land and riches and more exclusion, most immediately of Mexican Americans, Indians, and blacks.

NOTES

1. John L. O'Sullivan, "Manifest Destiny," *The United States Magazine and Democratic Review* 16 (1845): 7–10.

2. Lester G. Bugbee, "Slavery in Early Texas: I," *Political Science Quarterly* 13 (September 1898): 389–412.

3. Stephen F. Austin, at San Felipe de Austin, to Thomas F. Leaming of Philadelphia, June 14, 1830, Austin Papers, Center for American History, University of Texas at Austin; quoted in Eugene C. Barker, "The Influence of Slavery in the Colonization of Texas," *Mississippi Valley Historical Review* 11 (June 1924): 30.

4. *Cong. Globe*, 29th Cong., 1st sess., 1214–1217 (August 8, 1846).

5. Treaty of Guadalupe Hidalgo, February 2, 1848, in Hunter Miller, ed., *Treaties and Other International Acts of the United States*, 8 vols. (Washington, DC: GPO, 1931–1948), 5:220–221.

6. *Cherokee Nation v. Georgia*, 30 U.S. (5 Pet.) 1, 17 (1831).

7. California Land Settlement Act, 9 Stat. 631 (March 3, 1851).

8. See generally George Martinez, "Legal Indeterminacy, Judicial Discretion, and the Mexican American Litigation Experience, 1930–1980," *University of California–Davis Law Review* 27 (1994): 555–618.

DOCUMENTS

4.1.   "Unfit to be free, and incapable of self government," 1836

The Declaration of Independence that Texas settlers issued on March 2, 1836, illustrated their sense of Anglo-American superiority and separateness from Mexicans, even while living in Mexico and being subject to its constitution and laws. In large part the declaration criticized Mexico for not being America, for being Catholic and not Protestant; and it scorned Mexicans as inferiors "unfit to be free, and incapable of self government."

The Mexican government, by its colonization laws, invited and induced the Anglo-American population of Texas to colonize its wilderness under the pledged faith of a written constitution, that they should continue to enjoy that constitutional liberty and republican government to which they had been habituated in the land of their birth, the United States of America.

In this expectation they have been cruelly disappointed. . . . It denies us the right of worshipping the Almighty according to the dictates of our own conscience, by the support of a national religion. . . .

We appealed to our Mexican brethren for assistance. Our appeal has been made in vain. Though months have elapsed, no sympathetic response has yet been heard from the Interior. We are, therefore, forced to the melancholy conclusion, that the Mexican people have acquiesced in the destruction of their liberty, and the substitution therfor of a military government; that they are unfit to be free, and incapable of self government.

Source: Tex. Const. App. 478–481 (Vernon 1993).

4.2.   "We are the nation of progress," 1839

Credited with coining the phrase "Manifest Destiny" in 1845, journalist John L. O'Sullivan (1813–1895) had written early and often of the United States' having a special destiny based on its racial pluralism. Echoing the nation's Latin motto E pluribus unum *that the first Great Seal committee chose in 1776, O'Sullivan promoted the sense of America's strength lying in its "origin from many other nations" and, particularly, in its dedication to equality. He projected the nation's following "God's natural and moral law of equality, the law of brotherhood" into "the boundless future." What happened to those in the path of his vision of America's destiny appeared not to concern O'-Sullivan. His evangelical advocacy of American expansion appeared to countenance only conversion, not coexistence, and without a sense of contradiction, he appeared to see only people of a single color in his pluralism.*

The American people having derived their origin from many other nations, and the Declaration of National Independence being entirely based on the great principle of human equality, these facts demonstrate at once our disconnected position as regards any other nation. . . . [S]o far as regards the entire development of the natural rights of man, in moral, political, and national life, we may confidently assume that our country is destined to be the great nation of futurity.

It is so destined, because the principle upon which a nation is organized fixes its destiny, and that of equality is perfect, is universal. . . .

The far-reaching, the boundless future will be the era of American greatness. In its magnificent domain of space and time, the nation of many nations is destined to manifest to mankind the excellence of divine principles. . . .

Yes, we are the nation of progress, of individual freedom, of universal enfranchisement. . . . We must onward to the fulfilment of our mission—to the entire development of the principle of our organization—freedom of conscience, freedom of person, freedom of trade and business pursuits, universality of freedom and equality. This is our high destiny, and in nature's eternal, inevitable decree of cause and effect we must accomplish it. All this will be our future history, to establish on earth the moral dignity and salvation of man—the immutable truth and beneficence of God.

Source: "The Great Nation of Futurity," *The United States Magazine and Democratic Review* 6 (1839): 426–430.

4.3.   "The peaceful triumphs of the industry of our emigrants," 1845

Clamor over expansion dominated the U.S. elections of 1844. Texas ranked foremost as a topic, and the vision of the United States' extending throughout North America drove much of the popular and political imagination. Presidential victor James K. Polk (1795–1849) campaigned on aggressive expansionism that included more than annexing Texas. The former Tennessee governor and congressman who rose to be Speaker of the House of Representative pushed for the U.S. borders to extend to Alaska with his slogan "54-40 or fight!" In his inaugural address in March 1845, Polk exulted that "our domain extends from ocean to ocean." He insisted that peace and prosperity for all characterized American expansion, which he called "the peaceful triumphs of the industry of our emigrants." He nowhere mentioned Mexico or displacing Mexicans, and while mentioning Indians, he passed over them as nothing more than peoples whose title "to vast tracts of country has been extinguished."

I regard the question of annexation as belonging exclusively to the United States and Texas. . . .

Our Union is a confederation of independent States, whose policy is peace with each other and all the world. To enlarge its limits is to extend the dominions of peace over additional territories and increasing millions. The world has nothing to fear from military ambition in our Government. . . . [O]ur Government can not be otherwise than pacific.

Foreign powers should therefore look on the annexation of Texas to the United States not as the conquest of a nation seeking to extend her dominions by arms and violence, but as the peaceful acquisition of a territory once her own, by adding another member to our confederation, with the consent of that member, thereby diminishing the chances of war and opening to them new and ever-increasing markets for their products. . . .

[S]erious objections have at different times been made to the enlargement of our boundaries. These objections were earnestly urged when we acquired Louisiana. Experience has shown that they were not well founded. The title of numerous Indian tribes to vast tracts of country has been extinguished; new States have been admitted into the Union; new Territories have been created and our jurisdiction and laws extended over them. As our population has expanded, the Union has been cemented and strengthened. . . . It is confidently believed that our system may be safely extended to the utmost bounds of our territorial limits, and that as it shall be extended the bonds of our Union, so far from being weakened, will become stronger. . . .

[E]ighty years ago our population was confined on the west by the ridge of the Alleghanies. Within that period—within the lifetime, I might say, of some of my hearers—our people, increasing to many millions, have filled the eastern valley of the Mississippi, adventurously ascended the Missouri to its headsprings, and are already engaged in establishing the blessings of self-government in valleys of which the rivers flow to the Pacific. The world beholds the peaceful triumphs of the industry of our emigrants. To us belongs the duty of protecting them adequately wherever they may be upon our soil. The jurisdiction of our laws and the benefits of our republican institutions should be extended over them in the distant regions which they have selected for their homes.

Source: President James K. Polk, "Inaugural Address (March 4, 1845)," in *A Compilation of the Messages and Papers of the Presidents, 1789–1897* (New York: Bureau of National Literature, 1897), 2223–2232.

4.4.   "One of the principal causes of our disgraces," 1846

El Tiempo, *a newspaper in Mexico City, in its issue of February 5, 1846, offered a view from the Mexican capital of the events unfold-*

ing immediately to war and beyond to a relationship in which the
United States would be "one of the principal causes of our disgraces."
Replying in part to those who denigrated Mexico in comparison with
the United States, the Mexican editorial writer explained significant
differences separating Mexico and the United States and presciently
forecast a clash of culture and identity destined to leave the two na-
tions and their peoples with difficult relations. His comments on the
character and content of U.S. nationality reflected noteworthy ele-
ments of the heritage and environment of ethnicity and race.

The United States of the North have been, are, and will be for many years, directly or indirectly one of the principal causes of our disgraces. . . .

The surprising prosperity of the North Americans has dazzled many and has caused thinking men to consider the cause of these advances. Most of our countrymen who have visited that classic country of freedom, as they hyperbolically call it, have neither made nor been able to make an in-depth study of the cause of its progress. . . .

[O]ur conclusion [is] that the American union is a colossus with feet of clay. . . . [T]he search for gold [is] the only god which is worshiped in that civilized nation. . . .

Public spirit exists there only in matters which directly effect pecuniary interests. . . .

In that country, there is no nationality due to the astonishing immigration of Europeans, who fill the United States with "citizens," as it is very easy there to avoid the laws of citizenship. There, elections are in fact carried by the Irish, who have the vote a year after arriving. In that country, bad faith is more shameless than in any other part of the globe.

In that country, laws are ignored or flouted under the most absurd pretexts.

In that country, there is no morality of any kind, and if good families exist, as some indeed do, their virtue is the more meritorious, since there are no incentives for good in an environment completely open to evil influences.

In other words, in that exalted nation, there are no social ties, no moral scruples, no customs, and no laws that are treated with due respect.

That nation is composed of foreigners, and it is clear that if their material and monetary opportunities should disappear they would abandon that country without a thought for its soil, its interests, its honor and glory. . . .

For the time being, the American union stands as a colossus threatening to end our existence. If we do not want to become its prisoner, we must abandon our selfish complaints and establish a solid and stable government.

Source: *El Tiempo* (Mexico City, Mexico), from Impressa de Lara, January 24, 1846–June 7, 1846.

4.5.   "A doubtful state of quietness," 1847

The War with Mexico significantly shifted the situation of Indians
in the Southwest. The cry of Manifest Destiny with which the United

States dispossessed Mexico of almost half its territory echoed in a push to further dispossess Indians of their lands. In a June 1847 report, federal Indian agent Robert S. Neighbors (1815–1859) captured the state of affairs in Texas where white settlers quickly pressed upon Indians with what he projected as bleak consequences.

For the last few months our settlements have extended very rapidly, and, unless checked, will continue to do so; also, frequently large parties of surveyors penetrate many miles into the country now occupied by the Indians. These movements keep the Camanches and many other tribes in continual excitement; and unless some measures can be adopted by the department to check the surveyors, it will finally lead to serious difficulties.

From these causes the Camanches are in a doubtful state of quietness, and there is no telling how soon there will be a general outbreak among them.

The laws of Texas do not acknowledge that the Indians have any right of soil; and those persons holding land claims contend that they have the privilege of locating wherever they choose.

Source: Robert S. Neighbors to William Medill, June 2, 1847, quoted in Francis Paul Prucha, *The Great Father: The United States Government and the American Indians*, 2 vols. (Lincoln: University of Nebraska Press, 1984), 1:358–359.

4.6.   "A triumph of Christianity?" 1848

The escaped slave who named himself Frederick Douglass (1817–1895) and rose to be a preeminent abolitionist leader offered a black perspective on the War with Mexico and the reception it received in the United States, writing an editorial in his Rochester, New York, weekly newspaper The North Star *in March 1848, seven days after the U.S. Senate ratified the Treaty of Guadalupe Hidalgo to end the war officially. Douglass plumbed the racial overtones and undertow of the war and its aftermath. He highlighted the hypocrisy of white Americans' relations with others.*

PEACE! PEACE! PEACE!

The shout is on every lip, and emblazoned on every paper. The joyful news is told in every quarter with enthusiastic delight. We are such an exception to the great mass of our fellow-countrymen, in respect to everything else, and have been so accustomed to hear them rejoice over the most barbarous outrages committed upon an unoffending people, that we find it difficult to unite with them in their general exultation at this time; and for this reason, we believe that by *peace* they mean *plunder*.

In our judgement, those who have all along been loudly in favor of a vigorous prosecution of the war, and heralding its bloody triumphs with apparent rapture, and glorifying the atrocious deeds of barbarous heroism on the part of wicked men engaged in it, have no sincere love of peace, and are not now rejoicing over *peace*, but *plunder*.

They have succeeded in robbing Mexico of her territory, and are rejoicing over their success under the hypocritical pretence of a regard for peace. Had they not succeeded in robbing Mexico of the most important and most valuable part of her territory, many of those now loudest in their professions of favor for peace, would be loudest and wildest for war—war to the knife.

Our soul is sick of such hypocricy.

We presume the churches of Rochester will return thanks to God for peace they did nothing to bring about, and boast it as a triumph of Christianity!

That an end is put to the wholesale murder in Mexico, is truly just cause for rejoicing; but we are not the people to rejoice; we ought rather blush and hang our heads for shame, and in the spirit of profound humility, crave pardon for our crimes at the hands of a God whose mercy endureth forever.

Source: *The North Star* (Rochester, NY), March 17, 1848.

4.7.   "Hunted themselves like wild beasts," 1852

> To formally treat Indians in part of the territory acquired in the Mexican Cession, Congress adopted a revised Indian policy in March 1852. Edward F. Beale (1822–1893) was the first U.S. superintendent of Indians in California under the 1852 act, and in November 1852 he painted a sad portrait of conditions he found in his new assignment. He described what he called "frontier civilization" ravaging not merely hostile Indians but even peaceful Indians. They inconvenienced acquisitive settlers. The aftermath of the War with Mexico, he reported, then extended to further unhappy relations between American settlers and the former Mexicans and Indians whom they were impatient to dispossess.

Driven from their fishing and hunting grounds, hunted themselves like wild beasts, *lassoed*, and torn from homes made miserable by want, and forced into slavery, the wretched remnant which escapes starvation on the one hand, and the relentless whites on the other, only do so to rot and die of a loathsome disease, the penalty of Indians' association with frontier civilization.

This is no declamation—I have seen it; and seeing all this, I cannot help them. I know that they starve; I know that they perish by hundreds; I know that they are fading away with a startling and shocking rapidity, but I cannot help them.

Humanity must yield to necessity. They are not dangerous; therefore they must be neglected.

I earnestly call the early attention of the government to this condition of affairs. . . . It is a crying sin that our government so wealthy and so powerful, should shut its eyes to the miserable fate of these rightful owners of the soil.

What is the expense of half a million for the permanent relief of these poor people to a government so rich?

Source: Edward Fitzgerald Beale to Luke Lea, November 22, 1852, in S. Exec. Doc. No. 4, 33rd Cong., Special sess. 378 (1852); serial 688. See also 10 Stat. 2 (1852).

ANNOTATED RESEARCH GUIDE

Books

Horsman, Reginald. *Race and Manifest Destiny: The Origins of American Racial Anglo-Saxonism*. Cambridge, MA: Harvard University Press, 1981. Illustrates developing racialist ideology that fashioned white supremacy to dominate blacks, Indians, and Mexicans.

Keller, Gary D., and Cordelia Candelaria, eds. *Legacy of the Mexican and Spanish-American Wars: Legal, Literary, and Historical Perspectives*. Tempe, AZ: Bilingual Review/Press, 2000. Papers from 1998 Transhistoric Thresholds conference offer perspective and multidimensional comparison on the U.S. reach encompassing diversity of color and culture with long-ranging impacts.

Kreneck, Thomas H. *Stolen Heritage: A Mexican-American's Rediscovery of His Family's Lost Land-Grant*. Austin, TX: Eakin Press, 1986. Reaches back to a south Texas land grant of 1832 to illustrate the ongoing contentions over Mexican American dispossession of property and rights.

Langum, David J. *Law and Community on the Mexican California Frontier: Anglo-American Expatriates and the Clash of Legal Traditions, 1821–1846*. Norman: University of Oklahoma Press, 1987. Treats the U.S. War with Mexico as a clash of dreams ending in harsh realities creating Mexican Americans as a new U.S. ethnic group amid Anglo-American cultural aversion and legal hostility.

Morrison, Chaplain W. *Democratic Politics and Sectionalism: The Wilmot Proviso Controversy*. Chapel Hill: University of North Carolina Press, 1967. Remains a useful summary of 1840s events in the slavery extension controversy with its debate about slavery, racial suitability, and the future of the American nation.

Prucha, Francis Paul. *The Great Father: The United States Government and the American Indians*. 2 vols. Lincoln: University of Nebraska Press, 1984. An indispensable, massive, and comprehensive review of the formulation, implementation, and immediate results of federal Indian policy.

Utley, Robert M. *The Indian Frontier, 1846–1890*. Rev. ed. Albuquerque: University of New Mexico Press, 2003. Classic analysis of U.S.-Indian wars, but more than military history, it highlights the clash of cultures and the impacts of civil contacts from epidemic diseases to inexorable technologies, such as the railroad.

Web Sites

http://www.pbs.org/kera/usmexicanwar—links to online resources on the U.S. War with Mexico (1846–1848) as a bilingual companion to a documentary that KERA-TV Dallas/Fort Worth produced for PBS.

http://www.pbs.org/kera/usmexicanwar/dialogues/prelude/manifest/manifestdestiny.html—describes the cultural and racial elements and effects of Manifest Destiny as a push for expansion into the West.

http://www.pinzler.com/ushistory/mextimeline.html—offers a timeline to put in context the War with Mexico and the debate over American slavery and sectionalism and their meaning for race relations.

http://www.tsha.utexas.edu/handbook/online/articles/view/MM/pqmck.html—offers discussion and links to the controversy of civil and property rights of those who became Mexican Americans as a result of the 1848 treaty ending the U.S. War with Mexico.

5

Civil War: Slavery and Emancipation in Black and White

The Civil War (1861–1865) signaled a shift of profound significance in the history of race relations in the United States. Slavery figured prominently in the rhetoric of the war, but the war was not about slavery—not in the sense of being about the situation or suffering of enslaved blacks, not in the beginning nor in the end. The United States did not fight the Civil War to free slaves. To emphasize the federal government's commitment not to touch slavery in the South, Congress in March 1861 adopted and sent to the states for ratification a proposed constitutional amendment to prohibit forever any subsequent amendment to "abolish or interfere . . . with the domestic institutions" of the states.[1] Nevertheless, slavery did become a casualty of the war—not instantly, but eventually, perhaps ineluctably.

The Civil War was primarily a clash of divergent visions of and for the United States. Each vision claimed to be the true American one. It claimed to embody the true American way. It claimed for its proponents the title of true Americans. Neither vision was pure of elements of the other. Both shared much. Yet their distinct aspects—particularly their differences in outlook, politics, and social patterns—overwhelmed their commonality, at least for the bloody historical moment that was the Civil War.

One vision espoused a confined, deferential politics that elevated large-scale landholders. It rested on a world market–oriented economy geared to produce plantation commodities for export. It held fiercely to the preeminence of local authority and private direction to promote the general welfare. It rested on a subordinated black base. It predominated in the South, which held 94.9 percent of the nation's 4,427,276 blacks in 1860 and 99.9 percent of the slaves. It had only 29.5 percent of the nation's whites. In two slave states—Mississippi and South Carolina—blacks outnumbered whites.

The other vision espoused an increasingly fluid, popular politics that monied interests dominated. It rested on a developing domestic, mass market geared to produce industrial goods and services primarily for domestic consumption. It held fiercely to the preeminence of national authority and public direction to promote the general welfare. It rested on a base of white workingmen: Although 60.7 percent of the nation's total population lived outside the slave states, only 5.1 percent of the nation's blacks resided there in 1860.

Slavery figured prominently in each vision. For one, it was essential. For the other, it was anathema. Slaves formed the core of the South's plantation economy. Indeed, the slave system made the South what it was. Slavery infused the South's behavior, culture, and politics. It was more than economics. It was a worldview, a whole way of thinking and living based on a specific form of race relations. To the South, slavery was part of Manifest Destiny: Providence ordained the plantation system and placed blacks to slave for whites.

The North disagreed with the South not a wit on the issue of white supremacy. What the North abhorred was slavery's overpowering social consequences. The popular concern in the North was not blacks' condition but whites' condition. And Manifest Destiny was no less a feature in that vision, which also held that Providence indeed had ordained white supremacy. The difference was that the popular plan divined in the North included no blacks. Rather, it excluded blacks—and other nonwhites—as incompatible with America's high purpose of achieving a more and more perfect society through democratic self-government.

Republican presidential nominee Abraham Lincoln expressed the predominant view of non-slave states' whites in an 1860 speech at New Haven, Connecticut. Expressing the basis of his vision of what America should be, Lincoln explained, "When one starts poor, as most do in the race of life, free society is such that he knows he can better his condition; he knows that there is no fixed condition of labor, for his whole life."[2] But that was exactly what slavery decreed: A "fixed condition," not only for the slave's whole life but for the larger society's life. Slavery was a condition for blacks and whites. It constrained and condemned both. Repudiating such a condition lay at the heart of the white laboring and middle classes that Lincoln and his Republican Party hoped to represent.

The cast of the question then was not slavery as a concern for blacks. That was settled before the Republican Party emerged in 1854. The escaped slave and prominent abolitionist Frederick Douglass explained the point with absolute clarity in January 1849. "The Cry of Free Men was raised, not for the extension of liberty to the black man, but for the protection of the liberty of the white," he noted.[3] The weekly *True Democrat* of Cleveland, Ohio, succinctly articulated the point at the time of the Compromise of 1850. "The slave question is not a Negro question. It goes far beyond the colored race," the *True Democrat* editorialized in its issue of December 18, 1850. "It touches to the very quick the life and mind, the hopes and happiness, the prospects and progress, of our kith and kin, of every white man in the South," the newspaper stated.[4]

Much antislavery then was hardly pro-Negro. It was antislavery *and* anti-Negro. It clung to the notion of a white man's country of Manifest Destiny. Blacks ruined that vision. That was what many, if not most, whites opposed.

Small-scale white farmers and merchants, mechanics and ordinary day laborers, yearned to exclude blacks from their world. They wanted to eliminate black
competition. Such whites saw blacks, enslaved and unenslaved, as representing a substance and structure of society they rejected. The *National Era* newspaper published in Washington, D.C., reported the feelings of millions of such
whites early in the 1850s. They "would gladly abolish slavery today, if the
slaves could be removed to a foreign county," the *National Era* explained.[5] Such
white men from the North went to war in 1861 not for slavery or antislavery.
They went to war for their vision of the Union.

Newly elected President Abraham Lincoln well understood the sentiment.
He renounced any aim in regard to slavery in his inaugural address on Monday, March 4, 1861. "I have no purpose, directly or indirectly, to interfere with
the institution of slavery in the States where it exists," he declared. "I believe
I have no lawful right to do so, and I have no inclination to do so," he averred.

In the midst of the war, Lincoln held fast to his controlling aim: Preserving
the Union. He reiterated his personal and political objective in August 1862 in
a clear-cut statement to New York *Tribune* newspaper editor Horace Greeley,
known for his assertive antislavery sentiments. "My paramount object in this
struggle *is* to save the Union, and is *not* either to save or destroy slavery." Lincoln declared that

> If I could save the Union without freeing *any* slave I would do it; and if I could
> save it by freeing *all* the slaves I would it; and if I could save it by freeing some
> and leaving others alone I would also do that.[6]

Like most of his fellow Republicans, Lincoln was no friend of slavery nor
fully of slaves or other blacks. He occupied lesser ground. He opposed slavery
because of what he had described in 1837 as its "injustice and bad policy."[7] Be-
lieving as he did in natural rights, Lincoln asserted a black's right to be free
from slavery, to be free "in the right to eat the bread, without the leave of anybody else, which his own hand earns."[8] Yet he believed also in "a physical difference between the two [races], which in my judgment will probably forever
forbid their living together upon the footing of perfect equality," as he explained during his 1858 senatorial campaign with his famed debates with Illinois's incumbent U.S. senator, Stephen A. Douglas.[9]

Elevating blacks' legal standing and rights was at best a distant notion (and
more often a disagreeable concept) to most whites in the nation in 1860. Among
whites, only a minuscule fringe of radical abolitionists believed in true equality between blacks and whites. Lincoln himself rejected such equality. He believed in racial separation. He suggested compensated emancipation and
colonization to rid the nation of its black-white race relations problem. He
struggled also with emancipation as an act of war. The president early rejected
freeing slaves out of hand, as several Union field commanders proposed in
1861 and 1862. He feared such a policy might alienate the Border States—
Delaware, Kentucky, Maryland, and Missouri—and stiffen Confederate resistance to ending the rebellion. Indeed, the president countermanded army
commanders who issued field orders proclaiming emancipation.

As the president temporized, Congress adopted its own antislavery schedule. In March 1862, it suspended the federal Fugitive Slave Act of 1850 by adopting an article of war to bar members of U.S. Armed Forces from returning fugitive slaves to slaveholders. In April 1862, it abolished slavery in the District of Columbia. It provided compensation to loyal slaveholders and appropriated funds for "colonization" of former slaves to Haiti, Liberia, or other places outside the United States. In June 1862, Congress abolished slavery in all U.S. territories. In July 1862, Congress made emancipation a policy of war, enacting the Second Confiscation Act which declared "forever free" slaves of Confederate officials, both military and civilian.[10] It further declared forfeit and free slaves of any person engaged in or assisting the rebellion. Congress confined the emancipation it conferred to areas the U.S. Army occupied in the rebel states. It pressed further to authorize the president to employ "persons of African descent" in any capacity to suppress the rebellion. Congress was not yet so bold, however, as to accept blacks' repeated pleas to formally shoulder arms for the United States.

Blacks had soldiered for the United States in the War for Independence (1775–1783). Before then they bore arms for the colonies. They fought for the United States in the War of 1812 (1812–1814) and in the War with Mexico (1846–1848). Such service for the U.S. military had availed personal distinctions and rewards—including individual release from slavery—but it had occasioned no general improvement in blacks' status.

The Civil War promised otherwise. Blacks' future appeared clearly in the balance. New York City's weekly *Anglo-African* in September 1861 declared, "The South must be subjugated, or we shall be enslaved." The war sounded "a special call to defend our rights," the *Anglo-African* exhorted. It was "Liberty or Death," the black newspaper declared, paraphrasing the Virginia patriot Patrick Henry's famed 1775 cry from the American Revolution.

Blacks by the thousands were eager to heed the call to arms in 1861. But federal law barred blacks from state militia, and not a single recognizable black served in the U.S. Army. The prewar exclusion policy forced blacks to the sidelines at the start. It left them "to be on the alert to seize arms and drill as soon as the government shall be willing to accept our services," as the *Anglo-African* editorialized in September 1861.[11]

Yet blacks' service as soldiers was neither requested nor desired until federal manpower needs pressed hard on decision makers. Lincoln consistently disregarded calls for black troops for more than a year into the war. Congress led the president to enlisting blacks. Its Militia Act in July 1862 authorized employing "persons of African descent" in "any military or naval service for which they may be found competent." The act further attached such service to emancipation. It freed any slaves who served, if their slaveholders were not loyal. It also extended emancipation for such slaves to their wives and children.[12]

While Lincoln dawdled on enlisting blacks, he committed himself finally to follow Congress in linking the war and emancipation. In July 1862, he presented to his cabinet a draft of a presidential proclamation to free slaves in areas in rebellion. Crafting it as a threat, he linked issuing it to a suitable Union victory. That turned out to be Antietam on September 17, 1862. Five days later, Lincoln issued his preliminary Emancipation Proclamation. He declared,

That on the 1st day of January, A.D. 1863, all persons held as slaves within any State or designated part of a State the people whereof shall then be in rebellion against the United States shall be then, thenceforward, and forever free.[13]

If Lincoln viewed his proclamation as offering the South a choice between a carrot and a stick, he soon saw the South spurn both. On January 1, 1863, he issued his famed Emancipation Proclamation with full force.

While of little immediate practical effect to slaves, the Emancipation Proclamation in time ushered in fundamental changes in the shape of race relations in the United States. The proclamation itself instantly liberated not a single slave. In fact, it purported to affect only persons and places that the United States conceded it did not control. It left untouched all slaves within the control of the United States.

The proclamation proved more symbolic than substantive. Its actual effect awaited the force of federal arms. Its symbolic affect was more immediate. Blacks hailed the event. A meeting of "colored citizens" in Harrisburg, Pennsylvania, acclaimed "the 1st day of January, 1863, as a new era in our country's history—a day in which injustice and oppression were forced to flee and cower before the benign principles of justice and righteousness." Lincoln's limited scope did not escape their notice, however. "We would have preferred that the proclamation should have been general instead of partial," they lamented.[14]

Emancipation hardly thrilled everyone. Many northern whites vigorously opposed ending slavery. Antebellum antiabolitionism remained hardy during the war. Not merely slaveholders in the Border States condemned emancipation. Many throughout the North, outside of New England, remonstrated against it. Particularly Irish and German immigrants and former southerners, who had moved north or west, objected to emancipation as a purpose, goal, or result of the war. Moreover, the Democratic Party stood firmly against emancipation. Prominent were the so-called Peace Democrats and especially those Horace Greeley's New York *Tribune* in July 1861 dubbed "Copperheads," likening them to the stealthy snake known for striking without warning. Largely concentrated in Illinois, Indiana, and Ohio, Copperheads held no brief for blacks and wanted no part of emancipation. Consistent with their antebellum sentiment, they wanted no blacks in the Midwest.

The Oshkosh *Courier* in east-central Wisconsin clearly indicated its sentiment during the war's first year: "If this is a war . . . for abolition, then the sooner the Union goes to the devil the better," it declared in February 1862.[15] About 80 miles (130 kilometers) south-southeast, the Milwaukee *See-Bote* titled one of its many Negrophobic editorials "Abolition, the Worst Enemy of the Free White Laborer." In April 1862 it declared: "Workingmen! Be careful! Organize yourself against this element which threatens your impoverishment and annihilation."[16] Deep antiblack prejudice permeated city and countryside among whites who feared a flood of ex-slaves competing for jobs.

In assessing what for Republicans were disastrous elections in 1862, Horace Greeley's New York *Tribune* noted that labor competition was the most common argument against emancipation. Indeed, Republican setbacks in October and November voting emboldened emancipation opponents. Republicans nearly lost their majority in Congress and did lose key states such as New York.

The *Daily Empire* in Dayton, Ohio, virtually chortled, "The people of the great States of Ohio, Indiana, and Pennsylvania have spoken in thunderous tones through the ballot box against the fanatical Abolition legislation of the last Congress."[17] In November 1862, Springfield's Democratic *Illinois State Register* rebuked the preliminary Emancipation Proclamation and stated, "The Home of Lincoln Condemns the Proclamation."[18] Dayton's *Daily Empire* again expressed the perspective of many whites who supported the Civil War because they wanted to maintain race relations as they were between blacks and whites, not because they wanted to change them. Emancipation was the last thing they wanted. A white lawyer in Dayton bitterly summarized common opposition to emancipation in a January 1863 letter. "In my heart I believe our policy is best for the white race, the black race, the country, and humanity, and I can die on the scaffold if need be, but I cannot change my faith," he declared.[19]

In 1862, before the final Emancipation Proclamation, ex-slaves in South Carolina organized as the First S.C. Volunteers under command of the Massachusetts abolitionist minister Colonel Thomas Wentworth Higginson. By the war's end, about 200,000 blacks served in what the segregated U.S. Army designated as U.S. Colored Troops. Unequal pay and conditions indicated the government's official view of black troops. The army initially paid black soldiers $10 per month for all ranks, while paying white soldiers $13 per month for privates and larger amounts for higher ranks. Black insistence on equal rights in the ranks helped move the government in June 1864 to equalize pay, retroactive to January 1864 or to the time of enlistment for those not slaves when the war began. Yet putting blacks in arms for the Union agitated many whites. Some complained that recruiting blacks further proved the Union war effort had strayed from its purpose and become a "War for the Nigger."[20]

The federal Draft Act of March 1863 fed antiblack resentment about the war's purpose and prosecution. This first federal conscription law called for registering all able-bodied males of military age—without restrictions as to race or color—and designating them the "national forces of the United States."[21] It subjected registrants to being called to actual service for two years beginning on July 1, 1863. It allowed for paid substitutes, however, which with other provisions fostered doubt about its basic justice and wisdom.

The draft pushed race relations to the cutting edge. In northern cities such as Toledo, Cincinnati, Brooklyn, and Detroit, the strain of war had already led to ugly encounters between white workers and blacks. At opposite ends of Ohio, for example, Irish workers in Toledo and Cincinnati rioted against black competition on the docks in July 1862. Violence spilled from the piers and wharfs into the streets of the black sections as white workingmen attacked blacks of all ages, sexes, and conditions. In August 1862, an Irish mob set upon black tobacco factory workers in Brooklyn, New York. In March 1863, whites in Detroit destroyed much of the black section of the city, ransacking black homes and killing blacks randomly. The violence proved an ugly prelude.

In July 1863, one of the bloodiest riots in U.S. history erupted. It started at the New York City draft office in the sticky, morning heat on July 13. It lasted to the weekend and quickly became more than a draft protest. It was antiwar, antirich, antiestablishment, antiauthority. It was particularly anti-Negro.

During its four days the New York City Draft Riots of 1863 became one of the nation's worst race riots. Blacks became central targets of the mostly Irish-led mobs that terrorized Manhattan from the Bowery to Harlem. They hanged blacks from lampposts and telegraph poles. They attacked black homes and places that served black needs. In one of the ugliest scenes, the mob rolled a barrel of kerosene into the Colored-Orphan Asylum on Fifth Avenue and burned it to the ground. How many of the 300 housed there escaped was never clear. Turning from the young to the old, the mob also torched the Aged Colored-Woman's Home on 65th Street. Police data from the riot showed hundreds of buildings burned and ransacked. Property damage topped $1 million, a staggering sum at the time. Counts of the dead ranged from 300 to 1,200 whites, with an uncounted number of blacks dead. The magnitude of loss showed at least in part in the fact that Manhattan's black population that had numbered 12,472 in 1860 numbered only 9,945 in 1865.

New York City's Draft Riots evidenced whites' deep-seated prejudices. The turns of war had taken the nation to a place many whites wished not to go. Indeed, a majority cursed the war, even while fervently embracing the Union. They preferred a politics of expediency and peace by compromise. They were willing to allow the South its Peculiar Institution. They insisted only on the Union. If war was necessary to preserve the Union, then they wanted war limited to that objective. Human rights were no priority for them. To the degree they were antislavery, they were not necessarily pro-abolition. They were certainly not pro-Negro. Ending slavery was a consequence of the war, not a cause. Freeing blacks from white control was not the majority's aim. They were unready and unwilling to embrace blacks. Indeed, *The Methodist* magazine correspondent from London, England, wrote in 1862 that on many issues "the Southerners are more friendly to the colored race than the Northerners."[22]

So as slavery's end loomed, its aftermath for race relations nowhere appeared clear. To some, such as Massachusetts Republican U.S. Senator Charles Sumner, the end of slavery promised that "all persons are equal before the law."[23] Others, including the attorney general of the United States, thought the notion of "equality before the law" preposterous. Members of the U.S. House of Representatives in the 38th Congress (1863–1865) repeatedly resisted and rejected the proposed Thirteenth Amendment to prohibit slavery. They acquiesced only after November 1864 voting easily reelected Lincoln and increased Republican seats in the House from 102 to 149. In January 1865, with two votes to spare for the two-thirds majority required, the House approved the principle that "Neither slavery nor involuntary servitude, except as a punishment for crime whereof the party shall have been duly convicted, shall exist within the United States, or any place subject to their jurisdiction." In a flurry, eighteen states ratified the proposed amendment within twenty-five days. The next nine necessary to meet the three-fourths requirement for ratification among the then-thirty-six states followed by December 1865, when Secretary of State William Seward proclaimed the amendment ratified.

Opposition hardly died. Many balked at ending slavery. Many balked also at the amendment's providing that "Congress shall have power to enforce this article by appropriate legislation." Wide disagreement appeared on what would be appropriate. The hesitation was not only in strong slaveholding areas. New Jersey initially rejected the amendment. Delaware and Kentucky also rejected it. All three states in time would relent. New Jersey ratified in January 1866. Delaware did not until 1901. Kentucky took until 1976. Mississippi steadfastly refused its assent.

Thus, the Civil War moved the nation to a new place in race relations. It was a place without legally sanctioned slavery, but what place there was for blacks or their relations with whites remained unsettled.

NOTES

1. Joint Resolution to Amend the Constitution of the United States, J. Res. 13, 36th Cong., 12 Stat. 251 (1861).

2. Roy P. Basler, ed., *The Collected Works of Abraham Lincoln*, 9 vols. (New Brunswick, NJ: Rutgers University Press, 1953–1955), 1:75.

3. *The North Star* (Rochester, NY), January 12, 1849, 1.

4. Cleveland *True Democrat*, December 18, 1850, 1.

5. *National Era* (Washington, DC), August 12, 1852, 1.

6. Richard N. Current, ed., *The Political Thought of Abraham Lincoln* (New York: Bobbs-Merrill, 1967), 215.

7. Basler, *Collected Works of Abraham Lincoln*, 1:75.

8. Ibid., 3:16.

9. Ibid.

10. 12 Stat. 589 (July 17, 1862), officially titled "An Act to Suppress Insurrection, to Punish Treason and Rebellion, to Seize and Confiscate the Property of Rebels, and for Other Purposes." Among the other purposes was the forfeiture of slaves.

11. *Anglo-African*, September 14, 1861, 1.

12. 12 Stat. 589 (July 17, 1862).

13. 12 Stat. 1267 (September 22, 1862).

14. *Christian Recorder*, February 7, 1863.

15. Oshkosh *Courier*, February 21, 1862.

16. Milwaukee *See-Bote*, April 23, 1862.

17. Dayton *Daily Empire*, October 25, 1862; quoted in Frank L. Klement, "Midwestern Opposition to Lincoln's Emancipation Policy," *Journal of Negro History* 49 (1964): 178.

18. Springfield *Illinois State Register*, November 5, 1862; quoted in Klement, "Midwestern Opposition to Lincoln's Emancipation Policy," 179.

19. Thomas O. Lowe to "Dear Will" (his brother William Lowe), January 23, 1863, Dayton and Montgomery County Public Library; quoted in Klement, "Midwestern Opposition to Lincoln's Emancipation Policy," 183.

20. Mary Frances Berry, *Military Necessity and Civil Rights Policy: Black Citizenship and the Constitution, 1861–1868* (Port Washington, NY: Kennikat Press, 1977), 55.

21. "An Act for enrolling and calling out the national forces, and for other Purposes," 12 Stat. 731 (March 3, 1863).

22. *The Methodist*, September 27, 1862, 3.

23. Cong. Globe, 38th Cong., 1st sess., 134 (1864). Sumner introduced S. 99, "to secure equality before the law in the courts of the United States," on February 8, 1864.

DOCUMENTS

5.1. **"The withering influence of a nation's scorn and contempt," 1860**

In the 1860 elections that led the nation to civil war, New Yorkers voted on a suffrage referendum to amend the state constitution for black men to vote on the same basis as white men. The campaign revealed much about race relations of the day. The New York City and County Suffrage Committee of Colored Citizens championed the referendum with telling arguments that said much about the position of blacks and their perspectives. The results of the voting said much also about whites' feelings about blacks. About two in three (63.6 percent) of New York voters rejected the proposition.

Fellow Citizens: We have had, and still have, great wrongs of which to complain. A heavy and cruel hand has been laid upon us. As a people, we feel ourselves to be not only deeply injured, but grossly misunderstood. Our white countrymen do not know us. They are strangers to our characters, ignorant to our capacity, oblivious to our history and progress, and are misinformed as to the principles and ideas that control and guide us, as a people. The great mass of American citizens estimate us as being a characterless and purposeless people; and hence we hold up our heads, if at all, against the withering influence of a nation's scorn and contempt.

It will not be surprising that we are so misunderstood and misused, when the motives for misrepresenting us and for degrading us are duly considered. Indeed, it will seem strange, upon such consideration (and in view of the ten thousand channels through which malign feelings find utterance and influence), that we have not fallen even lower in public estimation than we have done; for, with the exception of the Jews, under the whole heavens there is not to be found a people pursued with a more relentless prejudice and persecution. . . .

What stone has been left unturned to degrade us? What hand has refused to fan the flame of popular prejudice against us? What American artist has not caricatured us? What wit has not laughed at us in our wretchedness? What songster has not made merry over our depressed spirits? What press has not ridiculed and condemned us?

Source: "The Suffrage Question," *The National Principia* (New York) 1 (October 20, 1860): 385–386.

5.2.   "The colored man will fight," 1861

African Americans saw the Civil War from its start as a signal event in present and future race relations. Black men clamored to join the U.S. Armed Forces on the battlefield to crush slavery. The Union early and often rejected their pleas to shoulder arms. Many blacks expected the day to come before long, however, when need would overcome prejudice. As with the anonymous author of the piece below, black men at once gave notice that they would be ready to soldier when the nation was ready to accept them to soldier. They asked only that the nation accept them also for what they were—Americans, patriots, fellow countrymen, rightful citizens.

Colored men calculate upon being yet in the midst of the fight as *soldiers*. We feel that our services will be needed: they will be forthcoming; but we must be discreet. They will be forthcoming when most needed. The colored man will fight,—not as a tool, but as an American patriot. He will fight most desperately, because he will be fighting against his enemy, slavery, and because he feels that among the leading claims he has to your feelings as fellow-countrymen, is, that in the page of facts connected with the battles for liberty which his country has fought, his valor—the valor of black men—*challenges comparison*; and because he feels that those facts have weight in causing his countrymen to award to him all his rights as an American citizen.

The colored man will go where duty shall call him, though not because he is colored. He will stand by the side of his white brave fellow-countrymen. They will together, if needs be, make "a great sacrifice of life." . . . Yes, all this for freedom, their common country, and the right. This he will do without price; but he would have his rights.

Source: Liberator, May 10, 1861, 1, reprinting item with no date from *The Boston Daily Atlas and Bee*.

5.3.   "You and we are different races," 1862

More than once Abraham Lincoln (1809–1865) announced himself of the mind that the "physical difference between the two [races] . . . will probably forever forbid their living together upon the footing of perfect equality." He consistently urged plans for blacks to exit America and live elsewhere. He urged a colonization plan on Delaware in November 1861, when it considered abolishing slavery. He proposed a colonization plan to Congress in March 1862 and applauded its providing $100,000 to colonize blacks freed when it abolished slavery in the District of Columbia in April 1862. In August 1862 he urged his views, reported below, on a group described as "Free Colored

Men" invited to hear him at the White House. Again in December 1862, with the final Emancipation Proclamation in the offing, he pressed provisions for colonization.

You and we are different races. We have between us a broader difference than exists between almost any other two races. Whether it is right or wrong I need not discuss; but this physical difference is a great disadvantage to us both, as I think.

Your race suffers very greatly, many of them, by living among us, while ours suffers from your presence. In a word, we suffer on each side. If this is admitted, it affords a reason, at least, why we should be separated. . . .

Your race are suffering, in my judgment, the greatest wrong inflicted on any people. But even when you cease to be slaves, you are yet far removed from being placed on an equality with the white race. . . .

The aspiration of men is to enjoy equality with the best when free, but on this broad continent not a single man of your race is made the equal of a single man of ours. . . .

It is better for us both, therefore, to be separated.

Source: Carl Sandburg, *Abraham Lincoln: The War Years*, 4 vols. (New York: Harcourt, Brace & Co., 1939), 1:574–575.

5.4.   "There is no country like our own," 1862

Blacks responded immediately and negatively to President Abraham Lincoln's urging their voluntary exiting America to live elsewhere under U.S.-backed colonization. In a mass meeting less than a week after Lincoln's remarks to an invited black audience at the White House on August 14, 1862, a mass meeting of blacks in Queens, New York, denounced colonization and chided the president for having "served the cause of our enemies" by urging "a mistaken policy." Acclaiming the United States as "our native country," the convened blacks declared the United States as "the country of our choice, being our fathers' country," and insisted on having their rights as Americans fully recognized and exercised without discrimination on account of race, color, or previous condition.

Whereas the President desires to know in particular our views on the subject of being colonized in Central America or some other foreign country, we will take the present opportunity to express our opinions most respectfully and freely, since as loyal Union colored Americans and Christians we feel bound to do so.

First. We rejoice that we are colored Americans, but deny that we are a "different race of people," as God has made of one blood all nations that dwell on the face of the earth, and has hence no respect of men in regard to color, neither ought men to have respect to color, as they have not made themselves or their color.

Second. The President calls our attention particularly to this question—"Why should we leave this country?" . . . We will answer this question by showing why we should remain in it. This is our country by birth. . . . This is the country of our choice, being our fathers' country.

Third. Again, we are interested in its welfare above every other country; we love this land, and have contributed our share to its prosperity and wealth. . . .

Fourth. Again, we believe, too, we have the right to have applied to ourselves those rights named in the Declaration of Independence. . . .

Our answer is this: There is no country like our own. Why not declare slavery abolished, and favor our peaceful colonization in the rebel States, or some portion of them? We would cheerfully return there, and give our most willing aid to deliver our loyal colored brethren and other Unionists from the tyranny of rebels to our government. . . .

Hence we conclude that the policy of the President toward the colored people of this country *is a mistaken policy*.

Source: *Liberator*, September 12, 1862.

5.5. "All persons held as slaves within said designated States, and parts of States, are, and henceforward shall be free," 1863

> *Abraham Lincoln (1809–1865) campaigned and entered the presidency holding that, as he stated in his 1861 inaugural address, "I have no purpose, directly or indirectly, to interfere with the institution of slavery in the States where it exists. I believe I have no lawful right to do so, and I have no inclination to do so." The war changed his position, as he showed in issuing his preliminary Emancipation Proclamation on September 22, 1862, and then in making it final on January 1, 1863. On completing the proclamation, Lincoln reportedly said: "I never, in my life, felt more certain that I was doing right than I do in signing this paper." Like the opening of the Civil War itself, the Emancipation Proclamation pushed race relations further into a new era.*

I, Abraham Lincoln, President of the United States, by virtue of the power in me vested as Commander-in-Chief, of the Army and Navy of the United States in time of actual armed rebellion against the authority and government of the United States, and as a fit and necessary war measure for suppressing said rebellion, do, on this first day of January, in the year of our Lord one thousand eight hundred and sixty-three, . . . [act] in accordance with my purpose so to do publicly proclaimed for the full period of one hundred days. . . .

By virtue of the power, and for the purpose aforesaid, I do order and declare that all persons held as slaves within said designated States, and parts of States, are, and henceforward shall be free; and that the Executive government of the

United States, including the military and naval authorities thereof, will recognize and maintain the freedom of said persons.

And I hereby enjoin upon the people so declared to be free to abstain from all violence, unless in necessary self-defence; and I recommend to them that, in all cases when allowed, they labor faithfully for reasonable wages.

And I further declare and make known, that such persons of suitable condition, will be received into the armed service of the United States to garrison forts, positions, stations, and other places, and to man vessels of all sorts in said service.

And upon this act, sincerely believed to be an act of justice, warranted by the Constitution, upon military necessity, I invoke the considerate judgment of mankind, and the gracious favor of Almighty God.

Source: Emancipation Proclamation, Proclamation 17, 12 Stat. 1268 (January 1, 1863).

5.6.   "This proclamation changed everything," 1863

> *The escaped slave and prominent abolitionist Frederick Douglass (1817–1895) years after the fact reflected on the Emancipation Proclamation's significance. The most noted black American of the nineteenth century, Douglass expressed much of blacks' thinking and feeling. His speeches spellbound many an audience. His* North Star *newspaper (later titled* Frederick Douglass's Paper*), published in Rochester, New York, starting in 1847, served its day as a font of black news and commentary. His 1845 autobiography,* Narrative of the Life of Frederick Douglass, an American Slave Written by Himself, *was a bestseller destined to become a literary classic and primary source on U.S. slavery from a onetime slave's perspective. In the book's 1881 revision and update retitled* Life and Times, *Douglass recalled his sense of the Emancipation Proclamation's context and significance.*

The first of January, 1863, was a memorable day in the progress of American liberty and civilization. It was the turning-point in the conflict between freedom and slavery. A death blow was then given to the slaveholding rebellion. Until then the federal arm had been more than tolerant to that relict of barbarism.

The secretary of war, William H. Seward, had given notice to the world that, "however the war for the Union might terminate, no change would be made in the relation of master and slave." Upon this pro-slavery platform the war against the rebellion had been waged during more than two years. It had not been a war of conquest, but rather a war of conciliation. McClellan, in command of the army, had been trying, apparently, to put down the rebellion without hurting the rebels, certainly without hurting slavery, and the government had seemed to coöperate with him in both respects. . . .

The whole anti-slavery phalanx at the North, had denounced this policy, and had besought Mr. Lincoln to adopt an opposite one, but in vain. Generals, in the field, and councils in the Cabinet, had persisted in advancing this policy through defeats and disasters, even to the verge of ruin. We fought the rebellion, but not its cause.

And now, on this day of January 1st, 1863, the formal and solemn announcement was made that thereafter the government would be found on the side of emancipation. This proclamation changed everything.

Source: Frederick Douglass, *The Life and Times of Frederick Douglass* (Hartford, CT: Park Publishing Co., 1881).

5.7. "An uneffaceable disgrace to the American people," 1863

"The Home of Lincoln Condemns the Proclamation," declared the Democratic newspaper Illinois State Register, *published in the state capital of Springfield, in January 1863. It reported that the Illinois legislature had moved to pass the following resolution to condemn President Abraham Lincoln's Emancipation Proclamation that went into effect on January 1, 1863. It denied that the proclamation had any legal basis, accused it of distorting the aims and objects of the Civil War, and decried it as a disgrace and a horrible social revolution.*

Resolved: That the emancipation proclamation of the President of the United States is as unwarrantable in military as in civil law; a gigantic usurpation, at once converting the war, professedly commenced by the administration for the vindication of the authority of the constitution, into the crusade for the sudden, unconditional and violent liberation of 3,000,000 negro slaves; a result which would not only be a total subversion of the Federal Union but a revolution in the social organization of the Southern States, the immediate and remote, the present and far-reaching consequences of which to both races cannot be contemplated without the most dismal foreboding of horror and dismay. The proclamation invites servile insurrection as an element in this emancipation crusade—a means of warfare, the inhumanity and diabolism of which are without example in civilized warfare, and which we denounce, and which the civilized world will denounce, as an uneffaceable disgrace to the American people.

Source: *Illinois State Register* (Springfield, IL), January 7, 1863, 1.

5.8. "A question reserved . . . for their own people," 1865

Congress's debate on a proposed Thirteenth Amendment to ban slavery in the United States captured much in persistent past discussion and presaged much in future discourse on the federal govern-

ment's authority and role in regard particularly to slavery and gener-
ally to race relations. The House of Representatives rejected the pro-
posed amendment until national elections in November 1864
resoundingly reelected President Abraham Lincoln and carried in a
Republican majority. In January 1865 the lame-duck session of the
House, with 2 votes to spare to reach the required two-thirds major-
ity, approved the proposed amendment 119 to 56. Speaking just be-
fore the vote, Wisconsin Democratic Representative James Sproat
Brown (1824–1878) repeated his personal and his party's objections
to the amendment. Insisting the Constitution privileged state's rights,
Sproat declared he was neither for slavery nor against blacks. He ar-
gued that both should be left to follow their own course, which in his
view was inevitable death for slavery. The issues and problems be-
longed to the individual states, not to the national government, Sproat
insisted.

The Constitution in its true spirit delegated certain powers of general interest in every State to the General Government; in no instance did it seek to interfere with the merely local interest or institutions of any State. Indeed, any
such interference would be entirely inconsistent with the declaration of the
Constitution itself as to its objects. . . . We are therefore on our oaths to declare
that interference with an institution local in its character is not merely an addition to the powers of the General Government as a destruction of the local
powers of the States, but is a matter necessary to the general weal of all parts
of the country. I cannot so hold. . . .

I am not now and never have been an apologist for slavery. I have never believed that it could be a permanent institution; the seeds of death were in its
nature. Had I lived in Maryland I should have voted to abolish slavery; I
should so have voted in Missouri; I would so vote in Kentucky. Their material
interests will undoubtedly be advanced by such abolition; but it is still a question reserved under the Constitution for their own people.

This is, however, not even a question of the practical abolition of slavery.
There are causes at work, which in any event will destroy it. . . . Thousands of
the most intelligent [slaves] have already escaped; new ideas as to liberty (a
word hitherto unknown to them) have through intermingling with our soldiers
been scattered among them; the patient drudge of former times (who then
scarce knew that he had a soul) will soon inquire into the reason why his bone
and sinews are the property of another; the wealth of the southerner in slavery, if it cannot take to itself wings, will at least take to itself legs and disappear.

Nor am I altogether indifferent to the effects upon national character of such
an amendment. It is a declaration upon our part that slavery is not merely a
local institution, but a national sin, sustained and upheld by the Constitution.
Our fathers carefully avoided the possibility of this charge; nowhere have they
used in the Constitution the word *slave.* In providing for their surrender it uses
the words "persons held to service or labor;" in depriving the South of full representation for slaves, it requires an enumeration of free persons, &c., and three
fourths [*sic*] of all others. So careful were they to avoid a recognition in any

way of slavery! We might fairly change these two provisions; but to ingraft upon the Constitution a provision abolishing slavery, is to declare upon our oaths that slavery was connected with the purposes and object of the Constitution, and belonged to the North as well as to the South. . . .

I cannot vote for the amendment.

Source: Cong. Globe, 38th Cong., 2nd sess. 527 (January 31, 1865) (comments of Rep. James Sproat Brown, D–WI).

ANNOTATED RESEARCH GUIDE

Books

Berlin, Ira, et al., eds. *Freedom's Soldiers: The Black Military Experience in the Civil War.* New York: Cambridge University Press, 1998. A collection of powerful documents treating the nearly 200,000 blacks, mostly freedmen, who served in the Civil War U.S. Army and Navy.

Berwanger, Eugene H. *The Frontier Against Slavery: Western Anti-Negro Prejudice and the Slavery Extension Controversy.* Rev. ed. Urbana: University of Illinois Press, 2002. Lays open whites-only prejudice that shaped the law and the social and political climates that before 1860 excluded blacks from most of the territories and states from the Ohio River Valley westward.

Bilotta, James D. *Race and the Rise of the Republican Party, 1848–1865.* New York: Peter Lang, 1992. Probes the racial thinking of the day with its pseudoscience backing of blacks as physically and mentally inferior to whites and shows how Negrophobia shaped congressional and presidential policies.

Blight, David W. *Race and Reunion: The Civil War and Reunion in American Memory.* Boston: Belknap Press, 2002. Explores the American culture of moral crusading that simultaneously pressed for black rights and white unity and the consequences of such culture and dissonance on continuing race relations.

Blight, David W., and Brooks D. Simpson, eds. *Union and Emancipation: Essays on Politics and Race in the Civil War Era.* Kent, OH: Kent State University Press, 1997. Considers the importance of race in defining the American nation, its mission, and its conception of freedom and rights in the time of crisis and its aftermath.

Greenberg, Martin Harry, and Charles G. Waugh, eds. *The Price of Freedom: Slavery and the Civil War.* Nashville, TN: Cumberland House Publishing, 2000. Moves through black perspectives on the coming of the war to their recruitment, enlistment, and military experience, including views on black women in the war effort and black aid to the Confederacy.

Guelzo, Allen C. *Lincoln's Emancipation Proclamation: The End of Slavery in America.* New York: Simon & Schuster, 2004. Treats the proclamation from genesis to aftermath in light of Lincoln's uppermost aim to restore the Union, not to emancipate slaves.

McPherson, James M. *Abraham Lincoln and the Second American Revolution.* New York: Oxford University Press, 1990. Seven provocative essays examining Lincoln's role as a conservative revolutionary whose leadership nevertheless triggered slavery's end and a transformation of the South.

———. *The Negro's Civil War: How American Negroes Felt and Acted during the War for the Union.* New York: Random House, 1965. A still fascinating documentary packed with illustrative materials on blacks' perceptions and practices during the war.

Quarles, Benjamin. *Lincoln and the Negro*. New York: Oxford University Press, 1962. Classic and still useful in its revealing anecdotes of the Great Emancipator's personal and political perspectives on U.S. race relations between blacks and whites.

Smith, John David, ed. *Black Soldiers in Blue: African American Troops in the Civil War Era*. Chapel Hill: University of North Carolina Press, 2002. A collection of original essays probing the immediate and eventual meaning of blacks' armed service in the Civil War.

Vorenberg, Michael. *Final Freedom: The Civil War, the Abolition of Slavery, and the Thirteenth Amendment*. New York: Cambridge University Press, 2001. An innovative examination of the struggles of U.S. legal thinkers, policymakers, and people in general to shape the meaning and measure of emancipation.

Web Sites

http://www.cr.nps.gov/history/online_books/rthg/chap5.htm—this National Park Service site probes the racial milieu that gave rise to the Civil War and shared its prosecution and aftermath.

http://www.pbs.org/wgbh/aia/part4/4narr5.html—using Part 4 of the PBS six-hour documentary series *Africans in America* (Boston: ROJA Productions, 1994), the site focuses on the role blacks played in the Civil War and on the problem of race as a cause and continuing consequence of the war.

6

After Slavery? Reconstruction and Segregation

The Thirteenth Amendment, ratified in December 1865, settled constitutional questions about the status of slavery. It did not, however, settle questions about the status of ex-slaves or blacks in general. Deciding what the amendment meant revealed sharp differences about the character of slavery, the character of African Americans, and the character of the American nation.

Among the immediate primary questions were: What did prohibiting slavery actually prohibit? What exactly was slavery, after all? What were the capacities of African Americans as Americans? Where could and should blacks fit in the scheme of American life? Were emancipation from slavery and civil equality for blacks to be synonymous? At the core were questions about fundamental rights and federal authority. At bedrock were questions about black-white race relations in view of "American" identity.

Nowhere in the United States prior to the Thirteenth Amendment had blacks as a group enjoyed full civil equality. Civil law had not recognized slaves as persons nor provided them much more standing than chattel—movable property like cattle. Nor had federal or state law recognized unenslaved blacks as having rights on the same basis as whites. Chief Justice Roger B. Taney stated the point bluntly in his infamous opinion in the 1857 Dred Scott case when he declared blacks "had no rights which the white man was bound to respect."[1] So merely announcing in 1865 that U.S. law no longer permitted slavery left unanswered in what capacity U.S. law would recognize blacks no longer enslaved.

The ending of slavery north of the Mason-Dixon line after the War for Independence (1775–1783) suggested how the South might handle its post–Civil War experience with ex-slaves. Northern states in the 1780s and 1790s, after what historians have called "the First Emancipation," largely replaced slavery with segregation as the racial boundary marker. "In virtually every phase of existence, Negroes found themselves systematically separated from whites," historian Leon F. Litwack noted in his classic study of blacks in the North from 1790 to 1860. Blacks "were either excluded from railway cars, omnibuses, stage-coaches, and steamboats or assigned to special 'Jim Crow' sections; they sat . . . in secluded and remote corners of theaters and lecture halls." Litwack explained further that "they could not enter most hotels, restaurants, and resorts, except as servants; they prayed in 'Negro pews' in white churches."[2]

Violence erupted in the antebellum North when whites perceived blacks' crossing barriers race relations imposed. A white mob in Philadelphia, Pennsylvania's "City of Brotherly Love," stoned to death an "uppity" black woman in 1819. Rioting whites in Cincinnati routed more than a thousand blacks from that Ohio city in 1829. In 1832 white Ohioans terrorized a group of recently manumitted slaves to stop them from settling in the state. In 1834 New York City erupted in three days of July rioting that systematically singled out for attack black homes and black leaders, such as the Reverend Peter Williams—the first black priest in the Episcopal Church. In their frenzy to keep blacks in a separate place, the New York rioters especially denounced black-white sex and intermarriage. Indeed, they singled out Williams on a rumor he had conducted an interracial marriage in his parish at the St. Phillip's African Episcopal Church on Center Street, where the mob also fixed its wrath. The rampage eerily presaged New York City's Draft Riots in July 1863, one of the bloodiest race riots in U.S. history.

Whites in the postbellum South also responded with violence to blacks in the aftermath of slavery. In May 1866, a murderous three-day riot in Memphis, Tennessee, left forty-six blacks and two whites dead. At least seventy-five more were shot. Ten others were severely beaten. White gangs raped at least five black females. White rioters destroyed twelve black schools, four black churches, and ninety-one homes—eighty-nine of blacks, one of a white man, and one of an interracial couple. Whites infuriated by the bold bearing of black Union army veterans in the city sparked the conflagration.

What sustained the rampage, however, was whites' rising rage over the rapid influx of blacks. Between 1860 and 1865, the number of blacks in Memphis jumped from 3,000 to at least 20,000; by some counts, it reached 25,000. Further down the Mississippi River a spectacle similar to that in Memphis occurred in July 1866. Resentful whites in New Orleans also spilled their anger into the streets and murdered at least 200 in rioting. There, too, the number of blacks had at least doubled since 1860, when the census recorded 24,074. The war-related influx of blacks further pressurized an already hostile environment.[3]

The 1866 riots in Memphis and New Orleans reflected much about the postbellum repositioning of black-white relations. The rapid rise in black population in both cities triggered white perceptions that blacks were out of control. And that was the crucial issue—control. Blacks saw the end of slavery as a start of self-determination. No longer would others decide their lives. They would decide for themselves. Thus, at the end of the Civil War, and even before then, blacks tested their freedom, by testing their mobility.

Moving was a means for many blacks to measure their emancipation. In their moving, "going to town" was a frequent direction. Before the war, free blacks strongly preferred urban areas. Indeed, free blacks were probably the most ur-banized of any group in antebellum America. The postbellum black surge to southern cities changed their black-white complexion and also the composition of their black communities. Rather than relatively self-sufficient artisans and their families forming the bulk of the black population, relatively needy for-mer fieldhands came to make up the bulk of many new urban black communi-ties in the South. The flow reflected blacks' desires to get away from dreaded slave fields and quarters and to dreamed-of work and accommodations.

Ex-slaves' relocation was part of restructuring their lives, particularly in re-gard to family, work, and church. Family clearly ranked first in ex-slaves' eyes. They hastened to escape the position in which, as a black newspaper in Austin, Texas, put it, "lawful wedlock was unknown . . . [as were] relations of husband and wife, parent and child."[4] Law had recognized no kindred ties among slaves. Ex-slaves insisted on having law recognize their marriages, their par-enting, their children, and their family rights. But whites resisted. Vagrancy and apprenticeship laws stripped blacks of their children on assertions that the parents lacked "the resources, or . . . refuse to provide and bear expense of those minors."[5] Getting black families sanctioned on the same legal basis as white families was not easy. Nor was it always encouraged by whites who in-sisted on pointing to blacks' disrupted legal kinship as a matter of blacks' pref-erences rather than as a result of practices and principles slavery fostered. It proved another rub in black-white relations.

Black churches were primary agents in pushing for recognition of the black family. As in the aftermath of emancipation in the North, the black church sprang to life with vigor in the postbellum South. As in the North, slaves in the South usually attended their slaveholders' churches—albeit in separate sec-tions or at separate services. And as in the North, after emancipation blacks generally refused such arrangements. Separate was not the same, and it was not acceptable. Thus blacks split from white churches.

Acting as a primary engine in developing black life after slavery, black churches provided a pattern of organization and leadership that figured in forming the basis of blacks' educational, political, and social experiences. Standing as a champion of black uplift, however, the church stood also as a canker for opponents of black independence. Black churches became prime tar-gets for white night riders and rioters who used the torch in protest. Burned black churches appeared somehow to remedy whites' grievances over blacks' assertiveness. Church buildings also represented blacks' accumulating prop-erty. That, too, angered some whites. So did black schools. Not infrequently, black churches housed black schools. Freedmen's Bureau schools were often in black church buildings. And churches ran their own schools.

Through one connection or another, in the immediate postbellum South church-related schools were the norm for blacks for primary or grade schools as well as for higher education. The bulk of black colleges grew from church roots—not unlike early American colleges such as Harvard, Yale, Princeton, and Brown, which religious denominations founded. Also, black colleges rep-resented notable black-white cooperation. To start, white Methodists founded Wilberforce in Ohio in 1856, as a college for blacks. Its naming honored the in-fluential English antislavery advocate William Wilberforce (1759–1833). The

African Methodist Episcopal (AME) Church acquired control of the college in 1863. Northern white groups such as the American Missionary Association (AMA) disbursed more than $250,000 to black schools in 1865 and 1866. Hampton, Howard, Fisk, Talladega, and New Orleans University all benefitted from church monies. Denominations created their own schools. The Protestant Episcopal Church founded St. Augustine's College in Raleigh, North Carolina, in 1867, for example. Georgia's Atlanta Baptist College bore its benefactor's name. Methodists promoted professional education, particularly in medicine, funding Meharry Medical School in Nashville, Tennessee, and Flint Medical College in New Orleans.

Blacks' efforts at establishing a new place for themselves clashed with whites' efforts to keep blacks "in their place." The clash pitted a place of whites' control against a place of blacks' choice. At extremes, one group wanted to change almost everything, and the other wanted to change almost nothing. Indeed, many whites saw any significant change in blacks' position as meaning the end of society as they knew it and wanted it to be. The stakes appeared to be life and death. Thus, they resisted. The result was violence.

The rioting in Memphis and New Orleans in 1866 merely sampled the white mob violence that became a primary and persistent feature of black-white race relations throughout the postbellum South. Rioting was whimsical. More predatory was the steady terror of white secret societies such as the Ku Klux Klan (KKK) that Confederate veterans in the south-central Tennessee town of Pulaski initiated in 1866 in the aftermath of the Memphis riot. Dedicated to white supremacy, the KKK and its fellow travelers, such as the Knights of the White Camelia, begun in Louisiana in 1867, premeditated death and destruction to strip blacks of freedom. Their symbol was the ultimate ugliness of lynching. The frenzied shootings, hangings, butcherings, burnings, bludgeonings, beatings, mutilatings, and dismemberings were only a part of the violence blacks faced. Not merely by extralegal means did whites vent their fury against blacks who appeared not to know their place.

While white rioters and vigilantes put blacks to death without legal sanction, states did no less deadly work. Their process was, however, dubbed legal. Southern prison populations bulged with blacks. Police brutality against blacks was rife. It triggered the Memphis riot. The incessant terror that maintained slavery shifted to maintain segregation as the system of white supremacy and black subordination. The South sought to establish the new system as law in a set of Black Codes.

Congress balked at transparent southern efforts to replace old Slaves Codes with new Black Codes. To clarify and protect blacks' rights, Congress in April 1866 passed the first federal Civil Rights Act over President Andrew Johnson's veto. The act sought to clear up basic issues, such as whether blacks were citizens. The infamous Dred Scott decision in 1857 had appeared to deny blacks' citizenship. Louisiana's high court in 1860 had declared more directly, "The African race are strangers to our Constitution."[6] Thus, the 1866 federal act opened by announcing that "all persons born in the United States and not subject to any foreign power, excluding Indians not taxed, are hereby declared to be citizens of the United States."[7]

Citizenship represented a basic first step toward rights. But by itself the title "citizen" provided few rights. White women were citizens, after all, but their rights were clearly restricted on the basis of their sex. Congress acted to make clear that citizenship rights were not to be restricted on the basis of race. It declared that

> citizens, of every race and color, without regard to any previous condition of slavery or involuntary servitude, except as a punishment for crime whereof the party shall have been duly convicted, shall have the same right, in every State and Territory in the United States . . . as is enjoyed by white citizens.[8]

Congress sought also to list some citizenship rights. It covered mostly what were then thought of as political rights. They involved persons more or less directly with the political system. They treated government operation in the courts, at the ballot box, or in some other public function. The 1866 act listed rights "to make and enforce contracts, to sue, be parties, and give evidence, to inherit, purchase, lease, sell, hold, and convey real and personal property, and to full equal benefit of all laws and proceedings for the security of person and property." Continuing challenge to the constitutional basis for establishing and enforcing such rights gave rise to the Fourteenth Amendment in 1868, with its guarantee of "equal protection of the laws."[9]

Resistance to blacks' rights, and especially to equal rights, was not merely southern. Nor was it only an issue for congressional debate. The states individually grappled with the issues and illustrated how unstable was the seeming support for embracing blacks as full members of the American community. A state convention of blacks in Illinois in 1866 noted how they continued to be relegated in the "land of Lincoln." The state had ratified the Thirteenth Amendment and repealed "part of her black code" but, the convention complained, continued to shut black children out of public schools and still barred blacks from voting. And Illinois was not peculiar. Blacks in New York in 1869 raised similar complaints of being "taxed without being represented" and of paying "to support common schools while their children are denied the privilege of attending."[10]

Suffrage and schooling revealed the parameters within which prevailing prejudice confined blacks' rights. Suffrage represented the foundational public right in U.S. political philosophy. It furnished the popular consent for constitutional sovereignty. Yet the vote was not granted to all persons, nor even to all citizens. Age, of course, acted as a bar. So did sex and race. The antebellum rally cry to reform voter qualifications had touted universal adult white male suffrage. At the time of the Civil War, only in New England did blacks have an unqualified right to vote. New York granted blacks a right to vote but qualified it to a degree that basically denied it and in referenda consistently refused to grant blacks the vote on the same terms as whites. Four other northern states had constitutions that barred blacks from voting. Eight others barred black voting by statute.

The results of the Civil War did not radically shift popular sentiment. Between 1865 and 1870, at least sixteen states outside the South put before their voters the issue of black suffrage. The proposition lost in fourteen. Only Minnesota and Iowa struck the "white only" requirement and allowed black males to vote on the same basis as whites. Thus the Fifteenth Amendment ratified in 1870 to outlaw "race, color, or previous condition of servitude" as a bar to voting was not merely a measure aimed at the South. It confronted a nationwide failure to embrace a basic element of freedom for blacks.

The Fifteenth Amendment's removing race as a legal bar to blacks' voting and enabling blacks to vote were different things. As so often in U.S. history, merely removing the label of race meant little more than cosmetic change. It signaled a start to a new stage of struggle, not an end of struggle. And with voting, the struggle was bloody. Blacks' seeking to exercise suffrage met violent resistance. Election seasons were primary times for marauders such as the KKK and other white vigilantes.

As intense as resistance to blacks' political rights was, it paled in comparison to resistance to what were called social rights attached to people's associating together. The pattern of segregation that accompanied slavery before the Civil War dominated popular thought and behavior among whites. They showed little inclination to change after the war. Not in the states that had maintained slavery in 1860 nor in any other part of the nation did whites generally embrace either the reality or rhetoric of accepting blacks as social equals.

Many whites saw indiscriminate association with blacks as but a prelude to intimate association with blacks. Miscegenation loomed large and ugly in many minds. The image primarily of black men having sex with white women overwhelmed many with fear and loathing. In the context of federalism, which ordinarily left legislation on social relations to states, Congress itself long resisted addressing social rights. It relented only as a tribute to Charles Sumner, Massachusetts's longtime Republican senator and civil right champion, when he died in March 1874.

The Civil Rights Act of 1875 that Congress passed, largely as tribute to Sumner, entitled "all persons . . . to the full and equal enjoyment of the accommodation, advantages, facilities, and privileges of inns, public conveyances on land or water, theaters, and other places of public amusement." But the act proved to be less than it appeared. It left unanswered the question of what "full and equal enjoyment" meant. Moreover, it failed to recognize a right blacks demanded as basic: The right to send their children to public schools without racial discrimination.

Segregated public schools were the rule in the antebellum North. Ohio (1838), Michigan (1841), Iowa (1846), Indiana (1850), New York (1850), Pennsylvania (1854), California (1855), and Illinois (1857) all provided by law for separate schools. Massachusetts offered the leading legal justification for the practice. In the 1849 case of *Roberts v. the City of Boston*, the commonwealth's celebrated Chief Justice Lemuel Shaw declared Boston's practice of separate schools for blacks was neither unreasonable nor illegal. He saw no useful purpose in "compelling colored and white children to associate together in the same schools." Common schooling would not lessen any "distinction and prejudice, existing in the opinion and feelings of the community," Shaw explained. Anti-Negro "prejudice, if it exists, is not created by law, and probably cannot be changed by law," he opined.[11]

Congress in 1875 appeared to agree with Shaw. The Civil Rights Act of 1875 reconnected pre-war antislavery rhetoric and ideals with postwar reality and the politics of race relations. The token Congress offered in tribute to Sumner proved to be worth little. Almost immediately the Supreme Court moved to curtail the 1875 act and with it Congress's authority over civil rights. In *United States v. Reese* and *United States v. Cruikshank* in March 1876 the Court stripped away the essential federal shield for blacks' basic political rights. In January 1878 in *Hall v. De Cuir*, the Court restricted states' power to protect blacks from discrimination. In 1883 the Court reached the 1875 act and finished its gutting of Congress's civil rights protections.

Writing for an 8–1 majority in *The Civil Rights Cases* (1883), Justice Joseph P. Bradley declared that neither the Thirteenth nor the Fourteenth Amendment authorized Congress to create or secure "what may be called the social rights of men and races."[12] The Thirteenth Amendment "simply abolished slavery," Bradley stated. Social discrimination had nothing to do with "any badge of slavery or servitude," in his view. "It would be running the slavery argument into the ground," he sneered, "to make it apply to every act of discrimination which a person may see fit to make."[13]

The only member of the Supreme Court to reject Bradley's view was Kentucky-born former slaveholder John Marshall Harlan. And he did so vigorously. He chided his brethren for taking so "narrow and artificial" a view as to make them virtually blind to the realities blacks faced in the aftermath of slavery. He insisted that blacks' "freedom necessarily involved immunity from, and protection against, all discrimination against them, because of their race, in respect of such civil rights as belong to freemen of other races." For the government to allow racial discrimination was for the government to allow classes among its citizens—a result fundamentally contrary to the U.S. Constitution. Harlan insisted that "there cannot be, in this republic, any class of human beings in practical subjection to another class."[14]

Whether segregation was legal or only "practical subjection," as Justice Harlan termed it, remained an issue after the Supreme Court's ruling in *The Civil Rights Cases*. An apparent majority of the nation accepted the practice. Southern states increasingly acted to sanction it by law. They moved to make public practice legal policy, to make de facto segregation de jure. Transportation led the way. Nine states moved between 1887 and 1892 to mandate that common carriers segregate passengers by race. The issue came to a head in a challenge to Louisiana's 1890 Separate Car Act that resulted in the landmark case of *Plessy v. Ferguson* (1896).

Massachusetts-born Justice Henry Billings Brown delivered the Court's 7–1 decision. He dismissed the challenge that the law of race was unreasonable and unconstitutional. In recognizing race and in requiring "equal but separate" accommodations based on race, Louisiana merely recognized "distinctions based upon physical differences," Brown wrote. He emphasized that race was a *fact*. It was a fact of life and of law that, in his view, "must always exist so long as white men are distinguished from the other race by color."[15] Requiring racial separation was both reasonable and legal, according to Brown and his brethren in the Court majority. The ruling dismissed with apparent contempt the idea "that the enforced separation of the two races stamps the colored race with a badge of inferiority." If inferiority existed, it was not because the law created it, the majority concluded.[16]

As he had in *The Civil Rights Cases* in 1883, Justice John Marshall Harlan vigorously challenged the majority's view in *Plessy v. Ferguson*. A state's recognizing race by law created classes among citizens, which violated the nation's fundamental principles, Harlan insisted. The United States was a place where, he wrote, "the law regards man as man, and takes no account of his surroundings or of his color when his civil rights as guaranteed by the supreme law of the land are involved." In a line destined to be often quoted, Harlan concluded, "Our constitution is color-blind, and neither knows nor tolerates classes among citizens."[17] His was a lonely voice raised against de jure segregation.

The *Plessy* decision confirmed the apparent sway of American-style apartheid and appeared to set the racial cast of the coming century. A generation of unprecedented immigration that between 1882 and 1910 averaged nearly 2 million persons a year, mostly from eastern and southern Europe, hardened the black-white divide. The new immigrants, many despised and considered racially suspect by native-born American whites, flailed to distance themselves from blacks. Frantic to prove their "whiteness," many out-bigoted homegrown nativists in promoting race to separate and structure group relations. Refusing to live, work, eat, ride, recreate, or go to school with blacks, many new immigrants exalted whiteness as a monolith that included them in the promise of American life while isolating blacks.

The U.S. foray into overseas empire in the advent and aftermath of the War with Spain in 1898 infused large elements of American popular opinion with a sense of what the jingoist English poet Rudyard Kipling dubbed "the white man's burden." Many white Americans more fervently than ever embraced a sense of white moral superiority, the inferiority of all nonwhite peoples, and foreordained racial segregation to preserve their sense of divinely ordained white civilization. Such formed the foundation of what moved the preeminent and prescient U.S. intellectual W.E.B. Du Bois in 1903 to declare that "the problem of the twentieth century is the problem of the color-line."[18]

NOTES

1. *Scott v. Sanford*, 60 U.S. 393, 408 (1857).

2. Arthur Zilversmit, *The First Emancipation: The Abolition of Slavery in the North* (Chicago: University of Chicago Press, 1967); Leon F. Litwack, *North of Slavery: The Negro in the Free States, 1790–1860* (Chicago: University of Chicago Press, 1961), 97.

3. United States Congress, House Select Committee on the Memphis Riots, *Memphis Riots and Massacres, 1866*, H.R. Rep. No. 101, 39th Cong., 1st sess. (1866); James Gilbert Ryan, "The Memphis Riots of 1866: Terror in a Black Community during Reconstruction," *Journal of Negro History* 62 (1977): 243–257; U.S. Bureau of the Census, *Population of the United States of 1860* (Washington, DC: GPO, 1864), 195.

4. *The Freedmen's Press* (Austin, TX), July 18, 1868, 2.

5. "An Act related to Apprentices and Indentured Servants," 1865 La. Acts 3.

6. *African Methodist Episcopal Church v. City of New Orleans*, 15 La. Ann. at 443 (1860).

7. "An Act to protect all Persons in the United States in their Civil Rights, and furnish the Means of their Vindication," 14 Stat. 27 (April 9, 1866).

8. Ibid.

9. Ibid. U.S. Const. Amend 14, sec. 1.

10. *Proceedings of the Illinois State Convention of Colored Men, Assembled at Galesburg* (Chicago: Church, Goodman and Donnelley, 1867); "Negro State Convention in Utica," New York *Daily Tribune*, August 20, 1869, 2.

11. *Roberts v. the City of Boston*, 59 Mass. (5 Cush.) 198 (1849).

12. 109 U.S. at 22.

13. Ibid., 24.

14. Ibid., 26, 36, 62.

15. 163 U.S. at 550, 543.

16. Ibid., 551.

17. Ibid., 559 (Harlan, J., dissenting).

18. W.E.B. Du Bois, *The Souls of Black Folk* (New York: A.C. McClurg, 1903), in the essay "Of the Dawn of Freedom," 10, revised from "The Freedmen's Bureau," *Atlantic Monthly*, March 1901, 354–365.

DOCUMENTS

6.1.   "Full equal benefit of all laws," 1866

Even as the proposed Thirteenth Amendment to prohibit slavery and involuntary servitude worked its way to ratification between February and December 1865, Congress saw the measure was insufficient to protect African Americans. Ex-Confederate states almost immediately after their surrender began enacting laws called Black Codes to replace the old Slave Codes. They subjected blacks to civil disabilities and legal burdens to subordinate by race. The Black Codes curtailed blacks' "rights in the pursuit of life, liberty, and property to such an extent that their freedom was of little value," U.S. Supreme Court Justice John Marshall Harlan later summarized. To combat the threat, Congress enacted the first federal Civil Rights Act, having to override President Andrew Johnson's veto to make it law in 1866. The act's title indicated its clear purpose. It outlined basic personal rights, including the right to citizenship, and offered a framework for race relations within U.S. law.

An Act to protect all Persons in the United States in their Civil Rights, and furnish the Means of their Vindication.

Be it enacted, That all persons born in the United States and not subject to any foreign power, excluding Indians not taxed, are hereby declared to be citizens of the United States; and such citizens, of every race and color, without regard to any previous condition of slavery or involuntary servitude, except as a punishment for crime whereof the party shall have been duly convicted, shall have the same right, in every State and Territory in the United States, to make and enforce contracts, to sue, be parties, and give evidence, to inherit, purchase, lease, sell, hold, and convey real and personal property, and to full equal benefit of all laws and proceedings for the security of person and property, as is enjoyed by white citizens, and shall be subject to like punishment, pains, and penalties, and to none other, any law, statute, ordinance, regulation, or custom, to the contrary notwithstanding.

Source: 14 Stat. 27 (April 9, 1866).

6.2.   "We have been promised our rights but have not yet received them," 1869

After the Civil War, blacks continued their prewar practice in the North of convening local, state, regional, and national conventions to discuss race relations, to develop solutions for targeted problems, and to publicize their grievances. A state convention of New York blacks meeting in the central, upstate city of Utica in August 1869 announced their sore displeasure at the continuing, nationwide denial of equal rights to blacks. They remonstrated against the full range of racial discrimination that sucked the substance from their citizenship and made the U.S. promise of liberty a lie. From lynching to voting to segregated public schools to discrimination in military service and in the court system, the black convention demanded an end to racial subordination and the start of full exercise of promised equal rights.

A large minority of the citizens of the United States are denied those rights which are given them by their Creator. They are taxed without being represented; they are subject to trials by juries which are not their peers; they are murdered without having redress; they are taxed to support common schools while their children are denied the privilege of attending those in their respective wards; they are called upon for military service of their country without receiving proper protection from the country, and without any incentives whatever of being commissioned officers.

These grievances belie the Declaration of Independence by which the American people profess to be governed. We have been laboring for the past two and a half centuries to enrich the country without having received a particle of remuneration. We have been promised our rights but have not yet received them. . . .

We demand all the rights and prerogatives enjoyed by our white fellow-citizens. We have lived here two and a half centuries, and know only this country as our home. Here we have a few cherished memories, and many sad ones; yet our country is dear to us with all her faults. We demand these rights as natives of this country. We demand them for our long unrequited toil; we demand them from our part in the recent Rebellion, without which, millions more of dollars and thousands more previous lives would have been spared; we demand them for the protection of our wives and children; we demand them as a large minority of the entire population of the country; we demand them for the safety of the Republican party with which we shall ally ourselves so long as it continues to battle for righteousness and justice; we demand them as men, children of a common father.

Source: New York *Daily Tribune*, August 20, 1869.

6.3.   "It is essential to just government we recognize the equality of all men before the law," 1875

Following their outlawing slavery in 1865, the nation's lawmakers struggled to determine what liberty and equality meant in principle and in practice. The Civil Rights Act of 1866 provided for "full equal benefit of all laws and proceedings for the security of person and prop-

erty." Such "benefits" touched and concerned what people of the day considered economic and political rights. They did not reach areas of interpersonal association then considered social rights. The Civil Rights Act of 1875 advanced into social areas by providing for "full and equal enjoyment" of public accommodations. Most blacks relished the broadened enunciation of equality that they saw as allowing them full and equal access to publicly available goods, services, and conveniences. But many whites raged against what they felt was a forced, unnatural, and demeaning consorting with blacks.

An act to protect all citizens in their civil and legal rights

Whereas, it is essential to just government we recognize the equality of all men before the law, and hold that it is the duty of government in its dealings with the people to mete out equal and exact justice to all, of whatever nativity, race, color, or persuasion, religious or political; and it being the appropriate object of legislation to enact great fundamental principles into law: Therefore,

Be it enacted by the Senate and House of Representatives of the United States of America in Congress assembled, That all persons within the jurisdiction of the United States shall be entitled to the full and equal enjoyment of the accommodations, advantages, facilities, and privileges of inns, public conveyances on land or water, theaters, and other places of public amusement; subject only to the conditions and limitations established by law and applicable alike to citizens of every race and color, regardless of any previous condition of servitude.

Source: 18 Stat. 335 (March 1, 1875).

6.4.   "Running the slavery argument into the ground," 1883

Resistance to the Civil Rights Act of 1875's equal accommodations provisions reached the U.S. Supreme Court in 1883. Before the Court were five cases—one each from the District of Columbia, Kansas, Missouri, New York, and Tennessee. Consolidated under the title The Civil Rights Cases, *they concerned denying blacks accommodations at an inn or hotel or at a theater or opera house or on a railroad. The legal question was whether Congress had authority to reach what many considered private actions. In a constitutional sense, the question touched the relation between racial discrimination and slavery. In prohibiting slavery, had the Thirteenth Amendment outlawed racial discrimination as part of what the law called "the badges and incidents" of slavery? The answer proved crucial to the structure and style of race relations in the United States. The Court majority held that racial discrimination was not necessarily unconstitutional.*

The thirteenth amendment has respect, not to distinctions of race, or class, or color, but to slavery. The fourteenth amendment extends its protection to races and classes, and prohibits any state legislation which has the effect of denying to any race or class, or to any individual, the equal protection of the laws. . . .

It would be running the slavery argument into the ground to make it apply to every act of discrimination which a person may see fit to make as to the guests he will entertain, or as to the people he will take into his coach or cab or car, or admit to his concert or theater, or deal with in other matters of intercourse or business. . . .

When a man has emerged from slavery, and by the aid of beneficent legislation has shaken off the inseparable concomitants of that state, there must be some stage in the progress of his elevation when he takes the rank of a mere citizen, and ceases to be the special favorite of the laws, and when his rights as a citizen, or a man, are to be protected in the ordinary modes by which other men's rights are protected. There were thousands of free colored people in this country before the abolition of slavery, enjoying all the essential rights of life, liberty, and property the same as white citizens; yet no one, at that time, thought that it was any invasion of their personal status as freemen because they were not admitted to all the privileges enjoyed by white citizens, or because they were subjected to discriminations in the enjoyment of accommodations in inns, public conveyances, and places of amusement. Mere discriminations on account of race or color were not regarded as badges of slavery. If, since that time, the enjoyment of equal rights in all these respects has become established by constitutional enactment, it is not by force of the thirteenth amendment, (which merely abolishes slavery,) but by force of the fourteenth and fifteenth amendments.

Source: The Civil Rights Cases, 109 U.S. 3 (1883) (Bradley, J., for the Court).

6.5.   **"To secure and protect rights belonging to them as freemen and citizens; nothing more," 1883**

Kentucky-born former slaveholder John Marshall Harlan (1833–1911) alone on the U.S. Supreme Court dissented in The Civil Rights Cases *in 1883. He argued eloquently that racial discrimination was part and parcel of slavery. The Thirteenth Amendment outlawed both in principle and practice and in public and private action, he insisted. While losing in his day and for decades to come, Justice Harlan's arguments offered a framework for decades of legal challenges that in time shifted how U.S. law saw and treated racial discrimination.*

It was determined, by a change in the fundamental law, to uproot the institution of slavery wherever it existed in this land, and to establish universal freedom. . . .

I do not contend that the thirteenth amendment invests congress with authority, by legislation, to regulate the entire body of the civil rights which citizens enjoy, or may enjoy, in the several states. But I do hold that since slavery, as the court has repeatedly declared, was the moving or principal cause of the adoption of that amendment, and since that institution rested wholly upon the inferiority, as a race, of those held in bondage, their freedom necessarily involved immunity from, and protection against, all discrimination against them, because of their race, in respect of such civil rights as belong to freemen of other races. Congress, therefore, under its express power to enforce that amendment, by appropriate legislation, may enact laws to protect that people against the deprivation, on account of their race, of any civil rights enjoyed by other freemen in the same state; and such legislation may be of a direct and primary character, operating upon states, their officers and agents, and also upon, at least, such individuals and corporations as exercise public functions and wield power and authority under the state. . . .

My brethren say that when a man has emerged from slavery, and by the aid of beneficent legislation has shaken off the inseparable concomitants of that state, there must be some stage in the progress of his elevation when he takes the rank of a mere citizen, and ceases to be the special favorite of the laws, and when his rights as a citizen, or a man, are to be protected in the ordinary modes by which other men's rights are protected.

It is, I submit, scarcely just to say that the colored race has been the special favorite of the laws. What the nation, through congress, has sought to accomplish in reference to that race is, what had already been done in every state in the Union for the white race, to secure and protect rights belonging to them as freemen and citizens; nothing more.

The one underlying purpose of congressional legislation has been to enable the black race to take the rank of mere citizens. The difficulty has been to compel a recognition of their legal right to take that rank, and to secure the enjoyment of privileges belonging, under the law, to them as a component part of the people for whose welfare and happiness government is ordained. At every step in this direction the nation has been confronted with class tyranny, which a contemporary English historian says is, of all tyrannies, the most intolerable, "for it is ubiquitous in its operation, and weighs, perhaps, most heavily on those whose obscurity or distance would withdraw them from the notice of a single despot." . . .

The supreme law of the land has decreed that no authority shall be exercised in this country upon the basis of discrimination, in respect of civil rights, against freemen and citizens because of their race, color, or previous condition of servitude. To that decree—for the due enforcement of which, by appropriate legislation, congress has been invested with express power—every one must bow, whatever may have been, or whatever now are, his individual views as to the wisdom or policy, either of the recent changes in the fundamental law, or of the legislation which has been enacted to give them effect.

Source: *The Civil Rights Cases*, 109 U.S. 3, 26–62 (1883) (Harlan, J., dissenting).

6.6.   "Where rests the responsibility for the lynch law," 1892

Mob murder of blacks stained the nation, particularly from the late 1860s to the 1920s. During the 1890s, the bloodiest decade recorded, white vigilantes beat, burned, hanged, stabbed, shot, stomped, or otherwise killed, on average, 113 blacks a year. In 1892 they lynched 161 blacks, prompting the aging champion of blacks' civil rights Frederick Douglass (1817–1895) to pen a magazine article titled "Lynch Law in the South." He noted the cry of black men raping white women as the usual, untrue excuse for white rage. He went further to cast lynching as not merely an act of a disorderly herd but a sanctioned act of social control chargeable to the whole of white society and the United States itself.

How can the South hope to teach the Negro the sacredness of human life while it cheapens it and profanes it by the atrocities of mob law? The stream cannot rise higher than its source. . . .

The crime which these usurpers of courts of law and juries profess to punish is the most revolting and shocking of any this side of murder. This they know is the best excuse, and it appeals at once and promptly to a prejudice which prevails at the North as well as the South. Hence we have for any act of lawless violence the same excuse—an outrage by a Negro upon some white woman. It is a notable fact, also, that it is not with them the immorality or the enormity of the crime itself that arouses popular wrath. . . .

For 200 years or more white men have in the South committed this offense against black women, and the fact has excited little attention, even at the North, except among Abolitionists; which circumstance demonstrates that the horror now excited is not for the crime itself, but that it is based on the reversal of color in the participants. . . .

Now, where rests the responsibility for the lynch law prevalent in the South? It is evident that it is not entirely the ignorant mob. The men who break open the jails and with bloody hands destroy human life are not alone responsible. These are not the men who make public sentiment. They are simply the hangmen, not the court, judge or jury. They simply obey the public sentiment of the South—the sentiment created by wealth and respectability, by the press and pulpit. A change in public sentiment can be easily effected by these forces whenever they shall elect to make the effort. Let the press and the pulpit of the South unite their power against the cruelty, disgrace and shame that is setting like a mantle of fire upon these lynch-law States, and lynch law itself will soon cease to exist.

Nor is the South alone responsible for this burning shame and menace to our free institutions. Wherever contempt of race prevails, whether against African, Indian or Mongolian, countenance and support are given to the present peculiar treatment of the Negro in the South. The finger of scorn at the North is correlated to the dagger of the assassin in the South. The sin against the Negro is both sectional and national, and until the voice of the North shall be heard in emphatic condemnation and withering reproach against these continued ruthless mob law murders, it will remain equally involved with the South in this common crime.

Source: Frederick Douglass, "Lynch Law in the South," *North American Review* 155 (July 1892): 117–124.

6.7.   "We cannot say . . . separation of the two races . . . is unreasonable," 1896

Persistent and pervasive popular white resistance to sharing public spaces with blacks succeeded in The Civil Rights Cases *(1883) to block Congress from outlawing racial discrimination in public accommodations. In* Plessy v. Ferguson *(1896), excerpted below, such white resistance again succeeded. It gained sanction for public accommodations that the U.S. Supreme Court directed to be "equal but separate." Over a vigorous, lone dissent by Justice John Marshall Harlan (1833–1911), the ruling allowed the accretion of racial segregation into an American-style apartheid that gripped the South and held sway throughout much of the United States, not merely as a folkway but as the law of the land until the 1950s and 1960s.*

This case turns upon the constitutionality of an act of the general assembly of the state of Louisiana, passed in 1890, providing for separate railway carriages for the white and colored races. . . .

The constitutionality of this act is attacked upon the ground that it conflicts both with the thirteenth amendment of the constitution, abolishing slavery, and the fourteenth amendment, which prohibits certain restrictive legislation on the part of the states.

That it does not conflict with the thirteenth amendment, which abolished slavery and involuntary servitude, except as a punishment for crime, is too clear for argument. Slavery implies involuntary servitude,—a state of bondage; the ownership of mankind as a chattel, or, at least, the control of the labor and services of one man for the benefit of another, and the absence of a legal right to the disposal of his own person, property, and services. . . .

A statute which implies merely a legal distinction between the white and colored races—a distinction which is founded in the color of the two races, and which must always exist so long as white men are distinguished from the other race by color—has no tendency to destroy the legal equality of the two races, or re-establish a state of involuntary servitude. . . .

As [far as] a conflict with the fourteenth amendment is concerned, the case reduces itself to the question whether the statute of Louisiana is a reasonable regulation, and with respect to this there must necessarily be a large discretion on the part of the legislature. In determining the question of reasonableness, it is at liberty to act with reference to the established usages, customs, and traditions of the people, and with a view to the promotion of their comfort, and the preservation of the public peace and good order. Gauged by this standard, we cannot say that a law which authorizes or even requires the separation of the two races in public conveyances is unreasonable, or more obnoxious to the fourteenth amendment than the acts of congress requiring separate schools for colored children in the District of Columbia, the constitutionality of which does not seem to have been questioned, or the corresponding acts of state legislatures.

We consider the underlying fallacy of the plaintiff's argument to consist in the assumption that the enforced separation of the two races stamps the colored race with a badge of inferiority. If this be so, it is not by reason of anything found in the act, but solely because the colored race chooses to put that construction upon it.

Source: *Plessy v. Ferguson*, 163 U.S. 537 (1896) (Brown, J., for the Court).

ANNOTATED RESEARCH GUIDE

Books

Ayers, Edward L. *The Promise of the New South: Life after Reconstruction*. New York: Oxford University Press, 1992. Typifies the new scholarship including poor whites in reconsidering the South's post-Reconstruction cultural, political, social, and racial history.

Belz, Herman. *Abraham Lincoln, Constitutionalism, and Equal Rights in the Civil War Era*. New York: Fordham University Press, 1998. Nine reprinted essays argue a conservative, state's rights perspective on civil rights' changes that emerged during and after the war.

Hahn, Stephen. *A Nation under Our Feet: Black Political Struggles in the Rural South from Slavery to the Great Migration*. Cambridge, MA: Belknap Press, 2003. Compellingly chronicles the groundwork rural southern blacks laid to exercise economic and political rights to reshape race relations in the face of violent white resistance.

Hyman, Harold M., and William M. Wiecek. *Equal Justice under Law: Constitutional Development, 1835–1875*. New York: Harper & Row, 1982. An excellent, broad-ranging synthesis of evolving legal doctrines, including those allowing persistent, state-backed racial discrimination.

Litwack, Leon F. *Been in the Storm So Long: The Aftermath of Slavery*. New York: Knopf, 1979. Reconstructs black and white perceptions and behaviors in the post–Civil War South, revealing the intensity and tenacity of the struggles of racial ordering.

Logan, Rayford W. *The Betrayal of the Negro: From Rutherford B. Hayes to Woodrow Wilson*. New York: Collier Books, 1965. Reprint, New York: Da Capo Press, 1997. Focuses on the problem of determining blacks' place following the Civil War in the context of America's self-image and its vision of justice, law, liberty, civilization, and Christianity.

Rabinowitz, Howard N. *Race Relations in the Urban South, 1865–1890*. Urbana: University of Illinois Press, 1980. Opens the milieu of the postbellum South in tracing the social-political movement from racial exclusion to segregation, with the city serving as a microcosm for larger issues of Reconstruction.

Rable, George C. *But There Was No Peace: The Role of Violence in the Politics of Recon-struction*. Athens: University of Georgia Press, 1984. Focuses on conservative white counterrevolutionary resistance to fundamental changes in race relations between blacks and whites in the immediate postbellum South.

Richardson, Heather Cox. *The Death of Reconstruction: Race, Labor, and Politics in the Post–Civil War North, 1865–1901*. Cambridge, MA: Harvard University Press, 2004. Illustrates how American ideals failed to accommodate the transition of 4 million former slaves into workable race relations in an industrializing nation increasingly accepting laissez-faire government.

Shapiro, Herbert. *White Violence and Black Response: From Reconstruction to Montgomery*. Amherst: University of Massachusetts Press, 1988. Focuses on violence as a tool of social control in race relations bent on whites' suppressing black, brown, red, and yellow peoples.

Trelease, Allen W. *White Terror: The Ku Klux Klan Conspiracy and Southern Reconstruction*. New York: Harper & Row, 1971. Reprint, Baton Rouge: Louisiana State University Press, 1995. Details immediate post–Civil War violence as a general tool of white social control and a particular tool of the southern Democratic Party that substituted Jim Crow apartheid for slavery as the basis of southern and national race relations.

Woodward, C. Vann. *The Strange Career of Jim Crow*. Commemorative ed. New York: Oxford University Press, 2001. This third revised edition of the classic study of post-bellum black-white relations in the South has all the prefaces from previous editions to trace its response to criticisms and subsequent research. It also has new comments on post-1965 developments.

Web Site

http://edsearch.pbs.org/Eas/2003/res_det.htm—in its TeacherSource, PBS's *The American Experience* series offers *The African American Odyssey: A Quest for Full Citizenship*, with a broad-ranging discussion of Reconstruction and its aftermath, using the Library of Congress multimedia exhibition to document blacks' coping with the daily and persistent structures of race relations.

7

Geronimo! Ending the Indian Wars

The Civil War (1861–1865) and its aftermath marked years of critical change in race relations, not merely between whites and blacks but also between whites and every other major racial group in the nation—Indians, Asians, and Mexican Americans. For Indians the Civil War reproduced something of their predicament during the War for Independence (1775–1783), when events pressed tribes to pick between their existing relations with Great Britain or establishing new relations with local rebels.

As Indians joined in the Civil War, choosing sides split tribes. Some went with the North, some with the South. The U.S. Army initially rebuffed Indians' offers to enlist to fight, as it also rebuffed blacks' initial offers. But, as with blacks, military necessity moved the U.S. government to reconsider and accept to arms able-bodied men of whatever color. In June 1862, the U.S. Army mustered two regiments largely of Creek and Seminole, together with some Cherokee, Delaware, and Osage. It enlisted the Indians, however, mostly to fight other Indians in the trans-Mississippi West.

The fighting for the most part continued the U.S. Army's campaign begun in the 1850s to smooth the way for settlement by pacifying local Indians. For with the end of the War with Mexico in 1848, Manifest Destiny began to overrun "Indian country." The envisioned perpetual reserve Congress created west of the Mississippi River in 1834 had taken on a new look. Once considered remote frontier, the area by 1850 appeared neither so distant nor undesirable. Visions of fabulous riches fixed on the new West. Vast fertile lands beckoned to farmers and herders. Gold and silver lodes summoned miners. Prospects of lucrative trade and transport enticed entrepreneurs. So the United States entered a round of new treaties. Federal policy aimed to have Indians again cede lands and retire farther into more confined areas.

The new policy appeared in 1851 in the first Treaty of Fort Laramie, which one historian described as "a landmark on the national path to a reservation system."[1] Signed with the Sioux, Cheyenne, and Arapaho—the most powerful Plains tribes, the treaty aimed to protect the central part of the rugged 2,000-mile (3,200-kilometer) northwest emigrant route called the Oregon Trail that ran from Independence, Missouri, to the Columbia River region. In December 1861, the United States moved to secure the major trading and travel route called the Santa Fe Trail. It signed a treaty with the Navajo, or Diné as they called themselves, who were the most populous Indians in the Southwest, if not the entire West.

Almost as the ink was drying on the new round of treaties, U.S. Army area commanders advised their superiors in Washington, D.C., "that there is now no choice between their [the Indians'] absolute extermination or their removal and colonization at points so remote from the settlements as to isolate them entirely from the inhabitants of the Territory."[2] As "the only permanent remedy" he saw, one federal Indian agent recommended, "Reservations should be at once located and the Indians forced to reside upon them."[3] In autumn 1862, one U.S. Army commander offered a simple vision of the problem and its solution. "The whole duty can be summed up in a few words," he wrote. "The Indians are to be soundly whipped."[4]

The army's first targets were Mescalero Apaches. Bands of these eastern Apaches ranged from the Rocky Mountains' southern segment in western Texas south to Mexico's state of Chihuahua. They took their name from a major source of their food, fabric, and drink—the mescal cactus, also called *peyote*. They had used the army's absence in 1861 to raid settlers.

The Navajo became the next target. Settled in their semisedentary style in northwestern New Mexico, northern Arizona, and southeastern Utah, the Navajo rejected army directives to move from their traditional homes.

The U.S. plan was to round up Apache and Navajo, whether as friendlies or prisoners, and settle them at a place early Spanish explorers called Bosque Redondo (round forest or woods), after a grove of cottonwoods on the Pecos River in the Great Plains section of eastern New Mexico. The army fort there was to be the center of a reservation where Indians were to be "fed and kept there under *surveillance*." The longer term goal was "to have them plant a crop" and become farmers who would no longer hinder white expansion.[5] The blunt message the army delivered indiscriminately to Indians, whether friend or foe, was, "Go to Bosque Redondo, or we will pursue and destroy you."[6]

Many architects and advocates of the emerging reservation policy viewed themselves as benefactors, not enemies of Indians. They viewed their policy as a humane alternative to Indian extinction. Where removal appeared reasonable before massive trans-Mississippi white migration, it no longer appeared practical by the 1850s. Increasingly, few remote places existed in U.S. territory to which to send Indians. Only lands Indians themselves inhabited remained. So rather than removing Indians wholesale in a vision akin to that of colonizing blacks, the view developed to relegate Indians to a portion of their present space. Such a vision saw Indians being saved rather than exterminated by the ineluctable tide described as white or Christian civilization. Yet moving Indians onto reservations hardly proved a civilized process. The forced march of more than 6,000 Navajo out of the rocky expanse of Canyon de Chelly in north-eastern Arizona in 1863–1864 amply demonstrated the point. The tragic trek to Bosque Redondo that Navajo lore remembered as "the Long Walk" rivaled the Cherokees' Trail of Tears in the 1830s.

Corralling Indians on reservations aimed to introduce them to civilization. It aimed to remove them from the wild and to remove the wild from them. Reformers touted education as the central character-changing process for reservation Indians, just as others at the time touted it for reconstructing blacks. Crucial in both visions was capturing youths before they learned their culture and traditions. "[T]each their children how to read and write; teach them the arts of peace; teach them the truths of Christianity," one advocate insisted, and the Indian problem would solve itself.[7] Nature would take care of the other end and complete the process. As one reformer explained, "[T]he old Indians will die off, and carry with them all latent longings for murdering and robbing; the young ones will take their places without these longings; and thus, little by little, they will become a happy and contented people."[8] Reservation schools and nonreservation boarding schools long persisted in this perspective.

While reformers expressed hope of remaking Indians in whites' likeness, the paternalistic reservation process made Indians dependent on the federal government—at least initially, if not perpetually. The paradox was, of course, that without whites' intrusions Indians had long been self-sustaining. Being constrained to follow whites' ways and to fit within whites' patterns reversed Indians' fortunes. Left on their own, they sustained themselves, as they had for millennia. But reformers insisted Indians could not be left on their own, for then they would stand in the way of progress—that is, in the way of civilization or at least of white expansion.

Congress cursed the cost. One estimate put the annual average Bosque Redondo outlay at about $2 million from 1863 to 1868. As with what became known as the Freedmen's Bureau that aided ex-slaves in the transition to emancipation after the Civil War, the reservation program became tagged as a wasteful welfare program. Confusion and corruption marked administration and operation. The federal government itself conceded that conditions were intolerable. In June 1868, federal officials signed a fresh Navajo Treaty to relocate the tribe on a reservation closer to its traditional lands in the Four Corners areas of what would become the states of Arizona, Colorado, New Mexico, and Utah. The federal aim was to cut costs by having the Indians be more self-sufficient and also by having the Navajo go to war no more.

The battle to quiet the so-called buffalo tribes on the northern Great Plains took similar turns. Inhabiting what became the states of Colorado, Kansas, Montana, Nebraska, North Dakota, South Dakota, and Wyoming, the Plains Indians impeded the emigrant flow along the Oregon Trail that reached from Missouri to the Pacific Northwest. So the U.S. Army pushed to pacify the Cheyenne and Arapaho, Kiowa and Comanche, and the Oglala and Brulé Sioux. Such an effort seemed especially needed after discovery of gold at Pikes Peak in 1858 produced a rush of whites into Indian lands.

Federal agents succeeded at Fort Wise, Colorado, in 1861 to renegotiate the lands earlier guaranteed to the Cheyenne and Arapaho. The treaty introduced a further twist to the reservation policy by allotting lands not in common for tribal ownership but in severalty to individual members. The approach intentionally attacked tribal identity, aiming to promote individualism at the expense of traditional collectivism. It aimed to change Indians' character and community and to induce habits of personal work and reward that reflected dominant white Americans' notions of economic enterprise and social organization.

Many Cheyenne and Arapaho rejected the radical Fort Wise plan. They refused to leave the buffalo paths and their hunting grounds. Thus, clashes continued. From Minnesota southward, U.S. officials, settlers, and migrants feared that intermittent Indian sorties boded a general uprising. That fear was fanned in August 1862 when Santee Sioux—or Dakota, as they call themselves—rose up in the Minnesota territory, killing 800 to 1,000 whites.

Panic gripped the Plains. To avenge the Santee uprising, the army rounded up hundreds of Indians and put 392 on trial before a five-man military commission that condemned 303 to death. In what has remained the largest official mass execution in U.S. history, thirty-eight Sioux were hanged in a public spectacle at Mankato the day after Christmas 1862. All the Santee and other local Indians, such as the Winnebago, suffered further for the uprising. It served as pretext for removing Indians from Minnesota to reservations in Nebraska. Neither the executions nor removal, however, quieted the Sioux or the settlers.[9]

The prevalent white view was that one way or another Indians had to go. The massacre at Sand Creek, Colorado, in November 1864 brutally illustrated one means to make Indians go. About 1,200 U.S. troops—mostly Colorado volunteers under Colonel John M. Chivington—slaughtered Arapaho and Cheyenne who had encamped to sue for peace near Fort Lyon. The Indians sat under both the U.S. flag and a white flag of truce. But the emblems availed little. A bloodbath covered Indian women and children, as well as men. More than a few were scalped. Whites danced in Denver and cheered parading cavalrymen as champions. As one of the foremost historians of U.S.-Indian relations summarized,

> The Sand Creek Massacre became a *cause célèbre*, a never-to-be-forgotten symbol of what was wrong with United States treatment of the Indians, which reformers would never let fade away and which critics today still hold up to view.[10]

Embarrassed by the Sand Creek massacre, federal officials proved eager to settle the situation. Vacillating between using treaties or troopers as the means to treat with Indians remained a problem, however. Treaty-making often proved misdirected as both the standing and meaning of treaties were often misperceived. White negotiators too often viewed a treaty as an end-all, as a point of no return, rather than as a point in a continuing process. Further, they too often misconceived the authority of Indian signers, who usually were headmen or chiefs with ceremonial or nominal authority at best and without command over all their people. White agents sometimes also disastrously misrepresented their own authority. Congress rejected out of hand more than a few treaties Indians were assured were done deals. Moreover, as treaties were not self-executing, they depended on good faith for enforcement. Frequently such was woefully lacking. Treaty contents and conditions became persistent points of contention. Indeed, it sometimes appeared no meeting of the minds had ever occurred. What Indians thought was agreed often proved almost entirely contrary with what whites thought was agreed.

Some in Congress and elsewhere conceived of treaties as a shield for both Indians and settlers. They thought that merely enforcing treaties would protect all and solve what newspapers increasingly referred to as the "Indian problem." They tended to see troopers as shield carriers who protected whites and Indians by securing the treaty grants and rights of both. To them, the frontier army stood as a police force. To others, the army was a sword. Perhaps more pointedly, it was a machete to clear the path for civilization. Proponents of neither view appeared willing to invest much for the army to plan or perform either mission at the close of the Civil War.

With postwar demobilization in place, Congress in 1866 reorganized the army and created a special force for frontier duty. Blacks filled a conspicuous spot in the force. Congress authorized four black units in the new regular army: the Ninth and Tenth Cavalry and the Twenty-fourth and Twenty-fifth Infantry. Commanded in the segregated service by white commissioned officers and black noncommissioned officers, the units formed about one-sixth to one-tenth of the postwar army's effective strength, which rarely exceeded 19,000. As armed black men were unwelcome in the East and especially in the South, the units operated in the West. Not infrequently, they formed the majority of the available army forces. Known as "Buffalo soldiers," black troopers fought particularly in the New Mexico territory. Indeed, more than 3,000 blacks served at eleven of the sixteen forts in the territory. Eighteen of the men won the Congressional Medal of Honor for their heroism fighting Indians.

Also of importance on the frontier were Indian scouts and auxiliaries also authorized in the 1866 army reorganization act. They served throughout the trans-Mississippi West. The practice was older than the United States, for colonials used Indian scouts and auxiliaries in their Indian wars. Colonel of New Mexico volunteers Christopher "Kit" Carson used Utes in his 1863–1864 campaign that led to the Navajo Long Walk.

The 1866 act for the first time provided for official enlistment of Indians in the regular U.S. Army. Indian service proved invaluable. A few turned on their own tribes, but they were exceptions. Usually, Indians fought traditional enemies of their tribes. The Crow and Pawnee, for example, scouted the Sioux. Utes hunted Navajo. After all, while whites may have viewed Indians collectively, Indians viewed themselves as distinctly separate peoples. They saw themselves not as fighting their own people. They saw themselves as fighting for their people, as fighting to advance their own band or tribe. They fought also to advance individual interests, which at times started simply with joining the Blue Coats so as to get off the reservation. They were no less segregated than blacks in service and often no more generally respected. Some commanders relied on Indian scouts and auxiliaries as indispensable; others forever suspected their loyalty.

Whether acting as shield or sword, the U.S. Army faced a tough task to implement federal Indian policy. Its conventional training and tactics, simply put, were ill-suited for the situation. Even with its Buffalo soldiers and Indian scouts and auxiliaries, as one expert noted, the army remained a "conventional military force trying to control, by conventional military methods, a people that did not behave like a conventional enemy and, indeed, quite often was not an enemy at all."[11] Further, the army faced not only a foe in the field but insidious second-guessing from almost every point along a spectrum that cast it by contrast as the vanguard of annihilating or civilizing Indians.

The military mission was both ambiguous and ambivalent. The Union hero of the Civil War, General Ulysses S. Grant, came himself to reflect the split personality of postbellum U.S. policy toward the Indians. As president from 1869 to 1877, Grant championed a "peace policy" announced in his remarkably brief first inaugural address. The policy reinforced the reservation approach and viewed segregation as the way to keep Indians from troublesome contacts with whites, while also allowing Indians to learn whites' ways. It elicited support from many who viewed themselves as humanitarians.

Like many others, Grant accepted that converting Indians to Christianity appeared their most likely salvation, morally and materially. Congress immediately adopted and augmented Grant's peace policy. In April 1869, it authorized a Board of Indian Commissioners to advise the president and to act at his direction "to promote civilization among said Indians, bring them, where practicable, upon reservations, relieve their necessities, and encourage their efforts at self-support."[12]

The board and its supporters believed missionaries could better pacify Indians than the military could. It aimed at cultural assimilation and promoted piety as the way to convert Indians. It aimed not merely to create Christians but to settle Indians as individual farmers and homesteaders who embraced private property and white culture. Spiritual guidance was thus to produce secular gain for all—except traditional tribal values, of course. The approach promoted a tough humanitarianism designed to do away with Indians as Indians in the cause of saving Indians.

Thus continued the two-faced character of federal policy. It offered the proverbial carrot and stick. Missionaries stood on one side, the military on the other. One welcomed Indians to "live upon reservations and become civilized."[13] The other promised death and destruction. William Tecumseh Sherman, commanding general of the U.S. Army from 1869 to 1884, gave force to the promise. Noted for applying the concept of total war to the South in his March to the Sea through Georgia and the Carolinas in 1864 and 1865, Sherman offered Indians the simple choice of complying with reservation policy or dying. He offered no sympathy. He promised to "use all the powers confided in me to the end that these Indians, the enemies of our race and of our civilization, shall not again be able to begin and carry out their barbarous warfare."[14]

Under Sherman the army became a force of last resort. It marched usually to clean up violent collapses of the announced "peace policy." The Modoc War along the Oregon-California border in 1872–1873 displayed the pattern. To clear the Cascades for settlement, the army came to scour the complex of caves and ravines of the California Lava Beds. Its mission was to capture a group of about eighty warriors and their families who insisted on leaving the reservation to return to traditional tribal lands. For the resistance, the army executed Modoc leader Keintpoos (aka Kintpuash), whom whites called Captain Jack. It exiled his band's remainder to Oklahoma. On the Southern Plains a similar scene led to the Red River War from July 1874 to February 1875.

Both the Modoc War and the Red River War reflected failed reservation policies and practices. Federal officials too often showed ignorance or insensitivity in lumping Indians together despite their differences. They forced traditional enemies such as the Modoc and Klamath together onto the same reservation. That created at least some of the friction that led to fighting. Also, federal agents frequently failed to deliver promised food and other supplies. They fostered miserable conditions that provoked Indians to "jump the reservation," as Cheyenne, Comanche, and Kiowa did in 1874 in Oklahoma and Texas.

While poor practices pushed Indians from reservations, even poorer practices failed to protect Indians on reservations from white encroachment. The discovery of gold in the Black Hills in 1874, for instance, brought a rush of whites and a surge of Sioux resistance. The relatively isolated region stretching from western South Dakota to northeastern Wyoming lay as sacred, traditional ground for the Sioux. The Treaty of Fort Laramie in 1868 guaranteed exclusive Indian possession of the Great Sioux Reserve in the Dakota territory west of the Missouri River. But with the gold rush, U.S. agents demanded Sioux removal. Most refused to go. Nevertheless, the federal government ordered them out by January 1876. Thus ensued perhaps the most noted of postwar Indian battles.

In June 1876, Colonel George Armstrong Custer led a column of the Seventh Cavalry detailed to herd the Sioux to places the government had fixed. Locating a camp on the Little Bighorn River in Montana, the impetuous Custer attacked. Only a single horse named Comanche survived from Custer's force of more than 200 troopers. The Hunkpapa Teton Dakota Tatanka Iyotake, whom whites called Sitting Bull, and the Oglala Ta-sunko-witko, whom whites called Crazy Horse, led Sioux and Cheyenne warriors in a victory that paradoxically sealed the Plains Indians' fate.

An embarrassed U.S. Army and enraged popular opinion required retribution. The Dakota wars forced the Sioux to relinquish their treaty rights to the Black Hills. Homestake Mine—the largest gold mine in the United States—replaced them as the Dakota region's primary possessor.

The final phase of the Indian wars played out with the Apache in southern New Mexico and Arizona. A brief peace came after 1872–1873 with the Chiricahua Chief Cochise. He left the reservation in 1872 when the government sought to remove him and his people to the Tularosa reservation in New Mexico. He returned only when the United States established a separate Chiricahua reservation that summer. Commonly called the greatest guerrilla fighter in U.S. history, Cochise eluded the U.S. Army for more than ten years in his stronghold in Arizona's Dragoon Mountains. He met his death at the hands of reservation guards in 1874. He was but one of many Indian leaders killed in custody or listed as "killed while trying to escape."

The last of the Apache leaders to surrender was the Chiricahua Goyathlay ("One Who Yawns"), known among whites as Geronimo. Like Cochise, Geronimo sampled reservation life more than once and repeatedly found it lacking.

In 1885 he led a band of about 150, most of whom were women and children, from the San Carlos reservation. For ten months he dodged across the U.S.-Mexico border. In March 1886 at Cañón de Los Embudos in Sonora, Mexico, he surrendered his exhausted people to General George Crook. On returning to U.S. territory, Geronimo appeared to reject a fate such as Cochise's—death by accident or incident on the reservation. He bolted with a handful of men. About 5,500 U.S. troops, including 500 Indian scouts and auxiliaries, chased him more than 1,500 miles for five months. In September 1886, at Skeleton Canyon in the Sonora Mountains of southwestern Arizona, Geronimo tendered his final surrender.

What the U.S. press hailed as "Geronimo's capture" signaled the end of a process begun in the 1600s and that determined much of the character of race relations between whites and Indians. It featured relentless dispossession and resistance. By the 1830s, the U.S. solution to the "Indian problem" was to remove Indians from east of the Mississippi to the West. The Trail of Tears marked the displaced Cherokee and other southeastern tribes dedicated to cultivating the soil. By the 1890s, the U.S. solution was to ship Indians from west to east, as Geronimo and others went from Arizona to Florida. The plan was to direct Indians to cultivate the soil and, thus, civilize them.

Geronimo's surrender ushered in the culminating phase of the U.S. reservation policy of supervised segregation begun in the 1830s. With Indians confined, federal policy turned to accelerate their assimilation. The General Allotment Act of February 1887 detailed the ends and means. Also called the Dawes Severalty Act after its sponsor, Massachusetts Republican U.S. Senator Henry L. Dawes, the law shifted federal policy from providing for tribal reservations as collectives to providing lands in several and distinct plots to Indians as individuals. Dawes's ethnocentric vision appeared aimed at re-creating the family farm society of his native Massachusetts. But it was to operate among Indians, most of whom had been removed to nonarable western lands. By treating with Indians as individuals rather than as tribes, the act aimed to destroy tribes by destroying tribal relations. The policy was to cease to recognize Indians and to see only individuals. That was to be the promised assimilation. It signaled an ultimate assault aimed to end Indians' traditional ways of living.

Culture replaced land as the primary U.S. target. Since colonial times, an inexorable white incursion had laid waste to much of Indians' life. Their resistance gave rise to recurrent calls for spiritual restoration. As in the 1760s with the Ottawa Chief Pontiac, so again in the 1880s and 1890s as Geronimo's capture signaled the end of an era, Indians embraced religious revivals as aids in their struggle against white encroachment. And that, too, turned deadly as the so-called Ghost Dance Uprising of 1890–1891 showed on the Great Plains.

The uprising erupted from a deliverance message that promised moral and material salvation. It centered on a messianic Paiute named Wovoka. In the 1880s he awakened among Plains Indians as far as the Dakotas belief in a resurrection of the ancestors and restoration of traditional tribal power by throwing off white ways. To effect the restoration required believers to perform rites collectively called the Ghost Dance.

The determination and delirium of Ghost Dance adherents alarmed whites. In December 1890, U.S. troops sought to suppress unrest associated with an ardent renewal of the dance on the Pine Ridge reservation in southwestern South Dakota. Several hundred Sioux took to the rugged gullies and buttes of the Dakota Badlands between the Cheyenne and White rivers. Leaving the reservation stamped them as "hostiles." Troopers tracked them down. On December 29, 1890, a quiet surrender turned tragic when a scuffle became a bloodbath near Wounded Knee Creek. Thirty troopers died. Close-range fire from automatic weapons that included Gatling machine guns slaughtered at least 144 Indians, more than a third women and children.

The 1890 massacre at Wounded Knee marked an ugly end of the era signaled in Geronimo's surrender. The times for Indians tolled with a motif resonant of what prompted the historian Rayford W. Logan to label the years from 1877 to 1901 "the nadir" for blacks.[15] The United States had reduced Indians to a point at which they were directed to cease to exist. Congress organized a more reduced Indian territory of about of 70,000 square miles (180,000 square kilometers) in 1890 and, using the Choctaw words *okla* (people) and *humma* (red), named the place Oklahoma. In 1907 it became the forty-sixth state. It was no longer the Indian territory. It was certainly not an Indian state. Indeed, recognition of Indians was on the wane. In the predominant public thought, the "Indian problem" was solved with the end of the Indian wars.

A determined but quieter pressure to remove Indians entirely persisted. Some cast it with humanitarian or reform impulses. Whatever the motive, the policy pressed Indians toward cultural amalgamation. They were to be saved from themselves by being refashioned into the image and likeness of whites. Their race relations with whites were to depend on the degree to which they blended into the American mass—one might say to the degree they were no longer identifiably Indians. They were instructed that their future lay in a natural order fixed by white supremacy fed at the time by a wave of worldwide imperialism and by waves of European immigrants eager to fix their place in American life.

NOTES

1. Robert M. Utley, *Frontiersmen in Blue: The United States Army and the Indians, 1848–1865* (New York: Macmillan, 1967), xi.

2. U.S. Army Colonel Edward R. S. Canby (1817–1873), then commander of the Department of New Mexico, to Assistant Adjutant General, December 1, 1861, in U.S. Department of War, *The War of the Rebellion: A Compilation of the Official Records of the Union and Confederate Armies*, series 1, 4 (pt. 1): 77–78.

3. [Indian Agent] Lorenzo Labadi to J. L. Collins, September 25, 1862, in *Condition of the Indian Tribes: Report of the Joint Special Committee, Appointed under Joint Resolution of March 3, 1865*, S. Rep. No. 156, 39th Cong., 1st sess., 391–392 (1867) (serial 1157).

4. General James H. Carleton, Commander of the Department of New Mexico, to Colonel of Volunteers Christopher "Kit" Carson, October 12, 1862, in *Condition of the Indian Tribes*, 99–101 (1867) (serial 1279); Carleton to Edwin A. Rigg, August 6, 1863, ibid., 124.

5. Carleton to [Adjutant General] Lorenzo Thomas, March 19, 1863, ibid., 101–102, 106.

6. Carleton to J. Francisco Chavez, June 23, 1863, ibid., 116; Carleton to Colonel Christopher Carson, September 19, 1863, *Records of the U.S. Army Continental Commands,*

1861–1870, Department of New Mexico, National Archives Record Group 393, Letters Sent, 14:104.

7. Carleton to Lorenzo Thomas, September 6, 1863, in *Condition of the Indian Tribes*, 134.

8. Ibid.

9. Pope to Henry Hastings Sibley, September 28, 1862, in *The War of the Rebellion*, series 1, 13:686; Francis Paul Prucha, *The Great Father: The United States Government and the American Indians* (Lincoln: University of Nebraska Press, 1984), 1:443; David A. Nichols, *Lincoln and the Indians: Civil War Policy and Politics* (Columbia: University of Missouri Press, 1978), 117; 12 Stat. 658 (February 21, 1863), "An Act for the Removal of the Winnebago Indians, and for the Sale of their Reservation in Minnesota for their Benefit."

10. Prucha, *The Great Father*, 461.

11. Robert M. Utley, *Frontier Regulars: The United States Army and the Indian, 1866–1891* (New York: Macmillan, 1973), 9.

12. 16 Stat. 13, 40 (April 10, 1869).

13. H.R. Exec. Doc. No. 1, 43rd Cong., 1st sess., pt. 5, iii–iv, "Report of the Secretary of the Interior, 1873" (serial 1601).

14. Utley, *Frontier Regulars*, 145.

15. Rayford Whittingham Logan, *The Negro in American Life and Thought: The Nadir, 1877–1901* (New York: Dial Press, 1954).

DOCUMENTS

7.1.   "The most humane course," 1862

*On taking command of the Department of New Mexico in Sep-
tember 1862, U.S. Army Brigadier General James H. Carleton (1814–
1873) announced a no-holds-barred policy for taking in hand the
Navajo and the Mescalero Apache tribes. The following excerpt from
his orders marked "confidential" to Colonel Christopher "Kit" Carson
(1809–1868) of the First New Mexican Volunteers described his policy and purpose unambiguously. His remark on New Mexico's being
"attacked by the Texans" referenced Confederate forays, showing the
Civil War's unsettling reach into Indian relations.*

Colonel:

All Indian men of that tribe [the Mescalero Apache] are to be killed whenever and wherever you can find them: the women and children will not be
harmed, but you will take them prisoners and feed them at Fort Stanton until
you receive other instruction about them.

If the Indians send in a flag and desire to treat for peace, say to the bearer
that when the people of New Mexico were attacked by the Texans, the
Mescaleros broke their treaty of peace, and murdered innocent people, and ran
off their stock: that now, our hands are untied and you have been sent to punish them for their treachery and their crimes: That you have no power to make
peace; that you are there to kill them wherever you can find them; that if they
beg for peace, their Chiefs and twenty of their principal men must come to
Santa Fe to have a talk here; but tell them fairly and frankly that you will keep
after their people and slay them until you receive orders to desist from these
Head Quarters; that this making of treaties for *them* to break whenever they
have an interest in breaking it, will not be done any more; that we believe if
we kill some of their men in fair open war, they will be apt to remember that
it will be better for them to remain at peace, than to be at war.

I trust that this severity in the long run will be the most humane course that
could be pursued toward these Indians.

Source: Brig. General James H. Carleton to Colonel Christopher Carson, 1st New Mex-
ican Volunteers, En route to Fort Stanton, NM, October 12, 1862, in *Records of the U.S.
Army Continental Commands, 1861–1870*, Department of New Mexico, National Archives
Record Group 393, Letters Sent, 13:76–77.

7.2.   "The Long Walk," 1863–1864

> *Navajo lore retells in many voices the story of "the Long Walk"—
> what others have called "the Kit Carson Campaign" or "the Last Great
> Navajo War." Under orders of U.S. Army Brigadier General James H.
> Carleton (1814–1873), Colonel Christopher "Kit" Carson (1809–1868)
> of the First New Mexican Volunteers marched into the last Navajo
> strongholds in the rocky expanse of Canyon de Chelly in northeast-
> ern Arizona in 1863–1864. He marched out with more than 6,000
> captives. Their 300-mile forced march ended at a desolate tract on the
> Pecos River in eastern New Mexico. The place was called Bosque Re-
> dondo. Carson explained the setting, his tactics, and some of the dif-
> ficulties of removing the Navajo from their ancestral homelands and
> of keeping them on a reservation. He offered the observations and rec-
> ommendations that follow in 1865 in testimony to a joint special com-
> mittee of Congress investigating Indian affairs.*

I consider the reservation system the only one to be adopted for them. . . .

When I campaigned against them eight months I found them scattered over
a country several hundred miles in extent. There is no suitable place in their
own country—and I have been all over it—where more than two thousand
could be placed. . . . If they were scattered on different locations, I hardly think
any number of troops could keep them on their reservations.

The mountains they live in in the Navajo country cannot be penetrated by
troops. There are cañons in their country thirty miles in length, with walls a
thousand feet high, and when at war it is impossible for troops to pass through
these cañons, in which they hide and cultivate the ground.

In the main Cañon de Chelly they had some two or three thousand peach
trees, which were mostly destroyed by my troops. Colonel Sumner, in the fall
of 1851, went into the Cañon de Chelly with several hundred men and two
pieces of artillery; he got into the cañons some eight or ten miles, but had to
retreat out of it at night.

In the walls of the cañon they have regular houses built in the crevices, from
which they fire and roll down huge stones on an enemy. They have regular
fortifications, averaging from one to two hundred feet from the bottom, with
portholes for firing. No small-arms can injure them, and artillery cannot be
used. In one of these crevices I found a two-story house. I regard these cañons
as impregnable. General Canby entered this cañon, but retreated out the next
morning.

When I captured the Navajoes I first destroyed their crops, and harassed
them until the snow fell very deep in the cañons, taking some prisoners occa-
sionally. I think it was about the 6th of January, after the snow fell, that I started.
Five thousand soldiers would probably keep them on reservations in their own
country.

The Navajoes had a good many small herds when I went there. I took twelve
hundred sheep from them at one time, and smaller lots at different times. The

volunteers were allowed one dollar per head for all sheep and goats taken, which were turned over to the commissary. I think General Carleton gave the order as an encouragement to the troops. I think from fifteen hundred to two thousand could subsist themselves in the Valley de Chelly.

At this point it took me and three hundred men most one day to destroy a field of corn. . . .

I am of the opinion that, in consequence of the military campaign and the destruction of their crops, they were forced to come in.

Source: United States Congress, *Condition of the Indian Tribes: Report of the Joint Special Committee, Appointed under Joint Resolution of March 3, 1865* (Washington, DC: GPO, 1867), 96–98.

7.3.   No more treaties, 1871

In the Indian Appropriations Act of 1871, Congress changed the traditional basis of federal relations with Indians. With a stroke, it denied essential Indian independence and sovereignty. It extended as a full legal fact Chief Justice John Marshall's 1831 pronouncement that Indians sat "in a state of pupilage." Marshall had declared that Indians' "relation to the United States resembles that of a ward to his guardian." Congress went further than had the chief justice in Cherokee Nation v. Georgia (1831). He left them as "domestic dependent nations." Congress in 1871 marked them simply as dependents. Yet it reiterated the nation's full faith in upholding all prior treaty obligations. The substance and reach of those treaty relations shaped much of future race relations between whites and Indians.

Hereafter no Indian nation or tribe within the territory of the United States shall be acknowledged or recognized as an independent nation, tribe, or power with whom the United States may contract by treaty: *Provided further*, that nothing herein contained shall be construed to invalidate or impair the obligation of any treaty heretofore lawfully made and ratified with any such Indian nation or tribe.

Source: Indian Appropriations Act of 1871, 16 Stat. 544, 566 (March 3, 1871).

7.4.   "Never been very desirable neighbors," 1886

Almost immediately on the news cast as Geronimo's "capture," popular cries arose to remove the Apache and other Indians entirely from areas of the Southwest and to take their reservation lands. The article excerpted below commented on the calls for removal and reflected more than usual sensitivity for Indians. It suggested some of

*the irony in sending western Indians east in the 1880s, as eastern In-
dians were sent west in the 1830s and 1840s. Yet it made the popular antipathy toward Indians clear. As President Andrew Jackson posed
in the 1830s, the popular choice most whites cast for Indians in the
1880s was removal or death. More than a few cast Indians as a
plague, and in calling for a remedy, they suggested a Spanish adage
that translated as "kill the dog, kill the disease." But not safety alone
elicited Indian removal. Profits were at issue. Indians occupied valuable lands, as the excerpt noted. It illustrated again that segregation,
colonization, and exclusion dominated the day's thinking about race
relations.*

Now that the news comes that Geronimo is really captured, and that he and
his immediate following will be sent East, the question of the removal of the
whole tribe will naturally be revived.

Since 1882, and even previously to that year, the Southwestern press and
people have clamored for a removal of the Apaches to some distant place,
where they might be either so hemmed in by populous surroundings as to render them powerless, or else so isolated as to make it almost impossible for them
to reach civilized settlements. In either case they intend to get the Indians out
of the way—good-naturedly, by persuasion and treaty, if possible, forcibly if
necessary. . . .

It matters not where the Apaches are removed to, once the transfer is
achieved. . . .

Why? Because the real cause of [whites'] clamor is not constant dread of out-
breaks; it is a desire on their part to own the lands now constituting the White
Mountain and San Carols Reservation. . . .

The Apache reservation is coveted by its neighbors. It contains coal measures, which the mining interests of the Globe districts may need.

Source: "Removal of the Apaches from Arizona," *The Nation*, September 9, 1886, 208–209.

7.5.   "Treat the nation's wards honestly," 1886

---

*Geronimo's final surrender in September 1886 accelerated discus-
sions of federal policy for the Indians' future. Popular consensus
among Indians' friends and foes in the U.S. capital touted assimilation as the only answer. If Indians were to have a viable future in the
United States, they needed to work, live, and be more like whites,
consensus held. Those who considered themselves friends of Indians,
as did the writer of the article excerpted below, insisted that to ensure
Indians' future the federal government must honor its treaties with Indians and protect their rights. Such protection began with lands. Preserving Indian ownership and occupation remained the flash point in
relations with whites, as it had been continuously from the beginning
of contact between Indians and European settlers. But what was there*

to safeguard Indians individually and collectively or to shield their economic interests? Those questions persisted as keys to race relations.

The two officers of the Government who are most directly concerned in the control and care of the Indians desire in the main to treat the nation's wards honestly, to protect them in their rights, and to hasten the day when the Indians, can maintain these rights as individuals, just as white citizens maintain theirs, and without the constant intervention of governmental protective power. . . .

The two questions regarding the Indians which excite most discussion, are the future of the Indian Territory and the division of Indian lands among individual owners instead of continuing to hold them for the tribes in common.

In his report last year [the interior secretary] said: "The practice of moving the Indian to more distant reservations can be continued no longer. He must make his final stand for existence where he is now." . . .

And yet [the secretary and the commissioner of Indian affairs] seek to find excuses for throwing open the Indian Territory [Oklahoma], more or less extensively, to the white man's use. Congress has asserted its right to grant rights of way through this Territory to railroad companies in the face of treaty obligations.

[The] Commissioner . . . waves aside such obligations by arguments like these: "These Indians have no right to obstruct civilization and commerce and set up an exclusive claim to self-government. . . . I repeat, to maintain any such view is to acknowledge a foreign sovereignty, with the right of eminent domain, upon American soil—a theory utterly repugnant to the spirit and genius of our laws, and wholly unwarranted by the Constitution of the United States." . . .

Justice and expediency, in a word, both require that our treaty obligations with the Indian Territory tribes be sacredly respected. It is by doing this, and not by proving to them the falsity of white men's promises, that they will be introduced to adopt the white man's system of government.

Much is said about the unnecessary amount of land which these Indians now possess. It is, in fact, counting good and poor, about 500 acres per capita. A white settler in Dakota can take up 480 acres. When we remember that the Indians have the right to this land, it does not seem as if their allowance is excessive, especially in view of the time, which their best friends hope is approaching, when the fathers' possessions may be allotted to the children and divided among them as are those of the whites.

Source: "The Indians and the Government," *The Nation*, December 23, 1886, 517.

7.6.   "Invigorated old heathen ideas," 1890

The so-called Ghost Dance or Messiah Craze on Sioux reservations in South Dakota stirred neighboring whites' fears of Indian violence in the newly created state during the summer and fall of 1890. Re-

sponding to the escalating fears and rumors of a planned Sioux up-
rising, President Benjamin Harrison (1833–1901) in November 1890
ordered the Sioux reservations put under military control. Newspapers
swirled with reports that the Sioux were taking to the warpath. Amid
the frenzy, William Hobart Hare (1838–1909), the Protestant Episco-
pal missionary bishop of South Dakota, counseled noninterference.
He did not preach religious freedom for Indians, but he confidently
expected that spreading Christianity would subdue the Ghost Dance
and traditional beliefs without force of arms. The bishop's comments
offered not only commentary on the Ghost Dance but a window on
race relations.

All have doubtless read more or less in the newspapers of the delusion which
has taken possession of the minds of the wilder element among the Indians.
The leaders in the movement have invigorated old heathen ideas with snatches
of Christian truth, and have managed to excite an amount of enthusiasm which
is amazing. They teach that the Son of God will presently appear as the avenger
of the cause of the wild Indian; the earth will shiver, a great wave of new earth
will overspread the present face of the world and bury all the whites and all
Indians who imitate their ways, while the real Indians will find themselves on
the surface of the new earth basking in the light. The old ways will be restored
in primitive vigor and glory and the buffalo, antelope, and deer will return. . . .
Of course this strange craze revives many dear memories and appeals
strongly to the race feeling even in the civilized Indians. In these old ideas the
being of many of them moves with the ease of old habit, like machinery well
oiled. In Christian thought and life, their natures, not yet thoroughly habituated to them, move like machinery when dry. Many of the Indians look upon
the whole movement, however, with disdain, and unless some unfortunate
move should precipitate organized resistance on the part of the deluded Indian, the craze like many other, will run its course and pass away.

Source: "Interference Dangerous: Bishop Hare's Views on the Treatment of the Delusion," *New York Times*, November 26, 1890, 2, reprinting an interview from the *Sioux
Falls Press* (Sioux, SD), November 20, 1890.

7.7.   "The alarming state of things," 1890

In a notice of the tragedy known as the Wounded Knee massacre,
The Times of London offered pointed perspective on Indian relations
in the United States. As one of the world's premier newspapers, it
flashed news of the killings that two days before New Year's Day in
1891 left thirty troopers and at least 144 Indians dead near Wounded
Knee Creek. The site near the Sioux Pine Ridge reservation in south-
western South Dakota came to symbolize a place and power of spir-
itual revivalism for at least two generations of Indians separated by

almost a century. In fixing blame, The Times *directed white Americans to look at themselves.*

The Americans must not be angry if we are inclined to suspect that the alarming state of things is due greatly to their injudicious and inconsiderate management of the Indians. Would this terrible struggle—certain to be attended with atrocious cruelties on one side and fearful vengenaces on the other, be raging now if the order had not been given to arrest Sitting Bull! The American policy has made the Indians what they are.

Source: *The Times* (London, UK), January 1, 1891; reprinted in the *New York Times*, January 1, 1891, 1.

ANNOTATED RESEARCH GUIDE

Books

Barrett, S. M. *Geronimo: His Own Story*. New York: Duffield, 1906. Rev. ed., reprint, New York: Plume Books, 1996. "Taken down and edited" from interviews, this as-told-to auto/biography relates the Apache chief's perspectives on Indians' struggles with whites in the context of the custom and history of his tribe.

Broderick, Johnson, ed. *Navajo Stories of the Long Walk Period*. Chinle, AZ: Dine College Press, 1973. Forty interviews from the 1960s offer attitudes and experiences captured in the folklore of Dïné storytellers.

Carlson, Leonard A. *Indians, Bureaucrats, and Land: The Dawes Act and the Decline of Indian Farming*. Westport, CT: Greenwood Press, 1981. Extensive economic models show the failed direction and results of the 1887 act that divided tribally owned reservations into individual homesteads for Indian families.

Cutler, Bruce. *The Massacre at Sand Creek: Narrative Voices*. Norman: University of Oklahoma Press, 1995. Tells a tale of violence and sadism depicting racial hatred of blood-lusting militia and the impact of their actions on Indian-white relations.

Iverson, Peter. *Diné: A History of the Navajos*. Albuquerque: University of New Mexico Press, 2002. Treats Navajo roots in the land bordered by their four sacred mountains and their relations and struggles with Spanish and other white settlers and includes an insightful account of the Long Walk era and exile.

Jensen, Richard E., et al. *Eyewitnesses at Wounded Knee*. Lincoln: University of Nebraska Press, 1991. A comprehensive collection of photographs with accompanying captions and essays on the context of the December 1890 massacre that became a tragic symbol of Indian-white relations.

Mooney, James. *The Ghost-Dance Religion and the Sioux Outbreak of 1890*. Washington, DC: GPO, 1896. Reprint, Lincoln: University of Nebraska Press, 1991. This anthropological classic details the dance ritual and the religious views and revivalist visions it represented.

Priest, Loring Benson. *Uncle Sam's Stepchildren: The Reformation of the United States Indian Policy, 1865–1887*. New Brunswick, NJ: Rutgers University Press, 1942. Reprint, New York: Octagon Books, 1969. Lays bare how the chicanery of national politics literally and morally bankrupted American Indian policy as it oscillated between palliatives and panaceas.

Prucha, Francis Paul. *American Indian Policy in Crisis: Christian Reformers and the Indian, 1865–1900*. Norman: University of Oklahoma Press, 1976. Shows how an American search for order relegated Indians as deviant and disorderly to reformation by assimilation and attempts at tribal disintegration that reduced their power, property, and cultural cohesion.

Roberts, David. *Once They Moved Like the Wind: Cochise, Geronimo, and the Apache Wars.* New York: Simon & Schuster, 1993. An engrossing tale of twenty years of tragic struggle between survival and settlement, rich with first-person nuggets from archives.

Utley, Robert M. *Frontiersmen in Blue: The United States Army and the Indian, 1848–1865.* New York: Macmillan, 1967. Reprint, Lincoln: University of Nebraska Press, 1981. Classic treatment of the small, underfunded regular army's efforts, along with local volunteers, from the Great Plains westward to manage the Indian problem.

Viola, Herman. *Trail to Wounded Knee: A Last Stand of the Plains Indians, 1860–1890.* Washington, DC: National Geographic, 2004. Richly illustrated narrative of the closing of the U.S. western frontier in a collision of cultures and demise of a way of life.

Web Sites

http://www.cr.nps.gov/nagpra/DOCUMENTS/ResMAP.htm—contains information on the Bureau of Indian Affairs, a tribal list, and a map of Indian reservations in the continental United States and other resources.

http://www.gbso.net/skyhawk/indianwa.htm—offers a quick overview of the Indian wars from colonial times to the 1890s.

http://pbsvideodb.pbs.org/programs/program.asp?item_id=7883—links to *Geronimo and the Apache Resistance*, a four-segment film (produced by Neil Goodwin and Lena Carr, Peace River Films, 1988) that covers the background of Chiricahua Apache, their negotiations and clashes with the U.S. Army, their resistance, and their ultimate removal as prisoners of war to Florida, Alabama, and Oklahoma.

8

Yellow Peril: Anti-Asian Animus from Exclusion to Internment

The arrival in the United States of significant numbers of Chinese in the 1850s added momentous dimension to the nation's race relations. The California Gold Rush that began in 1848 attracted the first hundreds of Chinese to the newly acquired territory of the United States. The attraction combined with repulsion for thousands fleeing the devastating Taiping Rebellion (1850–1864) that rampaged through China's richest provinces and routed or killed between 20 million and 40 million people in what was perhaps the most important event in nineteenth-century China. American sources drew on the displaced population. The contract labor provisions of the U.S. Immigration Act of 1864 coupled with the eastward building of railroads from Pacific seaports—particularly the Central Pacific from San Francisco, California—worked to increase the Chinese presence in America.

The Treaty of 1868 between China and the United States aimed to expand the Chinese American dimension by recognizing "free immigration and emigration" as an "inherent and inalienable right" of U.S. citizens and subjects of the emperor of China.[1] With "free immigration," more than 130,000 Chinese entered the United States between 1868 and 1877. Almost 75,000 Chinese lived in California by 1880. Roughly 1 in every 11 persons the federal census counted in the Golden State then were Chinese. Another 94,000 Chinese lived in the Pacific Northwest.

The growing Chinese presence precipitated a backlash primarily among white workingmen. Particularly the recently arrived young in lower occupational groups appeared angry at competing with Chinese for jobs. California proved a special hotbed of reaction. Golden State politicians began early to "yellow-bait." The Democratic Party used race there as an issue, as it did wherever it could to advantage. Race had worked for Democrats in eastern cities such as New York and Philadelphia. It worked for them in the South. So, too, in California Democrats positioned themselves as the white man's party. And they enjoyed success, as illustrated in their winning California's 1867 elections.

Anti-Chinese animus was more, however, than campaign rhetoric. Anti-Chinese riots swept Los Angeles in October 1871, killing at least nineteen Chinese. Similar violence rocked San Francisco in the July Days riots of 1877. From the July ashes arose the Workingmen's Party of California (WPC). It became something of an institution in the San Francisco Bay area from 1877 to 1880. It packed political punch for white workingmen's programs that included cutting Chinese competition.

Many WPC supporters and other white workingmen appeared more than embittered at the twists of the 1870s. For many, dark reality had replaced alluring dreams. Many felt trampled in the rush that had carried them to the Golden State. They had looked to step up in life. Almost from the start of the 1870s, however, rather than looking up, economics had turned down for them. Even before the full appearance of the depression called the Panic of 1873, times turned hard. Then in 1873 the whole economy appeared to collapse. The New York Stock Exchange closed for ten days. Factories shut. Railroads failed. Jobs evaporated. Wages gave way. Workingmen suffered. Reacting to their pain, many in California made Chinese convenient targets.

Irish-born immigrant Denis Kearney, a consummate demagogue who mixed anti-Chinese racism with populist and republican rhetoric, led the WPC in institutionalizing its protest as part of California's fundamental legal structure. Using violence and the threat of violence, as well as ballots, Kearney's party succeeded in having California's second constitution, adopted in May 1879, reflect the WPC animus. It essentially banned Chinese labor in the state. It forbade corporations from employing any Chinese. It directed the legislature to criminalize importing Chinese and particularly to penalize companies engaged in such importation. It annulled all so-called coolie labor contracts under which the majority of Chinese immigrated and worked until they paid off their debt for transportation to America in an indenture system. It also banned Chinese from public works employment.

The new constitution imposed conditions on where Chinese could legally reside, formally creating Chinese ghettos. It added to political disabilities the state's highest court had sanctioned. In *People v. Hall* (1854), the California Supreme Court declared Chinese incapable of testifying in court against whites. The constitution of 1879 added a bar on Chinese voting.

The anti-Chinese assault went beyond California. The nation itself formally spurned Chinese. In the case of *In re Ah Yup* (1878), the federal circuit court for the District of California denied Chinese any right to become naturalized citizens. Tracing U.S. naturalization acts, Judge Lorenzo Sawyer noted that U.S. law from the first required an alien to be "a free white person" in order to "be admitted to become a citizen."[2] Nor was there any avail for Chinese in Congress's 1870 Reconstruction era change to provide "[t]hat the naturalization laws are hereby extended to aliens of African nativity, and to persons of African descent."[3] Chinese were neither black nor white, Judge Sawyer noted. He concluded then that "it is entirely clear that congress intended by this legislation to exclude Mongolians from the right of naturalization."[4]

Congress indeed confirmed Judge Sawyer's conclusion, rallying in 1879 to the popular outcry against Chinese. Seeking unilaterally to abrogate the "free immigration" provisions of the 1868 treaty, it passed a bill to restrict Chinese entry to the United States. President Rutherford B. Hayes balked. Vetoing the bill, Hayes insisted that respect for treaty provisions required negotiating with China for any change. In November 1880, China and the United States did, in fact, negotiate a new treaty. Its provisions permitted the United States to "regulate, limit or suspend" immigration from China. In May 1881, the U.S. Senate approved what became known as the Chinese Exclusion Treaty.[5] The full Congress followed with the Chinese Exclusion Act of 1882, barring entry of Chinese laborers for ten years. (The act became the first in a series expanding and renewing restrictions until 1904 when Congress imposed a categorical ban that remained until repealed in 1943 to recognize China's status as a U.S. ally against Japan in World War II.)[6]

Chinese in the United States organized to defend themselves. Resisting discrimination at every turn, they proved adept in pursuing legal remedies in both state and federal courts. Before the Exclusion Act of 1882, Chinese litigants won more than half their cases in western states outside of California—at least in appeals courts. Turnabout came, however, with rising waves of popular hostility. After the 1882 act, Chinese prevailed in only about one-third of their cases in western states' appeals courts.[7]

Chinese challenged individual exclusion decisions at their major U.S. port of entry, San Francisco. Fighting usually to maintain residence already established in the United States, Chinese between 1882 and 1890 filed at least 7,080 petitions in federal courts at San Francisco challenging administrative decisions excluding their entry. They won reversals in 85 to 90 percent of the cases.[8] Other federal courts often proved not as well disposed toward Chinese. As both the president and Congress retreated from any promise of equal rights that may have been implied in Reconstruction, federal courts also retreated from challenges to the explicit and implicit white superiority standards in U.S. law. The Supreme Court's undercutting the Civil Rights Act of 1875, for example, sank not only blacks' hopes but also those of Chinese. The principle announced in the 1875 act, of "equal and exact justice to all, of whatever nativity, race, color, or persuasion," appeared not to be an idea whose time had come.[9]

In a series of six cases, often collectively called *The Chinese Exclusion Cases*, the U.S. Supreme Court from 1884 to 1893 appeared to succumb in the face of anti-Chinese frenzy.[10] The Court began well enough. Resisting lumping all Chinese as outcasts after 1882, the Court distinguished between Chinese who had established residence and "previously acquired rights" in the United States and those who had not arrived prior to 1882. The Court ruled that "no previously acquired rights are [to be] violated."[11]

In the 1886 case of *Yick Wo v. Hopkins*, the Court reinforced the view that it would uphold rights of resident Chinese. Treating not immigration exclusion but local and state hostility evidenced in a municipal ordinance excluding Chinese from operating laundry businesses, the Court held that San Francisco had gone too far in segregating Chinese. City and county supervisors had denied Yick Wo and 200 others municipal licenses to operate laundries although they met every legal requirement. "[N]o reason for it exists except hostility to the race and nationality," the Court found. Such exclusion "in the eye of the law is not justified," the Court ruled. It thus upheld Yick Wo and his brethren's right to equal protection of the laws under the Fourteenth Amendment—at least on the facts in that case.[12]

The decision in *Yick Wo* marked something of a high watermark. The Court soon faltered and appeared to endorse blanket Chinese exclusion from constitutional guarantees. In 1893, in what Justice Stephen J. Field in dissent dubbed the "Chinese Deportation Cases," the Court withdrew from resident Chinese the fundamental rule of U.S. law that presumed a person innocent until proven guilty. Upholding Congress's 1892 act to prohibit "the coming of Chinese persons into the United States," the Court allowed "any person of Chinese descent" to be deported unless he "shall establish, by affirmative proof . . . his lawful right to remain in the United States." Thus, the Court allowed Fong Yue Ting and others to be deported, although they were longtime, legal U.S. residents; indeed, Fong had resided in the United States since at least 1879.[13]

The Court's 6–3 majority in *Fong Yue Ting* appeared to lump all Chinese together. It found no distinction between deporting longtime, legal U.S. residents—Chinese persons admitted to, and living in, the United States before Congress passed any of the exclusion laws—and persons seeking to enter the United States after 1882. It allowed the power to prohibit to serve also as the power to expel. It admitted no impediment to deporting permanent U.S. residents who were Chinese. Such a deportation was not a punishment, the Court ruled. By its reasoning, no alien could ever have any right to residence in the United States: They remained forever on sufferance, liable to, and defenseless against, instant deportation.

Justices David J. Brewer and Stephen J. Field and Chief Justice Melville W. Fuller vigorously disagreed with the majority ruling in *Fong Yue Ting*. In turn, each argued that excluding entry was one thing and expelling lawful residents was another. Chinese who had entered the United States legally and become lawful residents were, Justice Brewer insisted, "within the protection of the Constitution, and secured by its guarantees against oppression and wrong." Deporting persons merely because of their descent, as the 1892 act provided and as the majority decision allowed, "deprives them of liberty and imposes punishment without due process of law, and in disregard of constitutional guarantees," Justice Brewer wrote in summary.[14] Justice Field, although an avid supporter of Chinese exclusion, echoed Brewer, whose sensitivities may have been heightened by his being born in Smyrna, Turkey, the son of American missionaries. Chief Justice Fuller dismissed the 1892 act as "in effect, a legislative sentence of banishment, and, as such, absolutely void."[15]

The deportations proceeded. The process reached beyond California or the Pacific coast. It ran nationwide. Fong Yue Ting and others in the 1893 Chinese deportation cases lived in New York City. Teeming with European immigrants, lower Manhattan had also attracted Chinese on its way to hosting the largest Chinatown in the United States. Violence in the West drove many Chinese to the East. Commercial lines and leanings led them further to the nation's top port and most populous city. But they found it, too, unwelcoming.

Japanese also became targets of exclusion. But they emerged more slowly. Only a slight presence until the late 1890s, they suffered from spillover against Chinese. The U.S. Census counted a mere 148 Japanese in the nation in 1880. In 1890 the count reached only 2,038. The earliest group had arrived in California in 1869 and set up in Gold Hill as a commercial community that called itself the Wakamatsu Tea and Silk Farm Colony. It aimed to grow tea plants, silk cocoons, mulberry trees, and bamboo roots. This start in commercial agriculture proved telling, for Japanese success in the area stirred envy. As white laborers resented competing with Chinese, white farmers and farmhands grew also to resent competing with Japanese. Indeed, some seemed unable or unwilling to distinguish between the Chinese and Japanese. In 1884 the San Francisco Board of Education segregated all Japanese, Korean, and Chinese students together in the Oriental School it established. It later added Asian Indian and Filipino children.

No specific U.S. statutory exclusion of the Japanese existed until the Immigration Act of 1924 established the national origins quota system and provided that "no alien ineligible to citizenship shall be admitted to the United States." By then Japanese exclusion was an acknowledged, decades-old U.S. policy. Efforts had begun in 1892 to use provisions barring Chinese entry to bar Japanese also.[16] But, of course, the two peoples were not the same. Separate measures arose against the Japanese after their number in the United States more than quintupled by 1900, rising to 12,000. Then an average of 6,000 to 7,000 Japanese annually entered the United States before the series of diplomatic exchanges called the Gentlemen's Agreement of 1907–1908 quietly shut U.S. entry to Japanese.

In 1910 the official number of Japanese in the United States was 72,157. That count missed at least 20,000. Indeed, one report in 1909 put the number of *employed* Japanese between 77,800 and 83,800. In 1920 the census counted 111,000 Japanese in the United States.[17] But the exploding numbers alone were not the central cause of anti-Japanese animus. Predominantly unmarried males, Japanese immigrants scattered throughout the western United States to various jobs from domestic service to railroad construction to foresting and mining. Of an estimated 77,800 to 83,800 Japanese employed in 1909 in the United States, 38,000 to 40,000 were located as agricultural laborers; 12,000 to 14,000 as shopkeepers or shop hands; 10,000 to 12,000 in domestic service; 10,000 in railroad jobs; 3,600 in canneries; 2,200 in lumber mills; and 2,000 in mines.[18] The tens of thousands who put down stakes in California agriculture—particularly in the valleys surrounding Los Angeles—proved remarkable. The intensity of their work and the success of their productivity provoked almost immediate reaction. California Labor Commissioner J. D. Mackenzie undertook a special statewide investigation of the Japanese in 1909. Their success as independent farmers especially targeted them for popular and public policy hostility.[19]

Beginning with California in 1913, at least ten western states enacted laws to exclude Japanese from lands. Known as the Alien Land Law, California's statute declared Japanese and other aliens who were ineligible for citizenship to be ineligible also to "acquire, possess, enjoy, transmit, and inherit real property, or any interest therein, in this state."[20] Violation forfeited the land to the state. Other states copied the California language in a movement aimed not only to block access to land—and thus to agricultural competition—but also to discourage Japanese settlement. The Alien Land Laws barred Japanese even from sharecropping, for it denied them the capacity to enter into any contract related to lands.[21]

Like Chinese residents before them, Japanese in the United States fought their segregation and exclusion. Their battles in court yielded less than the modicum of success Chinese won in the 1880s and early 1890s. State courts usually upheld the discrimination enacted in state laws. The U.S. Supreme Court also sustained such discrimination. In three notable decisions in 1923 the Court let stand state laws barring Japanese aliens from renting or owning land. In reasoning reminiscent of the 1896 decision in *Plessy v. Ferguson*, which upheld segregation against blacks, the Court in 1923 ruled that discrimination against Japanese aliens was "reasonable and germane" and within a state's "wide discretion."[22]

So the exclusion of Asians that began with Chinese embraced Japanese. Indeed, it embraced all Asians. The U.S. Supreme Court in 1923 declared expansively that U.S. immigration laws "excluded from admission into this country all natives of Asia." Similarly, U.S. naturalization law allowed only "free white persons" to be admitted to citizenship. Announcing a standard of " 'Caucasian' only as that word is popularly understood," the Court indicated its embrace of the tenor of the times.[23]

The racial cast of U.S. citizenship was clear, insisted Justice George Sutherland, himself an English-born immigrant and naturalized U.S. citizen. He concluded with a majority of the Supreme Court that race fundamentally, perhaps unalterably, distinguished people. Racial difference was "of such character and extent that the great body of our people instinctively recognize it and reject the thought of assimilation," Justice Sutherland declared.[24]

Race pushed Asian Americans—whether resident aliens or born in the United States—into legally sanctioned segregation, like that of African Americans. Indeed, in 1927 in a Mississippi school segregation case involving a child born in the United States of Chinese parents, the U.S. Supreme Court explicitly noted that persons of Asian heritage were relegated, as blacks were, to schools other than those whites attended.[25] Simply put, the principles and practices of white supremacy sat Asian Americans and African Americans together as "colored people." The U.S. majority excluded and reviled them as nonwhites.

The utmost spectacle of Asian American exclusion occurred during World War II. Japan's startling attack at Pearl Harbor in the then U.S. territory of Hawaii unleashed a horde of race-based resentment, especially on the U.S. West Coast. "Japs" became not merely U.S. enemies but despicable villains. In California and the Pacific Northwest, few appeared willing to distinguish between Americans of Japanese descent, who were citizens or permanent resident aliens, from the Imperial Japanese forces that attacked Hawaii.

Citing fears of sabotage, but transparently pandering to intense, regional racism, President Franklin D. Roosevelt initiated, and Congress confirmed, a War Relocation Authority (WRA) in March 1942. Operating in the West, the WRA established ten so-called relocation centers. There it herded more than 120,000 persons because of their Japanese descent. Most internees were native-born U.S. citizens. At least 17,600 of those held in the centers enlisted in the U.S. Armed Forces during the war. But the bulk languished in the centers often compared to concentration camps, until they closed in November 1945.

The historical racial climate, rather than any substantial fear of sabotage, prevailed in the WRC's action. Comparing what happened on the West Coast with what happened in Hawaii demonstrated the fact. Hawaii was an actual battle zone. It sat 3,000 miles closer to the fighting in the Pacific than California, Oregon, or Washington. Moreover, Japan's attack had left Hawaii's soil blood soaked. Yet even with one-third of its population of Japanese descent, Hawaii suffered no roundups as occurred on the West Coast.

Race, not citizenship or loyalty, dictated Japanese Americans' mistreatment on the West Coast. Their appeals for protection under the U.S. Constitution yielded them little solace. Most notably in *Hirabayashi v. United States* (1943) and *Korematsu v. United States* (1944), the Supreme Court upheld the detention program as "a valid military order." In *Korematsu*, Justices Owen J. Roberts, Robert H. Jackson, and Frank Murphy dissented. Justice Roberts termed the Japanese internment "a clear violation of Constitutional rights." Justice Roberts termed it "a military expedient that has no place in law under the Constitution." Justice Murphy denounced it as the "legalization of racism."[26]

In the Civil Liberties Act of 1988 the United States apologized for its Japanese internment. One congressional report on which the act rested publicly declared that "the actions were motivated largely by racial prejudice, wartime hysteria, and a failure of political leadership."[27] With the act, Congress and the president moved to provide "restitution to those individuals of Japanese ancestry who were interned." The sum per individual was more symbolic than substantive, as it was capped at $20,000. More significantly, the act moved to "acknowledge the fundamental injustice of the evacuation, [and] apologize on behalf of the people of the United States for the evacuation."[28] How much had the nation changed since the 1940s.

NOTES

1. Treaty of 1868 between the United States and China, referred to as the Ta Tsing Empire, 16 Stat. 739 (July 28, 1868).

2. See *In re Ah Yup*, 1 F. Cas. 223 (C.C.D. Cal. 1878) (No. 104).

3. 16 Stat. 256 (July 14, 1870). See also 18 Stat. 318 (February 18, 1875), designating in regard to naturalization that "[t]he provisions of this title shall apply to aliens being free white persons, and to aliens of African nativity, and to persons of African descent."

4. *In re Ah Yup*, at 224.

5. 22 Stat. 826 (May 5, 1881).

6. The repeal was more symbolic than a substantive return to "free immigration" or relative openness. The Act of December 17, 1943, ended exclusion but awarded China an annual quota of 105 immigrants to the United States.

7. John R. Wunder, "The Chinese and the Courts in the Pacific Northwest: Justice Denied?" *Pacific Historical Review* 52 (1983): 191.

8. Lucy Salyer, "Captives of Law: Judicial Enforcement of the Chinese Exclusion Laws, 1891–1905," *Journal of American History* 76 (June 1989): 91–117.

9. 18 Stat. 335 (March 1, 1875); *The Civil Rights Cases*, 109 U.S. 3 (1883).

10. See *Chew Heong v. United States*, 112 U.S. 536 (1884); *United States v. Jung Ah Lung*, 124 U.S. 621 (1888); *Chae Chan Ping v. United States*, 130 U.S. 581 (1889); *Fong Yue Ting v. United States, Wong Quan v. United States*, and *Lee Joe v. United States*, 149 U.S. 698 (1893).

11. *Chew Heong v. United States*, 112 U.S. 536, 560.

12. *Yick Wo v. Hopkins*, 118 U.S. 356, 374 (1886).

13. *Fong Yue Ting v. United States, Wong Quan v. United States*, and *Lee Joe v. United*

States, 149 U.S. 698 (1893); An act to prohibit the coming of Chinese persons into the United States, 27 Stat. 25 (May 5, 1892).

14. 149 U.S. at 733 (Brewer, J., dissenting).

15. Ibid., at 764 (Fuller, C. J., dissenting).

16. See *Nishimura Ekiu v. United States*, 142 U.S. 651 (1892) (twenty-five-year-old female Japanese alien from Yokohama detained at San Francisco upon the ground that she should not be permitted to land in the United States under the immigration act of March 3, 1891, 26 Stat. 827).

17. H. A. Millis, "Some of the Economic Aspects of Japanese Immigration," *American Economic Review* 5, no. 4 (December 1915): 787–804.

18. Ibid., 790.

19. Summary of California Labor Commissioner J. D. Mackenzie, Special State Investigation of 1909 of the Japanese in California, in Sidney L. Gulik, *The American Japanese Problem; A Study of the Racial Relations of the East and the West* (New York: C. Scribner's Sons, 1914), 316–323; Maxakazu Iwata, "The Japanese Immigrants in California Agriculture," *Agricultural History* 36 (January 1962): 25–37.

20. 1913 Cal. Stat. 206; 1921 Cal. Stat. 83.

21. See, for example, Washington's Anti-Alien Land Law, 1921 Wash. Laws 50. See also Dudley O. McGovney, "The Anti-Japanese Land Laws of California and Ten Other States," *California Law Review* 35 (1947): 7.

22. See *Terrace v. Thompson*, 263 U.S. 197 (1923); *Porterfield v. Webb*, 263 U.S. 225 (1923), and *Webb v. O'Brien*, 263 U.S. 313 (1923).

23. *United States v. Bhagat Singh Thind*, 261 U.S. 204, 215 (1923) (an Asian Indian the U.S. District Court described as "a high-caste Hindu" born in Armitsar, Punjab, who legally entered the United States at Seattle, Washington, on July 4, 1913, and served in the U.S. Army, was stripped of naturalized citizenship on grounds that he failed the "free white person" standards of the applicable statute—the Immigration Act of February 5, 1917, 39 Stat. 874).

24. *United States v. Bhagat Singh Thind*, at 214–215.

25. *Gong Lum v. Rice*, 275 U.S. 78 (1927) (petitioner Martha Lum, a child born in the United States in January 1915 of Chinese parents, through her father as what the law termed her "next friend" challenged Mississippi state education authorities for barring her attending a school with whites, classifying her with Negroes, and requiring her to attend school with blacks).

26. *Korematsu v. United States*, 323 U.S. 214, 225 (1944); ibid. (Roberts, J., dissenting); ibid., at 248 (Jackson, J., dissenting); ibid., at 242 (Murphy, J., dissenting).

27. H.R. Rep. No. 100-785 (1988), on a bill to implement the recommendations of the Commission on Wartime Relocation and Internment of Civilians.

28. Civil Liberties Act of 1988, Pub. L. No. 100-383, 102 Stat. 903 (1988).

DOCUMENTS

8.1.   "The Chinese Police Tax," 1862

Exemplifying race relations with the rising anti-Chinese animus in California, the state legislature in 1862 enacted a statute that indicated its character in its official title: "An Act to Protect Free White Labor Against Competition with Chinese Coolie Labor, and to Discourage the Immigration of the Chinese into the State of California." The U.S. Constitution barred the state from directly prohibiting immigrants from entry. Only Congress had such power. So California turned its taxing power into a cudgel to push Chinese from jobs and warn them away from the state. Akin to action southern states used in segregating blacks, California's law would over time lengthen the line of racial restrictions against Chinese and then against Japanese and other Asians.

The People of the State of California, represented in Senate and Assembly, do enact as follows:

There is hereby levied on each person, male and female, of the Mongolian race, of the age of eighteen years and upwards, residing in this State, except such as shall, under laws now existing, or which may hereafter be enacted, take out licenses to work in the mines, or to prosecute some kind of business, a monthly capitation tax of two dollars and fifty cents, which tax shall be known as the Chinese Police Tax.

Source: 1862 Cal. Stat. 462, § 1 (April 26, 1862).

8.2.   "Excluded by the term 'white person,'" 1878

Racial exclusion long blocked Chinese and other Asians from becoming naturalized U.S. citizens. The federal circuit court for California explained the law and its meaning in denying Ah Yup's naturalization petition in 1878. Describing him as "a native and citizen of the empire of China, of the Mongolian race," the court noted Ah Yup's meeting all the qualifications to be naturalized, except one—race. The court expanded on the significance of race, which it also referred to as "color." Extensively quoting debate in Congress on who was eligible to become a U.S. citizen, the court noted that Congress explicitly rejected the Chinese. It noted also fears expressed in Congress about a flood of Chinese immigrants creating unspecified "labor problems" and threatening American civilization itself. Other Asians also would fall into the excluded class for not being white.

The only question [before this court] is, whether the statute authorizes the naturalization of a native of China of the Mongolian race.

In all the acts of congress relating to the naturalization of aliens . . . the language has been "that any alien, being a free white person, may be admitted to become a citizen." . . .

Neither in popular language, in literature, nor in scientific nomenclature, do we ordinarily, if ever, find the words "white person" used in a sense so comprehensive as to include an individual of the Mongolian race. Yet, in all, color, notwithstanding its indefiniteness as a word of description, is made an important factor in the basis adopted for the distinction and classification of races.

I am not aware that the term "white person," as used in the statutes as they have stood from 1802 till the late revision, was ever supposed to include a Mongolian. . . . I find nothing in the history of the country, in common or scientific usage, or in legislative proceedings, to indicate that congress intended to include in the term "white person" any other than an individual of the Caucasian race. . . .

At the time of the amendment, in 1870, extending the naturalization laws to the African race, Mr. Sumner [Sen. Charles Sumner, Republican–MA] made repeated and strenuous efforts to strike the word "white" from the naturalization laws, or to accomplish the same object by other language. It was opposed on the sole ground that the effect would be to authorize the admission of Chinese to citizenship. Every senator, who spoke upon the subject, assumed that they were then excluded by the term "white person," and that the amendment would admit them, and the amendment was advocated on the one hand, and opposed on the other, upon that single idea.

Senator [Oliver] Morton [Republican–IN], in the course of the discussion said: "This amendment involves the whole Chinese problem. *** The country has just awakened to the question and to the enormous magnitude of the question, involving a possible immigration of many millions, involving another civilization; involving labor problems that no intellect can solve without study and time." . . .

Thus, whatever latitudinarian construction might otherwise have been given to the term "white person," it is entirely clear that congress intended by this legislation to exclude Mongolians from the right of naturalization. I am, therefore, of the opinion that a native of China, of the Mongolian race, is not a white person within the meaning of the act of congress. . . . The purpose undoubtedly was to . . . exclude the Chinese. It was intended to exclude some classes, and as all white aliens and those of the African race are entitled to naturalization under other words, it is difficult to perceive whom it could exclude unless it be the Chinese.

Source: *In re Ah Yup*, 1 F. Cas. 223 (C.C.D. Cal. 1878) (No. 104).

8.3.   "No Chinese shall be employed," 1879

In framing a new constitution in 1879, California seemingly stretched its rejection of Chinese to an extent that pointed with no possible misunderstanding about their being unwelcome. It denied them public and private employment. It voided their labor contracts. It sanctioned their removal and ban from "incorporated cities and towns." Indeed, it authorized prohibiting Chinese from being brought into the state. It reflected the "whites only" principle of race relations that permeated the nation, although usually associated only as a symbol of the South.

SEC. 2. No corporation now existing or hereafter formed under the laws of this State, shall, after the adoption of this Constitution, employ directly or indirectly, in any capacity, any Chinese or Mongolian. . . .

SEC. 3. No Chinese shall be employed on any State, county, municipal, or other public work, except in punishment for crime.

SEC. 4. The presence of foreigners ineligible to become citizens of the United States is declared to be dangerous to the well-being of the State, and the Legislature shall discourage their immigration by all the means within its power. Asiatic coolieism is a form of human slavery, and is forever prohibited in this State, and all contracts for coolie labor shall be void. All companies or corporations, whether formed in this country or any foreign country, for the importation of such labor, shall be subject to such penalties as the Legislature may prescribe. The Legislature shall delegate all necessary power to the incorporated cities and towns of this State for the removal of Chinese without the limits of such cities and towns, or for their location within prescribed portions of those limits, and it shall also provide the necessary legislation to prohibit the introduction into this State of Chinese after the adoption of this Constitution.

Source: Cal. Const., Article XIX, §§ 2–4 (1879).

8.4.   "The Chinese cannot assimilate with our people," 1884

The anti-Asian animus that focused initially on the Chinese because of their premier presence permeated the United States. Neither class nor region confined it. They were only the edge of broad-based aversion that Connecticut-born Justice Stephen J. Field (1816–1899) enlarged on in his dissent in Chew Heong v. United States *(1884), which upheld U.S. rights that Chinese had acquired prior to the 1882 Exclusion Act. Field made his fame and fortune in California, where he served in the state legislature and then on the state supreme court before being elevated to the U.S. Supreme Court. His view stereotyped*

Chinese as low-life, wage-cutting, labor-threatening laborers unable or unwilling to assimilate to American ways and who thus threatened American civilization. Justice Field asserted that his view formed the proper basis for race relations and reflected the perspective of "thoughtful persons who were exempt from race prejudices."

In view of these facts—that the Chinese cannot assimilate with our people, but continue a distinct race amongst us, with institutions, customs and laws entirely variant from ours; that the larger portion of persons termed Chinese laborers were imported under the labor-contract system; that no law to prevent their importation under this system had ever been passed by China; that competition with them tended to degrade labor, and thus to drive our laborers from large fields of industry; that the treaty was one-sided in the benefits it conferred as to residence and trade by the citizens or subjects of one country in the other, the condition of the people of China rendering any reciprocity in such benefits impossible—it is not surprising that there went up from the whole Pacific Coast an earnest appeal to Congress to restrain the further immigration of Chinese.

It came not only from that class who toil with their hands, and thus felt keenly the pressure of the competition with coolie labor, but from all classes. Thoughtful persons who were exempt from race prejudices saw, in the facilities of transportation between the two countries, the certainty, at no distant day, that, from the unnumbered millions on the opposite shores of the Pacific, vast hordes would pour in upon us, overrunning our coast and controlling its institutions. A restriction upon their further immigration was felt to be necessary to prevent the degradation of white labor, and to preserve to ourselves the inestimable benefits of our Christian civilization.

Source: *Chew Heong v. United States*, 112 U.S. 536, 568 (1884) (Field, J., dissenting).

8.5.   "The ugly abyss of racism," 1944

Girding the United States for war after Japan's attack on Pearl Harbor, Hawaii, on December 7, 1941, President Franklin D. Roosevelt in February 1942 issued Executive Order No. 9066. It authorized certain commanders to "prescribe military areas . . . from which any or all persons may be excluded." On that basis, the U.S. Army general commanding the western U.S. region excluded all persons of Japanese ancestry from the prescribed area—the entire Pacific Coast. Forced evacuation followed the exclusion, and the U.S. Army detained persons of Japanese ancestry in what were titled "relocation centers." Among those protesting their exclusion, evacuation, and detention was native-born U.S. citizen Fred Korematsu (1919–2005), a resident of San Leandro, California. Uncontradicted evidence proved him a loyal U.S. citizen. His Japanese ancestry alone was the basis for the action against him. A majority of the U.S. Supreme Court upheld the process against which Korematsu protested—one that interned him and 120,000 others of Japanese ancestry—as military necessity and denied it resulted from racial prejudice. Three members of the Court disagreed. Below Justice Frank Murphy (1890–1949) explained his view that racism designed and directed the internment process.

This exclusion of "all persons of Japanese ancestry, both alien and non-alien," from the Pacific Coast area on a plea of military necessity in the absence of martial law ought not to be approved. Such exclusion goes over "the very brink of constitutional power" and falls into the ugly abyss of racism. . . .

The judicial test of whether the Government, on a plea of military necessity, can validly deprive an individual of any of his constitutional rights is whether the deprivation is reasonably related to a public danger that is so "immediate, imminent, and impending" as not to admit of delay and not to permit the intervention of ordinary constitutional processes to alleviate the danger. Civilian Exclusion Order No. 34, banishing from a prescribed area of the Pacific Coast "all persons of Japanese ancestry, both alien and non-alien," clearly does not meet that test.

Being an obvious racial discrimination, the order deprives all those within its scope of the equal protection of the laws as guaranteed by the Fifth Amendment. It further deprives these individuals of their constitutional rights to live and work where they will, to establish a home where they choose and to move about freely. In excommunicating them without benefit of hearings, this order also deprives them of all their constitutional rights to procedural due process. Yet no reasonable relation to an "immediate, imminent, and impending" public danger is evident to support this racial restriction which is one of the most sweeping and complete deprivations of constitutional rights in the history of this nation in the absence of martial law.

It must be conceded that the military and naval situation in the spring of 1942 was such as to generate a very real fear of invasion of the Pacific Coast, accompanied by fears of sabotage and espionage in that area. The military command was therefore justified in adopting all reasonable means necessary to combat these dangers. In adjudging the military action taken in light of the then apparent dangers, we must not erect too high or too meticulous standards; it is necessary only that the action have some reasonable relation to the removal of the dangers of invasion, sabotage and espionage. But the exclusion, either temporarily or permanently, of all persons with Japanese blood in their veins has no such reasonable relation. And that relation is lacking because the exclusion order necessarily must rely for its reasonableness upon the assumption that all persons of Japanese ancestry may have a dangerous tendency to commit sabotage and espionage and to aid our Japanese enemy in other ways. It is difficult to believe that reason, logic or experience could be marshaled in support of such an assumption. . . .

The main reasons relied upon by those responsible for the forced evacuation, therefore, do not prove a reasonable relation between the group characteristics of Japanese Americans and the dangers of invasion, sabotage and espionage. The reasons appear, instead, to be largely an accumulation of much of the misinformation, half-truths and insinuations that for years have been directed

against Japanese Americans by people with racial and economic prejudices—
the same people who have been among the foremost advocates of the evacuation. A military judgment based upon such racial and sociological
considerations is not entitled to the great weight ordinarily given the judgments based upon strictly military considerations. . . .

The military necessity which is essential to the validity of the evacuation
order thus resolves itself into a few intimations that certain individuals actively
aided the enemy, from which it is inferred that the entire group of Japanese
Americans could not be trusted to be or remain loyal to the United States. No
one denies, of course, that there were some disloyal persons of Japanese descent on the Pacific Coast who did all in their power to aid their ancestral land.
Similar disloyal activities have been engaged in by many persons of German,
Italian and even more pioneer stock in our country. But to infer that examples
of individual disloyalty prove group disloyalty and justify discriminatory action against the entire group is to deny that under our system of law individual guilt is the sole basis for deprivation of rights. . . .

No adequate reason is given for the failure to treat these Japanese Americans on an individual basis by holding investigations and hearings to separate
the loyal from the disloyal, as was done in the case of persons of German and
Italian ancestry. It is asserted merely that the loyalties of this group "were unknown and time was of the essence." Yet nearly four months elapsed after Pearl
Harbor before the first exclusion order was issued; nearly eight months went
by until the last order was issued; and the last of these "subversive" persons
was not actually removed until almost eleven months had elapsed. Leisure and
deliberation seem to have been more of the essence than speed. And the fact
that conditions were not such as to warrant a declaration of martial law adds
strength to the belief that the factors of time and military necessity were not as
urgent as they have been represented to be. . . .

I dissent, therefore, from this legalization of racism. Racial discrimination in
any form and in any degree has no justifiable part whatever in our democratic
way of life. It is unattractive in any setting but it is utterly revolting among a
free people who have embraced the principles set forth in the Constitution of
the United States. All residents of this nation are kin in some way by blood or
culture to a foreign land. Yet they are primarily and necessarily a part of the
new and distinct civilization of the United States. They must accordingly be
treated at all times as the heirs of the American experiment and as entitled to
all the rights and freedoms guaranteed by the Constitution.

Source: Korematsu v. United States, 323 U.S. 214, 233–242 (1944) (Murphy, J., dissenting).
(Citations omitted.)

8.6.   "A grave injustice was done," 1988

---

*In 1980 Congress established the Commission on Wartime Reloca-
tion and Internment of Civilians (CWRIC) to review the facts and circumstances surrounding both President Franklin D. Roosevelt's*

decision to issue Executive Order No. 9066 and the order's actual implementation. The Civil Liberties Act of 1988 represented Congress's accepting the basic CWRIC results, reflected in the act's opening statement of findings and purpose offered below.

The Congress recognizes that, as described in the Commission on Wartime Relocation and Internment of Civilians, a grave injustice was done to both citizens and permanent residents of Japanese ancestry by the evacuation, relocation, and internment of civilians during World War II.

As the Commission documents, these actions were carried out without adequate security reasons and without any acts of espionage or sabotage documented by the Commission, and were motivated largely by racial prejudice, wartime hysteria, and a failure of political leadership.

The excluded individuals of Japanese ancestry suffered enormous damages, both material and intangible, and there were incalculable losses in education and job training, all of which resulted in significant human suffering for which appropriate compensation has not been made.

For these fundamental violations of the basic civil liberties and constitutional rights of these individuals of Japanese ancestry, the Congress apologizes on behalf of the Nation.

Based on the findings of the Commission on Wartime Relocation and Internment of Civilians (CWRIC), the purposes of the Civil Liberties Act of 1988 with respect to persons of Japanese ancestry included the following:

1) To acknowledge the fundamental injustice of the evacuation, relocation and internment of citizens and permanent resident aliens of Japanese ancestry during World War II;

2) To apologize on behalf of the people of the United States for the evacuation, internment, and relocations of such citizens and permanent residing aliens;

3) To provide for a public education fund to finance efforts to inform the public about the internment so as to prevent the recurrence of any similar event;

4) To make restitution to those individuals of Japanese ancestry who were interned;

5) To make more credible and sincere any declaration of concern by the United States over violations of human rights committed by other nations.

Source: Civil Liberties Act of 1988, Pub. L. No. 100-383, 102 Stat. 903 (1988).

ANNOTATED RESEARCH GUIDE

Books

Chan, Sucheng, ed. *Entry Denied: Exclusion and the Chinese Community in America, 1882–1943*. Philadelphia: Temple University Press, 1991. Collection of essays showing the relation of law and race, focusing primarily on Chinese coping as individuals and as a community in the United States.

Daniels, Roger. *Asian America: Chinese and Japanese in the United States since 1850*. Seattle: University of Washington Press, 1988. Offers a fresh chronicle of the immigrant experience focused on patterns of community, continuity, and change, along with U.S. socioeconomic and political reaction.

Gyory, Andrew. *Closing the Gate: Race, Politics, and the Chinese Exclusion Act*. Chapel Hill: University of North Carolina Press, 1998. Focuses on national concern for western regional worries, particularly among white workingmen, rather than nationwide racism or national labor pressure, as the prime mover of Chinese exclusion.

Houston, Jeanne, and James D. Houston. *Farewell to Manzanar: A True Story of Japanese-American Experience during and after the World War II Internment*. Boston: Houghton Mifflin, 1973. Details from firsthand experience of a seven-year-old from Long Beach of the scars of internment camp life.

Inada, Lawson Fusao, ed. *Only What We Could Carry: The Japanese-American Internment Experience*. San Francisco: California Historical Society, 2000. A mixed anthology offering autobiography, poetry, government documents, letters, and more, to convey the anguished experience and reality of the internment experience.

McClain, Charles, ed. *Chinese Immigrants and American Law*. New York: Garland Publishing, 1994. Articles and essays treating the legal confines, concerns, and impacts of Chinese immigration, community development, and racial discrimination.

Paul, Rodman W. *The Abrogation of the Gentlemen's Agreement*. Cambridge, MA: Harvard University Press, 1936. Explains how the view of Japanese as unassimilable figured in their being barred by the provisions of the Immigration Act of 1924.

Salyer, Lucy E. *Laws Harsh as Tigers: Chinese Immigrants and the Shaping of Modern Immigration Law*. Chapel Hill: University of North Carolina Press, 1995. Details the far-reaching legacy for U.S. society and immigration law of wrenching due process from the Chinese in their exclusion.

Wu, William S. *The Yellow Peril: Chinese Americans and American Fiction, 1850–1940*. Hamden, CT: Archon, 1982. Details images of Chinese Americans in U.S. fiction and whites' perceiving Asians as threats.

Yamamoto, Eric K., et al., eds. *Race, Rights, and Reparation: Law of the Japanese-American Internment*. Baltimore, MD: Aspen Publishers, 2001. A comprehensive course book treating historical and legal repercussions of the Japanese American internment during World War II.

Web Sites

http://us_asians.tripod.com/timeline-overall2.html—timeline of Asian American history including political, governmental, and cultural areas.

http://www.archives.gov/digital_classroom/lessons/japanese_relocation_wwii/japanese_relocation.html—provides background information, documents, and teaching resources for Japanese internment.

http://www.asianam.org/laws_against_asian-americans.htm—highlights Asian American encounters with the American legal system.

http://www.lib.berkeley.edu/MRC/chineseamvid.html—offers video resources on the Asian American experience.

9

From Nadir to New Negro: Segregation, Migration, and the New Deal

Advancing visions of white supremacy tightened U.S. race relations as the twentieth century dawned. In 1898 the nation established an empire largely over peoples of color. It acquired Puerto Rico, the Philippines, and Guam as a result of the War with Spain. It separately annexed Hawaii, also in 1898. It thus shouldered the "White Man's Burden" British imperial poet Rudyard Kipling in February 1899 stitched in verse to urge his vision of Anglo-Saxon civilization triumphant. The language of such domination resonated in America's overseas empire. At home its most visible twists showed in the segregation campaign that drove African Americans to what one historian described as the "nadir," while also propelling them in resistance to create a "New Negro."[1]

The nation's retreat from the true emancipation promised in Reconstruction exposed raw racism that insisted on white dominance and black subordination. Mimicking slavery and seeking to extend its hoary manners and means, segregation developed to keep blacks in their place, cut off from the core of the American dream of full self-realization. Segregation cut all in two. Recognizing only white and nonwhite, it scarred the nation. Especially in the South, where its strictures were not only fact but law, segregation maintained two Americas, separate and unequal.

The Supreme Court sanctioned segregation in deciding *Plessy v. Ferguson* in 1896. Upholding a Louisiana law mandating separate railway cars for white and colored people within the state, the Court cast legitimacy on a system of public and private privilege legally and popularly designated "for whites only." Exclusion was the real issue. And more than transportation was at stake, particularly in the South. States revived Black Codes. Several started with the most central and cherished of political rights—the vote. By 1910 the South sat close to where it was in 1860, with only white men allowed to vote or hold elected office. What started as sheer intimidation and violence against black voters shifted to legal barriers. Literacy tests, poll taxes, and other bent qualifications disproportionately removed blacks from voter rolls. Louisiana, for example, reduced its black voters to 5,320 (among 147,059 black adult males) by 1900. Earlier, blacks had formed a majority on the voting rolls in twenty-six of the state's sixty-three parishes (the equivalent of counties). Alabama at the same time reduced its black voters to fewer than 3,000 among 181,345 black males age twenty-one years or older. Alabama, along with Georgia, North Carolina, Oklahoma, and Virginia, by 1910 boasted constitutional provisions effectively barring black voters.

Segregation's bars were more than political. They reached schools, public accommodations, and even to the most private of relations—sex and marriage. What law left unmentioned, public sentiment usually covered. From housing to jobs to daily demeanor, self-styled vigilantes terrorized blacks. Lynch law enforced the social construction of white racial dominion. Between 1882 and 1889, for instance, lynch mobs murdered 534 blacks. In the 1890s, the carnage more than doubled to 1,111. It receded to 791 for 1900 to 1909.[2] The barbarism often excused under a banner of avenging defiled white womanhood from the sexual savagery of black brutes poorly masked the cruel cudgels of racial control. Southern women particularly rallied against the practice, and among their voices few were more active and powerful than that of Ida B. Wells-Barnett, a black journalist who in her tireless antilynching campaign detailed and documented atrocities.

White rioters in cities and towns added their own aggression to typically rural lynchings. Repeating an antebellum practice whites exercised in the North to set back blacks who appeared too forward in the 1830s and 1840s, white urbanites again attacked the growing black presence. Between 1898 and 1906, notable white riots wracked Wilmington, North Carolina, New Orleans, Louisiana, Statesboro, Georgia, Springfield, Ohio, Brownsville, Texas, and Atlanta, Georgia. In 1908 a riot in Springfield, Illinois, moved one commentator to describe the spectacle as "Race War in the North."[3]

The rioting pushed advocates against racism, segregation, and the violence they fed to advance broad-based coalitions to change America's dreadful race relations. The National Association for the Advancement of Colored People (NAACP) developed in direct reaction to the 1908 Springfield riot. It made common cause with black groups that refused to succumb to segregation's stranglehold system. It contrasted with the quiet conciliation for economic concessions that Booker T. Washington preached and for which the nation's dominant press organs anointed him *the* Negro's leader after the venerable Frederick Douglass's death and Washington's Atlanta Exposition Address in 1895.

For a moment in 1912 more than a few blacks confused the electioneering blandishments of Democratic candidate Woodrow Wilson with establishing promises of better days. Wilson's "New Freedom" resounded with long-sought equality. Indeed, Wilson directly addressed blacks' hopes in declaring, "I want to assure them that should I become President of the United States they may count upon me for absolute fair dealing, for everything by which I could assist in advancing the interest of their race in the United States."[4]

The Virginia-born Wilson proved truer to his cultural roots than to his campaign words, for he shepherded an onslaught of wholesale segregation throughout federal employment and facilities. He cut blacks off from civil service and insisted even on separate eating and toilet facilities throughout the capital. His disdain for dark-skinned peoples appeared not only at home. Abroad, he despatched U.S. Marines to bring "order" to Haiti in 1915, with a taunt that the black Caribbean island nation was incapable of self-rule.

Wilson's administrations offered little ground for blacks' hopes. Nor did the popular climate hint at hopeful winds. The success of director D. W. Griffith's 1915 movie *The Birth of a Nation* exhibited the baleful public mood. An instant sensation, the adaptation of bestselling novelist Thomas Dixon's 1905 *The Clansman* would become the highest-grossing and most viewed silent film ever. It recast the past to bait rabid racists. Its story line twisted the content and course of Reconstruction to cast blacks and their allies advocating racial equality as savages and scoundrels. It clothed the Ku Klux Klan's masked and hooded marauders as rescuers of white civilization. It virtually hailed race war and sanctioned white violence against blacks. The novel's initial sales sparked race riots in Philadelphia in 1906. The film's release in February 1915 set off storms of antiblack hostility. Yet the film fit well with spectacular lynchings in 1916 such as Jesse Washington's burning in Waco, Texas, and Anthony Crawford's mobbing for "impudence" in South Carolina.

The NAACP fought *The Birth of a Nation*'s showing, to little avail. The film set back the NAACP's national campaign against lynching. Indeed, it helped revive the KKK. Yet the NAACP's fledging Legal Defense and Educational Fund (LDEF) did begin to witness some success against segregation. In *Guinn v. United States* (1915), the U.S. Supreme Court blocked Oklahoma's blatantly race-based disfranchising under a so-called Grandfather Clause that based voters' eligibility on their grandfathers' qualifications. In *Buchanan v. Warley* (1917), the Court struck down municipally mandated residential segregation. Still, in and out of court, setbacks were more common than successes.

Among the ugliest setbacks was the 1917 riot that murdered at least forty blacks in East St. Louis, Illinois. Rallying against the riot and the general anti-Negro violence that lynched thirty-eight blacks in 1917, the NAACP arranged a Silent Protest Parade along New York City's Fifth Avenue in July 1917. Banners lettered "Mr. President, why not make America safe for Democracy" caught the incongruity of Woodrow Wilson's pronouncements on the U.S. entry into war to "make the world safe for Democracy."[5]

As in every war the nation fought from its start, blacks rushed to shoulder arms for America. Heeding the 1917 Selective Service Act's call, at least 700,000 blacks registered for service on opening day. In all, 2,290,525 registered and 367,000 served. While eager to enlist and serve, blacks suffered segregation in the U.S. Armed Services, as they had as civilians. The Marines excluded blacks altogether. The Navy used blacks only as menials. Only the Army allowed commissioned black officers—and then only after an insistent campaign. Nevertheless, all-black Army divisions served abroad with distinction, and black veterans returned home more insistent than ever to be accorded full rights and respect as U.S. citizens. W.E.B. Du Bois, as editor of the NAACP's *Crisis* magazine, echoed the battle-hardened soldiers' sentiments: *"We return. We return from fighting. We return fighting."*[6]

And fighting there was at home after the November 1918 armistice abroad. Twenty-two race riots erupted across the nation between April and October 1919. The summer of 1919 proved so bloody that NAACP Executive Secretary James Weldon Johnson named it "the Red Summer."[7] White mobs lynched seventy-six blacks in 1919. Race riots reached into Washington, D.C., for five days in July. Slaughter spilled in and around Elaine, Arkansas, in October, leaving an official count of twenty-five blacks and five whites dead. Even bloodier was the signal event of the Red Summer: thirteen days of escalating white attacks on blacks in Chicago, Illinois. It ended in a five-day, all-out race riot. It left at least twenty-three blacks and fifteen whites dead and another 537 persons injured.[8]

More than a few suggested that a fresh hubris, or uppityness, among Negroes caused the violence of the Red Summer. Few commented, however, on the institutionalized triggers of violence. The systemic pitting of ethnic Europeans, especially new immigrants, against blacks in industrial centers went unmentioned. Urban crowding and competition for housing and jobs appeared unnoticed. The common story blamed the victims. Negroes had been where they should not be. They had moved out of their place. They had acted out and suffered the consequences.

Reflecting such misplaced causation, one of the nation's leading newspapers lambasted what it lamented as new black militancy. "There had been no trouble with the Negro before the war when most admitted the superiority of the white race," the New York *Times* opined.[9] Two leading Negro newspapers of the day responded to whites' apparent surprise and suspicion at blacks' fighting desperately and effectively to defend themselves and their own. "As long as the Negro submits to lynchings, burnings, and oppressions—and says nothing[,] he is a loyal American citizen. But when he decides the lynchings and burnings shall cease even at the cost of some bloodshed in America, then he is a Bolshevist," the *Pittsburgh Courier* retorted. "If to fight for one's rights is to be Bolshevists, then we are Bolshevists and let them make the most of it," defiantly declared New Orleans's fiery weekly newspaper the *Crusader*.[10]

Insistent change was afoot. Du Bois and his cohort aggressively confronted the nation with demands to abandon segregation and its entire racist system. But counterresistance was no less aggressive. Revived in Atlanta in 1915, the KKK surged south to north. Touting by some counts 500,000 members in the 1920s, it boasted flourishing cells in Illinois, Indiana, Michigan, New York, and Oregon. It was bold, brash, and so well accepted that it paraded 40,000 ceremonially in the nation's capital in August 1925. Its call of "uniting native-born white Christians for concerted action in the preservation of American institutions and the supremacy of the white race" resonated profoundly in a nation turned in on itself with a misguided progressive sense of race-based privilege and xenophobia.[11]

With the Emergency Quota Act of 1921 and then the Immigration Act of 1924 (the national origins act which was U.S. policy until 1965), America turned its back on its Statue of Liberty's inscribed invitation. It barred all Asian immigrants and cut to a trickle immigration of Slavic and southern Europeans such as Poles, Russians, and Italians. In shutting out such peoples, policymakers and much of the population at large at least tacitly embraced pseudoscience adaptations of eugenics and biometrics to project immutable group differences that cast some peoples as suitable and superior and others as unsuitable and inferior. U.S. eugenics publicist Madison Grant's 1915 *The Passing of the Great Race; Or, the Racial Basis of European History* became something of a bible for the U.S. movement for exclusion and racial separation. Grant preached that people were what they were; and social, political, and economic policies and structures needed to obey the immutable realities of nature.

The anti-Negro mood thus reflected more than mobs. Backed by law and pushed publicly with an intellectual and pseudoscientific gloss as part of progressive social and political policy, blacks-in-their-place segregation enjoyed widespread support among whites in America. It shared nativistic ill-will and spread beyond native-born whites. Marginalized European immigrants such as the Italians, Irish, and Slavs expressed desperate needs to stand above somebody else on the socioeconomic ladder. They violently stood against blacks, pushing particularly to exclude them from where they lived and from where they worked. They feared any hint that they were on blacks' level.

"The Negro problem" once dubbed "the Southern problem" thus became increasingly national. Only 9 of every 100 blacks lived outside the South in 1890, and only 5 of every 100 blacks lived outside rural areas. Rapid and radical change called the Great Black Migration reshaped the distribution. Fifty-five of every 100 blacks would live outside the South by 1960, and 75 of every 100 blacks would live in urban areas. In 1910, not one U.S. city had at least 100,000 black residents; eighteen would by 1960.[12]

World War I accelerated the shift, especially to northern cities. It stopped the flow of European immigrants to industrial jobs, while spurring demand for production, particularly outside the South. Prevailing job conditions coupled with the depressing racial climate to produce a steady black exodus from the South. The 1915 Mississippi River floods helped the push. So did the crop-devastating 1914–1917 boll weevil outbreak in the South. Employment agents being paid to find factory workers helped pull blacks north. Black newspaper boosters such as Robert S. Abbott's *Chicago Defender* also drew the stream northward with information on how to make the journey and where to get a job. Between 1910 and 1920, at least 454,000 blacks left the South. Another 749,000 followed between 1920 and 1929, and 347,000 more left from 1930 to 1940.

Black migrants moved mostly along the rail lines. From Carolina and Georgia, they moved to New York City or Philadelphia. From Alabama, Louisiana, and Mississippi, they moved to Chicago, Detroit, and Cleveland. Black populations and racial tensions soared in such cities. Detroit's 611 percent increase between 1910 and 1920 topped the big city chart. Chicago's black population increased 148 percent. More modestly, Philadelphia's black population increased 59 percent. New York City's 66 percent increase amounted to 60,758 in actual number between 1910 and 1920. That number nearly tripled to 175,239 between 1920 and 1930.[13]

As blacks moved into neighborhoods, whites moved out. New York's Manhattan area called Harlem symbolized the shift and became something of a African American Mecca in the 1920s. It drew people and popular attention. It became a capital of an expressive resurgence of black culture that featured fresh attitudes, aspirations, and images. The central image was "the New Negro"—

a title Howard University philosophy professor Alain Locke popularized with his 1925 edited volume of essays, fiction, poetry, and art. Locke's "New Negro" was no caricature but a person of creativity, character, and activism. The black literary and artistic outpouring of the 1920s and 1930s took his book title for its own as "the New Negro Renaissance." It often became mistakenly localized in the title "Harlem Renaissance."

The Jamaica-born Marcus Garvey prefigured something of the New Negro's appearance. Arriving in New York City in 1916, he organized a branch of his Universal Negro Improvement Association (UNIA) and rallied black masses in bold self-assertion. He shared core ideas with Locke and Du Bois. His Pan-African outlook, for example, fit with Du Bois's work with various Pan-African congresses. It fit also with Locke's focus on African culture. Yet Garvey was distant from Locke and inimical to Du Bois, who considered him a bombastic buffoon.

Du Bois and Locke had their "talented tenth," as they dubbed the best and brightest blacks. Garvey had his people, claiming hundreds of UNIA chapters worldwide with 4 to 6 million members from 1920 to 1923. He collected millions of dollars for his community development programs and, especially, for his Back to Africa colonization schemes. Convicted and imprisoned for mail fraud in 1923, Garvey died in obscurity in London, England, in 1940. His populist legacy of black pride, black power, and black separatism hardly died with him. Garvey's energized black masses filled out the substance of the New Negro. His black-centered boldness and the NAACP's persistent petitioning for legal change displayed a character for all America and all the world to see. A placard carried in parade declared the image in bold capitals: "THE NEW NEGRO HAS *NO* FEAR."

The general economic collapse that began almost as the New Negro debuted in name in 1925 sharpened the ugly edge of race relations. Depression turned competition even more deadly. With unemployment reaching 15 million by 1932 and industrial production cut in half, white-dominated labor unions insisted on excluding blacks and pushed to protect their own—not infrequently with violence. White Illinois Central Railroad workers, for instance, killed ten black trainmen in 1932 to seize their workspace. "Whites only" was on the job and everywhere else.

The New Negro organized to resist racial subordination with renewed force that showed itself particularly in politics. The Great Migration that carried blacks out of the South also carried them back into the political arena as voters and officeholders. In cities such as Chicago, blacks' swelling numbers gave them voting power. Republican Oscar DePriest became the first black on Chicago's city council in 1915. Steadfast in what touted itself as the party of Lincoln and of emancipation, DePriest joined in Herbert Hoover's 1929 Republican victory to become the first black elected to Congress in the twentieth century and the first ever elected outside the South.

DePriest came to symbolize not only the New Negro's entry into politics but also the New Negro's shift in party as the black Democrat Arthur W. Mitchell unseated him in 1934. Outside the South, the Democratic Party shifted progressively to woo black voters in the 1920s as partisan competition boosted their swing position. But losses came with gains. The once receptive Republican Party shifted to lily-white, particularly in the South. And southern Democrats remained adamant against having blacks in their party or at the polls. Yet blacks' sheer numbers forced the National Democratic Party to make overtures that President Franklin D. Roosevelt negotiated in his 1930s New Deal coalition.

With nudges from his wife, Eleanor Roosevelt, and others, FDR appointed blacks to relatively high federal offices and reached beyond to rank-and-file jobs. Blacks on the federal payroll quadrupled from 50,000 to 200,000 during FDR's four terms as president. The federal works and relief agencies his New Deal established provided food, jobs, and training to blacks as part of the national effort to combat the Great Depression. And among blacks the need was great, as the weight of racism pressed them down and out of the economy. Almost twice the proportion of blacks (18.0 percent) compared to whites (9.5 percent) received relief aid. Not since the Civil War era Freedmen's Bureau had so much federal assistance flowed to blacks.[14]

FDR's efforts bowed, nevertheless, to southern Democrats who insisted on racial segregation. FDR refused to back the NAACP's call for a federal anti-lynching act or even to comment publicly on such an act. And when the outbreak of World War II in Europe jump-started the U.S. economy, FDR had to be pushed into combating blacks' exclusion from war industries jobs.

Radical social justice advocate and labor leader A. Philip Randolph more than anyone else insisted on putting FDR's feet to the fire on fairness to blacks in the Arsenal of Democracy's workplaces. Randolph demanded FDR's commitment to including blacks in booming defense employment. Drawing on his union organizing experience, Randolph threatened a 100,000-person-strong March on Washington, D.C., in July 1941 unless the president moved to end job discrimination in federal jobs and contract work.

With his Executive Order No. 8802 in June 1941, FDR purported to reaffirm a "policy of full participation in the defense program by all persons, regardless of race, creed, color, or national origin." The order created the Fair Employment Practices Committee (FEPC) to oversee compliance.

The New Negro hardly relied only on the president, the federal government, or anyone else. Old self-help sentiments surfaced in fresh forms. Blacks used the clout of their cash against job discrimination. They boycotted in New York City with a "Don't Buy Where You Can't Work" campaign. They made their votes count, too. If DePriest opened city councils in 1915, then Edward A. Johnson's 1917 election to the New York State Assembly opened state legislatures. In the 1930s and 1940s, blacks consistently won legislative seats in California, Illinois, Indiana, Kansas, Kentucky, New Jersey, New York, Ohio, Pennsylvania, and West Virginia.

Progress appeared at hand for blacks in politics and in jobs. Yet across the range of race relations the segregated status quo remained entrenched. Law in most places meant white order. The injustice southern law enforcement meted out to blacks stood starkly in the blatant lack of a fair trial for nine blacks aged twelve to nineteen years accused of raping two white women while riding a freight train in March 1931. The accused became known as the Scottsboro Boys because of the trial's Alabama locale. The drum-head state court's trial and electric chair convictions of all but the youngest within two weeks of the alleged crime became a national and international scandal. The U.S. Supreme Court twice required new trials.

The ordinary process of justice denied was clear for all the world to see. Lynch mobs murdered 119 blacks during the 1930s. Rioting, too, claimed a share. Whites continued to maraud and destroy black communities, as they did in Oklahoma's 1921 Tulsa Race Riot, demolishing the Greenwood District and the financial capital called Black Wall Street. Blacks rioted in return. New York's Harlem erupted in 1935. In 1943 riots rocked New York City again and reached to Beaumont, Texas, Detroit, Michigan, Mobile, Alabama, and Los Angeles, California.

Race relations remained ugly. Even as the United States battled the horror of racism rampant in Adolf Hitler's Nazi Germany, one observer noted that "no power in the world . . . could now force the Southern white people to the abandonment . . . of social segregation."[15] As more than 1.1 million blacks shouldered arms again for America, thoughts were that "[a] new Negro will return from the war" and return again "fighting."[16]

NOTES

1. Rayford W. Logan, *The Negro in American Life and Thought: The Nadir, 1877–1901* (New York: Dial Press, 1954); Alain Locke, *The New Negro, an Interpretation* (New York: Albert and Charles Boni, 1925).

2. U.S. Bureau of the Census, *Historical Statistics of the United States: Colonial Times to 1970* (Washington, DC: GPO, 1975), "Persons Lynched by Race, 1882 to 1970," Series 1168–1170, 422.

3. William E. Walling, "Race War in the North," *The Independent* 65 (September 3, 1908): 529–534.

4. Quoted in John Hope Franklin and Alfred A. Moss Jr., *From Slavery to Freedom: A History of African Americans*, 7th ed., 2 vols. (New York: McGraw-Hill, 1998), 2:324.

5. Schomburg Center for Research in Black Culture, "Harlem 1900–1940: The Silent Protest" (exhibition), http://www.si.umich.edu/CHICO/Harlem/text/silentprotest. html.

6. W.E.B. Du Bois, "Returning Soldiers," *The Crisis* 18 (May 1919): 13.

7. James Weldon Johnson, *Along This Way* (New York: Viking Press, 1935), 341.

8. William M. Tuttle Jr., *Race Riot: Chicago in the Red Summer of 1919* (New York: Atheneum, 1970), 32–73.

9. Quoted in Richard Wormser, "Red Summer (1919)," in PBS's *The Rise and Fall of Jim Crow: Jim Crow Stories*, http://www.pbs.org/wnet/jimcrow/stories_events_red. html.

10. Quoted in Franklin and Moss, *From Slavery to Freedom*, 2:353–354.

11. Kenneth T. Jackson, *The Ku Klux Klan in the City, 1915–1930* (New York: Oxford University Press, 1967).

12. Robert C. Twombly, *Blacks in White America since 1865: Issues and Interpretations* (New York: David C. McKay, 1971), 171–172.

13. Ibid.

14. U.S. Federal Emergency Relief Administration, "Color or Race of Persons in Re-

lief Families," in *Unemployment Relief Census: October 1933, U.S. Summary* (Washington, DC: GPO, 1934), 7–9.

15. Herbert Garfinkel, *When Negroes March* (Glencoe, IL: Free Press, 1959), 103, quoting U.S. Fair Employment Practices Committee member Mark Etheridge.

16. Lucille B. Milne, "Jim Crow in the Army," *New Republic* 110 (March 13, 1944): 339–342, offering letters the NAACP received from black soldiers.

DOCUMENTS

9.1.   "The friendship of the two races," 1895

In September 1895, at the opening of the Cotton States and International Exposition in Atlanta, Georgia, a little-known black educator, who in 1881 founded the Tuskegee Normal and Industrial Institute in Alabama, delivered a speech. It conveyed a smoothed-over summary of past black-white relations and offered a vision for mutually beneficial interracial cooperation. The speaker was Booker T. Washington (1856–1915). General white reaction to the speech known as the Atlanta Exposition Address cast on Washington the mantle of "the Negro's leader" that abolitionist and equal rights advocate Frederick Douglass (1817–1895) had carried until dying that February. Washington's speech to some seemed servile conciliation to placate whites rather than to protect or project blacks' rights. It did censure the contrived competition between European immigrants and blacks. It accepted social segregation of the races while arguing that whites and blacks were inextricably bound to rise or fall together, as least in the South.

One-third of the population of the South is of the Negro race. No enterprise seeking the material, civil, or moral welfare of this section can disregard this element of our population and reach the highest success. . . .

To those of the white race who look to the incoming of those of foreign birth and strange tongue and habits for the prosperity of the South, were I permitted I would repeat what I say to my own race, "Cast down your bucket where you are."

Cast it down among the eight millions of Negroes whose habits you know, whose fidelity and love you have tested in days when to have proved treacherous meant the ruin of your firesides.

Cast down your bucket among these people who have, without strikes and labour wars, tilled your fields, cleared your forests, builded your railroads and cities, and brought forth treasures from the bowels of the earth, and helped make possible this magnificent representation of the progress of the South.

Casting down your bucket among my people, helping and encouraging them as you are doing on these grounds, and to education of head, hand, and heart, you will find that they will buy your surplus land, make blossom the waste places in your fields, and run your factories. While doing this, you can be sure in the future, as in the past, that you and your families will be surrounded by the most patient, faithful, law-abiding, and unresentful people that the world has seen.

As we have proved our loyalty to you in the past, in nursing your children, watching by the sick-bed of your mothers and fathers, and often following them with tear-dimmed eyes to their graves, so in the future, in our humble way, we shall stand by you with a devotion that no foreigner can approach, ready to lay down our lives, if need be, in defence of yours, interlacing our industrial, commercial, civil, and religious life with yours in a way that shall make the interests of both races one.

In all things that are purely social we can be as separate as the fingers, yet one as the hand in all things essential to mutual progress.

There is no defence or security for any of us except in the highest intelligence and development of all. If anywhere there are efforts tending to curtail the fullest growth of the Negro, let these efforts be turned into stimulating, encouraging, and making him the most useful and intelligent citizen. Effort or means so invested will pay a thousand per cent interest. These efforts will be twice blessed—"blessing him that gives and him that takes."

There is no escape through law of man or God from the inevitable:—

> The laws of changeless justice bind
>   Oppressor with oppressed;
> And close as sin and suffering joined
>   We march to fate abreast.

Nearly sixteen millions of hands will aid you in pulling the load upward, or they will pull against you the load downward. We shall constitute one-third and more of the ignorance and crime of the South, or one-third its intelligence and progress; we shall contribute one-third to the business and industrial prosperity of the South, or we shall prove a veritable body of death, stagnating, depressing, retarding every effort to advance the body politic.

Source: Booker T. Washington, *Up from Slavery: An Autobiography* (New York: Doubleday, Page & Company, 1901), 218–222.

9.2.   "Why is mob murder permitted," 1909

> *Militant black journalist Ida B. Wells-Barnett (1862–1931) championed social and political justice, particularly in her crusade against lynching. She spared nothing to expose barbarous mob murders. She especially rallied church groups and women's clubs to stand up for justice and end lynching. Wells-Barnett offered the following speech at the 1909 conference from which the National Association for the Advancement of Colored People emerged and was instrumental in its national antilynching campaign.*

The lynching record for a quarter of a century merits the thoughtful study of the American people. It presents three salient facts:

First, lynching is color line murder.

Second, crimes against white women is the excuse, not the cause.

Third, it is a national crime and requires a national remedy.

Proof that lynching follows the color line is to be found in statistics for the past 25 years. . . .

Just as the lynch law regime came to a close in the West, a new mob movement started in the South. This was wholly political, its purpose being to suppress the colored vote by intimidation and murder. Thousands of assassins, banded together under the name of Ku Klux Klans, "Midnight Raiders," etc., spread a reign of terror by beating, shooting and killing colored people by the thousands. In a few years, the purpose was accomplished and the black vote was suppressed. But mob murder continued.

From 1882, when 52 were lynched, down to the present, lynching has been along the color line. Statistics show that 3,284 men, women and children have been put to death in this quarter of a century. . . . Twenty-eight human beings also burned at the stake, one of them a woman and two of them children; this is the awful indictment against American civilization—the gruesome tribute which the nation pays to the color line.

Why is mob murder permitted by a Christian nation? What is the cause of this awful slaughter? This question is answered almost daily—always [with] the same shameless, falsehood that "Negroes are lynched to protect womanhood." . . .

This is the never varying answer of lynchers and their apologists. All know that it is untrue. The cowardly lyncher revels in murder, then seeks to shield himself from public execration by claiming devotion to woman. But truth is mighty and the lynching record discloses the hypocrisy of the lyncher as well as his crime. . . .

Is there a remedy, or will the nation confess that it cannot protect its [own]. . . .

The only certain remedy is an appeal to law. . . . Federal protection of American citizenship is the remedy for lynching. . . .

Time was when lynching was sectional (regional), but now it is national—a blight upon our nation, mocking our laws and disgracing our Christianity. "With malice toward none but with charity for all" let us undertake the work of making the law effective and supreme upon every foot of American soil— a shield to the innocent and to the guilty punishment swift and sure.

Source: Mrs. Ida Wells-Barnett, "Lynching Our National Crime," in *Proceedings of the National Negro Conference 1909—New York, May 31 and June 1* (n.p., n.d.), 174–179. Thanks to the Library, Brigham Young University, Provo, Utah.

9.3.   "Heredity is the controlling factor in human development," 1915

Eugenics publicist Madison Grant (1865–1937) represented a broad strain inside and outside the Progressive Movement in the first part of the twentieth century. Grant and his cohort self-identified as the better sort who alone were true Americans. They feared blacks, along with immigrant hordes, were overrunning America. Preaching racial purity and Anglo-Saxon supremacy as absolute necessities, Grant joined with like-minded political and popular supporters to cut immigration to a trickle with the Emergency Quota Act of 1921 and then the Immigration Act of 1924, that established the national origins quota system. They virtually excluded immigrants from Africa, Asia, or almost anywhere outside northern and western Europe. Grant's 1915 book The Passing of the Great Race *sought to show America's danger in following Europe's path to decline by not securing its borders to protect the quality of its superior racial stock. To save America for true Americans the nation needed to shut out and segregate inferior peoples. Every people had their place and belonged there if America and, indeed, civilization were to survive and progress, in Grant's view represented below.*

The great lesson of the science of race is the immutability of somatological or bodily characters, with which is closely associated the immutability of psychical predispositions and impulses. This continuity of inheritance has a most important bearing on the theory of democracy and still more upon that of socialism, and those, engaged in social uplift and in revolutionary movements, are consequently usually very intolerant of the limitations imposed by heredity.

Democratic theories of government in their modern form are based on dogmas of equality formulated some hundred and fifty years ago, and rest upon the assumption that environment and not heredity is the controlling factor in human development.

Philanthropy and noble purpose dictated the doctrine expressed in the Declaration of Independence, the document which to-day constitutes the actual basis of American institutions. The men who wrote the words, "we hold these truths to be self-evident, that all men are created equal," were themselves the owners of slaves, and despised Indians as something less than human. Equality in their minds meant merely that they were just as good Englishmen as their brothers across the sea.

The words "that all men are created equal" have since been subtly falsified by adding the word "free," although no such expression is found in the original document, and the teachings based on these altered words in the American public schools of to-day would startle and amaze the men who formulated the Declaration.

The laws of nature operate with the same relentless and unchanging force in human affairs as in the phenomena of inanimate nature, and the basis of the government of man is now and always has been, and always will be, force and not sentiment, a truth demonstrated anew by the present world conflagration [World War I].

Source: Madison Grant, *The Passing of the Great Race; Or, the Racial Basis of European History*, 4th rev. ed. (New York: C. Scribner's Sons, 1926), ix–xi.

9.4.   "We return fighting," 1919

> *W.E.B. Du Bois (1868–1963), as editor of the National Association for the Advancement of Colored People's monthly magazine* Crisis, *articulated rough-and-ready sentiments not only of the 367,000 blacks who served in the U.S. Armed Forces during World War I but also of blacks at home, all veterans in struggling against the barbarism of lynching, rioting, segregation, and general racial discrimination. His column in May 1919 welcoming returning soldiers pronounced an insistent demand for change—a demand that turned President Woodrow Wilson's pronouncements on the U.S. entry into war to "make the world safe for Democracy" into a rebuke to "make America safe for Democracy."*

We are returning from war! The *Crisis* and tens of thousands of black men were drafted into a great struggle. For . . . America and her highest ideals, we fought in far-off hope; for the dominant southern oligarchy entrenched in Washington, we fought in bitter resignation. For the America that represents and gloats in lynching, disfranchisement, caste, brutality and devilish insult—for this, in the hateful upturning and mixing of things, we were forced by vindictive fate to fight also.

But today we return! We return from the slavery of uniform which the world's madness demanded us to don to the freedom of civil garb. We stand again to look America squarely in the face and call a spade a spade. We sing: This country of ours, despite all its better souls have done and dreamed, is yet a shameful land.

It lynches. . . .

It disfranchises its own citizens. . . .

It encourages ignorance. . . .

It steals from us.

It organizes industry to cheat us. It cheats us out of our land; it cheats us out of our labor. It confiscates our savings. It reduces our wages. It raises our rent. It steals our profit. It taxes us without representation. It keeps us consistently and universally poor, and then feeds us on charity and derides our poverty.

It insults us.

It has organized a nation-wide and latterly a world-wide propaganda of deliberate and continuous insult and defamation of black blood wherever found. . . .

This is the country to which we Soldiers of Democracy return. This is the fatherland for which we fought! But it is our fatherland. It was right for us to fight. The faults of our country are our faults. Under similar circumstances, we would fight again. But by the God of Heaven, we are cowards and jackasses if now that that war is over, we do not marshal every ounce of our brain and brawn to fight a sterner, longer, more unbending battle against the forces of hell in our own land.

We return.
We return from fighting.
We return fighting.
Make way for Democracy! We saved it in France, and by the Great Jehovah, we will save it in the United States of America, or know the reason why.

Source: W.E.B. Du Bois, "Returning Soldiers," *Crisis* 18 (May 1919): 13.

9.5.   "Black people should be given a country of their own," 1923

Jamaica-born Marcus Garvey (1887–1940) came to the United States in 1915. He was attracted by Booker T. Washington's theories of black economic development and especially by Washington's view of social separatism. Indeed, Garvey further developed notions of black separatism, returning in part to antebellum back-to-Africa colonization projects. He virtually repeated Martin R. Delany's 1852 declaration, "No people . . . can ever attain to greatness who lose their identity. We shall ever cherish our identity of origin and race." And although he shared with W.E.B. Du Bois a belief in Pan-Africanism and the sense that the race struggle was international and central to the twentieth century's course, Garvey and his separatism were anathema to Du Bois and organizations such as the National Association for the Advancement of Colored People. Below Garvey explains his view.

We love all humanity. We are working for the peace of the world which we believe can only come about when all races are given their due.

We feel that there is absolutely no reason why there should be any differences between the black and white races, if each stop to adjust and steady itself. We believe in the purity of both races. . . . It is a vicious and dangerous doctrine of social equality to urge, as certain colored leaders do, that black and white should get together, for that would destroy the racial purity of both.

We believe that the black people should have a country of their own where they should be given the fullest opportunity to develop politically, socially and industrially. . . . We believe that with the rising ambition of the negro, if a country is not provided for him in another 50 or 100 years, there will be a terrible clash that will end disastrously to him and disgrace our civilization.

We desire to prevent such a clash by pointing the negro to a home of his own. We feel that all well disposed and broad minded white men will aid in this direction. It is because of this belief no doubt that my negro enemies, so as to prejudice me further in the opinion of the public, wickedly state that I am a member of the Ku Klux Klan, even though I am a black man. . . .

Looking forward a century or two, we can see an economic and political death struggle for the survival of the different race groups. Many of our present-day national centres will have become over-crowded with vast surplus populations. The fight for bread and position will be keen and severe.

White men who have struggled for and built up their countries and their own civilizations are not disposed to hand them over to the negro or any other race without let or hindrance. It would be unreasonable to expect this. Hence any vain assumption on the part of the negro to imagine that he will one day become President of the Nation, Governor of the State or Mayor of the city in the countries of white men, is like waiting on the devil and his angels to take up their residence in the Realm on High and direct there the affairs of Paradise.

Source: Marcus Garvey, "The Negro's Greatest Enemy," *Current History* 18, no. 6 (September 1923): 956–957.

9.6.   "A new race-spirit is taking place," 1925

Howard University philosophy professor Alain Locke (1885–1954) attached an already bandied about name to the sense of racial awakening stirring among blacks after World War I. The spirit he and others sensed connected national and even international elements, as shown in renewed interest in Pan-Africanism—whether of the Marcus Garvey or W.E.B. Du Bois type. At home in America a "New Negro" reached back to echo the words of the nation's first black newspaper, New York City's Freedom's Journal *inaugurated in 1827 with the demand to "let the Negro speak for himself." The New Negro demanded adjustments in race relations that began with recognition of blacks' full identity and distinction.*

There is ample evidence of a New Negro in the latest phases of social change and progress, but still more in the internal world of the Negro mind and spirit. Here in the very heart of the folk-spirit are the essential forces. . . . Of all the voluminous literature on the Negro, so much is mere external view and commentary that we may warrantably say that nine-tenths of it is about the Negro rather than of him, so that it is the Negro problem rather than the Negro that is known and mooted in the general mind. . . .

Whoever wishes to see the Negro in his essential traits, must seek the enlightenment of that self-portraiture which the present developments of Negro culture are offering. . . . We shall let the Negro speak for himself. . . .

We are now presenting the New Negro in a national and even international scope. Although there are few centers that can be pointed out approximating Harlem's significance, the full significance of that event is a racial awakening on a national and perhaps even a world scale. . . .

Negro life is not only establishing new contacts and founding new centers, it is finding a new soul. There is a fresh spiritual and cultural focusing. We have, as the heralding sign, an unusual outburst of creative expression. There is a renewed race-spirit that consciously and proudly sets itself apart.

Source: Alain Locke, "Foreword," in *The New Negro, an Interpretation* (New York: Albert and Charles Boni, 1925), ix.

ANNOTATED RESEARCH GUIDE
Books

Arneson, Eric. *Black Protest and the Great Migration: A Brief History with Documents.* Boston: Bedford/St. Martin's Press, 2003. Shows World War I as a transformative event, not only for the nearly half-million blacks who relocated from south to north between 1915 and 1918 but for the accelerating demographic transformation of the U.S. countryside and city, north and south, and the experience of American race relations.

Brophy, Alfred L. *Reconstructing the Dreamland: The Tulsa Riot of 1921, Race, Reparations, and Reconciliation.* New York: Oxford University Press, 2002. Gripping account of an urban race riot such as those in East St. Louis and Chicago, Illinois, that illustrated the brutal repression resentful whites spewed on blacks in the early twentieth century.

Hale, Grace Elizabeth. *Making Whiteness: The Culture of Segregation in the South, 1890–1940.* New York: Pantheon Books, 1998. Absorbing cultural history of white southern racial construction of segregation as a postslavery system of dominance and subordination.

Jacobson, Matthew Frye. *Whiteness of a Different Color: European Immigrants and the Alchemy of Race.* Cambridge, MA: Harvard University Press, 1998. Traces the journey of eastern and southern European immigrants from being racial others, not relegated to being black but not accepted immediately as being white, as they pressed their way into a newly forged white monolith that stood as a symbol of the basic, black-white paradigm of U.S. race relations.

Kirby, John B. *Black Americans in the Roosevelt Era: Liberalism and Race.* Knoxville: University of Tennessee Press, 1980. Sketches the ideas and ideology of interracial cooperation in confronting and defining the "Negro problem" in the New Deal's response to the Great Depression.

Locke, Alain, ed. *The New Negro: Voices of the Harlem Renaissance.* New York: Athenaeum, 1925. Reprint, New York: Touchstone, 1999. Essays, fiction, poetry, drama, music, history, and more by prominent figures of the day showing a shifting vision of black identity, ideals, and race relations in the 1920s.

Martin, Tony. *Race First: The Ideological and Organizational Struggles of Marcus Garvey and the Universal Negro Improvement Association.* Westport, CT: Greenwood Press, 1976. Shows the parameters and problems of the first organized black mass movement in the United States from its start in 1914 to 1940, focusing on its ideology of liberation through racial exclusion.

Schneider, Mark Robert. *"We Return Fighting": The Civil Rights Movement in the Jazz Age.* Boston: Northeastern University Press, 2002. Captures the turbulence of post–World War I race relations as black veterans in the fight for democracy abroad refused to accept less than democracy at home.

Sitkoff, Harvard. *A New Deal for Blacks: The Emergence of Civil Rights as a National Issue.* New York: Oxford University Press, 1978. Details the developing force of the Civil Rights Movement in the 1930s, unfolding its importance for the strategies and successes of the 1950s and 1960s.

Tolnay, Stewart Emery, and E. M. Beck. *A Festival of Violence: An Analysis of the Lynching of African-Americans in the American South, 1882–1930.* Urbana: University of Illinois Press, 1995. Systematically analyzes antiblack southern mob violence in ten southern states and argues that economic erosion and threat more than anything else accounted for the brutality.

Web Sites

http://www.loc.gov/exhibits/african/afam008.html—the Library of Congress's African American Mosiac Exhibit contains detailed information on African American history and includes maps and other resources for charting blacks' Great Migration.

http://www.pbs.org/gointochicago/resources/biblio2.html—information on the 1991 PBS documentary film *Goin' to Chicago*, produced by George King and Associates, and other resources chronicling the first two twentieth-century waves of black migration from the agrarian, rural South to the industrial, urban North and West.

http://www.yale.edu/ynhti/curriculum/units/1979/2/79.02.04.x.html—this Yale–New Haven teacher's unit contains teaching tools and information on lynching and race riots.

10

"To Secure These Rights": From Desegregation to Long, Hot Summers

The atrocities *Der Fuhrer* Adolf Hitler led Nazi Germany and its collaborators to commit in the name of an asserted Aryan master race's purity and superiority turned many against racism and its legal manifestations. What Hitler labeled the "final solution" to race relations problems shocked and sickened many as an ultimate crime against humanity. The Holocaust slaughtered millions in state-sponsored, systematic exterminations based on racial classification and discrimination. The horror bled away much of racism's political and social attraction. Racial minorities and their advocates in the United States seized on revulsion against Nazi atrocities to assail racism and its legal manifestation in segregation.

The attack on racism at home in America replayed war propaganda and rhetoric with special emphasis, as blacks had done repeatedly since the American Revolution. During World War I, for example, black protests turned the U.S. war cry to "Make the World Safe for Democracy" into a cry to "Make America Safe for Democracy." So again in World War II black protest spotlighted the democratic symbols America paraded against Nazism. America's official Double V campaign that called for victory in Europe and victory in the Pacific took a twist in antiracists hands to become victory for democracy abroad and at home.

Protests stressed the gap between U.S. democratic rhetoric and racial realities in U.S. life. But racism's penetrating roots in American life and thought were not easily moved. That showed soon after the U.S. entry into war in December 1941. Racism proved a primary element in American hysteria that herded into concentration camps, known officially as "relocation centers," more than 120,000 U.S. citizens and residents because of their Japanese ancestry. In *Korematsu v. United States* (1944), U.S. Supreme Court Justice Frank Murphy denounced the treatment as the "legalization of racism."[1]

Even as their families sat interned, at least 17,600 Japanese Americans enlisted in the U.S. Armed Forces. Blacks, too, heeded the call as in every U.S. war. About a million blacks shouldered arms, and change came as they swelled the ranks. For the first time, the U.S. Marine Corps enlisted blacks—17,000 among a peak of 475,600 personnel by war's end. In the Army, more than infantry and support positions opened. Blacks entered artillery, tank, engineering, and medical units. Blacks became pilots. Black women served in the Women's Army Corps (WAC) and in the Women Accepted for Volunteer Emergency Services (WAVES). The Navy grudging let a few blacks serve as other than the traditional messmen. U.S. ground troops remained segregated as usual, however, until the final push into Germany in January 1945, when black units were put together with white units.

On the battlefield abroad and at home, segregation was under fire, but it was not retreating. "Whites Only" and "No Colored Allowed" remained fixed as law and custom throughout the nation. The tensions of challenging or changing the set racial order showed themselves in the bloody race riot in Detroit in June 1943 that left twenty-five blacks and nine whites dead. In August 1943 a race riot erupted also in New York's Harlem. Clearly volatile conditions marked the racial front at home.

World War II accelerated the Great Migration of blacks out of the South that World War I had quickened. More than 1.2 million blacks left the South during the 1940s. Another 1.5 million left during the 1950s. More than 2 in 3 of the 2.7 million moved to cities with factory jobs in Illinois, Michigan, New York, Pennsylvania, and Ohio or went way west to California. As blacks increased their presence outside the South, so too did black-white barriers rise as a national issue. A horror-weary black woman amid the aftermath of the 1943 Detroit riot offered her perspective on the nationalized race problem: "There ain't no North any more," she lamented. "Everything now is South."[2]

Racism lurked as ugly residue in the world that hobbled from war in 1945. The fully developing details of the Holocaust intensified aversion to the rhetoric of racial superiority. Racial domination and subordination became prime targets worldwide. In Africa, Asia, and America, resistance rose to white rule from afar and to minority white rule at hand. Both became international issues for the new world organization called the United Nations, chartered in June 1945 to promote "[u]niversal respect for, and observance of, human rights and fundamental freedoms for all without distinction of race, language, or religion." Taking a step many hoped for against racism, the United Nations in 1946 called South Africa's apartheid regime to account for its racial discrimination.

Buoyed by UN actions, a U.S. National Negro Congress (NNC) petitioned in 1946 for a UN hearing on conditions for blacks in the United States. Howard University Law School dean Charles H. Houston argued that U.S. denial of political rights to blacks was as much an international issue as any self-announced fascist or communist regime's denial of rights. Such comparisons resounded with deeper timbre in the creeping Cold War where America was again hoisting symbols of democracy—this time against what it dubbed the "international conspiracy" of the Iron Curtain.

The Cold War refreshed familiar dimensions of the African American struggle. Returning black veterans particularly demanded change. Foremost in their sights was the Armed Forces. The relatively new U.S. commander in chief, Harry S Truman, agreed. In his first message to Congress after Japan's surrender in September 1945, President Truman expanded FDR's New Deal agenda into a progressive domestic reform program called the "Fair Deal." Civil rights stood prominently among his "21 points." He called for a permanent Fair Employment Practices Act to prevent racial or religious discrimination in hiring. Moreover, he appointed a special committee to advise him on civil rights conditions. The committee reported its findings in *"To Secure These Rights"* (1947). Using a phrase from the Declaration of Independence as its title, the report roundly condemned segregation. Acting on it, President Truman focused a new committee on the Armed Services, and its 1948 report *Freedom to Serve* drew up steps to end segregation there.

America appeared unready to embrace desegregation as fundamental fairness or as essential to equal protection of the law. Political and popular leaders, especially in the South, spurned Truman's initiatives and other civil rights reforms. They rejected racial equality as unnatural and as subversive. Some cast civil rights initiatives as anti-American-inspired communism or socialism. They repudiated federal involvement as contemptuous of state's rights. They insisted that the basic structure of federalism guaranteed in the Constitution made civil rights a state issue, as slavery had been.

Something of a reprise of Civil War–era political splintering over the federal role in race relations appeared in the 1948 elections. Southerners bolted from the Democratic Party to oppose Truman and his civil rights program. They formed the States Rights Democrats, popularly known as Dixiecrats. They ran South Carolina Governor J. Strom Thurmond for president and Mississippi Governor Fielding Wright for vice president. Their platform labeled federal civil rights initiatives as "an effort to establish in the United States a police nation that would destroy the last vestiges of liberty enjoyed by a citizen." They won 1.2 million popular votes and 39 electoral votes, carrying Alabama, Louisiana, Mississippi, and South Carolina. With 24.1 million popular votes and 303 electoral votes, President Truman claimed reelection the pundits failed to anticipate. But his victory at the polls did not carry over into civil rights. With Dixiecrats—many of whom later turned Republican—in the forefront, Congress killed the president's civil rights initiatives.[3]

Truman did what he could through executive orders, but it was in federal courts that civil rights advanced most. It was there the National Association for the Advancement of Colored People focused. Its Legal Defense and Educational Fund, made independent in 1939, chipped away at segregation's legal basis. Its signal achievement came in a 1954 case from the District of Columbia and in four cases from Delaware, Kansas, South Carolina, and Virginia consolidated under the title *Brown v. Board of Education*. Chief Justice Earl Warren declared the Court's unanimous opinion that "in the field of public education the doctrine of 'separate but equal' has no place. Separate educational facilities are inherently unequal."[4] Finally, segregation's days seemed numbered.

If *Brown* dealt a death blow to de jure racial segregation in public schools, only a lingering death followed. The Court had announced a constitutional principle that, in 1955, it ordered carried out "with all deliberate speed." It left implementation in local hands. The sanction of law thus passed, but de facto segregation remained. Indeed, resistance rushed forth. Segregationists accelerated attacks on the broadening movement for civil rights and on the Supreme Court—the federal institution that had come to recognize the constitutional values inherent in and expressed by desegregation demands.

Recalcitrance to civil rights turned race relations even uglier. Many southern whites flatly rejected changed relations with blacks. They insisted on things as they were. They stood for and on segregation. The Supreme Court refused any retreat. In *Cooper v. Aaron* (1958), the justices unanimously declared that "constitutional rights . . . are not to be sacrificed or yielded to . . . violence and disorder." The Court warned that

> [t]he constitutional rights of children not to be discriminated against in school admissions on grounds of race or color declared by this court can neither be nullified openly and directly by state legislators or state executives or judicial officers, nor nullified by them through any evasive scheme for segregation.[5]

Blacks themselves brooked no retreat. They stood insistent. Indeed, they refused to be still or quiet. With rising urgency since World War II, blacks and others in common cause compelled America to attend to racial inequity and injustice. While *Brown* made its way through the courts, the Reverend Theodore J. Jemison, pastor of Mount Zion Baptist Church in Louisiana's capital of Baton Rouge, led blacks in an 8-day bus boycott to get first-come first-served seating from back to front for blacks. A similar bus boycott soon became national and international news. It too was in a southern capital—Montgomery, Alabama, the first home of old Dixie's Confederacy. It lasted 381 days. It started in December 1955 with local NAACP secretary Rosa Parks' refusing to yield her seat on a city bus to a white man as ordinance and custom decreed. Taken to court, Mrs. Parks and four other black women prevailed in *Browder v. Gayle* (1956), where a federal panel fully repudiated *Plessy* by finding "no rational basis upon which the separate-but-equal doctrine can be validly applied to public transportation."[6]

The Montgomery Bus Boycott nurtured broader links among local organizations that sustained black communities. It immediately produced the Montgomery Improvement Association (MIA). Many have marked it as the start of the modern Civil Rights Movement that was to last into the 1960s. It also elevated a new leader—the fresh twenty-six-year-old, second-year pastor of Montgomery's Dexter Avenue Baptist Church, the Reverend Dr. Martin Luther King Jr. As an MIA spokesman and later as head of the Atlanta-based Southern Christian Leadership Conference (SCLC) formed in 1957, King became a national figure. He was neither alone nor unchallenged in leading a vigorous reconfiguration of national race relations. The heads of old-line black organizations provided joint leadership. The NAACP's Roy Wilkins, the National Urban League's Whitney M. Young Jr., the Congress of Racial Equality's (CORE) James Farmer, and the labor organizer A. Philip Randolph, among others, contributed significantly. Everywhere, however, local leadership and organization proved crucial.

Differing voices enhanced King's public attraction. His calm marching into bloody, dog-biting police assaults and continuing to preach the Christian love feast of agape marked him as a much preferred alternative to those whom the U.S. popular press portrayed as fire-breathing radicals. Foremost among the branded extremists stood Nation of Islam (NOI) minister Malcolm X. The man who replaced his so-called slave name of Little with an X and later took the Islamic name El-Hajj Malik El-Shabazz exhorted separation in contrast to King's commonly labeled integration. He promised no Christian cheek-turning but violent self-defense. He talked of white devils, not of white brothers. Malcolm X reveled in the contrast with King and worked to sharpen America's black-white vision as a choice between what in April 1964 he called "the ballot or the bullet."[7]

For both King and Malcolm X—indeed, for the United States itself—a generation of surging impatience exerted the telling pressure in changing race relations. Younger blacks thrust the movement onto a new frontier. Adapting a 1930s labor strike tactic as a start, a group decided to sit rather than march. North Carolina College students in Durham tried it in August 1957. Four students at historically black North Carolina Agricultural and Technical (A & T) College in Greensboro, however, popularized the quick-spreading sit-in movement in 1960. It proved an effective boycott tactic. Economics and inconvenience pressured public accommodations and facilities across the South to yield. Sit-ins forced lunch counters, restaurants, libraries, beaches, hotels, and theaters to reflect new racial realities. In Greensboro, for instance, the sit-ins that began in February 1960 by July resulted in desegregated lunch counters.

Not blacks alone surged to end segregation. Other people of color joined the action, as did whites. CORE led the interracial direct action groups. Founded in 1942, CORE began in May 1961 to act as a movement center pressing on interstate transportation. It organized and operated what it called "freedom rides." Thousands would in time bus state-to-state throughout the South to test obedience to the U.S. Supreme Court's 1960 ruling in *Boynton v. Virginia* that no interstate transportation facilities could legally be segregated.[8] As with the students who sat in for desegregation, the freedom riders stirred anger and violence. Pro-segregation mobs pulled freedom riders from buses and terminals and left images bleeding into a spreading tableau that demanded federal action.

As desegregation inched forward under wary eyes, particularly those from the developing national medium of television, Federal Bureau of Investigation agents and U.S. marshals went south to try to prevent wholesale bloodletting. News stories marked successions of "firsts." Hamilton Holmes and Charlayne Hunter (later Hunter-Gault) in January 1961 became the first blacks to attend the University of Georgia, following a federal court order. James Meredith in 1962 became the first black to attend the University of Mississippi, after rioting to block him left two dead and President John F. Kennedy federalized the National Guard to secure Meredith's safe entry. Protesters massed for and against segregation across the South.

Bolder initiatives asserted black demands. Groups such as the Student Nonviolent (later National) Coordinating Committee (SNCC), organized in 1960, insisted on escalating direct action. From Albany, Georgia, to Birmingham, Alabama, in 1962 and 1963 sit-ins, boycotts, mass marches, and rallies demonstrated the spreading struggle's death grip in the South. A broad coalition joined in 1963 to seize the nation's attention. The planners revived A. Philip Randolph's 1941 campaign to focus public pressure for civil rights by marching on Washington. Randolph's deft lieutenant Bayard Rustin masterfully articulated the rationales and laid out the logistics.

On August 28, 1963, hundreds of thousands from across America met at the nation's capital to demand segregation's end with "Jobs and Freedom." The National Mall from the Lincoln Memorial to the Washington Monument overflowed with humanity. The old slave spiritual "We Shall Overcome," which black tobacco workers in South Carolina adapted for labor organizing in the 1940s, poured out in a 1960s version. It resounded as an anthem. The enduring sound of the moment arose unanticipated. Elevating himself to immemorial standing, Martin Luther King Jr. declared in what became his signature speech, "I have a dream." Listeners far and wide appeared to applaud King's eloquence and rhetoric and to accept his moral challenge for America to make good on what he called its "promise that all men would be guaranteed the inalienable rights of life, liberty, and the pursuit of happiness."[9] King's performance, along with his civil rights organizing and preaching nonviolent social change, led to his receiving the 1964 Nobel Peace Prize.

An accord appeared across America to condemn as immoral and unjust what King called "the manacles of segregation and the chains of discrimination."[10] National sentiment and, indeed, national lawmakers appeared persuaded to end segregation as a legal system 100 years after President Abraham Lincoln's 1863 Emancipation Proclamation appeared to promise to end slavery as a legal system. No harmony appeared, however, on what to do and how to do it. Many white southerners who saw segregation as essential to their way of life rejected the prospect of change, as many of their forebears had in the Civil War era. Yet one of their own with clear voice insisted on the need for change. "Until justice is blind, until education is unaware of race, until opportunity is unconcerned with the color of men's skins, emancipation will be a proclamation but not a fact," noted Vice President Lyndon B. Johnson (LBJ) in July 1963.[11]

More than the well-born, Massachusetts scion President John F. Kennedy (JFK), LBJ as a struggling son of Texas knew about race and poverty close up. He connected to the civil rights struggle personally. JFK's assassination in November 1963 put LBJ in position to turn his feelings into facts. Among his first initiatives, he exhorted Congress to pass far-reaching civil rights legislation JFK had been unable to secure. The legislation became the Civil Rights Act of 1964. Its eleven major parts called "titles" made major changes in law treating voting rights, discrimination in public accommodations, public facilities, and public education. It extended the U.S. Commission on Civil Rights, created in 1957, and created the Equal Employment Opportunity Commission (EEOC). It provided also for preventing discrimination in all federally assisted programs.[12]

The 1964 Civil Rights Act offered the appearance of victory in the long struggle for legal recognition and redress. Public segregation seemed outlawed. Full citizenship for all Americans seemed in the offing. To use the Constitution's phrase, "race, color, or previous condition of servitude" appeared no longer permissible as public bars to the full promise of American life. But the appearance proved illusion, not reality.

Racial resistance persisted. In places it stiffened. Atlanta Pickrick Restaurant owner Lester Maddox, for example, brazenly defied the 1964 act, refusing to serve blacks. (The attention won him Georgia's governorship in 1967.) And from standing in the schoolhouse door to defy federally ordered desegregation, Alabama Governor George C. Wallace took his campaign of "segregation today, segregation tomorrow, segregation forever" national as a 1964 presidential candidate.

Organizing and marching and protesting in an unyielding movement had changed America's law against segregation. Sweat, tears, and blood paid the ongoing price. Violence shadowed the Civil Rights Movement. Murder not infrequently marked the path. NAACP Mississippi field secretary Medgar Evers was shot in his home's driveway in June 1963. In September 1963, a dynamite bomb killed eleven-year-old Denise McNair as well as Cynthia Wesley, Carole Robertson, and Addie Mae Collins, all fourteen years old, at Birmingham's 16th Street Baptist Church. Civil rights workers James Earl Chaney, Andrew Goodman, and Michael Henry Schwerner were murdered on a Mississippi highway in June 1964. Viola Liuzzo and James J. Reeb were killed in the advent and aftermath of the so-called Bloody Sunday voting rights march in Selma, Alabama, in March 1965.

Outside the South, blacks showed spreading frustration at the racial subordination that persisted as America's standard practice. In July 1964, New York City's Harlem erupted after an off-duty policeman shot a fifteen-year-old black boy. Upstate, almost at the same time, an arrest of a seventeen-year-old black boy tipped Rochester to rioting. In August 1965, an arrest of a black man reportedly for drunk driving in Los Angeles's Watts district ignited six days of rioting that killed 34 persons, injured another 1,100, and cost an estimated $100 million in damage. While Watts burned, Chicago's Garfield Park neighborhood also erupted. What became feared as long, hot summers of racial unrest in American cities were under way.

Taunts of "Burn baby, burn" joined rising choruses of "Black Power" that former SNCC chairman Stokely Carmichael (later Kwame Turé) popularized in 1966. Bloody race rioting marred 1967 as fifty-nine riots erupted. Six days of rioting in Newark, New Jersey, killed 26 persons and injured at least 1,500 others. The deadliest riot was in Detroit, where 43 persons were killed. Stopping the violence took 4,700 U.S. Army troops. As he reluctantly despatched the troops, President Johnson appointed a National Advisory Commission on Civil Disorders to identify what happened and why, so as to quell repetition. The commission became known popularly as the Kerner Commission, after its chairman, Illinois Governor Otto Kerner. Seven months of investigation led the commission to conclude that the riots resulted from a worsening racial climate.

Frustrated blacks shunted into the nation's inner cities revolted at the dehumanizing deprivations of de facto segregation. Changes in law were not enough. Nor were President Johnson's 1964 declaration of a War on Poverty and invocations with a Great Society program. Hurting blacks demanded immediate, real-life changes. They wanted what the 1963 March on Washington had demanded—jobs and freedom. They wanted an end to their chronic poverty. They wanted an end to their always high unemployment and their poor education that contributed to their lack of decent jobs. They wanted better housing and health care. Most basically, they wanted human recognition and respect. An immediate rub was systematic police bias and brutality that so often triggered rioting. Black demands generated retorts from more than old-line segregationists who sneered, "What do blacks want now?" In a sentence that became its signature conclusion, the 1968 Kerner Commission *Report* warned that the nation was "moving toward two societies, one black, one white—separate and unequal."[13]

America's direction in race relations was at issue. Heartening change had occurred. The nation's images and institutions had taken on color since the lily-white-only days of World War II. The U.S. Armed Forces had desegregated. Jackie Robinson and Larry Doby broke Major League Baseball's color barrier in 1947. With them the complexion of American team sports shifted. Boxers such as heavyweight champions Jack Johnson and "Brown Bomber" Joe Louis and the 1936 Olympic track and field champion Jesse Owens had topped individual arenas. But segregation had excluded interracial teams—until the Brooklyn Dodgers played Robinson and the Cleveland Indians played Doby. The result showed in professional basketball (National Basketball Association [NBA]) and football (National Football League [NFL]). Cassius Clay's defeating world heavyweight boxing champion Sonny Liston in February 1964 and announcing himself a follower of the Nation of Islam to be called Muhammad Ali marked another new day for the nation. Ali exulted that he "shook up the world." In fact, much was shaken or at least stirred. Public school desegregation was changing college sports. A watershed fell in the 1966 National Collegiate Athletic Association (NCAA) Division I men's basketball championship when the all-black Texas Western (later Texas–El Paso) University squad beat segregationist Adolph Rupp's all-white, perennial powerhouse University of Kentucky team 72–65. On stage, screen, and television, professional entertainment also reflected a desegregating America. The nation's sights and sounds had become more colorful.

Government itself mirrored the change. In 1966 Massachusetts elected its former attorney general Edward W. Brooke the first black U.S. senator since Reconstruction and the first elected outside the South. That same year, President Johnson appointed Robert C. Weaver as the first black to hold a cabinet position. In 1968, New York's 12th Congressional District elected Shirley Chisholm the first black woman in the U.S. Congress. A surge in black voter registration in the South put blacks in local and statewide offices. Such change unsettled much. It was too slow and shallow from one perspective and too fast and far-reaching from another perspective.

"Where do we go from here—Chaos or Community?" Martin Luther King Jr. used that question as a 1967 book title.[14] It became no rhetorical query as events unfolded in 1968. King's evolving vision of civil rights had moved him to oppose the war in Vietnam and to press a Poor People's Campaign that aimed to emulate the 1963 March on Washington. His developing view of the need for economic justice put him on the road to support 1,300 striking black sanitation workers in Memphis, Tennessee. There at the Lorraine Motel on April 4, 1968, an assassin's bullet ended his life. At the news, rioting rocked more than 100 U.S. cities. The nation's capital itself went ablaze for three days with 12 killed, more than 1,200 reported injured, and about $30 million in damages. Frustration eclipsed hope among many, leaving the nation's race relations teetering on King's unanswered question.

NOTES

1. *Korematsu v. United States*, 323 U.S. 214, 242 (1944) (Murphy, J., dissenting).

2. Quoted in Alfred McClung Lee and Norman Humphrey, *Race Riot* (New York: Dryden Press, 1943), 141.

3. "Platform of the States Rights Democratic Party Unanimously Adopted at Oklahoma City, August 14, 1948," in Donald Bruce Johnson, *National Party Platforms, 1840–1972*, 5th ed. (Urbana: University of Illinois Press, 1973), 653; Emile B. Ader, "Why the Dixiecrats Failed," *Journal of Politics* 15 (1953): 356–369.

4. *Brown v. Board of Education*, 347 U.S. 483, 495 (1954). The D.C. case was *Bolling v. Sharpe*, 347 U.S. 497 (1954). See also *Brown v. Board of Education of Topeka*, 349 U.S. 294 (1955), called *Brown II*.

5. *Cooper v. Aaron*, 358 U.S. 1 (1958).

6. *Browder v. Gayle*, 142 F.Supp. 708 (M.D. Ala. 1956).

7. Celeste Michelle Condit and John Louis Lucaites, "Malcolm X and the Limits of the Rhetoric of Revolutionary Dissent," *Journal of Black Studies* 23 (1993): 292.

8. 364 U.S. 454 (1960) (reversing conviction of a black charged with trespassing in a "whites only" restaurant in the Richmond, Virginia, Trailways Bus Terminal).

9. Ed Clayton, *Martin Luther King, Jr.: The Peaceful Warrior* (New York: Pocket Books, 1968).

10. Ibid.

11. Press Release, "5/30/63, Remarks by Vice President, Memorial Day, Gettysburg, Pennsylvania," Statements File, Box 80, Lyndon Baines Johnson Library, University of Texas, Austin.

12. Civil Rights Act of 1964, Pub. L. No. 88-352 (July 2, 1964).

13. *Report of the National Advisory Commission on Civil Disorders* (New York: Dutton, 1968), 2.

14. Martin Luther King Jr., *Where Do We Go from Here: Chaos or Community?* (New York: Harper & Row, 1967).

DOCUMENTS

10.1.   "Basic civil rights," 1948

President Harry S Truman (1884–1972) sent Congress a special message with an ambitious ten-point program on civil rights in February 1948. Venturing where no president ever had, he openly confronted racial segregation. He called for an antilynching law, an anti–poll tax law, home rule for the District of Columbia, a U.S. Commission on Civil Rights, a permanent Fair Employment Practices Commission (FEPC), and desegregation of the armed forces, among other things. What he called for was realized in time. But he was far ahead of that time, and he knew it. His diary entry on the morning he sent his message anticipated Congress's rejection: "They, no doubt, will receive it as coldly as they did the State of the Union Message. But it needs to be said," he wrote.

In the State of the Union Message on January 7, 1948, I spoke of five great goals toward which we should strive in our constant effort to strengthen our democracy and improve the welfare of our people. The first of these is to secure fully our essential human rights. . . .

This Nation was founded by men and women who sought these shores that they might enjoy greater freedom and greater opportunity than they had known before. The founders of the United States proclaimed to the world the American belief that all men are created equal, and that governments are instituted to secure the inalienable rights with which all men are endowed.

In the Declaration of Independence and the Constitution of the United States, they eloquently expressed the aspirations of . . . mankind for equality and freedom. . . .

We believe that all men are created equal and that they have the right to equal justice under law.

We believe that all men have the right to freedom of thought and of expression and the right to worship as they please.

We believe that all men are entitled to equal opportunities for jobs, for homes, for good health and for education.

We believe that all men should have a voice in their government and that government should protect, not usurp, the rights of the people.

These are the basic civil rights which are the source and the support of our democracy. . . .

The Federal Government has a clear duty to see that Constitutional guarantees of individual liberties and of equal protection under the laws are not denied or abridged anywhere in our Union. That duty is shared by all three branches of the Government, but it can be fulfilled only if the Congress enacts modern, comprehensive civil rights laws, adequate to the needs of the day, and demonstrating our continuing faith in the free way of life.

I recommend, therefore, that the Congress enact legislation at this session directed toward the following specific objectives:

1. Establishing a permanent Commission on Civil Rights, a Joint Congressional Committee on Civil Rights, and a Civil Rights Division in the Department of Justice.

2. Strengthening existing civil rights statues.

3. Providing Federal protection against lynching.

4. Protecting more adequately the right to vote.

5. Establishing a Fair Employment Practices Commission to prevent unfair discrimination in employment.

6. Prohibiting discrimination in interstate transportation facilities.

7. Providing home-rule and suffrage in Presidential elections for the residents of the District of Columbia.

8. Providing Statehood for Hawaii and Alaska and a greater measure of self-government for our island possessions.

9. Equalizing the opportunities for residents of the United States to become naturalized citizens.

10. Settling the evacuation claims of Japanese-Americans.

Source: Special Message to the Congress on Civil Rights (February 2, 1948), in *Public Papers of the Presidents of the United States: Harry S. Truman 1948* (Washington, DC: GPO, 1963), 121–126.

10.2.   "Separate educational facilities are inherently unequal," 1954

In one of its most momentous decisions, the U.S. Supreme Court in May 1954 unraveled de jure racial segregation in public schools. Brown v. Board of Education *indeed left long lines of bitter battles. Some deemed it a start to a second American Civil War. It was surely a major move toward outlawing de jure racial segregation in every aspect of American life. It occasioned both massive resistance and mass demonstrations pressing blacks' call for full civil rights. It carried a potent message at a telling moment in U.S. race relations.*

We come then to the question presented: Does segregation of children in public schools solely on the basis of race, even though the physical facilities and other "tangible" factors may be equal, deprive the children of the minority group of equal educational opportunities? We believe that it does. . . .

To separate [children] from others of similar age and qualifications solely because of their race generates a feeling of inferiority as to their status in the community that may affect their hearts and minds in a way unlikely ever to be undone. The effect of this separation on their educational opportunities was well stated by a finding in the Kansas case by a court which nevertheless felt compelled to rule against the Negro plaintiffs. . . . Whatever may have been the extent of psychological knowledge at the time of Plessy v. Ferguson, this finding is amply supported by modern authority. Any language in Plessy v. Ferguson contrary to this finding is rejected.

We conclude that in the field of public education the doctrine of "separate but equal" has no place. Separate educational facilities are inherently unequal. Therefore, we hold that the plaintiffs and others similarly situated for whom the actions have been brought are, by reason of the segregation complained of, deprived of the equal protection of the laws.

Source: *Brown v. Board of Education of Topeka*, 347 U.S. 483, 493–495 (1954). (Citations omitted.)

10.3.   "The unwarranted decision of the Supreme Court," 1956

Georgia Democrat U.S. Senator Walter F. George (1878–1957) presented the statement dubbed "The Southern Manifesto" in March 1956. He and eighteen other senators endorsed it. So did eighty-one members of the U.S. House of Representatives. Responding to the "segregation cases," as many then called Brown v. Board of Education *(1954), the endorsers offered a southern state's rights view resting on their interpretation of the U.S. Constitution and on long custom and tradition. Resistance was their watchword. Violence was in the offing, they said, although they pointedly counseled those whom they called "our people" to "scrupulously refrain from disorder and lawless acts."*

DECLARATION OF CONSTITUTIONAL PRINCIPLES

The unwarranted decision of the Supreme Court in the public school cases is now bearing the fruit always produced when men substitute naked power for established law. . . .

We regard the decisions of the Supreme Court in the school cases as a clear abuse of judicial power. It climaxes a trend in the Federal Judiciary undertaking to legislate, in derogation of the authority of Congress, and to encroach upon the reserved rights of the States and the people.

The original Constitution does not mention education. Neither does the 14th Amendment nor any other amendment. The debates preceding the submission of the 14th Amendment clearly show that there was no intent that it should affect the system of education maintained by the States.

The very Congress which proposed the amendment subsequently provided for segregated schools in the District of Columbia.

When the amendment was adopted in 1868, there were 37 States of the Union. . . . Every one of the 26 States that had any substantial racial differences among its people, either approved the operation of segregated schools already in existence or subsequently established such schools by action of the same law-making body which considered the 14th Amendment. . . .

Though there has been no constitutional amendment or act of Congress changing this established legal principle almost a century old, the Supreme Court of the United States, with no legal basis for such action, undertook to exercise their naked judicial power and substituted their personal political and social ideas for the established law of the land.

This unwarranted exercise of power by the Court, contrary to the Constitution, is creating chaos and confusion in the States principally affected. It is destroying the amicable relations between the white and Negro races that have been created through 90 years of patient effort by the good people of both races. It has planted hatred and suspicion where there has been heretofore friendship and understanding. . . .

We pledge ourselves to use all lawful means to bring about a reversal of this decision which is contrary to the Constitution and to prevent the use of force in its implementation.

In this trying period, as we all seek to right this wrong, we appeal to our people not to be provoked by the agitators and troublemakers invading our States and to scrupulously refrain from disorder and lawless acts.

Source: 102 Cong. Rec. 4459–4460 (March 12, 1956).

10.4.   "Segregation forever," 1963

Alabama's George Corley Wallace (1919–1998) cast himself for a time as a symbol of segregation and, moreover, of defiance to federal desegregation mandates. His populist oratory dredged the South's rebel traditions on race and the meaning of America itself. To that tradition he added a theme of anticommunism. As governor in June 1963, he stood in the schoolhouse door to block black students from enrolling at the University of Alabama. He ran for president in 1964 to protest President Lyndon B. Johnson's civil rights stand. The sweep of Wallace's appeal showed in 1968. As the American Independent Party presidential candidate, he won 9.9 million votes, 13 percent nationally, and captured majorities in five southern states that yielded him forty-six electoral votes. Wounds from an attempted assassination during his 1972 presidential bid permanently paralyzed him below the waist. His first gubernatorial inaugural displayed his popular segregationist views.

Today I have stood, where once Jefferson Davis stood, and took an oath to my people. It is very appropriate then that from this Cradle of the Confederacy, this very Heart of the Great Anglo-Saxon Southland, that today we sound the drum for freedom as have our generations of forebears before us done, time and time again through history. . . . In the name of the greatest people that have ever trod this earth, I draw the line in the dust and toss the gauntlet before the feet of tyranny and I say segregation today, segregation tomorrow, segregation forever. . . .

The true brotherhood of America, of respecting the separateness of others and uniting in effort has been so twisted and distorted from its original concept that there is a small wonder that communism is winning the world.

We invite the negro citizens of Alabama to work with us from his separate racial station as we will work with him to develop, to grow in individual freedom and enrichment. We want jobs and a good future for BOTH races. . . . This is the basic heritage of my religion, in which I make full practice, for we are all the handiwork of God.

But we warn those, of any group, who would follow the false doctrine of communistic amalgamation that we will not surrender our system of government, our freedom of race and religion. That freedom was won at a hard price and if it requires a hard price to retain it, we are able and quite willing to pay it.

Source: Governor George C. Wallace, Inaugural Address (January 14, 1963), Alabama Governor, Inaugural Addresses and Programs, SP194, Alabama Department of Archives and History, Montgomery.

10.5.   "We are confronted primarily with a moral issue," 1963

> *Responding to Alabama Governor George C. Wallace's stand in the schoolhouse door in June 1963, President John F. Kennedy (1917–1963) delivered a radio and television address on civil rights to the nation. The country faced a moral crisis, the president said. Congress needed to respond by enacting legislation (what would become the Civil Rights Act of 1964). "But legislation," he advised, "cannot solve this problem alone. It must be solved in the homes of every American in every community across our country." Kennedy couched his call for civil rights in the context of both the Cold War struggle against communism and America's egalitarian principles laid out in the Declaration of Independence.*

This afternoon, following a series of threats and defiant statements, the presence of Alabama National Guardsmen was required on the University of Alabama. . . .

I hope that every American, regardless of where he lives, will stop and examine his conscience about this and other related incidents. This Nation was founded by men of many nations and backgrounds. It was founded on the principle that all men are created equal, and that the rights of every man are diminished when the rights of one man are threatened. . . .

This is not a sectional issue. Difficulties over segregation and discrimination exist in every city, in every State of the Union, producing in many cities a rising tide of discontent that threatens the public safety. Nor is this a partisan issue. In a time of domestic crisis men of good will and generosity should be able to unite regardless of party or politics. This is not even a legal or legislative issue alone. It is better to settle these matters in the courts than on the streets, and new laws are needed at every level, but law alone cannot make men see right.

We are confronted primarily with a moral issue. It is as old as the scriptures and is as clear as the American Constitution.

The heart of the question is whether all Americans are to be afforded equal rights and equal opportunities, whether we are going to treat our fellow Americans as we want to be treated. If an American, because his skin is dark, cannot eat lunch in a restaurant open to the public, if he cannot send his children to the best public school available, if he cannot vote for the public officials who will represent him, if, in short, he cannot enjoy the full and free life which all of us want, then who among us would be content to have the color of his skin changed and stand in his place? Who among us would then be content with the counsels of patience and delay?

One hundred years of delay have passed since President Lincoln freed the slaves, yet their heirs, their grandsons, are not fully free. They are not yet freed from the bonds of injustice. They are not yet freed from social and economic oppression. And this Nation, for all its hopes and all its boasts, will not be fully free until all its citizens are free.

We preach freedom around the world, and we mean it, and we cherish our freedom here at home, but are we to say to the world, and much more importantly, to each other that this is the land of the free except for the Negroes; that we have no second-class citizens except Negroes; that we have no class or caste system, no ghettoes, no master race except with respect to Negroes?

Now the time has come for this Nation to fulfill its promise. . . .

My fellow Americans, this is a problem which faces us all—in every city of the North as well as the South. Today there are Negroes unemployed, two or three times as many compared to whites, inadequate in education, moving into the large cities, unable to find work, young people particularly out of work without hope, denied equal rights, denied the opportunity to eat at a restaurant or lunch counter or go to a movie theater, denied the right to a decent education, denied almost today the right to attend a State university even though qualified. . . .

We cannot say to 10 percent of the population that you can't have that right; that your children cannot have the chance to develop whatever talents they have; that the only way that they are going to get their rights is to go into the streets and demonstrate. I think we owe them and we owe ourselves a better country than that. . . .

We have a right to expect that the Negro community will be responsible, will uphold the law, but they have a right to expect that the law will be fair, that the Constitution will be color blind, as Justice Harlan said at the turn of the century.

Source: President John F. Kennedy, Radio and Television Report to the American People on Civil Rights, The White House, June 11, 1963, transcript, John Fitzgerald Kennedy Library–Columbia Point, Boston, MA.

10.6.   "The Negro today asks justice," 1963

Vice President Lyndon B. Johnson (1908–1973) marked the centennial of the bloody July 1863 Civil War battle at Gettysburg, Pennsylvania, and the centennial of the Emancipation Proclamation by asking all Americans to focus on a responsible society's duty to remedy its history of racial injustice and inequality. He called for present and persevering action based on American principle to do justice to blacks.

On this hallowed ground, heroic deeds were performed and eloquent words were spoken a century ago....

We are called to honor our own words of reverent prayer with resolution in the deeds we must perform to preserve peace and the hope of freedom....

One hundred years ago, the slave was freed.

One hundred years later, the Negro remains in bondage to the color of his skin.

The Negro today asks justice.

We do not answer him—we do not answer those who lie beneath this soil—when we reply to the Negro by asking, "Patience."

It is empty to plead that the solution to the dilemmas of the present rests on the hands of the clock. The solution is in our hands. Unless we are willing to yield up our destiny of greatness among the civilizations of history, Americans—white and Negro together—must be about the business of resolving the challenge which confronts us now.

Our nation found its soul in honor on these fields of Gettysburg one hundred years ago. We must not lose that soul in dishonor now on the fields of hate.

To ask for patience from the Negro is to ask him to give more of what he has already given enough. But to fail to ask of him—and of all Americans—perseverance within the processes of a free and responsible society would be to fail to ask what the national interest requires of all its citizens.

The law cannot save those who deny it but neither can the law serve any who do not use it. The history of injustice and inequality is a history of disuse of the law. Law has not failed—and is not failing. We as a nation have failed ourselves by not trusting the law and by not using the law to gain sooner the ends of justice which law alone serves.

If the white over-estimates what he has done for the Negro without the law, the Negro may under-estimate what he is doing and can do for himself with the law.

If it is empty to ask Negro or white for patience, it is not empty—it is merely honest—to ask perseverance. Men may build barricades—and others may hurl themselves against those barricades—but what would happen at the barricades would yield no answers. The answers will only be wrought by our perseverance together. It is deceit to promise more as it would be cowardice to demand less.

In this hour, it is not our respective races which are at stake—it is our nation. Let those who care for their country come forward, North and South, white and Negro, to lead the way through this moment of challenge and decision.

The Negro says, "Now." Others say, "Never." The voice of responsible Americans—the voice of those who died here and the great man who spoke here—their voices say, "Together." There is no other way.

Until justice is blind to color, until education is unaware of race, until opportunity is unconcerned with the color of men's skins, emancipation will be a proclamation but not a fact. To the extent that the proclamation of emancipation is not fulfilled in fact, to that extent we shall have fallen short of assuring freedom to the free.

Source: Press Release, "5/30/63, Remarks by Vice President, Memorial Day, Gettysburg, Pennsylvania," Statements File, Box 80, Lyndon Baines Johnson Library, University of Texas, Austin.

ANNOTATED RESEARCH GUIDE

Books

Dudziak, Mary L. *Cold War Civil Rights: Race and the Image of American Democracy*. Princeton, NJ: Princeton University Press, 2002. Shows race as a strategic battleground in the superpower struggle that moved the United States to posture on the world stage in highlighting its better treatment of blacks as a promise of sincere friendship for Third World nations and peoples.

Fredrickson, Kari A. *The Dixiecrat Revolt and the End of the Solid South, 1932–1968*. Chapel Hill: University of North Carolina Press, 2001. Narrates the Dixiecrats' rise and repercussions from the 1930s and 1940s to the new southern Republican party in the 1960s with its old resistance to civil rights and racial change.

Gardner, Michael R. *Harry Truman and Civil Rights: Moral Courage and Political Risk*. Carbondale: Southern Illinois University Press, 2002. Highlights the Missourian as an unlikely but wholehearted champion of civil rights who pushed the U.S. Armed Forces to desegregate and laid the basis for progress in race relations in the 1950s and 1960s.

Klarman, Michael J. *From Jim Crow to Civil Rights: The Supreme Court and the Struggle for Racial Equality*. New York: Oxford University Press, 2004. Detailed probe of the political and social context of the high Court's rulings on race from 1896 to 1954, with an eye on their consequences and particularly violent confrontations that they provoked.

Kluger, Richard. *Simple Justice: The History of Brown v. Board of Education and Black America's Struggle for Equality*. New York: Knopf, 1976. Classic analysis and chronicle of the seminal case that marked the conclusion of more than a half century of work against separate but equal and the commencement of at least another half century of trying to realize equality as the basis of race relations.

Kryder, Daniel. *Divided Arsenal: Race and the American State during World War II*. New York: Cambridge University Press, 2000. Examines race relations in the U.S. military and broader society, describing the causes and consequences of race management policies and growing black discontent during World War II.

Mann, Robert. *The Walls of Jericho: Lyndon Johnson, Hubert Humphrey, Richard Russell, and the Struggle for Civil Rights*. New York: Harcourt, 1996. A former U.S. Senate press secretary reveals the behind-the-scenes fifteen-year battle that produced the 1964 Civil Rights Act.

McWhorter, Diane. *Carry Me Home: Birmingham, Alabama: The Climactic Battle of Civil Rights Revolution*. New York: Simon & Schuster, 2001. Discusses the southern Civil Rights Movement of the 1950s and 1960s from the perspective of hometown whites struggling with their own visions of self, society, and political position.

Rosenberg, Jonathan, and Zachary Karabell. *Kennedy, Johnson, and the Quest for Justice: The Civil Rights Tapes*. New York: W. W. Norton, 2003. Uses actual White House transcripts to show the presidential give-and-take to combat anti–civil rights racial violence in the two years before the Civil Rights Act of 1964.

Web Sites

http://pbsvideodb.pbs.org/resources/eyes/—links to *Eyes on the Prize*, a fourteen-part, critically acclaimed Public Broadcasting Service series (produced by Blackside Inc.) on the Civil Rights Movement. It aired first in January and February of 1987 with six programs titled *Eyes on the Prize: America's Civil Rights Years (1954–1965)*.

http://www.civilrights.org/research_center/civilrights101/desegregation.html—provides source for civil rights chronology and information on and texts of the various legal cases in the desegregation fight.

http://www.trumanlibrary.org/deseg1.htm—provides materials on the Truman administration and the desegregation of the U.S. Armed Forces.

11

Wounded Knee Again: The New Indian, Reservations, and Casinos

Race relations with Indians in the United States pivoted again in the 1960s and 1970s. "Red Power" echoed as a companion slogan to "Black Power" as Native Americans voiced their particular, persistent grievances. A Pan-Indian or supratribal sentiment galvanized collective action. It evoked the incipient strategic efforts of Ottawa Chief Pontiac (1720–1769) and Shawnee Chief Tecumseh (1768–1813) to forge intertribal alliances to repel advancing white occupation and to recapture traditional lands and ways of living. Responding to damage and distress to their collective and individual selves, Indians reaffirmed their tribal traditions, revived their sacred practices and rituals, and insisted on their legal rights.

American Indians had endured their historic nadir around the turn of the nineteenth century when the U.S. Census counted them as a mere 237,196 persons. Many then declared Indians on the road to extinction. What the popular press preferred to call Geronimo's "capture" in 1886—along with the official pronouncement of the closing of the frontier and the suppression of the Ghost Dance with the Wounded Knee massacre in 1890—marked the elimination of the "hostiles" in popular American imagination. In that vision, Indians became a vanishing breed slated for a path to oblivion—just as many had viewed the Negro as slated for extinction after abolition of slavery.

Indians, like blacks, managed to survive beyond popular expectations or hopes. The U.S. Census of 2000 counted the American Indian and Alaska Native population at 4.1 million (2.5 million reporting only Indian heritage and 1.6 million reporting mixed heritage).[1] The increase of 516,722, or 26 percent, between 1990 and 2000 was more than double the total number of Indians reported in 1900. Yet, again, like African Americans, American Indians had hardly thrived collectively. When compared with the general U.S. population at the middle of the twentieth century, Indians had far lower educational levels, higher unemployment rates, lower life expectancy at birth, and rampant preventable causes of death—from diseases of the heart, malignant tumors, diabetes, and cirrhosis and other chronic liver diseases.

In the era of strict racial segregation called American apartheid, Indians had remained shunted in a peculiar status outside the U.S. body politic. Almost at the same time that U.S. Chief Justice Roger B. Taney declared in the infamous 1857 Dred Scott Case that blacks were not and could never be U.S. citizens, U.S. Attorney General Caleb Cushing ruled that "Indians are domestic subjects of this Government . . . who are not therefore citizens."[2] While others born in the United States thereby became citizens under the Fourteenth Amendment, ratified in 1868, Indians were excluded from that citizenship provision, as the U.S. Supreme Court confirmed in *Elk v. Wilkins* (1884). Moreover, U.S. law barred Indians from naturalization open to foreigners. Only with the Indian Citizenship Act of 1924 did Congress provide finally that all "Indians born within the territorial limits of the United States" would be U.S. citizens.[3]

The impetus for the 1924 act was Congress's continuing assimilation policy. The idealized vision of absorbing Indians into an undifferentiated American mainstream had persisted as national policy. Not until the Indian Reorganization Act of 1934 initiated a so-called New Deal for Indians did Congress detour from what Department of the Interior official Lewis Meriam regarded as the failed assimilation policy of the Dawes General Allotment Act of 1887, which aimed to sever Indians from tribes. By treating Indians only as individuals, the Dawes Act aimed to destroy tribal relations and thus the tribes themselves.

The famous 1928 Meriam Report to the secretary of the interior on the economic and social condition of the American Indians significantly shifted the federal approach to better appreciating tribal substance and structures. The full force of the shift showed in the 1934 act, also called the Wheeler-Howard Indian Self-Government Act, for its sponsors U.S. Senator Burton K. Wheeler (Republican–MT) and U.S. Representative Edgar Howard (Democrat–NE). It pledged federal policy to promote the reconstitution of tribal government.

While shifting means and some ends, the 1934 act persisted in the aim of reducing federal costs for reservation administration by making Indians self-sufficient. Rather than the New England family farm model of the 1887 Dawes Act, the 1934 reorganization act broadened the scope for developing Indian lands and resources. It encouraged business formation to exploit market potential. It offered a credit system to provide seed capital for enterprises. And it provided for vocational education for training. Most important of all from the Indian perspective, the 1934 act provided for "Home Rule to Indians." It recognized tribal sovereignty and each tribe's "right to organize for its common welfare." In short, the act aimed "to grant to Indians living under Federal tutelage the freedom to organize for purposes of local self-government and economic enterprise."[4]

Since the U.S. founding, Indian independence, self-government, and sovereignty had consistently clashed as values and as realities with popular and political notions of American community and constitutional relations. So it was again following the 1934 act. By 1940, Congress had retreated from the autonomy it promised Indians in 1934. Fears found voice in Congress that the 1934 act aided Indians to "set up a state or nation within a nation."[5] President Andrew Jackson and others had uttered similar apprehensions in the advent and wake of the Indian Removal Act of 1830. Again, 100 years later, U.S. officials raised anxieties about Indian independence being "contrary to the intents and purposes of the American Republic."[6] So tribal sovereignty and especially tribes' authority to apply their own laws on their own lands and to their own members receded as federal policy. Total assimilation returned.

An apparent majority in Congress arose in the 1940s to remove Indian tribes and members to a position that allowed them to participate in "government in the same way as any domestic organization exists within a State or Commonwealth but not to be independent or apart therefrom."[7] Georgia had insisted on the same principle in the 1820s, when it moved against the Cherokee and other Indians. Removal had resulted in the infamous Trail of Tears. Pursuing what appeared to many as a new version of the old assimilation policy, Congress moved to terminate federal supervision over reservations. Indeed, a 1949 federal study recommended that the federal government transfer to the states all relations with Indians.[8] The proposed policy aimed to make Indians indistinguishable Americans "subject to the same laws and entitled to the same privileges and responsibilities" as all other U.S. citizens, as one congressional resolution declared in 1953.[9] At the same time, Congress enacted what became known as Public Law 280. It allowed states to exercise authority in Indian country. In fact, in many ways it put Indians under state jurisdiction.[10]

In 1954 the Department of the Interior, which housed the Bureau of Indian Affairs (BIA), began to withdraw aid and assistance from Indian groups deemed capable of self-governance. Loathed and loved from its inception in 1824, the BIA and its predecessors—starting in 1775 with the Continental Congress's Committee on Indian Affairs that Benjamin Franklin headed—administered almost every aspect of federal relations with Indians. From land to trade and transport, to supply of government provisions and services, it served as the federal agency for Indian affairs. Until the 1900s, perhaps only the War Department had closer contact with what the popular press often dubbed the "Indian problem."

The BIA grew to administer and manage more than 55 million acres of Indian trust lands. It acted as the Indians' leasing agent for lands and resources. It directed agricultural programs and was charged to protect Indians' water and land rights. It was also to aid and assist American Indians' and Alaska Natives' economic development. It supervised any effort to develop and maintain infrastructure on Indian lands. It was also to provide for health and human services. The BIA's extensive responsibilities and relatively meager federal funds made it a magnet for controversy and assertions of mismanagement. Indeed, charges of incompetence and corruption plagued the BIA, as they had Indian agents in the old West. The BIA's fundamental character remained in question. Was it an advocate for Indians or an enforcement agent for federal policy? It seemed perennially unable to satisfy any constituency.

Congress's reverting to an assimilation policy put further pressures on the BIA in the 1950s. In part paralleling blacks' civil rights demands, Indians found themselves faced with unwelcome calls in Congress for "complete integration."

Congress pushed the BIA to effectively decommission itself by moving to relinquish supervision over reservations. The push aimed to terminate federal
recognition of Indians. It encouraged Indians to leave reservations for city life.
Indeed, BIA relocation centers and grants acted as magnets to multiply Indian
populations in Chicago, Los Angeles, Minneapolis, Phoenix, Seattle, and other
urban centers. By 1985, less than half of American Indians would live on reservations. But the reservations did remain, to the consternation of the 1950s planners who aimed to make them go away in something of a reprise of the 1887
Dawes plan. The aim was to make Indians no longer exist officially. The plan,
as a 1953 congressional resolution suggested, was by decree to make Indians
indistinguishable Americans "subject to the same laws and entitled to the same
privileges and responsibilities."[11]

In the view of many, the 1950s federal rhetoric of integrating the Indian
masked a reality of cutting off selected tribes and groups not only from trust
supervision but also from essential services. The federal government appeared
again to be reneging on its promised relationship with, and responsibilities to,
Indians. In its treaties and historical pronouncements, the United States had
pledged itself to act in perpetuity as the guardian of Indians and to act in equity for Indians' benefit. In the 1950s the push appeared for the federal government to renounce guardianship and trusteeship. It sought to sever its special
relationship with Indians. That emerging framework set up a fresh round of
clashes.

Activists mounted the battle amid the Civil Rights Movement in the 1960s.
They combined resurgent ethnic pride among Indians to challenge federal Indian policy and practice. Their campaign aimed to reverse Indians' desperate
position within the United States. They especially targeted disease, illiteracy,
isolation, and poverty. Efforts centered on reorganizing Indian communities
politically and economically so as to reestablish tribal sovereignty and traditional values, while also developing beneficial market relations for Indian material resources, particularly land and labor.

The founding of the American Indian Movement (AIM) at Minneapolis, Minnesota, in 1968 signaled a new thrust of Red Power. AIM embodied bold militancy and fresh focus in attacking conditions that continued to devastate
Indians. It attended particularly to those off the reservation sites, where most
Indians were living. AIM laid the blame squarely on federal policy for abysmal
Indian health, education, and welfare. And AIM was hardly alone. Other Indian activists decried reduced federal services and slashed support for Indians. AIM and other Indian activists traced Indians' being in some of the
nation's worst living conditions to the mixed legacy of the Indian Reorganization Act of 1934 and to Congress's begrudging funding of Indian programs and
its delinquent trusteeship.

AIM insisted on immediate remedies. It demanded long-term solutions identified in a four-point platform. It aimed to revitalize traditional Indian cultures
and reestablish tribal autonomy. It asserted Indian legal rights, including those
to restore illegally taken tribal lands. And it aimed to establish Indian economic
independence. The platform sought to elevate successes and eliminate failures.
On lands under the Indian Claims Commission Act of 1946, tribes had begun
to reassert their property rights. Several won significant legal judgments that

returned lands to them or paid them for lands taken without adequate compensation. Among the monetary winners were two tribes from the "Trail of Tears" era of the 1830s and 1840s—the Cherokee Nation, awarded $14.8 million, and the Seminole, awarded $12.3 million. Other notable awards included the Crow tribe's $10.2 million, the Snake-Paiute of Oregon's $3.65 million, and the Nez Percé's $3 million.

To publicize the continuing failure of federal policy, AIM organized mass demonstrations and protests. It used symbolic events to motivate individual ethnic renewal and to produce publicity for systemic reforms. It grabbed national and international headlines in November 1969 by seizing Alcatraz Island in California's San Francisco Bay. It held the former federal prison site known as "the Rock" for nineteen months until June 1971. AIM again garnered attention in 1972 with what it called the "Trail of Broken Treaties" that culminated in a weeklong occupation of BIA offices in Washington, D.C. In February 1973, AIM members seized part of the South Dakota Oglala Sioux Pine Ridge reservation, site of the 1890 Wounded Knee massacre. A seventy-one-day siege followed. Tensions hardly subsided. In June 1975, a shoot-out erupted at Pine Ridge. AIM members faced off against more than 150 agents of the FBI and other national and local agencies. Two FBI agents died in the shooting. AIM co-founder Leonard Peltier was tried and sentenced to two consecutive life terms for the two killings.

While AIM took the warpath, other Indian organizations fought in other ways. Their efforts produced the Native American Rights Fund (NARF), which emerged in 1970 to provide legal services to Indians on a national level. Revitalized confederation sentiment launched the National Tribal Chairman's Association (NTCA) in 1971 to advance common causes. Control of economic resources headed the NTCA agenda. Its coffers and causes profited from developing casino gambling on Indian lands in the 1980s and 1990s. Indian gambling revenues reached $100 million in 1988. In 1993, gambling operations on Indian lands in twenty states took in revenues of about $6 billion. In 2000, the revenues exceeded $8 billion.

The casino bonanza marked a new round of struggles. Tribal sovereignty and treaty rights allowed tribes to offer on their lands gaming banned in the states surrounding them. Their enclaves became fresh magnates that drew many who wanted to take a chance either as investors or players. But gaming was only one of many areas in which Indians exercised their legal options. From insisting on fishing and hunting rights guaranteed by treaty to recovering resources and trust monies, Indians across America pressed their claims.

Indian gaming revenues appeared spectacular, but the benefits were not universal or clear. To start, only one in three Indians belonged to any of the 130 tribes with casinos. The other two in three belonged mostly to tribes locked in poverty. Also, only about 15 of every 100 gaming employees in Indian casinos were Indians. Even among tribes with casinos, economic problems persisted. Unemployment remained high. So did the levels of poverty, welfare rates, and incarceration rates for Native American men.

The poor condition of much of the Indian population contrasted sharply with the rich expectations many conjured. Indeed, casino gambling regenerated tensions between reservations and the states in which the reservations sat. The appearance of Indians' raking in big money hardly soothed neighboring populations or local and state politicians who eyed potential revenues. Cries of unconstitutional preferences for Indians resurfaced as non-Indian populations questioned why Indians were allowed to do what others were prohibited from doing. Centuries of invidious racial discrimination and the historical relationships between the federal government and Indian tribes settled little of the patent resentment. Nor did the idea of Indian autonomy quiet complaints. Assertion of Indian sovereignty in fact fueled anger against Indian self-government and any federal commitment to Indians as a separate and special constituent group.

Indians' places and positions in the American nation thus remained twisted within persistent historical tensions that trapped them as outsiders in the evolving United States. They continued as strangers in their native land. The rationale for Indians' occupying a special place or position in the nation remained a hotly debated issue of public policy. Whether Congress had a unique obligation toward Indians became as much an issue as the question of the character and content of any obligation that existed.

The nation exhibited similar wavering—not to say schizophrenic—treatment as it did with blacks, its other historic minority. Constructing frameworks to fit present relations within historical realities proved both delicate and difficult. America's first peoples continued in many regards captives in a colonialist past and present. Their tribal and territorial sovereignty, their local control, and protections promised them in successive treaties fell into disregard, if not disdain. The federal government asserted rights to exercise absolute authority over Indians without their consent. States too often refused to respect Indians' sovereignty. Indians thus stood as either outsiders or wards. No longer caricatured as fearful savages blocking civilization's progress, Indians sat no less derided as people with undeserved protections unable to cope without special accommodations.

The Indian Civil Rights Act (ICRA) of 1968 illustrated the straits in which external views pushed Indians. The act came with rhetoric of extending the U.S. Constitution's Bill of Rights to cover Indian country. Its supporters in Congress touted it as guaranteeing personal freedoms to Indians and to non-Indians on tribal lands. The reality beneath the rhetoric restricted Indian tribal sovereignty and disregarded Indians' cultural heritage. The ICRA required tribal governments to treat their members not in accord with their own cultural traditions but in accord with the U.S. view of certain basic individual rights. Congress decided the issue. It gave Indians no choice.

An onslaught of federal plenary power from the 1970s onward especially forced Indians to fend for self-definition and self-determination. The more than 300 federally recognized tribes found themselves in varying positions between being fully recognized and respected as units of governments and being merely a marginalized racial minority. Even where Congress retreated from further assault on Indian sovereignty, the Supreme Court took up the cudgel. The Court held, for example, that Indians had no special ceremonial or territorial rights in regard to free exercise of religion.[12] The Court limited tribal jurisdiction and in significant ways reverted to the failed assimilationism of the 1887 Dawes General Allotment Act. Following its 1978 decision in *Oliphant v. Suquamish In-*

dian Tribe, the Court repeatedly refused to recognize Indian sovereignty in Indian country over non-Indians and broadly diminished the geographic reach
of tribal sovereignty. In short, the Court came to recognize little, if any, special
or separate status for Indians. It appeared blind to Indians' historical identity.
Further, while curtailing tribal authority in Indian country, the Court also enlarged state authority.[13]

Moving into the twenty-first century then, American Indians found themselves again struggling to sustain and safeguard their cultural identity and
their communal resources. Gaming revenues, federal and state tax exemptions,
and valuable natural resource rights made Indians targets again for those eager
to milk their riches. Returning to a hoary vision of relations with Indians—one
shared with earlier land grabbers, gold seekers, and trappers—more than a few
Americans at the turn of the century imagined that wealth should flow from
Indians to whites. In that view, the phrase "Indian giver" expressed an accepted truth of race relations: Indians were to be givers. Others were to be tak-
ers. That was clear in the over 2.2 billion acres tribes had ceded to the United
States since 1778.

NOTES

1. Stella U. Ogunwole, "The American Indian and Alaska Native Population: 2000:
Census 2000 Brief," U.S. Census Bureau, http://www.census.gov/prod/2002pubs/
c2kbr01-15.pdf.

2. *Official Opinions of the Attorneys General of the United States* (Washington, DC: GPO,
1856), 7:749. See also *United States v. Rogers*, 45 U.S. 567, 572 (1846) (holding Indians
"subjects" of the U.S. government).

3. 43 Stat. 253 (June 2, 1924). Some Indians were U.S. citizens before 1924 by virtue
of (1) treaties, (2) special federal statutes, (3) military service, (4) acceptance of allot-
ments, or (5) for women, marriage to U.S. citizens.

4. 48 Stat. 984 (June 18, 1934).

5. *Hearings on S. 2103 before the Committee on Indian Affairs*, 76th Cong., 3rd sess.
(1940), quoted in Robert N. Clinton, Nell Jessup Newton, and Monroe E. Price, *American
Indian Law: Cases and Materials*, 3rd ed. (Charlottesville, VA: Michie Company, 1991), 156.
I gratefully thank my Arizona State University College of Law colleague Robert N. Clinton for his generous time and suggestions to aid and direct my understanding of Indian relations.

6. Ibid., 156–157.

7. Ibid., 157.

8. *Report to the Congress by the Commission on Organization of the Executive Branch of
the Government*, H.R. Doc. No. 55 (1949), 65.

9. H. Con. Res. 108, 83rd Cong., 1st sess., quoted in Clinton et al., *American Indian
Law*, 157.

10. 67 Stat. 588 (August 15, 1953).

11. H. Con. Res. 108, 83rd Cong., 1st sess., quoted in Clinton et al., *American Indian
Law*, 157.

12. See *Employment Div. v. Smith*, 494 U.S. 872 (1990) (holding Indians' ceremonial use
of peyote not protected under the Free Exercise Clause); *Lyng v. Northwest Indian Ceme-
tery Protective Ass'n*, 485 U.S. 439 (1988) (holding Indians' sacred area used for ceremonial purposes in a national forest not protected under the Free Exercise Clause from
disturbance by a logging road).

13. *Oliphant v. Suquamish Indian Tribe*, 435 U.S. 191 (1978) (holding that Indian tribes lacked inherent criminal jurisdiction over non-Indians on Indians lands). On diminution, see, for example, *South Dakota v. Yankton Sioux Tribe*, 522 U.S. 329 (1998); *Hagen v. Utah*, 510 U.S. 399 (1994); *Solem v. Bartlett*, 465 U.S. 463 (1984); *Rosebud Sioux Tribe v. Kneip*, 430 U.S. 584 (1977); *DeCoteau v. Dist. County Ct.*, 420 U.S. 425 (1975). See discussion in Clinton, "There Is No Federal Supremacy Clause for Indian Tribes," in *American Indian Law*, 218 ff.

DOCUMENTS

11.1.   "The status of the Indians," 1940

The Wheeler-Howard Act, often called the Indian Reorganization Act (IRA), 48 Stat. 984 (June 18, 1934), reversed the federal policy of seeking to assimilate Indians by dissolving tribal lands into allotted small farm holdings. The IRA reemphasized tribal governance and moved to incorporate such government in market-based management of tribal resources. Critics charged that federal policy recognizing tribal power encouraged communalism and perpetuated dependency. They asserted that the correct federal policy was for government to stop recognizing Indians as groups, to become blind to tribes, and to recognize only individuals. Below the U.S. Senate Committee on Indian Affairs reported its view of the IRA's failings and how to correct them.

Arguments advanced against the Wheeler-Howard Act in general, can be summarized as follows:

1. Acceptance of the act changed the status of the Indians from that of involuntary wardship to voluntary wardship.
2. The act provides for continued wardship of the Indians and gives the Secretary of the Interior increased authority.
3. The act is contrary to the established policy of the Congress of the United States to eventually grant the full rights of citizenship to the Indians.
4. The act provides for only one form of government for the Indians, viz. a communal government, with all property, real and personal, held in common; and it compels the Indians to live in communities segregated from the rest of American citizens.
5. The act itself and the administration of the act violates the rights of citizenship which the Indians have won through long years of efforts.
6. That the Indians prefer to be under the jurisdiction of the laws of the respective States where they reside.

CONCLUSION

Fundamentally the so-called Wheeler-Howard Act attempts to set up a state or a nation within a nation which is contrary to the intents and purposes of the American Republic. No doubt but that the Indians should be helped and given every assistance possible but in no way should they be set up as a governing power within the United States of America. They shall be permitted to have a part in their own affairs as to government in the same way as any domestic organization exists within a State or Commonwealth but not to be independent or apart therefrom.

Source: Hearings on S. 2103 before the Committee on Indian Affairs, 76th Cong., 3rd sess. (1940).

11.2.   "No longer a pure ethnic group," 1949

Advocates of treating Indians only as individuals and not as groups recurrently pushed the persistent question of racial identity in regard to Indians. Their basic question was, "Who is an Indian?" The section on Indian Affairs in a 1949 report to Congress from a commission former President Herbert Hoover (1874–1964) headed raised the issue and suggested that treating Indians as a group was impractical and unreasonable.

The Indian population is no longer a pure ethnic group. Rather it represents a melange of "full bloods" and persons of mixed ancestry. Persons classified as Indians under Federal policy and participating in tribal organizations are in many cases not Indians in the complete biological sense. This is illustrated by the following definition of "Indian" taken from the Indian Reorganization Act of 1934, the most recent definitive statement of Federal policy toward the Indians. . . .

The term "Indian" as used in this act shall include all persons of Indian descent who are members of any recognized Indian tribe now under Federal jurisdiction, and all persons who are descendants of such members who were on June 1, 1934, residing within the present boundaries of any Indian reservation, and shall further include all other persons of one-half or more Indian blood. For the purpose of this act, Eskimos and other aboriginal peoples of Alaska shall be considered Indians.

Government records recognize more than 100 tribes under distinct names and approximately 300 other groups who are separated either geographically or by linguistic stock. . . . The Indians' cultural and economic advances vary widely because of many special circumstances—land holdings, utility of land, and others.

Source: The Hoover Commission Report on Organization of the Executive Branch of the Government (New York: McGraw-Hill, 1949), 60–62.

11.3.   "Adequate educational opportunity," 1961

Education has been a much-discussed subject in American race relations. Sometimes as a panacea, sometimes as a more discrete or immediate problem solver, education has been offered as the leg up for the downtrodden or as the light of reason for those afflicted with racial

prejudice. In the following, one American Indian leader—the gover-
nor of the Gila River Pima-Maricopa tribes—offered his view of edu-
cational delivery and responsibilities among Indians and of Indians'
need to raise their educational levels as a means of individual and
tribal development.

I doubt that any of our Indian people could say they are satisfied with the education their tribe is now receiving when information from the 1950 census showed that Indians 25 years of age and older, living on Indian reservations, had on an average of between five and six years of schooling, while the average number of years of schooling for the same age group in the general population was in excess of ten years. . . . Probably less than 40% of Indian youth who enter high school today stay to graduate, while nearly 60% of all American youth now graduate from high school. . . .

What can be done to improve these conditions and whose responsibility is it?

I believe it is a responsibility involving many; namely, the State, the Bureau of Indian Affairs, tribal governments, community and parents, the school, the church and the students themselves. . . .

We place the State first because in this country education has been thought of as a State responsibility. . . .

We find school districts willing to accept Federal funds to build classrooms for Indian students, but unwilling to take into their districts reservation areas where these students live, without which Indians have no guarantee of continued use of such classrooms. . . .

We also look to the Bureau of Indian Affairs to see that our people have adequate educational opportunity and we do not want them to leave us until this opportunity is provided. We shall continue to look to them for help in solution of the foregoing problems and the operation of schools to meet our needs until such time as our people and the public schools are ready for a complete withdrawal of the Bureau. To force people into situations they are not ready for, and in which they are not wanted, will only intensify problems.

Tribal governments must take the lead in informing tribal members of the importance of education, and when possible and necessary give financial assistance. They must also work to raise the economic level of the Indian people, because our social, economic, and educational problems are too interrelated to be solved one at a time. We must advance on all fronts at the same time.

The community must develop a tradition of school attendance and achievement and foster it through parent-teacher groups, community clubs, organizations, churches, etc. Everyone must feel that education is important. Parents must be made to realize the importance of starting children to school at the proper age and seeing that they attend regularly. They must also realize that their responsibility does not end with placing and keeping a child in school. . . .

Schools also have a great responsibility for keeping students in school. Much can be done in this area by providing programs that are interesting and profitable to children with all levels of abilities. Many of our Indian students, as well as other groups, do not perform at the level of high achievement in programs that are geared mainly for non-Indians. . . .

Students themselves must overcome discouragement and prepare themselves for the long years ahead. All of this requires better counseling and guidance. . . .

Local control of schools is desirable. Indians must take an active part in the
support and control of schools. . . .

Perhaps one of the greatest needs of Indian people is a feeling of pride in
the many contributions Indians have made to our American society. The need
is just as great for non-Indians. There should be a place in our school programs
for the teaching of such understandings. Too often exposure to a new culture
has left the Indian with a feeling that all the old is bad. It has also left him un-
convinced that the new is good; therefore, he operates without a strong value
system. Native Indian Culture had much that was good and certainly that part
should be retained.

We must recognize, accept and defend the principle that man is a human
being entitled to the respect he earns. If we can understand this fact in the sense
that it is a common denominator, then the challenge is to develop the means
of a deeper understanding among all groups.

Source: Nelson Lose, "Why We Need Our Education," *Journal of American Indian Education* 1, no. 3 (May 1962): 23–25.

11.4.   "The overriding sovereignty of the United States," 1978

*The status of Indian tribes has been at issue repeatedly since the
earliest days of the United States. Central to the contention has been
the degree to which Indian tribes have standing as independent and
sovereign governments encompassing distinct cultures and societies
with the capacity and right of self-determination. Attached to that issue
has been the degree to which Indian tribes have legal control over
non-Indians on Indian lands. In 1978, the U.S. Supreme Court reviewed the law to express its view of diminished tribal sovereignty.*

Indian reservations are "a part of the territory of the United States." Indian
tribes "hold and occupy [reservations] with the assent of the United States, and
under their authority." Upon incorporation into the territory of the United
States, the Indian tribes thereby come under the territorial sovereignty of the
United States and their exercise of separate power is constrained so as not to
conflict with the interests of this overriding sovereignty. "[T]heir rights to complete sovereignty, as independent nations, [are] necessarily diminished." . . .

By submitting to the overriding sovereignty of the United States, Indian
tribes therefore necessarily give up their power to try non-Indian citizens of
the United States except in a manner acceptable to Congress. This principle
would have been obvious a century ago when most Indian tribes were characterized by a "want of fixed laws [and] of competent tribunals of justice." It

should be no less obvious today, even though present-day Indian tribal courts embody dramatic advances over their historical antecedents.

Source: *Oliphant v. Suquamish Indian Tribe*, 435 U.S. 191, 209–210 (1978). (Citations omitted.)

11.5.   "Their own innate sovereignty," 1997

Contention over tribal sovereignty intensified in the 1990s. Potential riches on Indian reservations with casino gambling and natural resources, particularly, rejoined the old struggle. With Supreme Court decisions tending to limit Indians' sovereignty, Congress again became a heated forum shaping fundamental relations with Indians. A bill titled the "Tribal Self-Governance Amendments of 1998," introduced in June 1997 in the 105th Congress, offered perspectives on restoring Indian sovereignty. The following House of Representatives report on the bill reviewed the failed termination policies enacted in the 1950s and the longer history of Indian sovereignty to draw correctives and conclusions for future relations.

The nature of Self-Governance is rooted in the inherent sovereignty of American Indian and Alaska Native tribes. From the founding of this nation, Indian tribes and Alaska Native villages have been recognized as "distinct, independent, political communities" exercising powers of self-government, not by virtue of any delegation of powers from the federal government, but rather by virtue of their own innate sovereignty. The tribes' sovereignty predates the founding of the United States and its Constitution and forms the backdrop against which the United States has continually entered into relations with Indian tribes and Native villages.

The present model of tribal Self-Governance arose out of the federal policy of Indian Self-Determination. The modern Self-Determination era began as Congress and contemporary Administrations ended the dubious experiment of Termination which was intended to end the federal trust responsibility to Native Americans.

The centerpiece of the Termination policy, House Concurrent Resolution 108, stated that "Indian Tribes and individual members thereof, should be freed from Federal supervision and control and from all disabilities and limitations specially applicable to Indians." While the intent of this legislation was to free the Indians from federal rule, it also destroyed all protection and benefits they received from the government. The same year, Congress enacted Public Law 280 which further eroded tribal sovereignty by transferring criminal jurisdiction from the federal government and the tribes to the state governments.

As a policy, Termination was a disaster. . . .

Sometimes we need to look to the past in order to understand our proper relationship with Indian tribes. More than two centuries ago, Congress set forth what should be our guiding principles. In 1787, Congress passed the North-west Ordinance. . . . Article Three set forth the Nation's policy towards Indian tribes:

> The utmost good faith shall always be observed towards the Indians; their land and property shall never be taken away from them without their consent * * * but laws founded in justice and humanity shall from time to time be made, for preventing wrongs being done to them * * *.

The founders carefully and wisely chose these principles to govern the conduct of this Nation in its dealing with American Indian tribes. Over the years, these principles have often been forgotten. Self-Government is but one of many ways to honor these principles. . . .

If we are to adhere and remain faithful to the principles that our Founders set forth—the principles of good faith, consent, justice and humanity—then we must continue to promote tribal self-government.

Source: H.R. Rep. No. 105-765 at 54–60 (1997), treating H.R. Res. 1833, 105th Cong. (1997). (Citations omitted.)

11.6.   "Looking for a person of American Indian descent," 2001

The 2000 U.S. Census pushed many race relations issues into sharp relief. Identity was high on the list. Among American Indians it connected with questions about residence and relation to reservations. It connected also with questions about casino gaming, as the May 2001 excerpted California news story from below illustrates.

If you are looking for a person of American Indian descent in San Diego County, you have better odds of finding him off the reservation, a review of the U.S. Census 2000 shows.

Only one of about every eight American Indians lives on one of the county's 18 reservations. . . .

But that's not news to tribal leaders, who say many of their members have left the reservations for better job opportunities and housing elsewhere. One reservation is unoccupied.

"In the past, the reservation was an austere and sparse place," said Mark Macarro, chairman of the Pechanga band, just south of Temecula in Riverside County. "About two or three generations ago many people moved away for jobs and only now are they beginning to come back."

California is now home to more American Indians than any other state, more than 333,000, up from 242,000 in 1990. Oklahoma has the second-largest population of American Indians.

In San Diego County, most of the American Indian population was concentrated in the cities rather than on the reservations, such as San Diego, 7,543; followed by Escondido, 1,646; and Oceanside, 1,370. . . .

Census numbers also suggest that more people are now willing to identify themselves as American Indians.

"I can't see the growth of the population as being a natural increase, but rather seems to indicate a change in people's sense of identity," said Al Schwartz, a professor of American Indian history at Cal State San Marcos. . . .

Overall, the number of people who identified themselves solely as American Indian and Alaska Natives in the United States grew by 26 percent during the 1990s to about 2.5 million last year. Add multicultural categories and the number of people claiming some American Indian ancestry is much larger.

Experts and tribal officials say many areas are getting a boost from American Indians returning to jobs and wealth provided by American Indian casinos, and others reclaiming their heritage. . . .

Tribal leaders say they hope newly built casinos . . . will revitalize their cultures and communities providing jobs, housing, better health care and education for their members.

Source: Edward Sifuentes, "More American Indians Living off Reservations," *The North County Times* (San Diego and Riverside, CA), May 24, 2001.

11.7.   "A person's identity as an Indian," 2002

> *Identity and the process of its official recognition for Indians, again connected to the 2000 U.S. Census, prompted discussion about criteria, which the Bureau of Indian Affairs sought to clarify, as in the following description.*

No single federal or tribal criterion establishes a person's identity as an Indian. Tribal membership is determined by the enrollment criteria of the tribe from which Indian blood may be derived, and this varies with each tribe. Generally, if linkage to an identified tribal member is far removed, one would not qualify for membership.

To be eligible for Bureau of Indian Affairs services, an Indian must (1) be a member of a tribe recognized by the federal government, (2) be of one-half or more Indian blood of tribes indigenous to the United States; or (3) must, for some purposes, be of one-fourth or more Indian ancestry. By legislative and administrative decision, the Aleuts, Eskimos and Indians of Alaska are eligible for BIA services. Most of the BIA's services and programs, however, are limited to Indians living on or near Indian reservations.

The Bureau of the Census counts anyone an Indian who declares himself or herself to be an Indian. In 1990 the Census figures showed there were 1,959,234 American Indians and Alaska Natives living in the United States (1,878,285 American Indians, 57,152 Eskimos, and 23,797 Aleuts). This is a 37.9 percent increase over the 1980 recorded total of 1,420,000. The increase is attributed to improved census taking and more self-identification during the 1990 count. . . .

There are more than 550 federally recognized tribes in the United States, including 223 village groups in Alaska. "Federally recognized" means these tribes and groups have a special, legal relationship with the U.S. government. This relationship is referred to as a government-to-government relationship.

A number of Indian tribes and groups in the U.S. do not have a federally recognized status, although some are state-recognized. This means they have no relations with the BIA or the programs it operates. A special program of the BIA, however, works with those groups seeking federal recognition status. Of the 150 petitions for federal recognition received by the BIA since 1978, 12 have received acknowledgment through the BIA process, two groups had their status clarified by the Department of the Interior through other means, and seven were restored or recognized by Congress.

Source: Bureau of Indian Affairs, U.S. Department of the Interior, "Facts about American Indians Today," http://www.infoplease.com/cgi-bin/id/A0192524.html.

ANNOTATED RESEARCH GUIDE

Books

Grounds, Richard A., et al., eds. *Native Voices: American Indian Identity and Resistance*. Lawrence: University Press of Kansas, 2003. Uses postcolonial theory in Indian-centered discussion of present predicaments and future needs to preserve and nurture Indian culture and community.

Hosmer, Brian, and Colleen O'Neill, eds. *Native Pathways: American Indian Culture and Economic Development in the Twentieth Century*. Boulder: University Press of Colorado, 2004. With historical perspective from the 1870s, casts Indian economic development in the context of modernity and cultural production considering the requirements of capitalism and tribal diversity and interests.

Johnson, Troy, Joane Nagel, and Wayne Champagne, eds. *American Indian Activism: Alcatraz to the Longest Walk*. Urbana: University of Illinois Press, 1997. Essays developing American Indian activism from the 1960s to the 1990s, giving voice to Indian perspectives on persistent problems and their solutions.

Lawrence, Bonita. *"Real" Indians and Others: Mixed-Blood Urban Native Peoples and Indigenous Nationhood*. Lincoln: University of Nebraska Press, 2004. Reconfigures the vanishing race theme to understand negotiated native identities not only off traditional tribal lands but within an urban environment that shifts status and entitlement and demands a reconstituted native community.

Lieder, Michael, and Jake Page. *Wild Justice: The People of Geronimo vs. The United States*. New York: Random House, 1997. Traces the Chiricahua Apache petitions before the Indian Claims Commission (ICC) from 1946 to 1970, illustrating how the claims process did and did not work as a newfound basis for Indian-white relations.

Lyman, Stanley David, et al. *Wounded Knee 1973: A Personal Account*. Lincoln: University of Nebraska Press, 1991. Pine Ridge Reservation Bureau of Indian Affairs superintendent's candid diary of the episode, with background materials.

Pasquaetta, Paul. *Gambling and Survival in Native North America*. Tucson: University of Arizona Press, 2003. Offers frameworks for understanding the meaning of Indian gambling far beyond casinos in reaching back to centuries of struggle over allocation of resources and riches where the usual flow made Indians losers.

Smith, Paul Chaat, and Robert Allen Warrior. *Like a Hurricane: The Indian Movement from Alcatraz to Wounded Knee*. New York: New Press, 1996. Treats the refocusing of national attention on Indians due to acts of radical resistance from 1969 to 1973.

Stern, Kenneth S. *Loud Hawk: United States versus the American Indian Movement*. Norman: University of Oklahoma Press, 1994. A firsthand account by a defense attorney detailing the continuing legal, political, and physical war over Indian self-determination and its elements of tribal sovereignty, economic self-sufficiency, cultural regeneration, and political independence.

Taylor, Theodore W. *The Bureau of Indian Affairs*. Boulder, CO: Westview Press, 1984. Offers a systematic description of BIA functions and structures, along with the interest groups and influences that formed and frustrated policy and practice.

United States House of Representatives. *Misplaced Trust: The Bureau of Indian Affairs' Mismanagement of the Indian Trust Fund: Seventeenth Report by the Committee on Government Operations*. Washington, DC: GPO, 1992. Details billions of dollars lost, if not stolen, from federal trust accounts of Indian property, underscoring contemporary Indian struggles for independent decision-making power and economic self-development.

Web Sites

http://www.aimovement.org/ggc/history.html—this "official Web site" of the American Indian Movement provides history and links to events.

http://www.ojp.usdoj.gov/ovc/help/ncai.htm—site of the National Congress of American Indians, founded in 1944 to serve as a forum for consensus-based policy development among its membership of over 250 tribal governments from every region of the country.

http://www.pbs.org/now/politics/indiangaming.html—provides information on the PBS program "Investigating the Indian Gaming Scandal" (*Now with Bill Moyers*, November 2004) and background on the history and expansion of Indian gaming in America.

12

Affirmative Action and "Reverse Discrimination" Backlash

Outlawing de jure racial segregation in America was one thing. Opening America to racial equality was quite another. Ending racial discrimination required adjusting attitudes, changing behaviors, and reordering basic structures. It reached to individuals and institutions. It encompassed every aspect of American life—the culture, economy, politics, and society. The task's dimensions daunted many. "The final battle against intolerance is to be fought—not in the chambers of any legislature—but in the hearts of men," President Dwight D. Eisenhower admonished as the civil rights efforts of the 1950s crested.[1] "The heart of the question is whether all Americans are to be afforded equal rights and equal opportunities, whether we are going to treat our fellow Americans as we want to be treated," President John F. Kennedy advised in 1963 when sending to Congress what became the Civil Rights Act of 1964. He noted that "law alone cannot make men see right."[2]

The work of getting the law to "see right" on de jure segregation appeared close to finished in 1967 when the U.S. Supreme Court decided *Loving v. Virginia*. The case treated Virginia's antimiscegenation law that criminalized interracial marriage as the ultimate horror of forbidden race-mixing. After decades of upholding such laws, the Court reversed itself and the nation's position on the source of centuries-old racial tensions. Sex, after all, surpassed even schools as a site of segregationist fears. The Court held racial discrimination as evidenced in Virginia's antimiscegenation law to be "odious to a free people." It declared, moreover, that state statutes providing for "invidious racial discrimination" could serve no "rational purpose."[3] Thus, such laws violated the Fourteenth Amendment's prohibition that no state "deny to any person within its jurisdiction equal protection of the laws." The "separate but equal" rule *Plessy v. Ferguson* ratified in 1896 and that *Brown v. Board of Educa-*

tion rejected in 1954 in public schooling was now rejected completely. America appeared finally and fully to repudiate the rationale of racial segregation by law.

The demise of segregation as a system of laws shifted the struggle to segregation as a system of life. Just as the legal prohibition of slavery in the 1860s had not stopped everyday practices of racial subordination, the legal prohibition of segregation in the 1960s did not stop everyday practices of racial subordination. Merely announcing a prohibition was not enough.

As ending slavery provoked dispute about what slavery was, so ending segregation provoked dispute about what segregation was. If slavery were merely a set of laws, then when the set of laws was gone, was slavery also gone? If segregation were merely a set of laws, then when the set of laws was gone, was segregation also gone? What if slavery or segregation were more than a set a laws? And what about their detritus or residue? Had slavery or segregation done damage that demanded repair? Had either done harm that required remedy? If so, what was damaged? Who was harmed? What was to be repaired, and how? Who was to receive any remedy? And who, if anyone, was to do the repair or supply the remedy? The questions were many.

President John F. Kennedy responded to some of the questions in March 1961. Issuing Executive Order No. 10925, he declared that

> it is the plain and positive obligation of the United States Government to promote and ensure equal opportunity for all qualified persons, without regard to race, creed, color, or national origin, employed or seeking employment with the Federal Government and on government contracts.

The president required federal agencies and contractors to "take affirmative action to ensure that applicants are employed, and that employees are treated during employment, without regard to their race, creed, color, or national origin."[4]

The phrase "affirmative action" took on a career of its own. It appeared to impose a duty to act. Further, the duty suggested a corresponding right. The Civil Rights Act of 1964 spelled out more fully the rights to be accorded "without regard to . . . race, creed, color, or national origin."[5] But the scope, substance, and standard for measuring the duty and corresponding rights were immediate issues.

President Lyndon B. Johnson in June 1965 addressed questions of scope. The problem of injustice against blacks was society wide, and the solution needed to be society wide too, he said. The nation and all its citizens had the duty to undertake affirmative action to achieve "equality as a fact and equality as a result," Johnson declared.[6] In September 1965, he issued Executive Order No. 11246 "to promote the full realization of equal employment opportunity through a positive, continuing program."[7]

President Johnson applied affirmative action to all aspects of federal employment and contracting. Jobs held the key to so much in U.S. life. Thus his push there made affirmative action personal for tens of millions of Americans who came to fear their jobs might be at risk. Since slavery times, whites had vehemently resisted black labor competition. Their resistance was no less in and after the 1960s.

When President Richard M. Nixon's 1969 Executive Order 11478 demanded that federal contractors show actual increases in minority employment with hiring "goals and timetables," sharp battle lines developed.[8] Critics attacked the approach as a quota system with arbitrary, fixed numbers that limited employers' choices and employees' chances to fill jobs by traditional standards. A major clash occurred over what became known as the Philadelphia Plan involving federal building projects in Pennsylvania's City of Brotherly Love. The white-only construction unions there, especially the crafts, flat out refused blacks' entry. Not being in the union meant not working on union sites. So federal contractors at such sites were caught between federal mandates and union resistance. Something had to give.

The structure and substance of employment, production, consumption, and distribution of wealth and privilege rested on race. Shifting the racial basics that favored whites and disfavored nonwhites, particularly blacks, and moving to equal opportunity meant drastic change. It demanded abandoning customary and standard practices based on race. Yet such practices formed much of doing business as usual. Affirmative action thus threatened the established order, and it was unwelcome among many.

A simple view cast affirmative action as redressing a balance between haves and have-nots, between those who because of their race traditionally were winners and those who were losers. Perhaps naturally those who saw themselves as haves resisted. Blessed with the property and promise of the best America offered, they were unwilling to surrender what they viewed as theirs by right. The rich tended to worry less about race. Their wealth buffered them from immediate concerns. The more restive and resistive were many at the economic and social middle margins. To these many, affirmative action appeared to mean losing their advantages. It appeared to jeopardize what they considered they had earned. It appeared to take what they considered they deserved because of what they personally had done. They did not see race as a basis for their having anything they had, and they refused to accept race as a basis for losing anything they had. Such persons might accept blacks and other nonwhites' being better off as a nice notion, but not at what they viewed as their expense. In short, resistance to the redress of affirmative action's promise of redistribution developed as resistance had to redress slavery after the Civil War.

Affirmative action became highly polarizing and political. Opponents castigated it as "reverse discrimination." They called it antithetical to the "equal protection of the laws" the Constitution promised. Proponents championed it as embodying and implementing equal protection. The argument turned on a basic question: What was racial discrimination? Was it an act, an intention, an effect, a pattern, a type of treatment, a result, or what? If it was an act, was it an act in isolation, or was the act to be considered in some context? If it was to be considered in context, what was the context to be? Would past practices of racial discrimination be part of the context? The questions were many. As the French observer Alexis de Tocqueville noted in the 1830s, "[S]carcely any political question arises in the United States which is not resolved, sooner or later, into a judicial question."[9] So it was with affirmative action. With government contracts, jobs, and schools dominating the subject matter in the often agonizing, bit-by-bit approach of the U.S. litigation process, a persistent procession headed to court, carrying kindling to already angry fires.

Early Supreme Court decisions, such as *Griggs v. Duke Power Co.* (1971), focused on outcomes or effects in construing Title VII of the Civil Rights Act of 1964. The antidiscrimination prohibitions required employers to eliminate what the Court called "artificial, arbitrary, and unnecessary barriers to employment that operate invidiously to discriminate on the basis of race."[10] The Court required no showing of discriminatory intent or purpose. It focused on results. It allowed disparate racial impact to prove illegal discrimination.

Reaffirmed in the Court's 1975 decision in *Albemarle Paper Company v. Moody*, disparate impact theory let proportional underrepresentation prove discrimination. Focusing on statistical imbalance, the ruling buoyed the Nixon approach of corrective goals and timetables. Outcry denounced the approach. Imbalances resulted not necessarily from discrimination but from differences in performance and preparation, disparate impact critics contended. Chief among the critics stood many white males. As Title VII and other federal law extended to protect women as well as nonwhites from discrimination, many white males increasingly felt their position and privilege besieged. They raged in challenge and went to court.

A series of workplace cases illustrated the affirmative action struggles in the 1970s and 1980s. Unions especially resisted displacing old job rules. They stood firm on seniority, for example. Much in the unionized workplace rested, after all, on the time-honored length-of-service system. Such a system entrenched privilege segregation had conferred by preferring only white men for many positions. Desegregating the workplace then meant confronting discriminatory effects of seniority systems. Yet the seniority system was not in itself illegal or necessarily objectionable. In enacting Title VII of the Civil Rights Act of 1964, Congress recognized the problem with seniority and specifically provided that a bona fide seniority system would not be unlawful under the act. So the issue was not seniority itself. Rather, seniority's discriminatory effects were at issue. Few denied past discrimination. The question was what to do about it.

Fashioning a remedy was the courts' problem. Vested rights workers gained through seniority clashed with rights segregation refused others by denying their opportunity to gain seniority. Simply destroying or diluting existing seniority lists was not a viable option. The law precluded such actions. So did union political clout. Doing nothing about past discrimination was not a viable option either. The wrongs were too clear to many who demanded immediate relief. Merely allowing a desegregated future to emerge in time failed to satisfy present demands and needs. Attempting to balance conflicting rights, courts and various advocates sought to create alternative qualifications for seniority. They fashioned synthetic seniority to blend with what already existed. That satisfied few, for the contending sides argued that such plans either surrendered too much or secured too little.

When unions agreed to compromise to make affirmative action work, their individual members not infrequently balked. In 1974, for example, the United Steelworkers of America (USWA) signed a collective bargaining agreement with Kaiser Aluminum & Chemical Corporation. It reserved for black employees one of every two in-plant craft training openings until Kaiser's black craftworkers moved from 1.8 percent to equal their approximately 39.0 percent in the local labor force. One of Kaiser's white production workers not accepted for craft training filed a class action suit. He asserted that reverse discrimination alone accounted for his and other whites' being rejected for training while having more seniority than selected black trainees. He argued that Kaiser and the union violated the Civil Rights Act of 1964 by discriminating in selecting trainees on the basis of race.[11]

The Supreme Court early settled that U.S. law protected whites as well as blacks from racial discrimination. So whom the law protected was not a primary issue. Rather, the issues focused on what action the law prohibited by whom. The law held governments and their agents to different standards than private persons. The Court ruled, for example, that Title VII did not condemn all private, voluntary, race-conscious affirmative action. Yet it offered no carte blanche in ruling against the white Kaiser worker in *United Steelworkers of America v. Weber* (1979).

There were permissible and impermissible affirmative action plans, the Court indicated. It drew no bright line to distinguish between the two, but it did sketch guidelines. Permissible plans aimed to break down old patterns of racial segregation. They aimed to open jobs in traditionally closed occupations. They did not "unnecessarily trammel the interests of white[s]." They required no firing of white workers to hire black replacements. They did not bar whites' advancement. They aimed to eliminate clear racial imbalance, not to create any rigid unchanging balance such as fixed quotas. Lastly, permissible plans were temporary.[12]

Private employers and unions now had guidance. So did state governments, at least in part. The Court's 1978 decision in *Regents of the University of California v. Bakke* had also treated claims of reverse discrimination. The context was public higher education, not a private workplace as in *Weber*. The University of California at Davis Medical School in 1973 and 1974 had denied admission to a white man named Allan Bakke. At the same time, the school admitted minority applicants—defined as American Indians, Asians, blacks, and Chicanos—with significantly lower scores than Bakke's. He sued, arguing that the school, a state agency, denied him admission on the basis of his race. That violated the Fourteenth Amendment's Equal Protection Clause, the California Constitution, and the Civil Rights Act of 1964, Bakke claimed.[13]

The California Supreme Court agreed with Bakke. It ordered his admission and barred consideration of race in the school's admissions process. On further appeal, the U.S. Supreme Court agreed with the California court, but only in part. It agreed that the medical school's minority admissions program violated equal protection because it excluded whites. It agreed also that Bakke be admitted to the medical school. It disagreed, however, on whether race could be considered in the school's admissions process.

The Court itself split sharply on using race as a factor in public higher education admissions. Justices John Paul Stevens, Potter Stewart, William H. Rehnquist, and Chief Justice Warren Burger refused to consider whether race could ever be a factor in an admissions policy, declaring the issue not to be then before the Court. Justices William J. Brennan Jr., Byron Raymond White, Thurgood Marshall, and Harry A. Blackmun insisted that the state's interest in overcoming substantial, chronic minority underrepresentation in the medical profession was sufficiently important to justify remedial use of race. Justice Lewis F. Powell Jr. tipped the balance, casting his view in terms of consideration of race being justified to achieve a diverse student body. Thus, "diversity" became an affirmative action catchword.

The decision hardly quieted complaints as the slumping 1970s economy deepened tensions. Calls for increased and equal minority and female access to, and actual participation in, the benefits of American life quickened. Resistence hardened. A supporter of federal civil rights legislation since the 1950s, Gerald R. Ford sought simultaneously to soothe growing white resentment while advancing affirmative action on becoming president in 1974. The question confronting the president and the nation was "How?" Numerical goals were proving to be political and practical problems, as *Bakke* illustrated. So how was the nation to achieve diversity? How were the vestiges of racism to be eliminated other than by race-conscious action?

Democratic President Jimmy Carter aggressively wielded his appointment power with federal hiring and contracting to advance affirmative action. Rather than a piecemeal, agency-by-agency approach, he consolidated affirmative action enforcement, centering it in the Labor Department and the Equal Employment Opportunity Commission. He appointed unprecedented numbers of blacks, Hispanics, and especially women to senior federal executive positions and to judgeships. He appeared determined to push the nation's commitment to civil rights to embrace economic justice as essential to legal equality. As part of the commitment, the Carter administration with Congress's cooperation more than doubled funds going to minority contractors.

In the Public Works Employment Act of 1977, Congress included a Minority Business Enterprise (MBE) provision that extended federal affirmative action. It required that state or local grantees of federal funds for public works buy at least 10 percent of their project services or supplies from minority-owned businesses. Congress defined minorities as U.S. citizens "who are Negroes, Spanish-speaking, Orientals, Indians, Eskimos, and Aleuts."[14] Several associations of construction contractors and subcontractors sued to block the program. The MBE was likely to cost them significant sums, and they argued it discriminated against them on illegal and unconstitutional racial bases.

To counter Carter's aggressive push, opponents of affirmative action more and more miscast it as illegal and immoral "preferential treatment." And they increasingly succeeded in confusing antipreference with antiaffirmative action. They ignored the fact that affirmative action was a means to end traditional preferences white males received. Yet increasingly partisan opponents such as Utah's Republican U.S. Senator Orrin Hatch mislabeled affirmative action as quotas and federally imposed "proportional representation" that threatened to "turn this country upside down." Responding to the miscasting, most Americans of whatever race, color, gender, or locale unsurprisingly rejected racial preferences.[15]

A shift was afoot. On his becoming president in 1981, Ronald W. Reagan's administration began to unravel nearly twenty years of court-sanctioned precedent for affirmative action. It touted color-blindness to replace color-consciousness. It cast affirmative action as quotas or proportional representation that undermined the American value and vision of assessment of individual merit. The president and his spokespersons insisted that government could not mandate equality or ensure results. Indeed, they argued that results should not be the issue in discrimination. Intention should be the sole measure, they contended. Thus, they applauded the Supreme Court's 1984 decision in *Firefighters Local Union No. 1794 v. Stotts*, which rejected disparate impact theory in upholding layoffs under a bona fide seniority system.

As Reagan gave way to his successor George H. W. Bush, his administration could take heart in having changed the Supreme Court's personnel and approach. The Court retreated from allowing affirmative action as a broad remedy for past discrimination. It moved also toward requiring intention rather than results to prove discrimination. Reagan appointee Justice Sandra Day O'-Connor illustrated the limiting approach in her opinion for the Court in *Richmond v. J. A. Croson Co.* (1989). She announced "strict scrutiny" for any race-conscious state action. Even given its history of racial discrimination, a city such as the old Confederate capital of Richmond, Virginia, could not enact public construction contract set-asides such as the federal 1977 minority business enterprise provisions as a broad affirmative action remedy. To be legitimate, a state plan had to target specific, not general, discrimination. Moreover, it needed to demonstrate a compelling governmental interest in using race and narrowly fit its action to the specific discrimination that compelled government remedial action, O'Connor wrote.[16]

Reagan Court appointee Antonin Scalia went further in *Croson*. He framed affirmative action as a narrow remedy only for de jure segregation. In Scalia's view, once a state eliminated its unlawful system it lost any authority for affirmative action. When the laws of slavery and segregation were gone, then slavery, segregation, and the unconstitutional discrimination attached to them were also gone. Their broad, lingering effects were not legal issues and not of compelling governmental interest to the states, Scalia argued. No constitutional authority allowed states to use race to remedy societal discrimination, he claimed. If a state had harmed someone, then the state could make amends, of course, but only to reach "identified victims of [its] discrimination." Further, he insisted that equal protection under the Fourteenth Amendment required that "strict scrutiny must be applied to all governmental classification by race, whether or not its asserted purpose is 'remedial' or 'benign'." The solution to the nation's history of racial problems was not affirmative action but what he termed a "raceneutral remedial program."[17] A fresh battle thus developed over state-based affirmative action. An ugly return to public higher education loomed, for it was a primary site of state spending and competition for places.

Fighting stiffened also on the federal level. Should federal affirmative action be judged by the same strict scrutiny as state action? By 5–4 the Court said no in *Metro Broadcasting Inc. v. Federal Communications Commission* (1990). It found reasonable FCC policies to enhance minority ownership to diversify broadcast media. Vigorously dissenting, the Court minority demanded applying the same strict scrutiny to federal acts as applied to state acts. Quoting from the Court's 1954 antisegregation rulings, the dissenters insisted that "it would be unthinkable that the same Constitution would impose a lesser duty on the Federal Government."[18]

In June 1995, the *Metro Broadcasting Inc.* dissenters prevailed. In *Adarand Constructors, Inc. v. Peña*, Justice O'Connor wrote for the 5–4 majority that federal, state, or local "government may treat people differently because of their race only for the most compelling reasons."[19] So the same strict scrutiny standards applied at all government levels. The majority thus upheld a white firm's challenge to a federal highway construction contract award to what the federal Small Business Administration, using racial criteria, identified as "disadvantaged" businesses. Justice O'Connor insisted that the decision was not fatal to affirmative action. "When race-based action is necessary to further a compelling interest," she wrote, "such action is within constitutional constraints."[20] While voting with the majority, Justices Scalia and Clarence Thomas disagreed with O'Connor. They declared race-based affirmative action dead.

President Bill Clinton claimed the *Adarand* decision "reaffirmed the need for affirmative action and reaffirmed the continuing existence of systematic discrimination in the United States."[21] Affirmative action needed to continue, he insisted. But its future was doubtful. Opponents had the upper hand. In *Hopwood v. Texas*, federal courts in 1994 and 1996 abandoned the *Bakke* diversity rationale, which sanctioned affirmative action. Instead, they adopted the views Justices Scalia and Thomas announced in *Adarand* that government could not recognize race as a criterion in distributing public benefits such as law school admission.

In November 1996 California voters passed Proposition 209, which proponents touted as barring the state from all forms of affirmative action. Washington state voters followed suit in December 1998, passing Initiative 200 to outlaw state affirmative action there. Florida followed by executive order in November 1999 to ban race as a factor in state employment, contracting, or school admissions. In June 2003, the U.S. Supreme Court revisited affirmative action in public higher education. In *Grutter v. Bollinger*, it rejected *Hopwood* and reaffirmed the *Bakke* diversity rationale. In *Gratz v. Bollinger*, it reaffirmed its ban on quotas or fixed formulas that precluded "individualized consideration."[22]

Where exactly was race headed as an issue of public policy as the United States entered a new century and a new millennium? Did race matter? Was race merely yesterday's concern? Was redressing the horrors of slavery and segregation appropriate, possible, or practicable? Was anyone owed anything by anyone in American society based on past injustice or the persisting effects of injustice? The questions percolated.

The culture wars entrenched in the nation from its beginning erupted anew. The contested terrain remained marked as ever—personal equality and opportunity. The banners on one side proclaimed that race remained a barrier to individual achievement. That continuing fact required government to act affirmatively. Government's duty was to ensure equal protection, not merely in the letter of the law but as a matter of fact. Banners on the other side proclaimed that antiwhite prejudice—and particularly antiwhite male prejudice—had subverted social justice and sent the nation further from reaching a color-blind goal. Whether the battle engaged affirmative action as such or used watchwords such as *diversity* or *multiculturalism*, the prize and problem remained intertwined in questions of who, if anyone, in America got special treatment and why. The search for answers continued to reach back to the nation's roots and to the reality of race found regularly in American life as a restriction or a reward.

NOTES

1. President Dwight D. Eisenhower, Address at the Hollywood Bowl, Beverly Hills, California (October 19, 1956), in *Public Papers of the Presidents of the United States: Dwight D. Eisenhower, 1956* (Washington, DC: GPO, 1956), 971, 976.

2. President John F. Kennedy, "Radio and Television Report to the American People on Civil Rights," The White House, June 11, 1963, http://www.cs.umb.edu/jfklibrary/j061163.htm.

3. 388 U.S. 1 (1967).

4. President John F. Kennedy, Executive Order No. 10925, 3 C.F.R. 481 (1959–1963), § 301 (1) (March 6, 1961) (establishing the President's Committee on Equal Employment Opportunity).

5. Title VII of the Civil Rights Act of 1964, 42 U.S.C. 2000e et seq.

6. President Lyndon B. Johnson, Commencement Address at Howard University: "To Fulfill These Rights," June 4, 1965, in *Public Papers of the Presidents of the United States: Lyndon B. Johnson, 1965* (Washington, DC: GPO, 1966), 2:635–640.

7. President Lyndon B. Johnson, Executive Order No. 11246, 3 C.F.R. 339 (1964–1965) (September 24, 1965) (providing for equal employment opportunity in federal government employment).

8. President Richard M. Nixon, Executive Order No. 11478, 3 C.F.R. 806 (1966–1970) (August 8, 1969) (providing for equal employment opportunity in federal government employment and contracting).

9. Alexis de Tocqueville, *Democracy in America*, trans. Henry Reeve, 4 vols. (London: Saunders and Otley, 1835–1840), 1:357–358.

10. *Griggs v. Duke Power Co.*, 401 U.S. 424, 429–433 (1971).

11. *United Steelworkers of America v. Weber*, 443 U.S. 193 (1979).

12. Ibid., at 200–208.

13. 438 U.S. 265 (1978). Note that § 601 of Title VI of the Civil Rights Act of 1964, 42 U.S.C.S. § 2000d, provided that "no person shall on the ground of race or color be excluded from participating in any program receiving federal financial assistance." The University of California at Davis Medical School received federal funds.

14. Public Works Employment Act of 1977, at 42 U.S.C.S. § 6705(f)(2).

15. Chester E. Finn Jr., " 'Affirmative Action' under Reagan," *Commentary* 73, no. 4 (April 1982): 17–28, quoting Hatch at 23. A 1977 Gallup survey found that only 11 percent of all respondents (including just 12 percent of women and 30 percent of nonwhites) condoned "preferential treatment in getting jobs and places in college," while 82 percent of all men, 80 percent of women, and 55 percent of nonwhites believed that "ability, as determined by test scores, should be the main consideration."

16. *Richmond v. J. A. Croson Co.*, 488 U.S. 469 (1989).

17. Ibid., at 520, 526 (Scalia, J., concurring).

18. Quoting *Bolling v. Sharpe*, 347 U.S. 497, 500 (1954) (holding racial segregation in the District of Columbia violated the due process guaranteed in the Fifth Amendment).

19. *Adarand Constructors v. Peña*, 515 U.S. 200, 227 (1995).

20. Ibid., at 237. The action needed only to satisfy the Court's "narrow tailoring" test. Ibid.

21. William Jefferson Clinton, "Remarks on Affirmative Action," July 19, 1995, Office of the Press Secretary, the White House, http://clinton3.nara.gov/Initiatives/One America/19970610-1444.html.

22. *Gratz v. Bollinger*, 539 U.S. 244 (2003) (holding 6-3 that the University of Michigan's undergraduate admissions program that awarded minorities additional points in the admission process was unconstitutional); *Grutter v. Bollinger*, 539 U.S. 306 (2003) (upholding, 5–4, the University of Michigan Law School's policy considering race as one of many factors in the admissions process because it furthers "a compelling interest in obtaining the educational benefits that flow from a diverse student body").

DOCUMENTS

12.1.   **"To encourage by positive measures equal opportunity," 1961**

The New Frontier ideal President John F. Kennedy (1917–1963) announced at his inauguration in 1961 projected a vision of America as a free, democratic society. The violence, pain, and grief of desegregation challenged that vision. Rising to the occasion with increasing vigor, JFK insisted on making U.S. ideals real in race relations. Using his executive authority to encourage equality and to move toward ending racial discrimination, in the document that follows he initiated affirmative action and established the President's Committee on Equal Employment Opportunity.

WHEREAS discrimination because of race, creed, color, or national origin is contrary to the Constitutional principles and policies of the United States; . . .

WHEREAS it is the plain and positive obligation of the United States Government to promote and ensure equal opportunity for all qualified persons, without regard to race, creed, color, or national origin, employed or seeking employment with the Federal Government and on government contracts; and

WHEREAS it is the policy of the executive branch of the Government to encourage by positive measures equal opportunity for all qualified persons within the Government; and

WHEREAS it is in the general interest and welfare of the United States to promote its economy, security, and national defense through the most efficient and effective utilization of all available manpower; and

WHEREAS a review and analysis of existing Executive orders, practices, and government agency procedures relating to government employment and compliance with existing non-discrimination contract provisions reveal an urgent need for expansion and strengthening of efforts to promote full equality of employment opportunity; and

WHEREAS a single governmental committee should be charged with responsibility for accomplishing these objectives:

NOW, THEREFORE, by virtue of the authority vested in me as President of the United States by the Constitution and statutes of the United States, it is ordered as follows:

There is hereby established the President's Committee on Equal Employment Opportunity.

Source: President John F. Kennedy, Executive Order No. 10925, 3 C.F.R. 481 (1959–1963), § 301 (1) (March 6, 1961).

12.2.   "To Fulfill These Rights," 1965

In June 1965, President Lyndon B. Johnson (1908–1973) dedicated his administration "to help the American Negro fulfill the rights which, after the long time of injustice, he is finally about to secure." He anticipated Congress's passing the Voting Rights Act that he signed into law on August 6, 1965. He also announced a White House conference with the theme and title of "To Fulfill These Rights." The theme became part of his vision of America as a "Great Society" resting on freedom for all, not merely as ideal but as real, as he indicated in the following document.

Freedom is the right to share, share fully and equally, in American society—to vote, to hold a job, to enter a public place, to go to school. It is the right to be treated in every part of our national life as a person equal in dignity and promise to all others.

But freedom is not enough. You do not wipe away the scars of centuries by saying: Now you are free to go where you want, and do as you desire, and choose the leaders you please.

You do not take a person who, for years, has been hobbled by chains and liberate him, bring him up to the starting line of a race and then say, "you are free to compete with all the others," and still justly believe that you have been completely fair.

Thus it is not enough just to open the gates of opportunity. All our citizens must have the ability to walk through those gates.

This is the next and the more profound stage of the battle for civil rights. We seek not just freedom but opportunity. We seek not just legal equity but human ability, not just equality as a right and a theory but equality as a fact and equality as a result.

For the task is to give 20 million Negroes the same chance as every other American to learn and grow, to work and share in society, to develop their abilities—physical, mental and spiritual, and to pursue their individual happiness.

To this end equal opportunity is essential, but not enough, not enough. . . .

Much of the Negro community is buried under a blanket of history and circumstance. It is not a lasting solution to lift just one corner of that blanket. We must stand on all sides and we must raise the entire cover if we are to liberate our fellow citizens. . . .

There is no single easy answer to all of these problems.

Jobs are part of the answer. They bring the income which permits a man to provide for his family.

Decent homes in decent surroundings and a chance to learn—an equal chance to learn—are part of the answer.

Welfare and social programs better designed to hold families together are part of the answer.

Care for the sick is part of the answer.

An understanding heart by all Americans is another big part of the answer. . . .

Its object will be to help the American Negro fulfill the rights which, after the long time of injustice, he is finally about to secure.

To move beyond opportunity to achievement.

To shatter forever not only the barriers of law and public practice, but the walls which bound the condition of many by the color of his skin.

To dissolve, as best we can, the antique enmities of the heart which diminish the holder, divide the great democracy, and do wrong—great wrong—to the children of God. . . .

For what is justice?

It is to fulfill the fair expectations of man. . . .

This is American justice. We have pursued it faithfully to the edge of our imperfections, and we have failed to find it for the American Negro.

So, it is the glorious opportunity of this generation to end the one huge wrong of the American Nation and, in so doing, to find America for ourselves, with the same immense thrill of discovery which gripped those who first began to realize that here, at last, was a home for freedom.

Source: President Lyndon B. Johnson, Commencement Address at Howard University: "To Fulfill These Rights," June 4, 1965, in *Public Papers of the Presidents of the United States: Lyndon B. Johnson, 1965* (Washington, DC: GPO, 1966), 2:635–640.

12.3.   "Freedom to marry," 1967

> *In* Loving v. Virginia *(1967), the U.S. Supreme Court squarely placed the rationale of racial segregation in the context of the Constitution's requiring "equal protection of the laws." Governmental use of racial classification itself was on trial. The Court rejected such classifications as the basis of prohibitions. And in treating miscegenation statutes, the Court reached into perhaps the most intimate of racially restricted areas—interracial sex and marriage. As indicated below, it found racial bans "violate[d] the central meaning of the Equal Protection Clause."*

There can be no question but that Virginia's miscegenation statutes rest solely upon distinctions drawn according to race. The statutes proscribe generally accepted conduct if engaged in by members of different races. Over the years, this Court has consistently repudiated "distinctions between citizens solely because of their ancestry" as being "odious to a free people whose institutions are founded upon the doctrine of equality." . . .

The fact that Virginia prohibits only interracial marriages involving white persons demonstrates that the racial classifications must stand on their own justification, as measures designed to maintain White Supremacy. We have consistently denied the constitutionality of measures which restrict the rights of citizens on account of race. There can be no doubt that restricting the freedom to marry solely because of racial classifications violates the central meaning of the Equal Protection Clause. . . .

Marriage is one of the "basic civil rights of man," fundamental to our very existence and survival. To deny this fundamental freedom on so unsupportable a basis as the racial classifications embodied in these statutes, classifications so directly subversive of the principle of equality at the heart of the Fourteenth Amendment, is surely to deprive all the State's citizens of liberty without due process of law. The Fourteenth Amendment requires that the freedom of choice to marry not be restricted by invidious racial discriminations. Under our Constitution, the freedom to marry, or not marry, a person of another race resides with the individual and cannot be infringed by the State.

Source: Loving v. Virginia, 388 U.S. 1, 8–12 (1967). (Citations omitted.)

**12.4.   "Potential for contribution to educational diversity,"
               1978**

In Regents of the University of California v. Bakke (1978), the U.S. Supreme Court confronted the clash of affirmative action and reverse discrimination complaints. The case arose from the Medical School of the University of California at Davis. In 1973 and 1974 the school ran a regular admissions program and a separate special admissions program for "economically and/or educationally disadvantaged" applicants who were American Indian, Asian, black, or Chicano. The special program admitted no disadvantaged whites. Allan Bakke, a white male applicant rejected in 1973 and 1974 under the regular admissions program, challenged the school's admission process. He alleged that the special program created a quota and sought to guarantee results not based on qualifications but on race in violation of the Fourteenth Amendment's Equal Protection Clause. Delivering the judgment in the case, excerpted below, Justice Lewis F. Powell Jr. bridged a yawning gap on the Court separating friends and foes of affirmative action. He condemned racial preference but allowed state colleges and universities to legitimately consider race in admissions decisions as an element indicating "potential for contribution to educational diversity."

The special admissions program is undeniably a classification based on race and ethnic background. To the extent that there existed a pool of at least minimally qualified minority applicants to fill the 16 special admissions seats, white applicants could compete only for 84 seats in the entering class, rather than the 100 open to minority applicants. Whether this limitation is described as a quota or a goal, it is a line drawn on the basis of race and ethnic status. . . .

It is settled beyond question that the "rights created by the first section of the Fourteenth Amendment are, by its terms, guaranteed to the individual. The rights established are personal rights". The guarantee of equal protection cannot mean one thing when applied to one individual and something else when applied to a person of another color. If both are not accorded the same protection, then it is not equal. . . .

The State certainly has a legitimate and substantial interest in ameliorating, or eliminating where feasible, the disabling effects of identified discrimination. The line of school desegregation cases, commencing with *Brown* [*v. Board of Education* (1954)], attests to the importance of this state goal and the commitment of the judiciary to affirm all lawful means toward its attainment. In the school cases, the States were required by court order to redress the wrongs worked by specific instances of racial discrimination. That goal was far more focused than the remedying of the effects of "societal discrimination," an amorphous concept of injury that may be ageless in its reach into the past.

We have never approved a classification that aids persons perceived as members of relatively victimized groups at the expense of other innocent individuals in the absence of judicial, legislative, or administrative findings of constitutional or statutory violations. . . . Without such findings of constitutional or statutory violations, it cannot be said that the government has any greater interest in helping one individual than in refraining from harming another. Thus, the government has no compelling justification for inflicting such harm. . . .

[A]ttainment of a diverse student body . . . clearly is a constitutionally permissible goal for an institution of higher education. . . . The freedom of a university to make its own judgments as to education includes the selection of its student body. . . . [I]t is not too much to say that the "nation's future depends upon leaders trained through wide exposure" to the ideas and mores of students as diverse as this Nation of many peoples.

Thus, in arguing that its universities must be accorded the right to select those students who will contribute the most to the "robust exchange of ideas," [the University of California] invokes a countervailing constitutional interest, that of the First Amendment. In this light, [the University] must be viewed as seeking to achieve a goal that is of paramount importance in the fulfillment of its mission.

It may be argued that there is greater force to these views at the undergraduate level than in a medical school where the training is centered primarily on professional competency. But even at the graduate level, our tradition and experience lend support to the view that the contribution of diversity is substantial. . . .

In summary, it is evident that the Davis special admissions program involves the use of an explicit racial classification never before countenanced by this Court. It tells applicants who are not Negro, Asian, or Chicano that they are totally excluded from a specific percentage of the seats in an entering class. No matter how strong their qualifications, quantitative and extracurricular, including their own potential for contribution to educational diversity, they are never afforded the chance to compete with applicants from the preferred groups for the special admissions seats. At the same time, the preferred applicants have the opportunity to compete for every seat in the class.

The fatal flaw in [this] preferential program is its disregard of individual rights as guaranteed by the Fourteenth Amendment. Such rights are not absolute. But when a State's distribution of benefits or imposition of burdens hinges on ancestry or the color of a person's skin, that individual is entitled to a demonstration that the challenged classification is necessary to promote a substantial state interest.

Source: *Regents of the University of California v. Bakke*, 438 U.S. 265, 289–290, 307–309, 311–313, 319–320 (1978) (Powell, J., announcing the judgment of the Court). (Citations omitted.)

12.5.   "We are just one race here," 1995

In Adarand Constructors v. Peña *(1995), the U.S. Supreme Court revisited whether government at any level could legitimately consider race in what Justice Lewis F. Powell Jr. in 1978 termed the "distribution of benefits or imposition of burdens." As in* Regents of the University of California v. Bakke *(1978), the Court judged the challenged program unconstitutional yet allowed that race-based governmental action could be constitutional in "compelling" circumstances. Justices Antonin Scalia and Clarence Thomas agreed with the judgment but disagreed with Justice Sandra Day O'Connor's opinion for the Court on whether "compelling" circumstances to justify race-based governmental action could ever exist. Below Justice Scalia explains his opinion. The next document presents Justice Thomas's opinion.*

In my view, government can never have a "compelling interest" in discriminating on the basis of race in order to "make up" for past racial discrimination in the opposite direction. Individuals who have been wronged by unlawful racial discrimination should be made whole; but under our Constitution there can be no such thing as either a creditor or a debtor race. That concept is alien to the Constitution's focus upon the individual, and its rejection of dispositions based on race, or based on blood. To pursue the concept of racial entitlement—even for the most admirable and benign of purposes—is to reinforce and preserve for future mischief the way of thinking that produced race slavery, race privilege and race hatred. In the eyes of government, we are just one race here. It is American.

Source: *Adarand Constructors v. Peña*, 515 U.S. 200, 239 (1995) (Scalia, J., concurring in part and concurring in the judgment). (Citations omitted.)

12.6.   "It is racial discrimination, plain and simple," 1995

Justice Clarence Thomas joined Justice Antonin Scalia in Adarand Constructors v. Peña *(1995), to disagree with Justice Sandra Day O'Connor's opinion for the Court on whether "compelling" circumstances could ever allow race-based governmental action. The lone black justice especially disagreed with the perspectives of others on the Supreme Court who backed affirmative action, which he called "racial paternalism."*

I agree with the majority's conclusion that strict scrutiny applies to *all* government classifications based on race. I write separately, however, to express my disagreement with the premise underlying JUSTICE STEVENS' and JUSTICE GINSBURG'S dissents: that there is a racial paternalism exception to the principle of equal protection. I believe that there is a "moral [and] constitutional equivalence," between laws designed to subjugate a race and those that distribute benefits on the basis of race in order to foster some current notion of equality. Government cannot make us equal; it can only recognize, respect, and protect us as equal before the law. . . .

[U]nder our Constitution, the government may not make distinctions on the basis of race. As far as the Constitution is concerned, it is irrelevant whether a government's racial classifications are drawn by those who wish to oppress a race or by those who have a sincere desire to help those thought to be disadvantaged. . . .

These [affirmative action] programs not only raise grave constitutional questions, they also undermine the moral basis of the equal protection principle. Purchased at the price of immeasurable human suffering, the equal protection principle reflects our Nation's understanding that such classifications ultimately have a destructive impact on the individual and our society. Unquestionably, "invidious [racial] discrimination is an engine of oppression." It is also true that "remedial" racial preferences may reflect "a desire to foster equality in society". But there can be no doubt that racial paternalism and its unintended consequences can be as poisonous and pernicious as any other form of discrimination. So-called "benign" discrimination teaches many that because of chronic and apparently immutable handicaps, minorities cannot compete with them without their patronizing indulgence. Inevitably, such programs engender attitudes of superiority or, alternatively, provoke resentment among those who believe that they have been wronged by the government's use of race. These programs stamp minorities with a badge of inferiority and may cause them to develop dependencies or to adopt an attitude that they are "entitled" to preferences. . . .

In my mind, government-sponsored racial discrimination based on benign prejudice is just as noxious as discrimination inspired by malicious prejudice. In each instance, it is racial discrimination, plain and simple.

Source: *Adarand Constructors v. Peña*, 515 U.S. 200, 240–241 (1995) (Thomas, J., concurring in part and concurring in the judgment). (Citations omitted.)

12.7.   "Equals without respect to race or gender," 1999

Announcing a campaign for "equity," Florida Governor Jeb Bush in November 1999 used the principles of nondiscrimination in the state constitution to outlaw affirmative action in state employment, educa-

tion, and contracting. His action followed similar moves in California, where voters in November 1996 passed Proposition 209, which its proponents touted as barring the state from all forms of affirmative action, and in Washington state, where voters in December 1998 passed Initiative 200 to outlaw state affirmative action.

WHEREAS, the Florida Constitution provides that all natural persons, female and male alike, are equal before the law and that no person shall be deprived of any right because of race or national origin; and

WHEREAS, Florida's government has a solemn obligation to respect and affirm these principles in its policies relating to employment, education and contracting; and

WHEREAS, the use of racial and gender set-asides, preferences and quotas is generally inconsistent with the obligation of government to treat all individuals as equals without respect to race or gender; and

WHEREAS, the use of racial and gender set-asides, preferences and quotas is considered divisive and unfair by the vast majority of Floridians, produces few, if any, long-term benefits for the intended beneficiaries, and is of questionable legality; and

WHEREAS, the laudable goal of increasing diversity in Florida's government and institutions of Higher Education, and in the allocation of state contracts, can and should be realized without the use of racial and gender set-asides, preferences and quotas; . . .

[T]he obligation of Florida's government to root out vestiges of discrimination can and should likewise be accomplished without resort to remedies involving the use of racial and gender set-asides, preferences and quotas.

Source: Governor Jeb Bush, Executive Order No. 99-281 (November 9, 1999) (banning race, gender, or national origin as a factor in state employment, contracting, or school admissions).

12.8.   "Educational benefits flow from a diverse student body," 2003

In June 2003, the Supreme Court revisited race in admissions at state institutions of higher education. It decided two cases arising from practices at the University of Michigan. One challenged undergraduate admissions, the other law school admissions. In Gratz v. Bollinger, *the Court found the undergraduate admission program's use of race acted as "the functional equivalent of a quota" and held it thus unconstitutional. In* Grutter v. Bollinger, *the Court in a 5–4 opinion by Justice Sandra Day O'Connor reiterated Justice Lewis F. Powell Jr.'s diversity rationale from* Regents of University of California v. Bakke *(1978). The ruling, excerpted below, upheld the law school's use of race as one factor "in a highly individualized, holistic review of each applicant's file, giving serious consideration to all the ways an applicant might contribute to a diverse educational environment."*

[W]e turn to the question whether the Law School's use of race is justified by a compelling state interest. . . . [The University of Michigan and its officials] assert only one justification for their use of race in the admissions process: obtaining "the educational benefits that flow from a diverse student body." In other words, the Law School asks us to recognize, in the context of higher education, a compelling state interest in student body diversity.

We first wish to dispel the notion that the Law School's argument has been foreclosed, either expressly or implicitly, by our affirmative-action cases decided since *Bakke*. It is true that some language in those opinions might be read to suggest that remedying past discrimination is the only permissible justification for race-based governmental action. But we have never held that the only governmental use of race that can survive strict scrutiny is remedying past discrimination. Nor, since *Bakke*, have we directly addressed the use of race in the context of public higher education. Today, we hold that the Law School has a compelling interest in attaining a diverse student body.

The Law School's educational judgment that such diversity is essential to its educational mission is one to which we defer. The Law School's assessment that diversity will, in fact, yield educational benefits is substantiated. . . . Our scrutiny of the interest asserted by the Law School is no less strict for taking into account complex educational judgments in an area that lies primarily within the expertise of the university. . . .

We take the Law School at its word that it would "like nothing better than to find a race-neutral admissions formula" and will terminate its race-conscious admissions program as soon as practicable. It has been 25 years since Justice Powell first approved the use of race to further an interest in student body diversity in the context of public higher education. Since that time, the number of minority applicants with high grades and test scores has indeed increased. We expect that 25 years from now, the use of racial preferences will no longer be necessary to further the interest approved today.

In summary, the Equal Protection Clause does not prohibit the Law School's narrowly tailored use of race in admissions decisions to further a compelling interest in obtaining the educational benefits that flow from a diverse student body.

Source: *Grutter v. Bollinger*, 539 U.S. 306, 327–328, 341–343 (2003) (O'Connor, J., for the Court). (Citations omitted.)

ANNOTATED RESEARCH GUIDE

Books

Beckwith, Francis J., and Todd E. Jones, eds. *Affirmative Action: Social Justice or Reverse Discrimination?* Amherst, NY: Prometheus Books, 1997. Provides fifteen articles debating the meaning of equality, the social standards of racial equality, and whether a need exists for affirmative action in labor markets and other arenas.

Carter, Dan T. *From George Wallace to Newt Gingrich: Race and the Conservative Counterrevolution, 1963–1994.* Baton Rouge: Louisiana State University Press, 1999. Explains the pandering and prodding of a politics of fear to promote social attitudes and issues that encoded race into divisive language that stymied nationwide development in race relations.

Curry, George E., ed. *The Affirmative Action Debate*. Reading, MA: Addison-Wesley, 1996. Twenty-nine essays representing both sides of the issues, debating process and result in seeking to understand the meaning of equality.

Durr, Kenneth D. *Behind the Backlash: White Working-Class Politics in Baltimore, 1940–1980*. Chapel Hill: University of North Carolina Press, 2003. Paints a localized portrait of white blue-collar populism with grievances that reflect anxieties over desegregation, deindustrialization, and demographic changes and that raise persistent questions about the meaning and reach of race as a social and political divider.

Eastland, Terry. *Ending Affirmative Action: The Case for Colorblind Justice*. New York: Basic Books, 1996. One-time Reagan administration Justice Department official argues the legality, morality, and politics of affirmative action, which he casts as racial preferences.

Edley, Christopher. *Not All Black and White: Affirmative Action and American Values*. New York: Farrar, Straus and Giroux, 1998. One-time Clinton administration adviser discusses the law, morals, and policy of affirmative action, which he views as continuing to be useful.

Meyer, Stephen Grant. *As Long as They Don't Move Next Door: Segregation and Racial Conflict in American Neighborhoods*. New York: Rowman & Littlefield, 2000. In the sensitive area of housing, illustrates race relations' problems from rejection of racial access by methods including mob violence and intimidation, realtor steering, mortgage lender red-lining, restrictive covenants, and white flight.

Robinson, JoAnn Ooiman, ed. *Affirmative Action: A Documentary History*. Westport, CT: Greenwood Press, 2001. Provides nearly 400 documents to trace the development of policy and practice reaching not only race but also gender and disability.

Sowell, Thomas. *Affirmative Action around the World: An Empirical Study*. New Haven, CT: Yale University Press, 2004. A broad empirical survey emphasizing inequitable consequences of affirmative action as a preferential program embraced for its idealized goals and rationales rather than for its real results.

Web Sites

http://pbsvideodb.pbs.org/resources/eyes/—links to *Eyes on the Prize*, a fourteen-part, critically acclaimed Public Broadcasting Service series (produced by Blackside Inc.) on the Civil Rights Movement. It aired first in January and February of 1987 with six programs titled *Eyes on the Prize: America's Civil Rights Years (1954–1965)*. The eight-part sequel, *Eyes on the Prize II: America at the Racial Crossroads (1965–1985)*, aired in 1990.

http://www.affirmativeaction.org/resources/index.html—American Association for Affirmative Action offers resources and links for information on federal laws and regulations, enforcement agencies, and court decisions about affirmative action.

13

Race on Trial in the 1990s

The criminal and civil trials of Orenthal James "O.J." Simpson, a black Pro Football Hall of Famer and media celebrity, unveiled continuing racial division in American life as the twentieth century closed. In June 1994, California authorities arrested Simpson on charges of murdering his thirty-five-year-old ex-wife Nicole Brown Simpson and her twenty-five-year-old friend Ronald Lyle Goldman. Police found the two stabbed and slashed to death outside Nicole's condominium in Los Angeles's affluent Brentwood section. O.J.'s celebrity drew sensational coverage from first discovery of the crime's connection to him. His relentlessly televised double-murder trial became an American fascination exported to millions worldwide. By one estimate, attention on O.J. generated goods and services that exceeded in value the gross domestic product of the Caribbean nation of Grenada in 1994. When the jury acquitted O.J. after about four hours' deliberation, the American populace appeared split in delight or disgust. The agitation persisted to 1999, first in a wrongful death civil suit and then in a battle for custody of O.J. and Nicole's two children. The saga became a tale of the place and position of race in the U.S. legal system and, most of all, of how Americans moving toward the twenty-first century saw and acted on race as an element in their everyday lives.

O.J.'s trials played as a made-in-America melodrama. It featured violence, sex, money, celebrity, and race, mixed in sensational and romantic parts. O.J. became larger than his life. He became more than simply an individual on trial. He became an ambiguous symbol in a society straining to fix race amid ideals of progressive social justice and traditional law and order. His image touched painful and raw patches in America's race-conscious social space.

Emotion seeped from the frayed but resilient taboo of interracial sex. It spewed also from the historical bête noire, as projections of Nicole's brutal

death at O.J.'s hand fit hoary views of the black male beast savaging unpro-
tected white womanhood. It recalled America's ugly history of lynching black
men to the hue and cry usually of falsely reported rape. It also scraped sore-
ness over a criminal justice system in which blacks, particularly black men, figured by huge disproportion.

In 1994, when O.J. went on trial for murder, the U.S. correctional system held
2,018,000 black adults. That was 89 of every 1,000 black adults.[1] The contrasting number was 19 per 1,000 for whites. Since the 1980s the system had put
more black men behind bars than in classrooms. Black men in college outnumbered black men behind bars by a ratio of more than 3 to 1 in 1980. By
1994, the ratio had dwindled to 1 to 1. It continued to worsen. By 2000, black
men behind bars outnumbered those in college by a ratio of 13 to 10.[2]

Did the imbalance show problems in blacks or in the criminal justice system? An easy majority agreed the system had serious problems. Differences
ran deep, however, on what exactly the problems were. Many said the system
let criminals off altogether or too leniently. Others insisted that the system victimized victims and used race and class to scapegoat.

O.J.'s trials seemed to say something about race to Americans everywhere.
Reactions demonstrated almost daily that race mattered in American life—as
it always had. Popular sentiment held that race determined O.J.'s predicament.
It triggered and controlled what happened in the criminal justice system. It colored his casting in the national media. It determined his outcome. For some,
the conversation carried more than a hint of O.J.'s being an uppity black man
who had forgotten, or tried to forget, his identity and place. He had divorced
his black wife, Marguerite Whitley, who bore him three children, to embrace a
white, golden-haired American dream girl. He had forsaken his own and was
paying the price. At least a few insisted race was irrelevant. It mattered not
who or what O.J. was. It mattered only what he had done or not done in the
double murder on June 12, 1994. The issue was not what society had done or
not done. It was not what police or others in the criminal justice system had
done or not done. What had O.J. done? That was the question from this view.
It was an individual, not a group, issue. Race was not in it. In legal terms, of
course, the issue in O.J.'s criminal trial was, "What had prosecutors proven to
the jury 'beyond a reasonable doubt'?"

Americans appeared overwhelmingly to see the criminal trial's outcome in
terms of race relations. And their view was not favorable. Asked immediately
after the verdict in October 1995, "Do you think the O.J. Simpson trial has done
more to help or hurt race relations in this country?" 74 percent of respondents
in a nationwide telephone Gallup poll of 1,225 adults said the trial had done
more to hurt. Only 15 percent said it had done more to help.[3]

More than feelings about O.J.'s episode figured in the calculus about national
race relations in the mid-1990s. U.S. society sat conflicted. It pondered whether
race mattered. It argued whether affirmative action remained necessary. It debated whether amalgamation marked the road to a color-blind society. What
were the children of racial intermarriage: What was their race? What was their
identity? Were they America's integrated future, exhibiting the end of race? Or
were mixed-race persons simply "others" forced into one or another of the traditional U.S. categories? With whom did such mixed-race children belong?

Should O.J. and Nicole's children be brought up black or white? And what kind of question was that? What did it mean? Did it mean that people of "mixed heritage" were the solution to the race question? Views varied. More than that, they clashed.

O.J.'s criminal trial occurred in a national memory still tender from the twists and violence of a grainy videotape that for nineteen seconds in March 1991 caught baton-swinging Los Angeles Police Department (LAPD) officers beating a black man named Rodney Glen King as he writhed on the ground. The beating appeared senseless. Its airing on national television conjured up outrageous images of brutalized blacks during and after slavery. It appeared to show how far America had *not* advanced.

The trial of four white LAPD officers involved in the King beating further solidified the worst view. Removed from Los Angeles to nearby Simi Valley—something of a white enclave that its Chamber of Commerce touted as "so close and yet so far" from polyglot Los Angeles—the trial ended in April 1992 with the predominantly white jury finding the officers "not guilty." The verdict seemed contrary to the clear visual evidence. Many found it simultaneously incredible and all too credible. Self-righteous anger scored the verdict as a disgrace. Fury fed riots in South Central Los Angeles, killing 54 persons and injuring another 2,000. When the predominantly black jury found O.J. not guilty in October 1995, more than a few saw the verdict as payback for Rodney King.

The notion of race as a get-out-of-jail card rankled many. Yet to many it played in contrast to the notion of race as a go-to-jail card imprisoning minority men. In one view, being black had privileged O.J. In another view, being white had privileged the majority since America's beginning. A sense of reverse discrimination figured in both views. At least some of the anger at the O.J. verdict reflected a festering attitude that civil rights agitation aimed not to end racial discrimination but, rather, to promote blacks at whites' expense.

Anxiety over affirmative action expanded antipathy. In the angry view of a world-turned-on-its-head, black preference supplanted the appropriate American goal of a color-blind society. And in the tough economic times from the late 1970s through the 1990s, white men feeling discriminated against on the basis of their race and their gender, too, turned bellicose. In such a view, the O.J. verdict proved the social system had gone wrong.

Landmark legal cases scored the struggle against what opponents denounced as preferences and quotas. Public higher education figured prominently in the cases. And no schools were more prominent than California's. In fact, as the O.J. trial heated up in the summer of 1995, the higher education admissions battleground centered on the Regents of the University of California. There black regent Ward Connerly, whom Republican Governor Pete Wilson appointed in 1993, moved to end use of race as a factor in the university system's admissions. The regents adopted the policy in July 1995.

Connerly rose to celebrity status as hero or dupe in his self-announced "fight against race preferences." He and a growing number of self-styled black conservatives asserted that color-blindness, not affirmative action, best solved race relations' problems. Economist Thomas Sowell had served since the 1970s as a leader of blacks who shared this perspective. They formed an anti–civil rights color blind chorus. They vociferously denounced as sham and shameful old-line civil rights leaders and organizations. Their stinging critiques cast government actions to ameliorate disadvantage, discrimination, or prejudice as out-of-date and counterproductive. Race was neither the problem nor the solution, they insisted. The problem was behavior. More broadly, it was a pattern of behavior that might be called "culture." Blacks needed to change their culture. They needed to think and act differently, black conservatives insisted. Black self-correction was in order, not societal redirection.

To many, confronting black (mis)behavior was exactly what had not been done in O. J.'s case. Color had been allowed to cloud everything. Race became an excuse. Worse, said critics who echoed black conservatives, it became a misguided apology. America needed to stop its "excessive national self-flagellation" over race and particularly over blacks' disfavored position, insisted controversial social critic Dinesh D'Souza in his much-talked-about 1995 book *The End of Racism*. Crassly peddling racist theories long dismissed, he asserted that behavior and biology relegated blacks to where they were. "Substantial innate differences raise the prospect of a multicultural society characterized not by benign equality, but rather by a natural hierarchy of groups: whites or Asians concentrated at the top, Hispanics in the middle, and blacks at the bottom," maintained D'Souza—himself a son of immigrants from India.[4]

Outcry denounced D'Souza's crudities. Similar clamor also met the innate differences message Richard Herrnstein and Charles Murray offered as science in their incendiary 1994 book *The Bell Curve*. It talked of genetics rather than race, of "cognitive ability" (more simply called intelligence) rather than undifferentiated biological elements. Their explosive thesis argued that substantial differences in intelligence separated individuals and groups in U.S. society. The distribution of rewards in position, salary, status, or other measures followed the differences, they said. The outcome was natural. It emerged from genetic endowment. Applied to the public debate on race relations, Herrnstein and Murray's message suggested that if America were a society (or wanted to be a society) where success or failure rested on individual achievement, then public policy should let the chips fall as they may and not try to rearrange outcomes by affirmative action or like measures that the natural order doomed to fail. Neither government policy nor anything else could do much about racial results, they concluded.[5]

Many rejected letting things stay as they were. They believed change could and should make a difference in racial positions and in race relations. They accepted racial change as necessary, from within and from without. Blacks needed to change. So did America. The call and response to such change continued to split Americans. Indeed, the nation wrestled with a massive call for change a day short of two weeks after O. J.'s acquittal in October 1995, when hundreds of thousands of black men rallied in a "Million Man March" at the nation's capital.

Much about the event proved controversial. Disputes flared even about the number that attended. Central in most of the contention stood Nation of Islam Minister Louis Farrakhan. He envisioned and evoked the march in a call for

spiritual atonement and personal and community reconciliation. His leadership proved a lightning rod. The anti-Semitism, hatred of whites, and exclusionist racism attributed to Farrakhan sparked fears that the event would be a
stage for a "message of malice and division," as President Bill Clinton anxiously put it.[6]

Many struggled to separate the message from the messenger. U.S. Army General Colin L. Powell, the first black to serve as chairman of the U.S. Joint Chiefs
of Staff (1989–1993), on the day of the event frankly admitted on the nationally
televised *CBS This Morning* show that "I wish somebody else had thought of
the idea of the 'Million Man March' rather than Minister Farrakhan." He explained, "I deplore, I condemn, the racist and anti-Semitic expressions that Minister Farrakhan has made over the years." Making an O. J. connection, as the
trial and verdict remained fresh, Powell compared Farrakhan to Mark
Fuhrman, an ex-LAPD detective whose testimony—particularly his taped racist
remarks—proved something of a turning point in the case. "Racism in any form
is deplorable," Powell insisted, "whether it comes from Minister Farrakhan or
a Mark Fuhrman, it's the same thing." Powell emphasized a positive vision of
"hundreds of thousands of black men coming together . . . to begin to uplift
black men and uplift African Americans to be part of an inclusive America."[7]

What exactly was "an inclusive America"? Was it one that recognized race
and racial differences in public and private actions? Or was an inclusive America one that at least publicly refused to recognize race and racial differences?
The California Civil Rights Initiative (Proposition 209) that Ward Connerly
pushed in 1996 appeared to put the questions to a popular referendum. The
proposition moved to amend California's constitution to say, "The state shall
not discriminate against, or grant preferential treatment to, any individual or
group on the basis of race, sex, color, ethnicity, or national origin in the operation of public employment, public education, or public contracting."[8] In November 1996, California voters adopted the proposition 54.6 to 45.4 percent.

Offered as a "color-blind, treat everyone equally" measure, Proposition 209's
success moved other states to act similarly. Washington's 1998 no-preference
statute was a prime example as a majority of Americans appeared fed up with
race issues. The view of many appeared to be that if race were not a past issue,
then it was time to declare it past, now that government-imposed racial segregation was gone. Integration had become a reality. Race was irrelevant. Look
at the phenomenal success of Halle Berry, Michael Jordan, Colin Powell, Denzel Washington, or Oprah Winfrey. Being black had not held them back, proponents of this view said.

Was the television world of talk-show host Oprah, or that of celluloid sex
symbols Berry and Washington, or NBA star Jordan, or the U.S. Armed Forces
any true test of American society? The color comity cast in television, movies,
and advertising apparently served to satisfy many that America had achieved
the integration and equality perceived as the ends of the Civil Rights Movement of the 1950s and 1960s. Others cast such a view as a glittering mirage.
Racial comity was not reality in America. Patterns in housing, education, and
culture (particularly the urban/suburban/ex-urban chasms) showed persistent
divides and revealed that the overwhelming majority of whites simply pre-

ferred blacks at a distance. They appeared eager to accept virtual reality rather than deal with the ugly persistence of systemic disadvantages.

The persistence of the black-white divide—what some called the black-white paradigm—moved many to doubt the relevance of race in the offing of the twenty-first century. Americans of Asian or Central and South American heritage, for example, recognizing their personal and peculiar group disadvantages in U.S. society, increasingly rejected dichotomy as a legitimate approach to race relations. America to them was not merely white or nonwhite. With them, it was more. Yet it was not the "rainbow" of the Reverend Jesse Jackson's coalition. Culture rather than color, language rather than lineage, appeared primary issues. Many distanced themselves from blacks, not only as a matter of culture but also in regard to common cause. They rejected being classed with blacks who were historically and persistently the bottom of U.S. society. For many nonwhite/nonblack Americans, pursuing the American dream involved only that single American ideal color—the color of money.

Class displaced color as a policy focus in many eyes. Poverty reappeared as a central issue. Talk shifted from race to "the truly disadvantaged," the "underclass," and the "inner city."[9] But questions remained about underlying reality. *Inner city*, for instance, appeared a color-coded term. It signaled a predominantly nonwhite, and usually black, urban area. It was synonymous with *ghetto*. It was a place of substandard housing, jobs, and social services. It was a heart of darkness where common sense said wise men (or was that white men), and certainly wise women, should fear to tread—never after dark, for sure. Popular writer Tom Wolfe rode the images to bestsellerdom with his 1987 novel *Bonfire of the Vanities*.

The inner city developed in large part from white flight beginning in the 1950s. Some called the phenomenon suburbanization. It was broad based. It reflected class, of course. But a significant aspect remained racial. More than that, it remained black and white. Inside and outside America's cities, the fact remained black/white racial separation. Distance was not class or income so much as simply black/white. Others of color—such as Asian Americans or Hispanic or Latino Americans—with a third-grade education were more likely to live in a neighborhood with whites than was a black with a Ph.D.

President Clinton noted the continuing black/white rift. He saw both old and new faces in the nation's race relations. He also saw more diversity. Moving to advance the nation toward his vision of racial unity, he announced in June 1997 "One America in the 21st Century: The President's Initiative on Race" (PIR). He centered the effort on a yearlong national conversation on race, racism, and reconciliation.[10]

Opponents trashed Clinton's PIR as a throwback. It reprised quotas, set-asides, and traditional assumptions about race and race relations. Such thinking was destined to "divert us and make it harder to solve problems," said Republican Speaker of the U.S. House of Representatives Newt Gingrich of Georgia. "Racism will not disappear by focusing on race," he insisted. "Racism will disappear by focusing on achievement and finding a way for every citizen to be an achiever." Pushing the conservative view, Gingrich declared that the solutions to the nation's race relations problems were not group remedies but, rather, "individual economics and education."[11]

As the twentieth century closed, the United States had much to ponder. Had race ceased to be a public policy issue? Had it become merely another issue of private, personal relations? Were there systemic and social problems attached to race that required public action? Views diverged. What was past, what was present, what was future appeared fraught with old fears and stereotypes. As with the lingering reaction to O. J.'s trials that came to something of a close in May 1999, with his negotiating a custody arrangement for the two children he had with Nicole, a split remained visible. In fact, a divide yawned.

Race persisted as a prop in an incessant struggle to define America, to prioritize its values, to decide which was foremost, individualism or social justice. If many in America wished to push it behind, to mark it as something in the past, race refused to lie low as America faced the twenty-first century. Catastrophic hurricane Katrina and its aftermath violently made the point in late summer 2005. It threw up in black and white issues of who counted, of governmental care and concern, of public policy and practice. Apparent overt racism in scenes from flooded New Orleans, Louisiana, provoked more than a few to reconsider the intermingling dynamics of class and race in how the federal government in particular responded or failed to respond. The crisis devastated what was then the thirty-fifth largest U.S. city. With 462,000 residents, a majority of them blacks, it was the birthplace and home of jazz, blues, and so much more in African American and American culture and identity. Immediate reactions to the horror split along racial lines, as a CNN/USA Today/Gallup poll demonstrated in mid-September 2005, two weeks after the storm hit. Six in 10 blacks responding in the poll said the federal government responded slowly and inadequately because most of the victims were black. Only about 1 in 8 whites polled agreed with that view. As in the nation's past, the presence of race and its impact persisted as a source of deep disagreement among Americans.

NOTES

1. Bureau of Justice Statistics Correctional Surveys (The National Probation Data Survey, National Prisoner Statistics, Survey of Jails, and The National Parole Data Survey) as presented in Correctional Populations in the United States, 1997. "Percent of adults under correctional supervision by race, 1986–97," http://www.ojp.usdoj.gov/bjs/glance/tables/cpracepttab.htm.

2. Justice Policy Institute, "Cellblocks or Classrooms? The Funding of Higher Education and Corrections and Its Impact on African American Men," http://www.justicepolicy.org/article.php?id=3.

3. Roper Center for Public Opinion Research at the University of Connecticut, Public Opinion Online, ACCESSION NUMBER: 0243478; QUESTION NUMBER: 022. The remainder were 6 percent "neither" and 5 percent "did not know" or refused to answer. http://www.ropercenter.uconn.edu/ss_cs.html.

4. Dinesh D'Souza, *The End of Racism: Principles for a Multiracial Society* (New York: Free Press, 1995), 437.

5. Richard J. Herrnstein and Charles Murray, *The Bell Curve: Intelligence and Class Structure in American Life* (New York: Free Press, 1994).

6. Zachary R. Dowdy, "Black Men Hear Appeal to Action; Farrakhan Asks Throng to Atone, Take Control," *Boston Globe*, October 17, 1995, 1.

7. Elizabeth Shogren, "Million Man March; Powell Praises Positive Parts of Gathering," *Los Angeles Times*, October 17, 1995, A11.

8. Cal. Const., Article I, § 31 (a) (1996).

9. William Julius Wilson, ed., *The Ghetto Underclass: Social Science Perspectives* (Newbury Park, CA: Sage Publications, 1989); Wilson, *The Truly Disadvantaged: The Inner City, the Underclass, and Public Policy* (Chicago: University of Chicago Press, 1987).

10. *One America in the 21st Century: Forging a New Future—the President's Initiative on Race, the Advisory Board's Report to the President* (Washington, DC: GPO, 1998).

11. Cragg Hines, "Gingrich Predicts Failure of 'Traditional' Panel on Race," *Houston Chronicle*, June 14, 1997, A5.

DOCUMENTS

13.1.   "I pledge," 1995

On October 16, 1995, a day short of two weeks after O. J. Simpson's acquittal on charges of double murder, hundreds of thousands of black men converged on the U.S. capital in a "Million Man March." Across the nation, many wrestled with the sight and significance of the rally. Most discussions featured something about the Nation of Islam's firebrand, Minister Louis Farrakhan (1933–). He had envisioned and evoked the march with themes of spiritual atonement and personal and community reconciliation. Yet focus on Farrakhan's long notorious preaching of black separateness, "white devils," and "oppressive Jews" moved many to fear the march would carry what President Bill Clinton anxiously called a "message of malice and division." In his speech at the rally, Farrakhan exhorted black men to take a pledge (repeated below) that he suggested expressed the central meaning of the Million Man March and exhibited a program for moving blacks and the American nation toward progress in race relations.

I pledge that from this day forward I will strive to love my brother as I love myself. I, from this day forward, will strive to improve myself spiritually, morally, mentally, socially, politically and economically for the benefit of myself, my family and my people.

I pledge that I will strive to build businesses, build houses, build hospitals, build factories and enter into international trade for the good of myself, my family and my people.

I pledge that from this day forward I will never raise my hand with a knife or a gun to beat, cut, or shoot any member of my family or any human being except in self-defense.

I pledge from this day forward I will never abuse my wife by striking her, disrespecting her, for she is the mother of my children and the producer of my future.

I pledge that from this day forward I will never engage in the abuse of children, little boys or little girls for sexual gratification. For I will let them grow in peace to be strong men and women for the future of our people.

I will never again use the "B word" to describe any female. But particularly my own black sister. I pledge from this day forward that I will not poison my body with drugs or that which is destructive to my health and my well-being.

I pledge from this day forward I will support black newspapers, black radio, black television. I will support black artists who clean up their acts to show respect for themselves and respect for their people and respect for the ears of the human family. I will do all of this so help me God.

13.2.   "The ultimate test of our democracy," 1995

On October 16, 1995, black men by the hundreds of thousands gathered on the Mall in Washington, D.C., in a "Million Man March" for spiritual atonement and personal and community reconciliation. The prospect of the gathering provoked anxiety and controversy. More than a few feared what so many black men might do together in one place and time. Many also wondered what it meant that so many black men had come together. The fact that Nation of Islam Minister Louis Farrakhan—whom much of the national media cast as a rabid racist—called the march further disturbed many. Among those seeking to make sense of it all was President Bill Clinton, who on the day of the march delivered the following speech on race relations at the University of Texas at Austin.

I believe the march in Washington today spawned such an outpouring because it is a reflection of something deeper and stronger that is running throughout our American community. I believe that in millions and millions of different ways our entire country is reasserting our commitment to the bedrock values that made our country great and that make life worth living.

The great divides of the past call for and were addressed by legal and legislative changes. They were addressed by leaders like Lyndon Johnson, who passed the civil rights act and the voting rights act.

And, to be sure, this great divide requires a public response by democratically elected leaders, but today we are really dealing and we know it, with problems that grow in large measure out of the way all of us look at the world with our minds and the way we feel about the world with our hearts.

And therefore while leaders and legislation may be important, this is work that has to be done by every single one of you.

And this is the ultimate test of our democracy, for today the house divided exists largely in the minds and hearts of the American people. And it must be united there, in the minds and hearts of our people.

Yes, there are some who would poison our progress by selling short the great character of our people and our enormous capacity to change and grow.

But they will not win the day. We will win the day.

13.3.   "The state shall not discriminate," 1996

> In November 1996, California voters had before them ballot Propo-
> sition 209. It was titled the California Civil Rights Initiative. Among its
> chief supporters was Ward Connerly (1939–), a black member of
> the Regents of the University of California. He succeeded in July 1995
> to move his fellow regents to ban using race as a factor in the uni-
> versity system's admissions. Fresh from that victory in what he termed
> his antiaffirmative action "fight against race preferences," Connerly
> campaigned for what he touted as color-blind public policy through-
> out the state. The proposition he promoted promised to eliminate state
> or local government's use of sex, race, or ethnicity as factors in hir-
> ing, promotion, training, recruitment, or public contracts. Voters
> adopted the proposition—reproduced below—5,268,462 (54.6 per-
> cent) to 4,388,733 (45.4 percent).

This initiative measure is submitted to the people in accordance with the provisions of Article II, Section 8 of the [California] Constitution. . . .

Section 31 is added to Article I of the California Constitution as follows:

SEC. 31. (a) The state shall not discriminate against, or grant preferential
treatment to, any individual or group on the basis of race, sex, color, ethnicity,
or national origin in the operation of public employment, public education, or
public contracting.

(b) This section shall apply only to action taken after the section's effective
date.

(c) Nothing in this section shall be interpreted as prohibiting bona fide qualifications based on sex which are reasonably necessary to the normal operation
of public employment, public education, or public contracting.

(d) Nothing in this section shall be interpreted as invalidating any court
order or consent decree which is in force as of the effective date of this section.

(e) Nothing in this section shall be interpreted as prohibiting action which
must be taken to establish or maintain eligibility for any federal program,
where ineligibility would result in a loss of federal funds to the state.

(f) For the purposes of this section, "state" shall include, but not necessarily
be limited to, the state itself, any city, county, city and county, public university system, including the University of California, community college district,
school district, special district, or any other political subdivision or governmental instrumentality of or within the state.

(g) The remedies available for violations of this section shall be the same, regardless of the injured party's race, sex, color, ethnicity, or national origin, as
are otherwise available for violations of then-existing California antidiscrimination law.

(h) This section shall be self-executing. If any part or parts of this section are
found to be in conflict with federal law or the United States Constitution, the
section shall be implemented to the maximum extent that federal law and the

United States Constitution permit. Any provision held invalid shall be severable from the remaining portions of this section.

Source: Attorney General of the State of California, "Proposition 209: Text of Proposed Law" (Sacramento, CA: Attorney General's Office, 1996).

13.4.   "A long and tortured road," 1997

> *Ward Connerly (1939–   ) was a prime mover of California's anti–affirmative action Proposition 209. Golden State voters ratified the proposed constitutional amendment in November 1996. That success spotlighted Connerly as something of a national figure in the struggles over affirmative action. Below is an excerpt of what Connerly offered as a reminiscence of his December 1997 visit at the White House with President Bill Clinton. The occasion provided Connerly an opportunity to recall his mental impressions of the position of his fellow blacks and the nation's recent history with race. It also provided an opportunity for him to critique what the nation needed to do in what he termed the "fight against race preferences."*

I also had a sense of the distance we have traveled as a nation, of what a long and tortured road we have walked in our search for racial fairness and how, in recent times, we seemed to have doubled back again on our own tracks. A generation ago, when Martin Luther king, Jr. stood . . . he brought with him a simple and eloquent plea for equal treatment under the law for all Americans, black and white. . . . But now, after almost forty years of national introspection and determined civic and political action had made America a different country from what it had been, the situation was reversed. I had come to Washington to reaffirm King's message, but I knew I would be opposed by a president who, although he claimed that his views had been formed by the moral urgencies of the civil rights movement, nonetheless insisted that race mattered even more today than it did in the distant past, and that equality under the law was no longer enough. . . .

As I see it, the generation of black people before my own would do anything to get ahead—dig ditches, clean houses, whatever. No job was too small and no day too long. In a brief thirty years, programs such as welfare had changed all this, replacing these heroic efforts at self-betterment with a culture of dependence. And affirmative action was the kissing cousin of welfare, a seemingly humane social gesture that was actually quite diabolical in its consequences—not only causing racial conflict because of its inequities, but also validating blacks' fears of inferiority and reinforcing racial stereotypes. As the brilliant writer Shelby Steele once noted, affirmative action is *a white man's notion of what a black man wants*—at its best, a Tammany of grievances; at its worst, a form of racial racketeering.

Proposition 209 was anathema to the Clintonites precisely because it unmasked affirmative action for what it had become over the last quarter century: not a "subtle plus" that imperceptibly affirmed black ambition, but a regime of systematic race preferences that put the government back in the same discrimination business it had been in when Thurgood Marshall, as lead attorney in *Brown vs. Board of Education* in 1954, wrote, "Distinctions by race are so evil, so arbitrary and insidious that a state bound to defend the equal protection of the laws must not allow them in any public sphere."

By winning in California, we had shown that the people of this country now accepted these once-controversial sentiments as simple common sense; that they were right to say they smelled the rat of sophistry in formulations such as "we must take race into account to get beyond race"; and that they were ready once and for all to get beyond the numbers games and the obsession with group identity and make the vision once articulated by Martin Luther King and Thurgood Marshall and others a reality.

Source: Ward Connerly, *Creating Equal: My Fight against Race Preferences* (San Francisco: Encounter Books, 2000), 1–4.

13.5.   "Rethinking Racial Identity," 1999

> *Preparations for the 2000 U.S. Census intensified discussion of the government's categories for racial identification and, indeed, of the meaning of race itself. As the nation's population leader and pacesetter in political and popular response to contemporary issues, California found itself the scene of significant discussion. Andre Mouchard, a writer at one of California's prominent newspapers, in the excerpt below illustrated aspects of the census identity discussion.*

The next census will let people check off more than one racial category, a process destined to reshape ideas about race in America.

Forget Tiger Woods.

Even though he's probably America's best-known multiracial person—a guy who once told Oprah that he is "Cablinasian" because he is part Caucasian, part black, part Indian and part Asian—the golf pro who grew up in Cypress might be too old to be a true example of our racial future.

He is, after all, 23.

Instead, for a peek at what America will look like in the next century, check out the parking lot at Turtle Rock Preschool in Irvine.

There, most school-day mornings, a few dozen toddlers pop out of their parents' luxury cars, minivans and SUVs. The well-groomed parade could be a United Nations meeting in miniature—Asian kids, Hispanic kids, white kids, African-American kids.

And, most of all, multiracial kids.

Well, probably most of all.

Nobody knows for sure.

"I don't know if (multirace kids) is the most common race here or not, to be honest, but they definitely are right up there," said Kristen Bold, the school's assistant director.

Turtle Rock, like most private schools, doesn't ask its customers about race or ethnicity. Even if it did, the school probably wouldn't track multiracial kids. In America, hardly anybody does.

Until now.

The next census, slated to begin in about a year, will include new rules that figure to drastically change many things—the national head count, the growing gap between rich and poor, and, perhaps, our definition of race.

Orange County—as it has, quietly, for the past 30 years—figures to be at the leading edge of America's changing racial identity.

Instead of picking a single race, as previous censuses have required, Americans will be allowed to check off all the race boxes that apply to them.

The result is expected to be a first-time look at the size and nature of a previously uncounted minority—multiracial people.

The new rules aren't perfect.

Census Bureau officials say the option to check off more than one race creates 32,000 possible racial combinations, up from 15 in 1990. . . .

What it all might mean is anybody's guess. But, ready or not, experts say many traditional ideas of race are about to change forever.

"The racial classifications in this country have, until now, been bipolar—black and white, and, more recently, nonwhite and white," said Margo Anderson, a census expert and professor of urban studies at the University of Wisconsin.

"Now, the questions are these: What's the new melting pot going to include, and what's it going to look like?"

Source: Andre Mouchard, "Rethinking Racial Identity," *Orange County Register*, April 25, 1999, L1.

13.6.   "The state shall not classify," 2003

In October 2003, California voters again had before them a ballot proposition on race. Called the Racial Privacy Initiative (Proposition 54), it aimed to stop California from recognizing or using any racial classification system. California would stop asking race-based questions and collecting any race-based data. It would allow race no official place in the state. Advocates claimed that the proposition, reproduced below, would be a step toward a color-blind society. Opponents claimed the proposition made the state simply blind. Voters rejected the proposition by 5,538,270 (63.9 percent) to 3,141,951 (36.1 percent). A similar measure in Michigan failed to qualify as a ballot measure in the 2004 elections.

PROHIBITION AGAINST CLASSIFYING BY RACE BY STATE AND OTHER PUBLIC ENTITIES

Section 32 is added to Article I of the California Constitution as follows: Sec. 32.

(a) The state shall not classify any individual by race, ethnicity, color or national origin in the operation of public education, public contracting or public employment.

(b) The state shall not classify any individual by race, ethnicity, color or national origin in the operation of any other state operations, unless the legislature specifically determines that said classification serves a compelling state interest and approves said classification by a 2/3 majority in both houses of the legislature, and said classification is subsequently approved by the governor.

(c) For purposes of this section, "classifying" by race, ethnicity, color or national origin shall be defined as the act of separating, sorting or organizing by race, ethnicity, color or national origin including, but not limited to, inquiring, profiling, or collecting such data on government forms.

Source: California Secretary of State, "Statewide Special Election, October 7, 2003," "Proposition 54: Text of Proposed Law" (Sacramento: California Secretary of State, 2003).

ANNOTATED RESEARCH GUIDE

Books

Crosby, Faye J., and Cheryl VanDeVeer, eds. *Sex, Race, and Merit: Debating Affirmative Action in Education and Employment*. Ann Arbor: University of Michigan Press, 2000. A rich anthology drawn from various sides of the affirmative action debate, focused particularly on higher education and employment.

Graves, Joseph L. *The Emperor's New Clothes: Biological Theories of Race at the Millennium*. New Brunswick, NJ: Rutgers University Press, 2002. Traces thinking about human genetic diversity in debunking the idea of race as biologically determined, arguing that divorcing race from biology is an essential first step to eliminating racism.

Helms, Janet E., ed. *Black and White Racial Identity: Theory, Research, and Practice*. Westport, CT: Greenwood Press, 1990. Offers theories of black and white racial identity as part of social relations and connections to personality development and realization.

Hunt, Darnell M. *O. J. Simpson Facts and Fiction: New Rituals in the Construction of Reality*. New York: Cambridge University Press, 1999. Explores the courtroom and public opinion spectacle, focusing on how race and other elements of social identity shaped perceptions of Simpson and his trials' implications for U.S. race relations.

Jacobs, Ronald N. *Race, Media, and the Crisis of Civil Society: From Watts to Rodney King*. New York: Cambridge University Press, 2000. Probes how journalists and society framed racial issues from the 1960s through the 1990s, focusing on the media's power and roles.

Jacoby, Russell, and Naomi Glauberman, eds. *The Bell Curve Debate: History, Documents, Opinions*. New York: Times Books, 1995. Taps the national controversy the best-selling book *The Bell Curve* ignited over the roles and impact of class, intelligence, and race in democratic practice in multiracial America.

Johnson, Kevin R., ed. *Mixed Race America and the Law: A Reader*. New York: New York University Press, 2002. Explores a new understanding of race in America through the mixed race experience with essays that range from interracial adoption to miscegenation, and racial classification.

Kennedy, Randall. *Race, Crime, and the Law*. New York: Pantheon Books, 1997. Examines the ferocious racial politics surrounding race and crime and how perceptions of inequity and injustice persist as problems in the complex of race relations.

Omi, Michael, and Howard Winant. *Racial Formation in the United States: From the 1960s to the 1990s*. 2nd ed. New York: Routledge, 1994. Connects the 1992 presidential election, the Los Angeles riots, and Clinton administration policies to historial development of U.S. race relations.

Walker, Samuel, et al. *The Color of Justice: Race, Ethnicity, and Crime in America*. Belmont, CA: Wadsworth, 1996. Probes patterns of crime and racial discrimination in the U.S. criminal justice system.

Wilson, William Julius. *The Truly Disadvantaged: The Inner City, the Underclass, and Public Policy*. Chicago: University of Chicago Press, 1987. Examines the profound impact of economics and politics on racial positioning and social policy with a special focus on black inner-city poverty.

———. *The Declining Significance of Race: Blacks and Changing American Institutions*. 2nd ed. Chicago: University of Chicago Press, 1980. Integrates historical perspective with social theory and research on contemporary trends to explain and project how changing economics and politics affect discussion of race, class, and social policy.

Web Sites

http://www.clinton5.nara.gov/textonly/Initiatives/OneAmerica/america_onrace.html—links to President Bill Clinton's initiative on race, inaugurated in 1997, with materials on the prospects of race relations in the 1990s and beyond.

http://www.courttv.com/casefiles/simpson—the CourtTV site links to various aspects of the criminal and civil trials of O. J. Simpson, with courtroom and other documents and multimedia materials.

http://www3.cnn.com/US/9510/megamarch/march.html—CNN site provide links to multimedia views of the Million Man March and its coverage in related stories.

ville, Texas, to San Diego, California, appeared a salient insecurity—although the longer U.S. border with Canada was even less guarded. Control of this southern U.S. border emerged over time as a sharp domestic and diplomatic issue. A surge of illegal immigration after 1945 focused attention on it. The size of the actual flow defied exact reporting, almost by definition. Numbers the U.S. Department of Justice reported apprehended provided a measure, however. From an annual average of about 11,000 apprehended crossing the U.S.-Mexico border illegally from 1934 to 1943, the number nearly tripled to 31,174 in 1944. It more than doubled in 1945 to 69,165. In 1954, it peaked at 1,089,583.[5]

A booming U.S. economy acted as a magnet. With legal immigration just about closed, illegal means remained the most practical entry for many. The stark contrast between poverty and plenty across what came to be called La Frontera from Mexico to the United States moved many. The *braceros* program proved to satisfy neither side then. Mexican workers and American employers wanted a larger flow than the program provided. The tension between opportunity and legal openings did not lessen when the Immigration and Nationality Act of 1965 provided for a labor certification program that offered permanent status to cross-border laborers.

As the United States entered its civil rights crisis in the 1950s and 1960s, Mexican Americans found themselves in an ambiguous posture. While many were generations-old, native-born U.S. citizens, they found themselves increasingly cast wholesale with guest workers or with suspected illegal immigrants. Public perceptions made few distinctions. Indeed, public perceptions failed further to distinguish among persons labeled merely Hispanic or Latino. *Hispanic*, after all, marked only a Spanish-speaking commonality Similarly, *Latino* marked only common origin from Latin America. Differences abounded among the peoples so labeled. Even the U.S. Census Bureau used the term *Hispanic* (and less often *Latino*) as a synonym for a racial category. American perception and practice treated those labeled Hispanic or Latino as both more and less a race.

As the largest and longest-storied of those labeled Hispanic, Mexican Americans showed the ways of racial discrimination and determined protest. They suffered segregation in Texas and Arizona, for example. Placed in segregated schools, they were also shunted in public accommodations such as swimming pools, restrooms, restaurants, movies, and other theaters. They lived apart in separate neighborhoods. They worked only in designated jobs and levels. As with others deemed nonwhites, Mexican Americans suffered from de facto practices even more than de jure policies.

By U.S. law, regardless of coloring or complexion, Mexican Americans were classified as white—which proved both a help and a hindrance in fighting the social distance and legal distinctions used to discriminate against them. As nominal whites, they were routinely denied Fourteenth Amendment claims against racial discrimination. The Texas Court of Criminal Appeals illustrated the spurious reasoning in its 1951 decision in *Sanchez v. State*. It rejected Mexican Americans' due process and equal protection challenges against their exclusion from jury service. The court declared that "no ground for discussing the discrimination" existed because Mexican Americans "are not a separate

14

At the Border Again? New Immigrants and Old Worries

Who gets to be an American? Much in U.S. race relations has centered on that question. And it was no less so as the nation entered a new millennium. In 1776 the Declaration of Independence railed against King George III's "obstructing the Laws for Naturalization" and refusing to encourage immigration to America. The document's final version suggested, however, that not all immigrants were welcome. The Africans whom drafter Thomas Jefferson called "a distant people" were dropped from the official version. Without mentioning the "distant people" by name, the Constitution drafted in 1787 set them to be banned from entering the United States after 1808. And the nation's first federal law determining who "may be admitted to become a citizen" pointedly restricted the privilege to "a free white person."[1]

Race persisted as an acknowledged aspect of constructing U.S. citizenship. It joined from time to time with nativism. When coupled, the two opposed the racial other along with the nonnative newcomer and outsider, labeling them "un-American." Such racialized nativism resurged in the 1990s. The racist, antiimmigrant brunt targeted particularly persons of Mexican descent and their fellow Hispanics and Latinos. They stood publicly scorned with contempt similar to that inflicted on Chinese and Japanese during the so-called Yellow Peril at the turn of the nineteenth century. The same cry echoed: These people are unassimilable. They cling to culture, customs, and language that are not American. If they are not stopped, they will overrun America and turn it into something it should not be, screamed naysayers.

One reputed expert on American culture and public policy at the opening of the twenty-first century projected current immigration patterns to mark "the end of the America we have known for more than three centuries." Moreover, he cast developments in battle terms as something of a rewaging of the 1840s

U.S. War with Mexico. "Demographically, socially and culturally, the 'reconquista' (re-conquest) of the Southwest United States by Mexican immigrants is well under way," he wrote. "This trend could consolidate the Mexican-dominant areas of the United States into an autonomous, culturally and linguistically distinct, and economically self-reliant bloc within the United States," he asserted.[2]

Reconquista concerns and similar worries have consistently revealed the racialized context of the persistent U.S. culture wars that from the nation's beginning have contested for its body and soul. Immigration policy has served as a pivotal ground in the conflict. It exposed the location of both larger political stories and smaller human interest stories personalizing battles against local and national prejudices. Fears of being displaced or overrun have abounded in the parochialism that has victimized millions on the basis of race, religion, or regional, national, and ethnic origin.

The national quota acts of the 1920s gave full voice to frightful exclusionist cries. Yet they were hardly original. Racial bars reached back at least to Chinese exclusion in the 1880s. World War I unleashed further restraints, as the Immigration Act of 1917 showed in excluding as "undesirables" sweeping categories of persons, including all Asians. The 1921 Act capping immigration at an annual limit of 3 percent of each nationality counted in the United States in 1910 laid the basis for the national origins scheme completed with the immigration acts of 1922 and 1924. Internal pressures against nonwhites, non-Europeans, non–western Europeans, non-Christians, and non-Protestants have throughout U.S. history exploded against persons of African and Asian descent and against persons from other areas of the Americas south of the United States. Beginning in the 1960s, the explosive pressures exerted fresh force in U.S. race relations.

The outlines of the developing battle emerged in the clamor over immigration reform in the early 1960s. It chorused with swelling cries for civil rights, and it, too, joined in the Great Society President Lyndon B. Johnson orchestrated. "A change is needed in our laws dealing with immigration," LBJ told Congress in January 1965. "The principal reform called for is the elimination of the national origins quota system. That system is incompatible with our basic American tradition," he declared.[3] But what, exactly, was the nation's oft-touted immigrant tradition? Was the nation really receptive to immigration or only to selected immigrants? And if selection were the issue, what were appropriate criteria? Eliminating national origins quotas hardly answered the myriad questions.

In the triumphal reformist air of the day, the Immigration and Nationality Act of 1965 signaled a shifting of national policy. Over three years, it phased in an ostensible first come, first served system. Yet the America that touted itself as a nation of immigrants showed little inclination of the "world-wide welcome" engraved on the Statute of Liberty. The new law limited immigration to a ceiling of 170,000 a year for persons outside the Western Hemisphere and 120,000 a year for persons inside the Western Hemisphere. Even doubling that number to 600,000 admissions annually in the 1980s represented only 1 immigrant per 400 U.S. residents. During the peak immigration years from 1905 to 1914, the United States annually accepted more than 1 million immigrants, or

1 for every 83 U.S. residents. So the reform was more restrictive than receptive, and its changes highlighted core questions of the nation's perception of the place of immigration and of immigrants in its present and future.

The 1965 act's impact showed what was at stake in the nation's immigration policy. Almost immediately after the act, the origins of immigrants shifted from northern Europe to Asia, southern Europe, and the Caribbean. Indeed, Asia supplied about four in ten of all legal immigrants to the United States between 1965 and 1985. China, Hong Kong, India, and the Philippines dominated the flow. Filipinos especially jumped in number, as their proportion rose to more than one-third (37 percent) of Asian immigrants, who collectively rose from being about 13 percent of all U.S. immigrants in the 1960s to approach 50 percent by 1990. That shift increasingly changed U.S. population characteristics. And it engendered political and social contention, much of it ringing with racial rhetoric about American character.[4]

Some cloaking themselves as defenders of American culture resisted what popular idiom dubbed "the new immigration." They especially decried the rising influx from Asia, the Caribbean, and Central and South America. They preferred northern and western Europeans, with whom they felt cultural and historical ties. They spoke of protecting not only U.S. culture but also the economy and labor. They announced fears that the English language would be lost in the United States, and they pressed for formal adoption of English as the official U.S. language. They fought bilingual education and governmental recognition of any rights to use languages other than English in public proceedings or even in private workplaces. The themes repeated persisting divides and a constant apprehension of a foreign flood that would wipe away America's essence.

Immigrants' impact on local and national labor markets, and on the broader political economy, was hotly contested—as it had been periodically since the 1800s. Complaints of immigrants snatching jobs from previous residents or depressing wages filled Boston in the 1840s, New York in the 1850s, and San Francisco in the 1860s and 1870s. Race and ethnicity resounded in those instances, marking the Irish and Chinese, for example. The post-1965 new immigrants sparked similar clamor. Unemployed and underemployed U.S. residents rarely saw any need for immigrants. Employers in several sectors almost routinely insisted, however, on their desperate need for immigrants to do jobs they claimed went begging.

Agriculture stood as a prime example. Shortage of labor to develop crops had served as an old and honored explanation. It had served the slave trade, and the rationale persisted that furnishing labor to fill need was essential to economic development. Such thinking laid the framework for the United States to import workers from Mexico as *braceros*, or "helping hands," in the farm labor shortages during World War II (1939–1945). Yet stark reality underlay the *braceros* program. While it appeared to facilitate labor mobility for potential employees from Mexico and potential employers in the United States, the program aimed in large part to curb and regularize the U.S. flow of Mexican workers, which to some seemed out of hand.

Some Americans came to view Mexicans as threats. The nearly 2,000-mile-long (3,140 kilometers), virtually open border stretching west from Browns-

race but are white people of Spanish descent."[6] As other whites sat on juries, Mexican Americans had no claim that whites were discriminated against the court ruled.

Texas courts insisted on a dichotomous view of race. It selectively chose, however, not the broad, traditional white and nonwhite division. When convenient, Texas courts used a narrow, technical black-and-white division. The view sought to trap persons who in practice were treated as nonwhites but who scrambled for any distance they could manage from being classified with blacks. Such use of racial dichotomy served increasingly as a weapon in a divide-and-conquer strategy to scatter nonwhites and to distance them among themselves. Each group was directed to nurse its own sense of peculiar grievances. Each was directed to cultivate its own set of remedies. Each was directed to view itself as special and separate and without need to share with other nonwhites, lest nonwhites mass to oppose the discriminations privileging whites. Thus, the Mexican American campaign against discrimination steered sharply from the ongoing African American campaign against discrimination.

Mexican Americans appeared to crave their own separate victory. They achieved it in part in the U.S. Supreme Court with *Hernandez v. Texas*. Decided in May 1954, exactly two weeks before the landmark desegregation decision in *Brown v. Board of Education of Topeka* (1954), *Hernandez* held that discrimination was a question of fact determined by examining actual practice, not merely by reference to any dichotomous race theory. Mexican Americans hailed the decision with a sense of community vindication. But basic questions remained unsettled about where Mexican Americans stood or wanted to stand in regard to race and segregation. The questions reached self-identity and social identity. They asked who was in and who was out. And there immigration questions loomed large.

The scale and structure of the immigrant flow from the 1960s forward challenged old external and internal race-coded communities. The so-called new immigrants included Vietnamese, Laotians, Koreans, South Asian Indians, Soviet Jews, Salvadorans, Dominicans, Cubans, Haitians, and a host of others that expanded old categories such as Asian Americans, who were earlier typified as Chinese or Japanese. The host of Spanish speakers made the Hispanic/Latino cluster a hodgepodge.

Concentrating mostly in three states—California, New York, and Texas—and then in cities, new immigrant clusters mimicked classic patterns of early-twentieth-century ethnic enclaves. "Little India" in Jackson Heights, Queens in New York City, the Dominicans of Manhattan's Washington Heights, and the "Little Saigons" in California's Orange and Santa Clara counties illustrated a redeveloping urban ecology. Relating to their physical surroundings and to one another, new immigrants often set aside old differences of culture, language, and religion for new identities in the U.S. racial prism. A sort of pan-ethnicity, for example, bonded South Asian Indians, Pakistanis, Bangladeshis, and Sri Lankans. In places, common interests among Spanish speakers also created something of an ethnic transnationalism that challenged old racial stereotypes and further stirred agitation about the reality and relevance of race as a continuing factor in American life.

Competing elements of distinction also distanced groups. The Cuban influx following Fidel Castro's rise to power in 1959 illustrated aspects of identity clashes within lumped pan-ethnic or transnational groups. Waves of Cuban exiles—first from 1959 to 1962 and then from 1965 to 1973—developed an emigré community that altered South Florida's face. Received with officially open arms in the U.S. contention with Castro, the first waves were something of political pawns. Subsequent waves—such as the Mariel boatlift people of 1980 and the raft-borne *balseros* of the early 1990s—shifted sentiments about the Cuban community and within the Cuban community itself. As with other immigrants historically, splits developed between older and newer arrivals. Older arrivals sometimes harbored feelings that their own hard-won position and degree of acceptance in place were being undermined by newer arrivals.

Over time the Cuban enclave's clearly permanent and growing presence also pushed anxieties about shifting power relations and consequent public policy. The flood of 30,000 Haitian refugees in 1992 added weight to worries. Overloaded state and federal agencies failed to accommodate the influx. Costs of public programs for adjustment and growing nativist cries about newcomers not assimilating in a narrow vision of Americanism increased agitation. Contrasting treatment of earlier more affluent, more typically European-featured Cubans with later flows of poorer and more typically African-featured Haitians fueled racial fires sometimes covered in smoke from discussions of biculturalism, multiculturalism, or diversity.

More than a million Southeast Asians from the U.S. war there—mainly Vietnamese, Laotians, Khmer, Hmong, and Chinese—added to the mix. As refugees, they fit a special category of U.S. immigrants claiming asylum as persecuted persons. Some Salvadorans also were refugees, but they and many Dominicans and others from the Caribbean and Central and South America arrived in the 1970s and later in growing waves of what were popularly called "the undocumented."

Coinciding with a surge of domestic discontent in the late 1970s and 1980s, the surge of newcomers elevated immigration again to being a national political issue. Policy and policing became hot topics. America's traditional touting of itself as a nation of immigrants blocked direct assault on immigration itself. Instead, focus fell on *illegal* immigration. Particularly, it hit persons described in the parlance of the U.S. Immigration and Naturalization Service (INS) as "entered without inspection" (EWI) or "undocumented." Comparatively little focus then fell on the complementary category of "visa abusers," considered as "documented" illegal immigrants. The focus highlighted the U.S.-Mexico border and Hispanics and Latinos in Texas, New York, and California. More than half of all new arrivals, and an estimated seven in ten of all illegal arrivals, congregated in the three states in the 1980s. California proved a special magnate. At least one in five foreign-born new arrivals lived in the Los Angeles area.

National concern dictated presidential-level discussions of how to define and deal with immigration issues. Consensus fixed on illegal immigration as the problem. The accepted solution was to secure the borders, especially the U.S.-Mexico border. What to do with illegal immigrants already here proved to be a thornier problem. The Immigration Reform and Control Act (IRCA) of 1986 aimed to handle both problems and more. It increased penalties against employers who hired illegal immigrants. Also, it offered controversial amnesty provisions that allowed illegal aliens to regularize their status if they documented their continuous residence in the United States before 1982. Opponents complained about lawbreakers being rewarded with the fruits of their crime. Proponents claimed that only by having illegals come forward could the government see the full dimensions for fashioning effective policy and policing. The act satisfied neither side.

About 2 million applied for amnesty under the 1986 act. The INS expected more than twice the number. Many eligible feared coming forward, however. They suspected a trap where they would be deported once they revealed themselves. Many who had already regularized their status de facto saw no need for the de jure process amnesty offered. The count shed little light on overall dimensions. It did fix Hispanics/Latinos as the bulk of illegal immigrants. Of every 100 amnesty applicants, 71 were from Mexico. El Salvador contributed 8 and Guatemala 3. Colombia, the Dominican Republic, Haiti, Nicaragua, the Philippines, Poland, and Iran each contributed 1 applicant. The count also confirmed California as the primary site for illegals, with 54 of every 100 applicants.[7]

Immigration opponents seized the 1986 amnesty results as proof of federal failure. They turned to state action, starting in California. Reacting to their fear of an Hispanic/Latino takeover, they pushed a 1986 ballot proposition to declare English the official language. But that was only a start. They pressed beyond language to issues of money. They claimed illegal immigrants cost the Golden State $2.5 billion annually. Paying for public services such as education, health care, and prisons for illegals drained income from every legitimate Californian, they argued. Their solution became "Proposition 187"—a 1994 state ballot initiative. Officially titled "Illegal Aliens. Ineligibility for Public Services. Verification and Reporting," Proposition 187 declared illegal aliens ineligible for state services. Moreover, it directed state and local workers to report suspected illegals to the state attorney general and the INS.

Hotly argued, Proposition 187 won by a margin of 59 to 41 percent of Californians' voting in November 1994. Analysis showed racial/ethnic divides and resentments in the voting. The 57 percent of California's 1990 population who were white/Anglos provided strongest support. They turned out in droves to make up 81 percent of the 1994 voters. They carried the northern California counties, where they were overwhelmingly dominant in number. They provided strong support also in southern and south-central counties, where the state's 26 percent Hispanic/Latino population concentrated. In contrast, opposition to Proposition 187 came in central/coastal counties where California's 9.5 percent Asian Americans and 7.5 percent African Americans created with Hispanic/Latinos more than average heterogeneity.[8]

The racial/ethnic divide revealed in the Proposition 187 voting proved not peculiar to California. It appeared across the nation. Similar voting issues and patterns arose in Arizona, Colorado, Florida, and Texas. An us/them rhetoric resonated in many, if not most, political discussions. A nativism at one time considered extremist in its espousal of white, Anglo-Saxon, Nordic, Protestant racial/ethnic stock and ethics found apparent popular respectability. *Forbes* magazine senior editor Peter Brimelow, himself a U.S. immigrant from England, espoused the theme in his alarmist 1995 book *Alien Nation: Common Sense about America's Immigration Disaster*. Political gadfly and sometimes presidential candidate Pat Buchanan joined the chorus with his 2002 book *The Death of the West: How Dying Populations and Immigrant Invasions Imperil Our Country and Civilization*. Harvard University pundit Samuel P. Huntington chimed in with his antiimmigrant *Who We Are* in 2004. Identity politics became a weapon, and again illegal immigration stood as an easy target.

Public reaction to the nation's changing racial/ethnic composition reflected sharp splits over America's symbols and substance. Was the United States a nation of created cultural choices or compelled cultural conformity? What did the nation's motto *e pluribus unum* mean in principle and in practice? What, if any, were the commonalities of American community? Was speaking English, for example, such a commonality? Proponents of English as the nation's official language argued yes. English as a language was, they contended, essential to Americanness. Apparently so were some set of beliefs and behaviors. But what exactly were *the* essential American beliefs and behaviors?

The image of cultural pluralism had become divisive at the turn of a new millennium. With all the contingent dynamics and social complexities among Americans, broad differences emerged. Political elites, public opinion leaders, and ordinary people clashed over fundamental images and issues of Americanness. With emotions high after the shock of 9/11 and the subsequent "War on Terrorism," the U.S. government and its leaders were compelled to consider a world abroad and at home where race—identified as color, culture, ethnicity, nationality, or religion—dominated discourse. If many seemed wary of saying it publically, contemporary struggles in many minds resolved into an old politics of race to determine dominance and distribution of wealth and other rewards. Thus, the United States confronted old worries as it faced new immigration.

Race-based identity politics since the 1950s had proved an effective political strategy to empower disadvantaged nonwhites. White power had worked for centuries, after all. And it appeared not about to stop. Was race to have repeating resonance in the U.S. future? In the competition for economic and social privilege, was the United States returning to issues that had made race so potent a force in its history? Many asked if the rising call for color-blind public policy echoed old messages of not recognizing people of color. Skeptics and critics cast the color-blind call as a reactionary political strategy of entrenched whites to disrupt and resist advances of disadvantaged nonwhites by discrediting the reality of race as a socially constructed identity in America. As the nation moved into the twenty-first century, the ultimate question again appeared to be, Who was to get what on what basis?

NOTES

1. Naturalization Act, 1 Stat. 103 (March 26, 1790).
2. Samuel P. Huntington's *Who We Are* (New York: Simon & Schuster, 2004), excerpted in "The Hispanic Challenge," *Foreign Policy* 30 (March–April 2004): 30–45.

3. President Lyndon B. Johnson, Message to the Congress on Submitting Proposed Immigration Legislation, January 13, 1965, in *Public Papers of the Presidents of the United States: Lyndon B. Johnson* (Washington, DC: GPO, 1965), 1:37–39.

4. *The [1986] Annual Report of the Council of Economic Advisers* (Washington, DC: GPO, February 1986), "The Economic Effects of Immigration," 215.

5. U.S. Department of Justice, Immigration and Naturalization Service (INS), *Annual Reports* (Washington, DC: GPO, 1931–1981); INS, *1985 Statistical Year Book* (Washington, DC: GPO, 1986), 177–179; Vernon Briggs Jr., "Methods of Analysis of Illegal Immigration into the United States," *International Migration Review* 18, no. 3 (1984): 626.

6. *Sanchez v. State*, 156 Tex. Crim. 468, 469, 243 S.W.2d 700, 701 (Tex. Crim. App. 1951).

7. Barry R. Chiswick, "Illegal Immigration and Immigration Control," *Journal of Economic Perspectives* 2, no. 3 (Summer 1988): 110.

8. For voting and population data analysis, see Caroline J. Tolbert and Rodney E. Hero, "Race/Ethnicity and Direct Democracy: An Analysis of California's Illegal Immigration Initiative," *Journal of Politics* 58 (1996): 806, 808, 816.

DOCUMENTS

14.1. "No ground for discussing the discrimination," 1951

*A Texas jury southwest of Houston found Mexican American An-
iceto Sanchez guilty of murder. In rejecting his appeal challenging his
conviction, the Texas Court of Criminal Appeals indicated the state's
judicial view of the status of Mexican Americans and their protections
against discrimination. The U.S. Supreme Court in 1954 roundly rejected the Texas court's reasoning reproduced below.*

[Appellant Sanchez] complains that there was violation of the [Fourteenth
Amendment's] due process clause in that there was a systematic, continual,
and uninterrupted practice in Fort Bend County of discriminating against the
Mexican-Americans as a race, and people of Mexican extraction and ancestry
as a class, in the selection of grand jury commissioners and grand jurors.

Appellant has filed quite an exhaustive brief on the subject in which he discusses decisions of other jurisdictions which, either intentionally or loosely,
refer to Mexican people as a different race. They are not a separate race but are
white people of Spanish descent, as has often been said by this court. We find
no ground for discussing the question further and the complaint raised by this
bill will not be sustained.

Source: Sanchez v. State, 156 Tex. Crim. 468, 243 S.W.2d 700 (Tex. Crim. App. 1951).

14.2. "Community prejudices are not static," 1954

*Texas juries indicted and convicted Mexican American Pete Her-
nandez for murder. When Hernandez challenged his indictment and
conviction on appeal, the Texas Court of Criminal Appeals rejected
his discrimination claims. Texas conceded the fact that "for the last
twenty-five years there is no record of any person with a Mexican or
Latin American name having served on a jury commission, grand jury
or petit jury in Jackson County," where Hernandez was indicted and
convicted. Yet the Texas appeals court recognized no discrimination
under the Fourteenth Amendment. Mexicans were whites by law. "In
so far as we are advised, no member of the Mexican nationality challenges that statement," the Texas court noted. So as long as whites
were on juries, Mexican Americans had no legal complaint, the court
insisted. In its view, "the equal protection clause of the Fourteenth
Amendment contemplated and recognized only two classes as com-*

ing within that guarantee: the white race, comprising one class, and the Negro race, comprising the other class." Exactly two weeks before its landmark desegregation decision in Brown v. Board of Education of Topeka *(1954), U.S. Chief Justice Earl Warren delivered the opinion of a unanimous Supreme Court rejecting Texas's view and according Mexican Americans and all other Americans Fourteenth Amendment protections against systematic discrimination, whether by law, intention, or fact.*

[Petitioner Hernandez] alleged that persons of Mexican descent were systematically excluded from service as jury commissioners, grand jurors, and petit jurors, although there were such persons fully qualified to serve residing in Jackson County. The petitioner asserted that exclusion of this class deprived him, as a member of the class, of the equal protection of the laws guaranteed by the Fourteenth Amendment of the Constitution. . . .

In numerous decisions, this Court has held that it is a denial of the equal protection of the laws to try a defendant of a particular race or color under an indictment issued by a grand jury, or before a petit jury, from which all persons of his race or color have, solely because of that race or color, been excluded by the State, whether acting through its legislature, its courts, or its executive or administrative officers. Although the Court has had little occasion to rule on the question directly, it has been recognized since Strauder v. West Virginia, 100 U.S. 303, that the exclusion of a class of persons from jury service on grounds other than race or color may also deprive a defendant who is a member of that class of the constitutional guarantee of equal protection of the laws.

The State of Texas would have us hold that there are only two classes—white and Negro—within the contemplation of the Fourteenth Amendment. The decisions of this Court do not support that view. And, except where the question presented involves the exclusion of persons of Mexican descent from juries, Texas courts have taken a broader view of the scope of the equal protection clause. . . .

Throughout our history differences in race and color have defined easily identifiable groups which have at times required the aid of the courts in securing equal treatment under the laws. But community prejudices are not static, and from time to time other differences from the community norm may define other groups which need the same protection. Whether such a group exists within a community is a question of fact. When the existence of a distinct class is demonstrated, and it is further shown that the laws, as written or as applied, single out that class for different treatment not based on some reasonable classification, the guarantees of the Constitution have been violated. The Fourteenth Amendment is not directed solely against discrimination due to a "two-class theory"—that is, based upon differences between "white" and Negro.

Source: Hernandez v. Texas, 347 U.S. 475, 476–479, 482 (1954) (Warren, C.J., for the Court). (Citations omitted.)

14.3.   "A change is needed in our laws dealing with immigration," 1965

> *In a message to Congress in January 1965, excerpted below, President Lyndon B. Johnson proposed fundamental changes in U.S. immigration policy to eliminate the national origins quota system that barred U.S. entry on the basis of race and ethnicity. Invoking what he termed the "fundamental longtime American attitude" of accepting individuals on their "personal qualities," not on their ancestry, Johnson scored the prejudices that "men and women from some countries are, just because of where they come from, more desirable citizens than others." But holding fast to such prejudices, critics at the time and over time insisted that including some and excluding others on the basis of race and ethnicity were essential to producing and preserving what they viewed as American character and culture.*

A change is needed in our laws dealing with immigration. Four Presidents have called attention to serious defects in this legislation. Action is long overdue. . . .

The principal reform called for is the elimination of the national origins quota system. That system is incompatible with our basic American tradition.

Over the years the ancestors of all of us—some 42 million human beings—have migrated to these shores. The fundamental longtime American attitude has been to ask not where a person comes from but what are his personal qualities. On this basis men and women migrated from every quarter of the globe. By their hard work and their enormously varied talents they hewed a great nation out of a wilderness. By their dedication to liberty and equality, they created a society reflecting man's most cherished ideals.

Long ago the poet Walt Whitman spoke our pride: "These States are the amplest poem. We are not merely a nation but a 'Nation of nations'."

Violation of this tradition by the national origins quota system does incalculable harm. The procedures imply that men and women from some countries are, just because of where they come from, more desirable citizens than others. We have no right to disparage the ancestors of millions of our fellow Americans in this way. Relationships with a number of countries, and hence the success of our foreign policy, is needlessly impeded by this proposition.

The quota system has other grave defects. Too often it arbitrarily denies us immigrants who have outstanding and sorely needed talents and skills. I do not believe this is either good government or good sense.

Source: President Lyndon B. Johnson, Message to the Congress on Submitting Proposed Immigration Legislation, January 13, 1965, in *Public Papers of the Presidents of the United States: Lyndon B. Johnson* (Washington, DC: GPO, 1965), 1:37–39.

14.4.   "Yellow Power," 1969

The civil rights revolution of the 1950s and 1960s that gave rise to the cry "Black Power" moved other people of color to raise their self-identified voices in cries of power. A prime example was Asian Americans' call for "Yellow Power." Particularly Asian American college students such as Amy Uyematsu issued their own telling manifestos of raised community consciousness, as illustrated in the excerpt below. The articulation revealed informative perspectives on the racial cast and construction of the United States, historically and at the moment of utterance.

Asian Americans can no longer afford to watch the black-and-white struggle from the sidelines. They have their own cause to fight, since they are also victims—with less visible scars—of the white institutionalized racism.

A yellow movement has been set into motion by the black power movement. Addressing itself to the unique problems of Asian Americans, this "yellow power" movement is relevant to the black power movement in that both are part of the Third World struggle to liberate all colored people. . . .

In the process of Americanization, Asians have tried to transform themselves into white men—both mentally and physically. Mentally, they have adjusted to the white man's culture by giving up their own languages, customs, histories, and cultural values. They have adopted the "American way of life" only to discover that this is not enough.

Next, they have rejected their physical heritage, resulting in extreme self-hatred. Yellow people share with the blacks the desire to look white. Just as blacks wish to be light-complected with thin lips and unkinky hair, "yellows" want to be tall with long legs and large eyes. The self-hatred is also evident in the yellow male's obsession with unobtainable white women, and in the yellow female's attempt to gain male approval by aping white beauty standards. Yellow females have their own "conking" techniques—they use "peroxide, foam rubber, and scotch tape to give them light hair, large breasts, and double-lidded eyes."

The "Black is Beautiful" cry among black Americans has instilled a new awareness in Asian Americans to be proud of their physical and cultural heritages. Yellow power advocates self-acceptance as the first step toward strengthening personalities of Asian Americans. . . .

The problem of self-identity in Asian Americans also requires the removal of stereotypes. The yellow people in America seem to be silent citizens. They are stereotyped as being passive, accommodating, and unemotional. Unfortunately, this description is fairly accurate, for Asian Americans have accepted these stereotypes and are becoming true to them.

The "silent" Asian Americans have rationalized their behavior in terms of cultural values which they have maintained from the old country. . . .

The yellow power movement envisages a new role for Asian Americans. . . .

Asian Americans . . . take much false pride in their own economic progress
and feel that blacks could succeed similarly if they only followed the Protestant ethic of hard work and education. Many Asians support S. I. Hayakawa,
the so-called spokesman of yellow people, when he advises the black man to
imitate the Nisei: "Go to school and get high grades, save one dollar out of
every ten you earn to capitalize your business." But the fact is that the white
power structure allowed Asian Americans to succeed through their own efforts
while the same institutions persist in denying these opportunities to black
Americans.

Asian Americans are perpetuating white racism in the United States as they
allow white America to hold up the "successful" Oriental image before other
minority groups as the model to emulate. White America justified the blacks'
position by showing that other non-whites—yellow—have been able to
"adapt" to the system. The truth underlying both the yellow's history and that
of the blacks has been distorted. In addition, the claim that black citizens must
"prove their rights to equality" is fundamentally racist. . . .

Although it is true that some Asian minorities lead all other colored groups
in America in terms of economic progress, it is a fallacy that Asian Americans
enjoy full economic opportunity. If the Protestant ethic is truly a formula for
economic success, why don't Japanese and Chinese who work harder and have
more education than whites earn just as much? . . .

The myth of Asian success is most obvious in the economic and social position of Filipino Americans. In 1960, the 65,459 Filipino residents of California
earned a median annual income of $2,925, as compared to $3,553 for blacks and
$5,109 for whites. Over half of the total Filipino male working force was em-
ployed in farm labor and service work; over half of all Filipino males received
less than 8.7 years of school education. Indeed, Filipinos are a forgotten minority in America. Like blacks, they have many legitimate complaints against
American society.

Source: Amy Uyematsu, "The Emergence of Yellow Power in America," *Gidra*, October
1969, from *Roots: An Asian American Reader*, ed. Amy Tachiki et al. (Berkeley: UCLA
Asian American Studies Center, 1971), 9–13.

14.5.   "Illegal aliens knowingly defy American laws," 1986

*The importance of immigration as a national political topic in the
mid-1980s moved President Ronald W. Reagan's Council of Economic
Advisers to include a chapter titled "The Economic Effects of Immigration" in its Annual Report delivered in February 1986 and excerpted below. Its moderated language sought to straddle a divide by
touting the economic benefits of immigration, on one hand, and de-
nouncing illegal immigration, on the other. It appeared aimed to re-
assure Americans that they were not being overrun nor being
displaced from jobs by immigrants, whether legal or illegal, who were
draining public resources.*

National concern has arisen about the effect of international migration, especially illegal migration, on the United States. Immigration policy and the ability to control the country's borders have serious implications for the definition of national sovereignty. Although many illegal aliens are productive members of society who have established strong community ties, their presence violates U.S. law. Concerns exist as well regarding the social, political, and environmental consequences of immigration. . . .

For much of the Nation's history, U.S. immigration policy has been based on the premise that immigrants have a favorable effect on the overall standard of living and on economic development. Analysis of the effects of recent migrant flows bears out this premise. Although an increasing number of migrants, including many illegal aliens, have entered the country in recent years, inflows are still low relative to population and relative to U.S. labor force growth.

International migrants have been readily absorbed into the labor market. Although some displacement may occur, it does not appear that migrants have displaced the native-born from jobs or have reduced wage levels on a broad scale. There is evidence that immigration has increased job opportunities and wage levels for other workers. Aliens may also provide a net fiscal benefit to the Nation, often paying more in taxes than they use in public services. Immigrants come to this country seeking a better life, and their personal investments and hard work provide economic benefits to themselves and to the country as a whole.

The economic gains provided by international migration, however, do not justify the presence or employment of aliens in the United States on an illegal basis. Illegal aliens knowingly defy American laws while their presence establishes claims to economic opportunity and Constitutional protections. As a sovereign Nation, the United States must responsibly decide not only who may cross its borders, but also who may stay.

Source: The [1986] Annual Report of the Council of Economic Advisers (Washington, DC: GPO, February 1986), "The Economic Effects of Immigration," 234.

14.6.   "A lack of understanding," 1992

Following up its 1989 Asian Roundtable Conferences, the U.S. Commission on Civil Rights—created in 1957 as an independent federal fact-finding and investigative agency monitoring discrimination and denial of constitutionally guaranteed equal protection of the laws—issued a report noting discriminatory barriers Asian Americans faced historically and in the present. The report, excerpted below, evidenced widespread barriers, discrimination, prejudice, and racially motivated violence that beset Asian Americans. Emphasizing the diversity among Asian Americans, the report documented race-based challenges and harassment that affected the broad range of Asian Americans from low-skilled new immigrants to longer resident, highly educated professionals. The report took aim particularly at the "model minority" stereotype of Asian Americans.

Contrary to the popular perception that Asian Americans have overcome discriminatory barriers, Asian Americans still face widespread prejudice, discrimination, and denials of equal opportunity. In addition, many Asian Americans, particularly those who are immigrants, are deprived of equal access to public services, including police protection, education, health care, and the judicial system.

Several factors contribute to the civil rights problems facing today's Asian Americans. First, Asian Americans are the victims of stereotypes that are widely held among the general public. These stereotypes deprive Asian Americans of their individuality and humanity in the public's perception and often foster prejudice against Asian Americans. The "model minority" stereotype, the often-repeated contention that Asian Americans have overcome all barriers facing them and that they are a singularly successful minority group, is perhaps the most damaging of these stereotypes. This stereotype leads Federal, State, and local agencies to overlook the problems facing Asian Americans, and it often causes resentment of Asian Americans within the general public. . . .

The root causes of bigotry and violence against Asian Americans are complex. Racial prejudice; misplaced anger caused by wars or economic competition with Asian countries; resentment of the real or perceived success of Asian Americans; and a lack of understanding of the histories, customs and religions of Asian Americans all play a role in triggering incidents of bigotry and violence. The media have contributed to prejudice by promoting stereotypes of Asian Americans, especially the model minority stereotype; by sometimes highlighting the criminal activities of Asian gangs; and by failing to provide the indepth and balanced coverage that would help the public to understand the diverse Asian American population. Furthermore, the media give little attention to hate crimes against Asian Americans, thereby hindering the formation of a national sense of outrage about bigotry and violence against Asian Americans, a critical ingredient for social change. Schools contribute to the problem by not teaching students about the histories, cultures, experiences, and contributions of Asian Americans. Political leaders contribute to the problem when they unthinkingly lash out at Japan as the cause of United States economic difficulties. More important, political and government leaders have yet to make it a national priority to prevent and denounce anti-Asian prejudice and violence.

Source: U.S. Commission on Civil Rights, *Civil Rights Issues Facing Asian Americans in the 1990s* (Washington, DC: GPO, 1992), 190–191.

ANNOTATED RESEARCH GUIDE
Books

Daniels, Roger. *Coming to America: A History of Immigration and Ethnicity in American Lives*. New York: HarperPerennial, 1991. A three-part survey providing a frame-

work for considering trends in demographic flows, politics and legislation, nativistic responses, and community development and transmission.

———. *Guarding the Golden Door: American Immigration Policy and Immigrants since 1882.*
New York: Hill and Wang, 2004. Probes the contentious and convoluted immigration debates with their often hyperbolic rhetoric and misleading statistics to
detail the law and demography treating U.S. policy before and after 1965.

Goldin, Liliana R., ed. *Identities on the Move: Transnational Processes in North America and
the Caribbean Basin.* Austin: University of Texas Press, 2000. Results of a 1996 conference with interdisciplinary and multimethodological perspectives on con-
structions of individual and communal identities that reform complex questions
in the politics of race relations.

Jaynes, Gerald D., et al., eds. *Immigration and Race: New Challenges for American Democracy.* New Haven, CT: Yale University Press, 2000. Fourteen essays tightly focused
on immigration policy and its affect on race relations, particularly in regard to
blacks.

Lee, Joann Faung Jean. *Asian-Americans: Oral Histories of First to Fourth-Generation Americans from China, the Philippines, Japan, India, the Pacific Islands, Vietnam and Cam-
bodia.* New York: New Press, 1992. Stories of striving and struggle from the
mouths of those who came from Asia and have persisted in creating various ethnic and national communities influencing U.S. race relations.

Perea, Juan F., ed. *Immigrants Out! The New Nativism and the Anti-Immigrant Impulse in
the United States.* New York: New York University Press, 1997. Prompted by California's 1994 Proposition 187, discusses the historical context of nativism, the
movement for official English, and the southern border question in the political
contention over the shape and substance of American community with its long-
standing sets of racial animus.

Suarez-Orozco, Marcelo, et al., eds. *The New Immigration: An Interdisciplinary Reader.*
New York: Routledge, 2004. Reflects the renewed inquiry and intense policy debate confronting the post-1965 immigrants as the largest influx in U.S. history in
the context of transnational change deeply affecting individual, national, and
racial identities.

Wu, Frank H. *Yellow: Race in America beyond Black and White.* New York: Basic Books,
2002. Surveys the Asian American past and the model minority myth in America while slicing into the debate on racial identity with astute commentary on the
damaging persistence of anti-Asian animus and racial stereotyping.

Yans-McLaughlin, Virginia, ed. *Immigration Reconsidered: History, Sociology, and Politics.*
New York: Oxford University Press, 1990. Moving beyond the too simplistic dichotomy of assimilation and pluralism, these essays probe structural conditions,
recruitment systems, and cooperative networks and strategies that suggest collective transformations of individual identities and group relations.

Web Sites

http://en.wikipedia.org/wiki/California_Proposition_187_(1994)—contains background information and links to Proposition 187 text and related legal issues.

http://www.besthistorysites.net/USHistory_Immigration.shtml—provides links to
various sites offering documents, lesson plans, teacher guides, and more on immigration to the United States.

http://www.census.gov/population/www/socdemo/race/racefactcb.html—offers
background and policy on racial and ethnic classifications the United States has used.

15

From Teheran to Baghdad: Facing Race with Arabs and Muslims

What has become known simply as 9/11 notched another measuring point for race relations in U.S. history. The assaults on September 11, 2001, triggered American political and popular reactions that reached beyond four hijacked airliners.[1] They set off revulsion that spilled beyond nineteen Arab men who combined homicide and suicide in seizing the planes as weapons.[2] The attacks mangled a section of the U.S. Department of Defense's headquarters—the five-sided National Defense Building in Arlington, Virginia, popularly known as the Pentagon. More spectacularly, the attacks collapsed each of the twin, 110-story towers of the World Trade Center in New York City. American reactions to the attacks retraced in bold strokes the shades and shadows connecting foreign and domestic dimensions in U.S. race relations.

The deadliest foreign attack ever on U.S. soil—with its toll nearing 3,000 dead—spilled racial and religious hatreds hundreds of years old in American thought and practice. The channels it gouged reached not only backward but, more important, pointed to portents for U.S. race relations in the twenty-first century. It illustrated anew how U.S. foreign relations have persistently shaped both the appearance and substance of U.S. domestic race relations. Treatment of Japanese Americans during World War II fully illustrated the blunt force of foreign features setting the content and context of domestic race relations. More than simple ethnicity, the element of race has repeatedly magnified hatred at home of those whom U.S. officials have tagged "enemies." Similarly, those tagged "friends" have been drawn closer, if not embraced, abroad and at home when U.S. foreign relations required—as illustrated during the 1950s and 1960s in U.S. reception of African Americans in their civil rights struggles while wooing decolonizing Africans as strategic allies in the Cold War. The advent and aftermath of 9/11 lethally displayed how U.S. foreign relations have shifted the domestic positions of distinct groups popularly cast as races.

The events of 9/11 capped at least a half century of intensifying anti-Arab and anti-Muslim repugnance in the United States. In the aftermath of the proclamation of the State of Israel in May 1948, anti-Arab and anti-Muslim rhetoric increasingly percolated in American public discourse to justify the Jewish homeland and U.S. support for its creation and existence on Palestinian Arabs' lands. The brew further bubbled and bittered with the hardening U.S. position in the ongoing Israeli-Palestinian conflict and in the five wars Israel fought against neighboring Arabs from 1948 to 1982. U.S. policy embracing Israel cast at least the appearance of greater domestic acceptance of Jews—despite America's history of deeply ingrained anti-Semitism with it traditional Christian roots. It deepened the historical cast of Arab and Muslim Americans as "others" in their identity and place in U.S. race relations.

Arabs entered the United States as "others" from the start. Before 1920 the U.S. Census recorded Arabs with Armenians, Turks, and other non-Arabic-speaking people. It also counted some as "other Asians" or as "other Africans." Variable application and meaning continually cast the term *Arab* as a generalized category for more than natives of the mostly desert peninsula in southwestern Asia called Arabia. *Arab* has encompassed Arabic-speaking peoples. Thus, it has ranged far, reaching with the language across northern Africa and throughout the part of western Asia often called the Middle East. Among other places, it has included not only the modern nation of Syria but also the Ottoman Empire's province of Syria. And from there came a significant wave of Semitic peoples classified as Arabs: They would number between 100,000 and 200,000 from 1880 to 1920. Mostly Eastern rite and Orthodox Christians (Maronite and Melkite) from the Middle East's Lebanon Mountains area, these immigrants applied to themselves limited regional identities. Their own self-references gave prominence to lineage, locality, and sect. They did not immediately call themselves Syrians or Arabs.

In the U.S. scheme of identity, the persons classified generally as Arabs and more specifically Syrians commonly became lumped in the lower half of the dichotomous racial taxonomy that recognized only whites and nonwhites or "colored persons." An early 1920s' Alabama election handbill that a local candidate distributed in Birmingham pushed the popular classification of Syrians, locating them with the commonly understood lowest touchstone—blacks. "They have disqualified the Negro, an American citizen, from voting in the white primary," the candidate noted. "[T]he Syrian should also be disqualified," he exhorted. "I DON'T WANT THEIR VOTES," his flier declared. "If I can't be elected by white men, I don't want the office."[3]

The economic position of the 1880–1920 immigrants called Syrians also set them apart. Quickly identified with pack peddling, as were itinerant German Jews, the Syrians found themselves not respected as merchants but instead scorned as mongers. Criticized for being drifters, they were commonly viewed as having no fixed place and no community. They were scorned as making no legitimate or positive contribution to the American community. They were not accorded even the status of sojourners, much less settlers.

Caught in the antiimmigrant and nativist backlash at the start of the twentieth century, they were repeatedly rejected as ineligible for U.S. citizenship. The Syrian American Associations of the United States joined in a 1914 challenge to a U.S. District Court decision in South Carolina that excluded them from being naturalized because they did not belong to the "white race."[4] The court sketched a blurry distinction to reinforce the conclusion that certain persons by race or ethnicity lacked the character for U.S. citizenship.

Syrians were Asians and as such excluded under U.S. immigration law, the court ruled. A higher court reversed the decision to allow the petitioning Syrians to become naturalized citizens. The court explained that

> the consensus of opinion at the time [1873–1875] of the enactment of the statute now in force was that they [Syrians] were so closely related to their neighbors on the European side of the Mediterranean that they should be classed as white.[5]

That proved grudging acceptance, at best.

Adding the hoary conflation and confusion of religion to race effaced the Arab American position even more. For while most of the early Syrians shared Christianity with the U.S. majority, significant numbers were Muslim. Indeed, significant—if publicly unrecognized—numbers of Muslims had long been in the United States. They came during the colonial era. They came in the transAtlantic slave trade, during which at least 2 million Muslims were sold into slavery in the Americas. Their Islamic cultural behaviors and practices distinguished them and in many places made them unwelcome. Their higher literacy rate and what one scholar has termed their "tradition of defiance and rebellion" cast Muslim slaves especially as undesirables in what became the United States.[6]

The old, bloody religious wars that reached back before the Crusades (1096–1270) cast Muslims not simply as outsiders but as enemies among Americans who cast themselves as a chosen Christian people. The view drew on Christian European animosities that decried Islam as vicious and virulent. It viewed Islam as a menace to western European civilization and as a threat to worldwide Christianity. Moreover, being connected with Africans and slaves and other spurious sorts that U.S. naturalization law excluded from citizenship almost hopelessly intermixed negative attributes in a popular American view of Arabs and Muslims. And in that view, Arabs and Muslims often stood as interchangeable.[7]

The popular and official U.S. take on world affairs after 1948 pushed Arabs and Muslims further beyond the pale in American eyes. The result stemmed not simply from a pro-Israel stance. It accumulated from a succession of events and errors. And it occurred at about the same time as a fresh wave of Arabs immigrated to the United States. They were successively displaced by World War II, by the creation of Israel, and by unrest in Egypt, Syria, and Iraq. The wave swelled in the 1960s, drawn in part by the U.S. Immigration and Nationality Act of 1965 that ended the old quota system that favored Europeans. It was driven also by the Arab-Israeli 1967 war, violence in Iraq, including the Kurd-Iraqi War of the 1960s, civil war in Lebanon, and unrest in Iran. A sense of Arabs inserting themselves into domestic U.S. life made at least some Americans anxious.

The 1956 Suez Crisis sparked a flickering aversion to uppity Arabs personified at that moment by Egyptian President Gamal Abdel Nasser. Divesting French and British interests, Nasser nationalized the 101-mile Mediterranean to Red Seas connection that since being completed in 1869 was one of the world's most heavily trafficked shipping lanes. It provided the shortest sea route between Europe and East Asia. Nasser's bold act propelled Arab nationalism into a feared force.

While not wholly Arab, the character of the Organization of Petroleum Exporting Countries (OPEC), formed in 1960–1961, made it at least appear an Arab proxy. So when OPEC increased oil prices 70 percent on average in September–October 1973, the consternation that rumbled from shaking economic fundamentals in the United States and elsewhere in the industrialized world fell on Arab heads. U.S. media vilified OPEC as greedy price-gougers bent on controlling world economics or at least on ruining the United States and western Europe. Portrayals virtually urged Americans to blame Arabs for any pain felt from a barrel of crude oil rising in price from $3.00 in 1973 to $30.00 in 1980.

Almost at the same time, Americans increasingly saw an image of Arabs and Muslims as terrorists. The Popular Front for the Liberation of Palestine's 1968 hijacking of an Israeli El Al airliner from Italy to Algeria propelled the image. Black September's notorious kidnapping and killing of Israeli athletes in Germany at the 1972 Munich Summer Olympics made Arabs more popularly despised in the United States. Perhaps the stroke that shifted most American sentiment from generalized revulsion to direct antipathy involved not Arabs but Muslims. It was the Teheran Hostage Crisis (1979–1980) that followed the fall of U.S. ally Shah Mohammad Reza Pahlavi in the Iranian Revolution of 1979–1980. The seizure of the U.S. embassy in Teheran in November 1979 and the holding of 52 Americans until the crisis ended after 444 days outraged Americans and set the stage for incoming U.S. President Ronald W. Reagan's anti-Arab, anti-Muslim jingoism.

More ugly anti-Arab and anti-Muslim associations with terrorism ensued for Americans as U.S. foreign policy directed U.S. Armed Forces into the Middle East. A truck-bomb attack in October 1983 effectively ended a U.S. peace mission in Lebanon, killing 243 U.S. Marines at their Beirut barracks. In April 1986, a group calling itself the Arab Revolutionary Cell exploded a terrorist bomb aboard TWA Flight 840 on its approach to Greece's Athens Airport, killing 4 U.S. citizens. Later in April 1986, President Reagan ordered U.S. air strikes on Libya for its alleged connections to terrorism. He directly targeted the anti-U.S., Libyan leader Muammar al-Qaddafi. Terrorism with an Arab and Muslim face continued to kill Americans, as on Pan Am flight 103 over Lockerbie, Scotland. A terrorist explosion killed all 259 persons aboard the December 1988 flight and 11 others on the ground. Almost immediately, U.S. forces again clashed with Libya as the United States accused Qaddafi of producing chemical weapons of mass destruction.

Iraq's Saddam Hussein replaced Qaddafi as a primary U.S. target when the United States led a coalition of nations to repulse Hussein's Iraqi invasion and occupation of neighboring Kuwait in August 1990. President George H. W.

Bush deployed U.S. forces in Operation Desert Shield to deter further Iraqi expansion. Following Iraq's refusal to withdraw in line with UN Security Council dictates, the U.S.-led Operation Desert Storm (with 540,000 U.S. troops in a total force of 700,000) launched the Persian Gulf War (1990–1991). Coalition air attacks began in mid-January 1991. By March 1991, Iraqi resistance completely collapsed, and President Bush proclaimed a cease-fire.

The hostilities stirred anger and antagonism against Arabs and Muslims in the United States. Arson, assault, and other hate crimes against Arab Americans, Muslim Americans, and persons mistaken as Arabs or Muslims rose. The Arab-Muslim image in political cartoons, comic strips, and video games reflected demeaning hostility. Antipathies intensified when an explosives-packed van detonated at noontime in the underground garage of Two World Trade Center in New York City, killing 6 and injuring another 1,000 persons in February 1993. Federal attorneys tried and convicted 12 members of the radical group Jama'at al-Jihad and its leader, the blind Egyptian Muslim Shaikh Omar Abdel Rahman, for the bombing.

An accelerating train of events then carried Americans to the terrible images of 9/11 and open anti-Arab, anti-Muslim belligerence. In June 1996, a truck bomb killed 19 and wounded hundreds in the multinational peacekeeping force at the Khobar Towers barracks in Dhahran, Saudi Arabia. In August 1998, almost simultaneous truck-bomb explosions at the U.S. embassies in Nairobi, Kenya, and Dar es Salaam, Tanzania, killed 224 and injured thousands. In October 2000, an explosives-laden boat gashed the USS *Cole* in the harbor at Aden, Yemen, killing 17 and wounding more than 30 other U.S. Navy crew.

The 1998 Twentieth Century-Fox film titled *The Siege: Freedom Is History*, starring two strong, U.S. box-office attractions (Denzel Washington and Bruce Willis), dramatized spiraling anti-Arab, anti-Muslim sentiment in the United States. Against the backdrop of a national security crisis erupting from major terrorist attacks in New York City, the movie depicted growing public intolerance at home. It focused on a clash between the principles of civil liberties and civil rights and the practices of law enforcement using racial profiling to target and confine as prisoners persons identified as Arabs, much as those identified as Japanese were interned in the United States during World War II.

Then came the real thing. The aftermath of 9/11 made *The Siege* appear a living reality. Arab and Muslim Americans fell under invariable official and popular distrust as enemies. They became apparent targets of vengeance, abroad and at home, in the "War on Terrorism" President George W. Bush declared three days after the terrorist attacks. As the nation girded for battle, old lines of racial and religious distrust and fear swelled. Feeding the frenzy, Congress rushed sweeping changes into U.S. law. The centerpiece was the October 2001 statute with the obviously contrived title "Uniting and Strengthening America by Providing Appropriate Tools Required to Intercept and Obstruct Terrorism." Known by its initials as the USA Patriot Act, the law spread roughly 350 pages. Its announced aim was to enhance domestic security. Its provisions wiped out decades of protections for personal rights against government intrusion. Immigrants especially felt the change, which the Homeland Security Act of November 2002 compounded. Not simply made to feel uninvited and unwelcome, immigrants—particularly those of darker hues and Middle Eastern origins—suffered by the tens of thousands in wholesale detentions and deportations.

Almost daily scenes in the deepening terrorism crisis connected to frightful images in U.S. history. What some have called a "new crusade" or a "clash of cultures" cast the United States as targeting and scapegoating racial and religious minorities and immigrants. U.S. officials have appeared again, as in past times of perceived crisis, to fail to protect civil liberties and civil rights. Mosques became surveillance sites. Investigations and prosecutions virtually closed American Arab and Muslim charities. Charges of racial profiling conjured up ugly faces of public and private oppression—not in distant lands but in the American homeland.

Using race or religion to decide whether to suspect, investigate, or prosecute anyone in the United States appeared at least to some Americans to hearken back dangerously to the racist doctrines and public policies of slavery, segregation, sealed reservations, and internment camps. What was America? What was America becoming? Such questions abounded in the face of the U.S. detaining incommunicado at the U.S. Naval Station Guantánamo Bay, Cuba, and other locations kept secret those it labeled "enemy combatants" following the U.S. invasion of Afghanistan in January 2002. Torture of prisoners at Abu Ghraib and other sites in Iraq after the U.S. invasion there in March 2003 deepened fears that the hoary lessons of race relations that defined the U.S. character remained unlearned. As throughout U.S. history, the response that what was happening was not about race but about national security, survival, and self-protection returned to the fundamental point that race relations have always been about group power and position. The crucial question was, How would Americans choose to treat race relations in the new century and new millennium?

NOTES

1. The airliners were two Boeing 757s and two Boeing 767s. American Airlines flight 11 departed Boston, Massachusetts, for Los Angeles, California, at 7:45 A.M. and crashed into the North Tower of the World Trade Center at 8:45 A.M. United Airlines flight 175 departed Boston for Los Angeles at 7:58 A.M. and crashed into the South Tower of the World Trade Center at 9:05 A.M. American Airlines flight 77 departed Washington Dulles International Airport in northern Virginia for Los Angeles at 8:10 A.M. and crashed into the Pentagon at 9:39 A.M. United Airlines flight 93 departed Newark, New Jersey, for San Francisco at 8:01 A.M. and crashed in Stony Creek Township, Pennsylvania, at 10:10 A.M. (All times are local.) See U.S. Department of Justice, Federal Bureau of Investigation, "Press Release 101," September 14, 2001.

2. Ibid. U.S. officials identified 19 hijackers—15 from Saudi Arabia, 2 from the United Arab Emirates, 1 from Egypt, and 1 from Lebanon. See also Ben Fenton and Toby Helm, "Seven Pilots Were Among 19 Hijackers," *The Daily Telegraph* (United Kingdom), September 15, 2001, 1.

3. Alan Dehmer, "Birmingham, Alabama: The Politics of Survival," in *Taking Root/Bearing Fruit: The Arab-American Experience*, ed. James Zogby (Washington, DC: American-Arab Anti-Discrimination Committee, 1984), 38–39. As his source for the quotation, Dehmer cites Philip K. Hitti, *The Syrians in America* (New York: George H. Doran Col, 1924), but gives no page.

4. *In re Dow*, 213 F. 355, 356 (D.C. E.D. S.C. 1914), referencing "section 2169 of the U.S. Revised Statutes as amended in 1875, and first used in the Statute of 1790." This decision was reversed on appeal.

5. *Dow v. United States*, 226 F. 145, 148 (4th Cir. 1915), holding, "At the date of the

new acts and amendments, especially the act of 1873, with its amendment of 1875, it seems to be true beyond question that the generally received opinion was that the inhabitants of a portion of Asia, including Syria, were to be classed as white persons."

6. Michael A. Gomez, *Exchanging Our Country Marks: The Transformation of African Identities in the Colonial and Antebellum South* (Chapel Hill: University of North Carolina Press, 1998), 145.

7. See, in particular, Janice J. Terry, *Mistaken Identity: Arab Stereotypes in Popular Writing* (Washington, DC: American-Arab Affairs Council, 1985).

DOCUMENTS

15.1.   **"Not . . . fit to . . . the right to be admitted a citizen,"**
             1914

---

*The following excerpts a February 1914 decision of U.S. District
Judge Henry Augustus Middleton Smith (1853–1924). Sitting in South
Carolina, Smith denied an application by a "Syrian" to become a naturalized U.S. citizen. He expressed a broad view of the meaning of
race as a qualification for U.S. citizenship. He also expressed particular views of the place of "Syrians" and others "Asiatics" in the U.S.
racial mix as he fixed on the meaning of "white persons" in U.S. law.
He declared "that 'white' was used in the sense of European." It meant
"the fair complexioned people of European habitancy and descent."
It excluded others.*

This is an application for naturalization. The applicant is a native of a place
called by him Batroun, in Syria in Asia. He has performed all the necessary for-
malities and would apparently from his intelligence and degree of information
of a general character be entitled to naturalization.

In color he is darker than the usual person of white European descent, and
of that tinged or sallow appearance which usually accompanies persons of descent other than purely European. . . . If rejected he can only be so upon the
ground that under the statute by reason of his nativity and descent he is not
entitled to be admitted as a citizen of this country. . . . [H]is application depends
upon whether he is a free white person.

Is a Syrian of Asiatic birth a free white person within the meaning of the
statute approved March 26, 1790? . . .

Do the words "free white persons" mean persons white in color? Is the definition to be determined by the colorization of the applicant to be ascertained
by ocular inspection by the court? . . .

The next question is whether the definition is racial; that is, whether the
words "white persons" are a racial designation. And that "white" is to be interpreted as meaning Caucasian, so called, or Indo-European. If racial, is any
one entitled to be admitted who belongs to a nation that speaks one of the languages spoken by the peoples heretofore denominated Caucasian, whether or
not his color be the very reverse of white. This would mean the admission of
all the mixed Asiatic races which speak a tongue the descendant of one of the
so-called Indo-European tongues, whether that tongue may have been forced
upon them or inherited by a very mixed transmission in point of race. . . .

The next definition may be termed a geographical one. Does the word
"white" in the statute refer to the peoples who were then commonly known in
this country as the peoples inhabiting Europe and whose descendants at the

time of the passage of the act of 1790 formed the inhabitants of the United States, excluding from such consideration the African descendants who were then slaves. If we give to the term "white" this geographical definition, that it means European, that "white" was used in the sense of European, the statute becomes one judicially speaking plain, understandable by the multitude as well as by the learned, and not difficult of enforcement.

The words "free white persons" would then mean all the fair complexioned people of European habitancy and descent commonly termed in 1790 the white races. That would appear to be what was intended by the terms of the act of 1790. It intended . . . to admit to citizenship in this country the people generally known as white; that is to say, the inhabitants of Europe and their descendants. . . . And such alone, are entitled to be admitted to naturalization under the terms of that clause of the statute.

This exclusion is no reflection upon the applicant, intellectual, moral, or racial. It simply means that the lawmaking power has not seen fit to admit to citizenship, under the clause mentioned, persons other than of European habitancy or descent. The court has no hesitation in saying that the applicant now before it would apparently be qualified to form a more desirable citizen than very many of those we now have as citizens, whether by birth or naturalization.

No race in modern times has shown a higher mentality than the Japanese. To refuse naturalization to an educated Japanese Christian clergyman and accord it to a veneered savage of African descent from the banks of the Congo would appear as illogical as possible, yet the courts of the United States have held the former inadmissible and the statute accords admission to the latter. This refusal is no reflection upon the excluded Japanese. The statute presents what may appear to be the startling discrimination that it forbids the privilege of citizenship to a Chinese or a Japanese descendant of two historic races that have accomplished so much in the constructive intellectual work of the world, and extends the privilege to a member of a savage negro tribe.

The admission of a foreigner to the privilege of citizenship in a country is wholly a matter for the people of that country. They may be as capricious and unreasonable as they see fit about it. It is a voluntary donation to be extended or denied according to the whims of the donor if he shall see fit to allow his action to be controlled by caprice or whim. He has certainly a right to be controlled by his ideas of prudent or wise policy towards himself in making the donation. . . .

The court does not undertake to say what races of mankind in matter of complexion should or should not be classed as white. There is a vast range in shades of white between the Northern Scandinavian and the Southern Portuguese. The only point decided is that the applicant is not that particular free white person to whom the act of Congress has donated the privilege of citizenship in this country with its accompanying duties and responsibilities. . . .

The applicant being an Asiatic does not come within the terms of the statute, and, whatever may be his other qualifications, Congress has not seen fit to endow him with the right to be admitted a citizen of the country.

Source: *Ex parte Dow*, 211 F. 486 (D.S.C. 1914).

15.2.   "The zone of danger," 1994

Anti-Arab tensions fast stiffened to strangling during the 1980s with increasing American focus on terrorism. University of Michigan graduate anthropologist Nabeel Abraham explained, in the excerpt below, how the tensions were manifested in racist anti-Arab violence across the United States during the decade, reaching a highwater mark in 1985 and 1986.

For the better part of the 1980s, Arab-Americans lived in an increasing state of apprehension as the Reagan administration waged its "war on international terrorism." The fear reached its zenith in 1985 and 1986.

The hijacking on June 14, 1985, of TWA Flight 847 to Beirut by Lebanese Shiite gunmen highlighted the predicament. The hijacking began with the beating death of a young American aboard the plane, and ended seventeen days later with the release of thirty-nine remaining U.S. hostages.

The incident received extensive coverage in the news media, much of it unashamedly sensationalist and hysterical. An editorial in the Richmond, Virginia, *News Leader*, for example, suggested one Lebanese Shiite prisoner be executed every fifteen minutes until the hostages were released (June 21, 1985). The *New York Post*, famous for its shrill tone, ran a front page photo of a Dearborn, Michigan, man of Lebanese Shiite ancestry posing with the likeness of an AK-47 machine gun, wearing a camouflage vest, bandoliers, and bullets under a banner headline, " 'U.S.-Nation under Attack'/Beirut U.S.A." (June 19). The photo was obtained by an unscrupulous reporter who persuaded the Lebanese-American to pose for his camera. According to the accompanying article, the Dearborn man allegedly boasted that 5,000 armed Lebanese Shiites were poised to defend themselves in the Detroit suburb. Even the normally staid *Wall Street Journal* was not immune to the hysteria of the hour. In an editorial titled, "The Next Hijacking," the *Journal* unabashedly called for U.S. military retaliation, starting with "strikes against Syrian military targets inside Lebanon" (June 18).

The media hype may have contributed to the outbreak of violent attacks against Arab-Americans and Middle Easterners that coincided with the hijacking, making 1985 a milestone in the history of violence against Arabs and other Middle Easterners. According to the Los Angeles Human Relations Commission, twelve (16.9 percent) out of a total of seventy-one religiously motivated incidents that took place in Los Angeles County in 1985 "were directed against Islamic mosques, centers or individuals of the Islamic faith." Commission officials noted this was the first time that any anti-Islamic incidents had been recorded in the six years for which records had been kept. According to the commission's annual report the anti-Muslim incidents appear "to have been provoked by a number of events in the Middle East. . . . In each case, Americans were killed."

Between June 16 and 22 Islamic Centers in San Francisco, Denver, Dearborn, and Quincy, Massachusetts, were vandalized or received telephone threats.

Arab-American organizations in New York and Detroit were also threatened. On June 22 the Dar as-Salaam Mosque in Houston was firebombed, resulting in $50,000 worth of damage. A week later on June 30, a woman known to be dating a Palestinian was raped in Tucson by two men who lightly carved a Star of David on her chest. On August 16 a bomb placed outside the door of the Boston office of the American-Arab Anti-Discrimination Committee (ADC) detonated, severely injuring the two policemen called to remove it. . . .

Do anti-Arab racism and hate violence exist in contemporary U.S. society? The answer, unfortunately, is in the affirmative. Moreover, far from being a fringe phenomenon, anti-Arab racism is found at the highest levels of mainstream society. In magnitude, anti-Arab racism and hate violence is minuscule compared with the racist violence directed at African-Americans and other minorities. Yet anti-Arab racism is unique in that it has been largely tolerated by mainstream society.

Source: Nabeel Abraham, "Anti-Arab Racism and Violence in the United States," in *The Development of Arab-American Identity*, ed. Ernest McCarus (Ann Arbor: University of Michigan Press, 1994), 161–162. (Citations omitted.)

15.3.   "A new crisis of identity," 1996

> *Arab Americans became something of a "mobilized diaspora" in the 1980s and 1990s as external thrusts forced an "Arab American" identity upon individuals of Arab descent in the United States, shaping amorphous self-defined sets of persons into a perceived "Arab American" community. Its members found assimilation available if they divested themselves of their Arabness but not if they insisted on standing out ethnically or religiously. Arab American experience illustrated again the dynamism and dimensions with which foreign affairs have influenced domestic race relations in the United States. It also illustrated how the U.S. racial prism has collapsed personal identity into something of an ethnic transnationalism that bonds the focal persons into a challenged racial stereotype. Very particularly, the following excerpt shows how the group politics of the U.S. environment created "Arab Americans."*

Recent Middle Eastern and global developments, including the Gulf War, the Middle East peace process, and the spread of radical Islam, have presented the Arab-American community and its mainstream institutions with a new crisis of identity and political purpose, forcing community leaders to redefine their domestic and foreign policy agendas. For the last three decades, the agenda of U.S. Arabs has been monopolized by the Arab-Israeli conflict; indeed, given the diversity of the community—in terms of quasi-national homelands, religions, and ideological persuasions—the Palestinian cause could be said to have provided the very foundation for pan-Arab ethnic identity in America. . . .

Like members of other ethnic groups, Arab-Americans may identify with symbols of their old country without maintaining an interest in its domestic or foreign affairs, while others may not identify at all as members of the community. In fact, the notion of pan-Arab ethnic solidarity and the appellation "Arab-American" took hold only after the 1967 Arab-Israeli war. Before that war, Arab-American identity was amorphous and dormant. As members of many subnational and religious groupings with unclear ethnic boundaries, Arab-Americans generally either assimilated as individuals or retreated to their ethnic and religious communities. Most of them were second generation Americans and Christians of Syrian-Lebanese origin who, while often retaining some sentimental affinity toward the countries and villages of their parents or grandparents' birth, remained apolitical.

Prior to the establishment of the Palestine Liberation Organization (PLO) and the 1967 Arab-Israeli war, Arab-Americans had no ideological core, national political organizations, or funding. Even Palestinian-Americans who came to the United States after 1948 with a strong sense of homeland loyalty did not retain a broad Palestinian identity. They focused primarily on family and village networks and were largely incognizant of the Palestinian cause as a whole. Moreover, until 1967 Arabs in America "generally refrained from identification with 'Arab' issues, considering that the (American) political process was closed on such issues, and fearing that they would be subject to social and economic repercussions by challenging Zionist and pro-Israeli sentiments."

The ethnopolitical awakening of Arab-Americans coincided with the civil rights movement and the increasing tolerance of ethnicity in American society after the 1965 Immigration Act. Its real impetus, however, was the traumatic defeat in 1967 and Israel's occupation of the West Bank and Gaza. Meanwhile, anti-Arab feeling in the United States was on the rise, exacerbated by the 1973 Arab oil embargo (and subsequent series of OPEC price hikes), the U.S. boycott of the PLO in 1975, and the increasing power of the pro-Israel lobby. The 1978 FBI Abscam operation, in which FBI agents disguised as Arabs sought to corrupt members of Congress, galvanized Arab-Americans politically. As activist James Zogby said, "while Palestinians [in the United States] were absorbed with issues 'over there' [in Palestine], we [Americans of Arab descent] were mainly concerned with issues 'over here' [in America]."

In the 1970s and 1980s, activists helped develop a minority consciousness that reflected frustration with the caricature of the Arab culture and the Muslim religion in America. They established Arab American institutions—the National Association of Arab Americans (NAAA) in 1972, the American-Arab Anti-Discrimination Committee (ADC) in 1980, the Arab-American Institute (AAI) in 1985—that drew heavily on the energies and frustration of the post-1967 Palestinian immigrants and refugees "with the homeland still fresh in their minds [who] were ready to be foot soldiers in the tedious, frustrating task of lobbying U.S. policy makers." How representative these institutions ever were is an open question, since the engine driving ethnic community activism is always made up of "core members" or organizing elites, the vast majority of the community being "silent members."

Israel's invasion of Lebanon in 1982 was a watershed in terms of Arab-American public protest. Many Arab-Americans were recruited by ADC and NAAA to protest the Israeli assault on Beirut, the Sabra and Shatila massacre, and America's perceived lack of response. The summer of 1982 may have been the diaspora's "finest hour," but internal divisions within the organizations and the failure to translate communal mobilization and the American public's support into political gains—such as congressional condemnation of Israel's role in Sabra and Shatila, a halt in the arms flow to Israel, or a cut in aid—led to disillusionment and retreat.

Americans of Arab descent wishing to downplay their ancestral roots have found assimilation in the United States to be firmly within reach. Yet Arab-Americans who have ventured to stand out ethnically or religiously have faced difficult times finding their way in America's multicultural society.

Source: Yossi Shain, "Arab-Americans at a Crossroads," *Journal of Palestine Studies* 25, no. 3 (Spring 1996): 46–48. (Citations omitted.)

15.4. **"Noxious mix of religious bigotry and anti-Muslim demagoguery," 2002**

> *Significant public discussion cast the announced U.S. "War on Terrorism" as something of a crusade—a religious struggle between Christians and Muslims. Attacks against Islam's beliefs, its adherents, and even its founder played in the news. A low point appeared early in October 2002 when the Rev. Jerry Falwell declared, "I think Mohammed was a terrorist." The conservative Baptist Falwell stood as a national political force who in 1979 founded the Moral Majority, Inc., to engage the Christian evangelical movement in U.S. politics through lobbying and endorsing candidates for public office. In response to Falwell's remark, the Washington, D.C.–based Council on American-Islamic Relations spokesman Ibrahim Hooper retorted, "Anybody is free to be a bigot if they want to. What really concerns us," Hooper emphasized, "is the lack of reaction by mainstream religious and political leaders, who say nothing when these bigots voice these attacks." One of the leading U.S. news organizations adopted and further elaborated the point in its editorial that follows.*

ONE OF THE high-water marks after Sept. 11 last year was President Bush's leadership in urging Americans not to condemn Islam because of the actions of extremists in the name of their faith. He set aside his war planning to visit the mosque at the Islamic Center of Washington, where he reminded the nation that "Islam is peace" and admonished Americans not to take out their anger on innocent American Arabs and Muslims. In an appearance before a joint session of Congress, Mr. Bush denounced the terrorists as traitors to their faith. The preachings of Osama bin Laden, he said, were a grotesque distortion of a great religion. And despite several highly publicized incidents of threats and lashing out at people thought to be Muslim, most Americans have heeded the president's message, resisting the ugly lure of religious intolerance and hate.

The same, however, cannot be said of some key leaders of the religious right in America who are counted among President Bush's closest political allies. And on their noxious mix of religious bigotry and anti-Muslim demagoguery, Mr. Bush's silence is deafening.

We have in mind several religious conservative leaders who count Mr. Bush as one of their own. There is the Rev. Franklin Graham, Billy Graham's son and successor and a participant in the president's inauguration, who has declared Islam a "very evil and wicked religion." And there is Christian Coalition founder and television evangelist Pat Robertson, who said that "to think that Islam is a peaceful religion is fraudulent." Mr. Robertson, in full attack mode himself, called the prophet Muhammad "an absolute wild-eyed fanatic . . . a robber and brigand . . . a killer." And, in an appearance on the CBS program "60 Minutes" to be broadcast tonight, the Rev. Jerry Falwell completes the demonization of a religion by smearing the prophet of Islam as "a terrorist."

These are not just the words of a fringe movement. The speakers are leaders among the religious right in America, a movement close to a president who speaks their language. Their embrace is mutual. It therefore falls to the president to break his silence on their gross distortion and to put some distance between their rhetoric and his own professions of tolerance. To avert his gaze from their actions is to permit the Falwells, Robertsons and Grahams to legitimize their own perverse teachings through their association with the president of the United States. If their words are not his, then the president must say so.

Source: Editorial, "Defaming Islam," *Washington Post*, October 6, 2002, B6. © 2002, The Washington Post. Reprinted with permission.

15.5.   "A serious backlash," 2002

The American-Arab Anti-Discrimination Committee Research Institute (ADCRI) based in Washington, D.C., surveyed the experiences of the Arab American community in the year after the terrorist attacks of 9/11. The report detailed over 700 violent incidents targeting Arab Americans and Muslim Americans, or those perceived to be Arabs or Muslims, in the first nine weeks after September 2001. It noted another 165 violent incidents from January 1 to October 11, 2002. The report also detailed discrimination in immigration policies and civil liberties concerns, particularly those stemming from provisions of the 2001 USA Patriot Act. What follows were the report's conclusions.

Arab Americans suffered a serious backlash following September 11, 2001.

The worst elements of this backlash, including a massive increase in the incidence of violent hate crimes, were concentrated in the first nine weeks following the attacks.

Arab Americans continue to suffer from increased levels of discrimination from their fellow citizens in many fields, while the government has shown a real commitment to uphold the law and punish offenders.

Arab Americans, especially immigrants from the Arab world, have been the principal focus of new government powers that restrict individual freedoms and protections, and infringe upon civil liberties.

Defamation against Arabs and Muslims, particularly attacks on Islam as a faith, has steadily increased in intensity and frequency during the entire period covered by this Report, laying the groundwork for potential future waves of hate crimes.

In spite of numerous expressions of support for the community from public figures and thousands of private citizens, Arab Americans remain exceptionally vulnerable to hate crimes, discrimination, extreme vilification by prominent persons, and derogations of civil rights and liberties.

Source: American-Arab Anti-Discrimination Committee Research Institute (ADCRI), *Report on Hate Crimes and Discrimination against Arab-Americans: The Post-9/11 Backlash*, available at http://www.adc.org/hatecrimes/contents.htm.

ANNOTATED RESEARCH GUIDE

Books

American-Arab Anti-Discrimination Committee. *Report on Anti-Arab Hate Crimes*. Washington, DC: American-Arab Anti-Discrimination Committee, 1992. This and other committee publications, such as *Congressional Hearings on Anti-Arab Violence: A Milestone for Arab-American Rights* (Washington, DC: The Committee, 1986), offer data, commentary, and perspectives on Arab Americans' positions and race relations.

Boosahda, Elizabeth. *Arab-American Faces and Voices: The Origins of an Immigrant Community*. Austin: University of Texas Press, 2003. Reflects the struggle of individual and communal identity not only in the post-9/11 context of heightened tensions but historically since the immigration at the opening of the twentieth century.

Citino, Nathan J. *From Arab Nationalism to OPEC: Eisenhower, King Sa'ud and the Making of US-Saudi Relations*. Bloomington: Indiana University Press, 2002. Traces the substitution of U.S. capitalism for British imperial hegemony as the dominant framework for order in the Middle East and its impact on U.S.-Arab perceptions and relations.

Haddad, Yvonne Yazbeck. *Not Quite American? The Shaping of Arab and Muslim Identity in the United States*. Waco, TX: Baylor University Press, 2004. Explores Arab and Muslim immigration and integration with the struggles against exclusion based on nationality, religion, and race.

Haddad, Yvonne Yazbeck, and John L. Esposito, eds. *Muslims on the Americanization Path?* New York: Oxford University Press, 2000. Probes the contentions and contradictions Muslims face in a reluctantly plural U.S. society that traditionally appeared to ask for sacrifice of other identity to be accepted as American.

Hagopian, Elaine C., ed. *Civil Rights in Peril: The Targeting of Arabs and Muslims*. London: Pluto Press, 2004. Exposes the post-9/11 War on Terror's targeting of Arabs and Muslims based on racist stereotypes that assault civil liberties.

Naff, Alixa. *Becoming American: The Early Arab Immigrant Experience*. Carbondale: Southern Illinois University Press, 1985. Documents through oral histories, photographs, and other artifacts the Arab immigrants' struggle for place and recognition in America's structure of racial identity.

Paust, Jordan J., et al., eds. *The Arab Oil Weapon*. Dobbs Ferry, NY: Oceana Publications, 1977. Reprints articles and documents dated from 1933 to 1976 illustrating the strategic importance of petroleum, the growing sense of its use in developing Arab communities, and the affect on perceptions of Arabs internationally and in the United States.

Said, Edward W. *Covering Islam: How the Media and the Experts Determine How We See the Rest of the World*. Rev. ed. New York: Vintage Books, 1997. Updated from 1981, this work examines how U.S. popular media have used and perpetuated biased images of Muslims so as to miscast them as a common enemy of America.

Shaheen, Jack G. *Arab and Muslim Stereotyping in American Popular Culture*. Washington, DC: Center for Muslim-Christian Understanding: History and International Affairs, Edmund A. Walsh School of Foreign Service, Georgetown University, 1997. A brief but pointed analysis of how U.S. media portray Arab countries and Islam and in the process perpetuate misunderstanding.

———. *Reel Bad Arabs: How Hollywood Vilifies a People*. New York: Olive Branch Press, 2001. Dissects more than 900 films to detail how the U.S. film industry abuses, defames, and disparages Arab peoples and thereby destroys opportunities for better American understanding of Arabs and their culture.

Suleiman, Michael W., ed. *Arabs in America: Building a New Future*. Philadelphia: Temple University Press, 2000. Offers twenty-one wide-ranging essays on the complexity and diversity of Arab American identity and its prospects in a continuing context of U.S. hostility.

Web Sites

http://usinfo.state.gov/products/pubs/muslimlife/—U.S. State Department site on international programs offering views on Muslim life in America, in light of Islam's being one of the fastest-growing religions in the United States today.

http://www.adc.org/index.php?id=283&no_cache=1&sword_list[]=stereotypes—American-Arab Anti-Discrimination Committee site treating images of Arabs and practices associated with Arabs, fostering stereotypes and continuing problems in race relations.

http://www.americanmuslims.info/—the site of the Council on American-Islamic Relations (CAIR), designed in its words "to foster greater understanding of Islam and to counter a rising tide of anti-Muslim rhetoric in the United States."

http://www.askasia.org/teachers/Instructional_Resources/FEATURES/AmericasCrisis/BG1/backlash.htm—lists resources and teaching guides ranging from anti-Asian sentiment in the 1940s through post-2001 anti-Arab sentiment.

http://www.islamamerica.org/—presents material on the emerging U.S. Muslim community and the roles of Muslims as citizens contributing to America and improving its social fabric.

Selected Bibliography

Adams, Francis D., and Barry Sanders. *Alienable Rights: The Exclusion of African Americans in a White Man's Land, 1619–2000.* New York: HarperCollins, 2003.

Allen, Theodore W. *The Invention of the White Race.* New York: Verso, 1994.

Anderson, Elijah, and Douglas S. Massey, eds. *Problem of the Century: Racial Stratification in the United States.* New York: Russell Sage Foundation, 2001.

Andolsen, Barbara Hilkert. *"Daughters of Jefferson, Daughters of Bootblacks": Racism and American Feminism.* Macon, GA: Mercer University Press, 1986.

Arthur, John, and Amy Shapiro. *Color, Class, Identity: The New Politics of Race.* Boulder, CO: Westview Press, 1996.

Barber, Lucy G. *Marching on Washington: The Forging of an American Political Tradition.* Berkeley: University of California Press, 2002.

Bayor, Ronald H., ed. *Race and Ethnicity in America: A Concise History.* New York: Columbia University Press, 2003.

Beckwith, Francis J., and Todd E. Jones, eds. *Affirmative Action: Social Justice or Reverse Discrimination?* Amherst, NY: Prometheus Books, 1997.

Bell, Derrick A. *Faces at the Bottom of the Well: The Permanence of Racism.* New York: Basic Books, 1992.

———. *Race, Racism, and American Law.* 4th ed. Gaithersburg, MD: Aspen, 2000.

———. *Silent Covenants:* Brown v. Board of Education *and the Unfulfilled Hopes for Racial Reform.* New York: Oxford University Press, 2004.

Berlin, Ira. *Many Thousands Gone: The First Two Centuries of Slavery in North America.* Cambridge, MA: Harvard University Press, 1998.

Bodnar, John E., Roger Simon, and Michael P. Weber. *Lives of Their Own: Blacks, Italians, and Poles in Pittsburgh, 1900–1960.* Urbana: University of Illinois Press, 1982.

Bonilla-Silva, Eduardo. *Racism Without Racists: Color-Blind Racism and the Persistence of Racial Inequality in the United States.* Lanham, MD: Rowman & Littlefield, 2003.

———. *White Supremacy and Racism in the Post–Civil Rights Era.* Boulder, CO: Lynne Rienner Publishers, 2001.

Brooks, James F., ed. *Confounding the Color Line: The Indian-Black Experience in North America*. Lincoln: University of Nebraska Press, 2002.

Brown, Michael K., et al. *Whitewashing Race: The Myth of a Color-Blind Society*. Berkeley: University of California Press, 2003.

Browning, Rufus P., Dale Rogers Marshall, and David H. Tabb, eds. *Racial Politics in American Cities*. 2nd ed. New York: Longman, 1997.

Bukhari, Zahid H., et al. *Muslims' Place in the American Public Square: Hope, Fears, and Aspirations*. Walnut Creek, CA: AltaMira Press, 2004.

Callaway, Colin G. *First Peoples: A Documentary Survey of American Indian History*. Boston: Bedford/St. Martin's, 1999.

Caraway, Nancie. *Segregated Sisterhood: Racism and the Politics of American Feminism*. Knoxville: University of Tennessee Press, 1991.

Carson, Claiborne, et al. *The Eyes on the Prize Civil Rights Reader: Documents, Speeches, and Firsthand Accounts from the Black Freedom Struggle, 1954–1990*. New York: Viking Penguin, 1991.

Carter, Dan T. *From George Wallace to Newt Gingrich: Race in the Conservative Counterrevolution, 1963–1994*. Baton Rouge: Louisana State University Press, 1996.

Chang, Iris. *The Chinese in America: A Narrative History*. New York: Viking Books, 2003.

Chen, Yong. *Chinese San Francisco, 1850–1943: A Trans-Pacific Community*. Stanford, CA: Stanford University Press, 2000.

Clinton, William J. *President's Initiative on Race: One America in the 21st Century: The President's Initiative on Race*. Washington, DC: The Initiative, 1997.

Conniff, Michael L., and Thomas J. Davis. *Africans in the Americas: A History of the Black Diaspora*. New York: St. Martin's, 1994. Reprint, Caldwell, NJ: The Blackburn Press, 2002.

Cose, Ellis. *Color-Blind: Seeing Beyond Race in a Race-Obsessed World*. New York: Harper-Collins, 1997.

Cottrol, Robert J., Raymond T. Diamond, and Leland B. Ware. Brown v. Board of Education: *Caste, Culture, and the Constitution*. Lawrence: University Press of Kansas, 2003.

Crenshaw, Kimberlé, et al. *Critical Race Theory: The Key Writings that Formed the Movement*. New York: New Press, 1995.

Cross, William E. *Shades of Black: Diversity in African-American Identity*. Philadelphia: Temple University Press, 1991.

Cruse, Harold. *Plural but Equal: A Critical Study of Blacks and Minorities and America's Plural Society*. New York: William Morrow, 1987.

Daniel, G. Reginald. *More than Black? Multiracial Identity and the New Racial Order*. Philadelphia: Temple University Press, 2002.

Daniels, Roger. *Asian America: Chinese and Japanese in the United States since 1850*. Seattle: University of Washington Press, 1988.

———. *Guarding the Golden Door: American Immigration Policy and Immigrants since 1882*. New York: Hill and Wang, 2004.

———. *Not Like Us: Immigrants and Minorities in America, 1890–1924*. Chicago: Ivan R. Dee, 1997.

Daniels, Roger, and Harry H. L. Kitano. *American Racism: Exploration of the Nature of Prejudice*. Englewood Cliffs, NJ: Prentice-Hall, 1970.

Daniels, Roger, Sandra C. Taylor, and Harry H. L. Kitano, eds. *Japanese Americans, from Relocation to Redress*. Salt Lake City: University of Utah Press, 1986.

Darder, Antonia, and Rodolfo D. Torres. *After Race: Racism after Multiculturalism*. New York: New York University Press, 2004.

Davis, F. James. *Who Is Black? One Nation's Definition*. University Park: Pennsylvania State University Press, 1991.

Delgado, Richard, and Jean Stefancic. *Critical White Studies: Looking Behind the Mirror.* Philadelphia: Temple University Press, 1997.

Dennis, Sam Joseph. *African-American Exodus and White Migration, 1950–1970: A Comparative Analysis of Population Movements and Their Relations to Labor and Race Relations.* New York: Garland Publishing, 1989.

Doane, Ashley W., and Eduardo Bonilla-Silva. *White Out: The Continuing Significance of Racism.* New York: Routledge, 2003.

Dobratz, Betty A., and Stephanie L. Shanks-Meile. *"White Power, White Pride!" The White Separatist Movement in the United States.* New York: Twayne Publishers, 1997.

Dodson, Howard, and Sylviane A. Dique. *In Motion: The African-American Migration Experience.* Washington, DC: National Geographic and the Schomburg Center for Research in Black Culture, 2005.

Dorinson, Joseph, and Joram Warmund, eds. *Jackie Robinson: Race, Sports, and the American Dream.* Armonk, NY: M. E. Sharpe, 1998.

D'Souza, Dinesh. *The End of Racism: Principles for a Multiracial Society.* New York: Free Press, 1995.

Du Bois, W.E.B. *Against Racism: Unpublished Essays, Papers, Addresses, 1887–1961.* Edited by Herbert Aptheker. Amherst: University of Massachusetts Press, 1985.

Dudziak, Mary L. *Cold War Civil Rights: Race and the Image of American Democracy.* Princeton, NJ: Princeton University Press, 2000.

Ellen, Ingrid Gould. *Sharing America's Neighborhoods: The Prospects for Stable Racial Integration.* Cambridge, MA: Harvard University Press, 2000.

Entman, Robert M., and Andrew Rojecki. *The Black Image in the White Mind: Media and Race in America.* Chicago: University of Chicago Press, 2000.

Feagin, Joe R., and Eileen O'Brien. *White Men on Race: Power, Privilege, and the Shaping of Cultural Consciousness.* Boston: Beacon Press, 2003.

Feagin, Joe R., Hernán Vera, and Pinar Batur. *White Racism: The Basics.* 2nd ed. New York: Routledge, 2001.

Finkelman, Paul, ed. *Race, Law, and American History, 1700–1990: The African-American Experience.* 11 vols. New York: Garland, 1992.

———. *Slavery and the Founders: Race and Liberty in the Age of Jefferson.* 2nd ed. Armonk, NY: M. E. Sharpe, 2001.

Franklin, John Hope, and Genna Rae McNeil, eds. *African Americans and the Living Constitution.* Washington, DC: Smithsonian Institution Press, 1995.

Franklin, John Hope, and Alfred A. Moss Jr. *From Slavery to Freedom: A History of African-Americans.* 8th ed. New York: Knopf, 2000.

Frazier, John W., Florence M. Margai, and Eugene Tettey-Fio. *Race and Place: Equity Issues in Urban America.* Boulder, CO: Westview Press, 2003.

Fredrickson, George M. *The Black Image in the White Mind: The Debate on Afro-American Character and Destiny, 1817–1914.* New York: Harper & Row, 1972.

Fuchs, Lawrence H. *The American Kaleidoscope: Race, Ethnicity, and the Civic Culture.* Middletown, CT: Wesleyan University Press, 1990.

Gee, Emma, et al., eds. *Counterpoint: Perspectives on Asian America.* Los Angeles: Asian American Studies Center, University of California, 1976.

Goldberg, David Theo. *Racial Subjects: Writing on Race in America.* New York: Routledge, 1997.

Gonzalez, Gilbert G., and Raul A. Fernandez. *A Century of Chicano History: Empire, Nations, and Migration.* New York: Routledge, 2003.

Gordon-Reed, Annette, ed. *Race on Trial: Law and Justice in American History.* New York: Oxford University Press, 2002.

Gracia, Jorge J. E., and Pablo De Greiff, eds. *Hispanics/Latinos in the United States: Ethnicity, Race, and Rights.* New York: Routledge, 2000.

Graves, Joseph L., Jr. *The Race Myth: Why We Pretend Race Exists in America*. New York: Dutton, 2004.

Gulick, Sidney L. *American Democracy and Asiatic Citizenship*. New York: Scribner, 1918.

Gyory, Andrew. *Closing the Gate: Race, Politics, and the Chinese Exclusion Act*. Chapel Hill: University of North Carolina Press, 1998.

Haddad, Yvonne Yazbeck, ed. *The Muslims of America*. New York: Oxford University Press, 1993.

———. *Not Quite American? The Shaping of Arab and Muslim Identity in the United States*. Waco, TX: Baylor University Press, 2004.

Hall, Ronald E. *The Scientific Fallacy and Political Misuse of the Concept of Race*. Lewiston, ME: Edwin Mellen Press, 2004.

Haller, John S., Jr. *Outcasts from Evolution: Scientific Attitudes of Racial Inferiority, 1859–1900*. Urbana: University of Illinois Press, 1971.

Hartman, Chester, ed. *Challenges to Equality: Poverty and Race in America*. Armonk, NY: M. E. Sharpe, 2001.

Hill, Herbert, and James E. Jones Jr., eds. *Race in America: The Struggle for Equality*. Madison: University of Wisconsin Press, 1993.

Hill, Mike. *After Whiteness: Unmaking an American Majority*. New York: New York University Press, 2004.

Hochschild, Jennifer L. *Facing up to the American Dream: Race, Class, and the Soul of the Nation*. Princeton, NJ: Princeton University Press, 1995.

Hodes, Martha Elizabeth. *Sex, Love, Race: Crossing Boundaries in North American History*. New York: New York University Press, 1999.

Hsu, Madeline Yuan-yin. *Dreaming of Gold, Dreaming of Home: Transnationalism and Migration Between the United States and South China, 1882–1943*. Stanford, CA: Stanford University Press, 2000.

Huang, Fung-Yea. *Asian and Hispanic Immigrant Women in the Work Force: Implications of the United States Immigration Policies since 1965*. New York: Garland Publishing, 1997.

Hundley, Norris, Jr., ed. *The Asian American: The Historical Experience*. Santa Barbara, CA: Clio Books, 1976.

Jacobs, Ronald N. *Race, Media, and the Crisis of Civil Society: From Watts to Rodney King*. New York: Cambridge University Press, 2000.

Jacobson, Matthew Frye. *Whiteness of a Different Color: European Immigrants and the Alchemy of Race*. Cambridge, MA: Harvard University Press, 1998.

Jacoby, Russell, and Naomi Glauberman, eds. *The Bell Curve Debate: History, Documents, Opinions*. New York: Times Books, 1995.

Jennings, James, ed. *Blacks, Latinos, and Asians in Urban America: Status and Prospects for Politics and Activism*. Westport, CT: Praeger, 1994.

Johnson, Kevin R. *How Did You Get to Be a Mexican? A White/Brown Man's Search for Identity*. Philadelphia: Temple University Press, 1999.

———, ed. *Mixed Race America and the Law: A Reader*. New York: New York University Press, 2003.

Jordan, Winthrop D. *The White Man's Burden: Historical Origins of Racism in the United States*. New York: Oxford University Press, 1974.

Joseph, Antoine L. *The Dynamics of Racial Progress: Economic Inequality and Race Relations since Reconstruction*. Armonk, NY: M. E. Sharpe, 2005.

Katznelson, Ira. *When Affirmative Action Was White: An Untold History of Racial Inequality in Twentieth-Century America*. New York: W. W. Norton, 2005.

Kincheloe, Joe L., et al. *White Reign: Deploying Whiteness in America*. New York: St. Martin's Press, 1998.

King, Desmond S. *Making Americans: Immigration, Race, and the Origins of the Diverse Democracy*. Cambridge, MA: Harvard University Press, 2000.

Kitano, Harry H. L., and Roger Daniels. *Asian Americans: Emerging Minorities*. 2nd ed. Englewood Cliffs, NJ: Prentice Hall, 1995.

Kivisto, Peter. *Americans All: Race and Ethnic Relations in Historical, Structural, and Comparative Perspectives*. Belmont, CA: Wadsworth Publishing Company, 1995.

Klarman, Michael J. *From Jim Crow to Civil Rights: The Supreme Court and the Struggle for Racial Equality*. New York: Oxford University Press, 2004.

Klinkner, Philip A., with Rogers M. Smith. *The Unsteady March: The Rise and Decline of Racial Equality in America*. Chicago: University of Chicago Press, 1999.

Knobel, Dale T. *America for the Americans: The Nativist Movement in the United States*. New York: Twayne Publishers, 1996.

Korgen, Kathleen Odell. *From Black to Biracial: Transforming Racial Identity among Americans*. Westport, CT: Praeger, 1998.

Koshy, Susan. *Sexual Naturalization: Asian Americans and Miscegenation*. Stanford, CA: Stanford University Press, 2004.

Krenn, Michael L., ed. *Race and U.S. Foreign Policy*. 5 vols. New York: Garland Publishing, 1998.

Lapchick, Richard Edward. *Smashing Barriers: Race and Sport in the New Millennium*. Updated ed. Lanham, MD: Madison Books, 2001.

Lee, Erika. *At America's Gates: Chinese Immigration during the Exclusion Era, 1882–1943*. Chapel Hill: University of North Carolina Press, 2003.

Lee, James Kyung-Jin. *Urban Triage: Race and the Fictions of Multiculturalism*. Minneapolis: University of Minnesota Press, 2004.

Lee, Robert G. *Orientals: Asian Americans in Popular Culture*. Philadelphia: Temple University Press, 1999.

Lemann, Nicholas. *The Promised Land: The Great Black Migration and How It Changed America*. New York: Knopf, 1991.

Levin, Michael E. *Why Race Matters: Race Differences and What They Mean*. Westport, CT: Praeger, 1997.

Lieberman, Robert C. *Shifting the Color Line: Race and the American Welfare State*. Cambridge, MA: Harvard University Press, 1998.

Lott, Juanita Tamayo. *Asian Americans: From Racial Category to Multiple Identities*. Walnut Creek, CA: AltaMira Press, 1998.

Loury, Glenn C. *The Anatomy of Racial Inequality*. Cambridge, MA: Harvard University Press, 2002.

Lyman, Stanford M., ed. *The Asian in North America*. Santa Barbara, CA: ABC-Clio Books, 1977.

Lyons, Oren. *Exiled in the Land of the Free: Democracy, Indian Nations, and the U.S. Constitution*. Santa Fe, NM: Clear Light Publishers, 1992.

Malcomson, Scott L. *One Drop of Blood: The American Misadventure of Race*. New York: Farrar, Straus and Giroux, 2000.

Maly, Michael T. *Beyond Segregation: Multiracial and Multiethnic Neighborhoods in the United States*. Philadelphia: Temple University Press, 2005.

Massey, Douglas S., and Nancy A. Denton. *American Apartheid: Segregation and the Making of the Underclass*. Cambridge, MA: Harvard University Press, 1993.

Meyer, Stephen Grant. *As Long as They Don't Move Next Door: Segregation and Racial Conflict in American Neighborhoods*. Lanham, MD: Rowman & Littlefield, 2000.

Moran, Rachel F. *Interracial Intimacy: The Regulation of Race and Romance*. London: University of Chicago Press, 2001.

Morín, José Luis. *Latino/a Rights and Justice in the United States: Perspectives and Approaches*. Durham, NC: Carolina Academic Press, 2005.

Moses, Michele S. *Embracing Race: Why We Need Race-Conscious Education Policy*. New York: Teachers College Press, 2002.

Naff, Alixa. *Becoming American: The Early Arab Immigrant Experience*. Carbondale: Southern Illinois University Press, 1993.

Nash, Gary B. *Race and Revolution*. Madison, WI: Madison House, 1990.

———. *Race, Class, and Politics: Essays on American Colonial and Revolutionary Society*. Urbana: University of Illinois Press, 1986.

Nash, Gary B., and Richard Weiss, eds. *The Great Fear: Race in the Mind of America*. New York: Holt, Rinehart and Winston, 1970.

Norrell, Robert J. *The House I Live In: Race in the American Century*. New York: Oxford University Press, 2005.

O'Brien, Gail Williams. *The Color of Law: Race, Violence, and Justice in the Post–World War II South*. Chapel Hill: University of North Carolina Press, 1999.

Oswalt, Wendell H. *This Land Was Theirs: A Study of Native North Americans*. 8th ed. New York: Oxford University Press, 2005.

Palumbo-Liu, David. *Asian/American: Historical Crossings of a Racial Frontier*. Stanford, CA: Stanford University Press, 1999.

Parrillo, Vincent N. *Strangers to These Shores: Race and Ethnic Relations in the United States*. 5th ed. Boston: Allyn and Bacon, 1997.

Peacock, Anthony A., ed. *Affirmative Action and Representation:* Shaw v. Reno *and the Future of Voting Rights*. Durham, NC: Carolina Academic Press, 1997.

Post, Robert, and Michael Rogin, eds. *Race and Representation: Affirmative Action*. New York: Zone Books, 1998.

Prucha, Francis Paul, ed. *Documents of United States Indian Policy*. 3rd ed. Lincoln: University of Nebraska Press, 2000.

———. *The Great Father: The United States Government and the American Indians*. 2 vols. Lincoln: University of Nebraska Press, 1984.

Reed, Ishmael. *Another Day at the Front: Dispatches from the Race War*. New York: Basic Books, 2003.

Richardson, Theresa R., and Erwin V. Johanningmeir. *Race, Ethnicity, and Education: What Is Taught in School*. Greenwich, CT: Information Age Publishing, 2003.

Richter, Daniel K. *Facing East from Indian Country: A Native History of Early America*. Cambridge, MA: Harvard University Press, 2001.

Rodriguez, Clara E. *Changing Race: Latinos, the Census, and the History of Ethnicity in the United States*. New York: New York University Press, 2000.

Rodriguez, Richard. *Brown: The Last Discovery of America*. New York: Viking, 2002.

Root, Maria P. P., ed. *The Multiracial Experience: Racial Borders as the New Frontier*. Thousand Oaks, CA: Sage Publications, 1996.

Rosaldo, Renato. *Assimilation Revisited*. Stanford, CA: Stanford Center for Chicano Research, Stanford University, 1985.

Rosales, F. Arturo. *Chicano! The History of the Mexican-American Civil Rights Movement*. Houston: Arte Publico Press, 1996.

———, ed. *Testimonio: A Documentary History of the Mexican-American Struggle for Civil Rights*. Houston: Arte Publico Press, 2000.

Rose, Peter I., et al. *Through Different Eyes: Black and White Perspectives on American Race Relations*. New York: Oxford University Press, 1973.

Rothenberg, Paula S., ed. *White Privilege: Essential Readings on the Other Side of Racism*. 2nd ed. New York: Worth Publishers, 2005.

Rushton, J. Philippe. *Race, Evolution, and Behavior: A Life History Perspective*. New Brunswick, NJ: Transaction Publishers, 1995.

Said, Edward W. *Covering Islam: How the Media and the Experts Determine How We See the Rest of the World*. Rev. ed. New York: Vintage Books, 1997.

Saunders, Kay, and Roger Daniels, eds. *Alien Justice: Wartime Internment in Australia and North America*. St. Lucia: University of Queensland Press, 2000.

Schaefer, Richard T. *Racial and Ethnic Groups: Census 2000 Update*. 8th ed. Upper Saddle River, NJ: Prentice Hall, 2002.

Scheckel, Susan. *The Insistence of the Indian: Race and Nationalism in Nineteenth-Century American Culture*. Princeton, NJ: Princeton University Press, 1998.

Schrieke, B.J.O. *Alien Americans: A Study of Race Relations*. New York: Viking Press, 1936. Reprint, San Francisco: R and E Research Associates, 1971.

Schutte, Gerhard. *What Racists Believe: Race Relations in South Africa and the United States*. Thousand Oaks, CA: Sage Publications, 1995.

Scott-Childress, Reynolds J., ed. *Race and the Production of Modern American Nationalism*. New York: Garland Publishing, 1999.

Shaheen, Jack G. *Arab and Muslim Stereotyping in American Popular Culture*. Washington, DC: Center for Muslim-Christian Understanding: History and International Affairs, Edmund A. Walsh School of Foreign Service, Georgetown University, 1997.

———. *Reel Bad Arabs: How Hollywood Vilifies a People*. New York: Olive Branch Press, 2001.

Sheehan, Bernard W. *Seeds of Extinction: Jeffersonian Philanthropy and the American Indian*. Chapel Hill: University of North Carolina Press, 1973.

Shoemaker, Nancy. *A Strange Likeness: Becoming Red and White in Eighteenth-Century North America*. New York: Oxford University Press, 2004.

Shropshire, Kenneth L. *In Black and White: Race and Sports in America*. New York: New York University Press, 1996.

Smedley, Audrey. *Race in North America: Origin and Evolution of a World View*. 2nd ed. Boulder, CO: Westview Press, 1999.

Smelser, Neil J., William Julius Wilson, and Faith Mitchell, eds. *America Becoming: Racial Trends and Their Consequences*. Washington, DC: National Academy Press, 2001.

Smith, Jane I. *Islam in America*. New York: Columbia University Press, 2000.

Smith, John David, ed. *When Did Segregation Begin?* New York: Palgrave, 2002.

Smith, Robert Charles. *Racism in the Post–Civil Rights Era: Now You See It, Now You Don't*. Albany: State University of New York Press, 1995.

Sollors, Werner, ed. *Interracialism: Black-White Intermarriage in American History, Literature, and Law*. New York: Oxford University Press, 2000.

Spears, Arthur K. *Race and Ideology: Language, Symbolism, and Popular Culture*. Detroit: Wayne State University Press, 1999.

Spickard, Paul R. *Mixed Blood: Intermarriage and Ethnic Identity in Twentieth-Century America*. Madison: University of Wisconsin Press, 1989.

Spickard, Paul R., and G. Reginald Daniel, eds. *Racial Thinking in the United States: Uncompleted Independence*. Notre Dame, IN: University of Notre Dame Press, 2004.

Steinberg, Stephen. *The Ethnic Myth: Race, Ethnicity, and Class in America*. 3rd ed. Boston: Beacon Press, 2001.

Steiner, Stan. *The New Indians*. New York: Harper & Row, 1968.

Steinhorn, Leonard, and Barbara Diggs-Brown. *By the Color of Our Skin: The Illusion of Integration and the Reality of Race*. New York: Dutton, 1999.

Stokes, Curtis, Theresa Meléndez, and Genice Rhodes-Reed, eds. *Race in 21st Century America*. East Lansing: Michigan State University Press, 2001.

Suleiman, Michael W., ed. *Arabs in America: Building a New Future*. Philadelphia: Temple University Press, 2000.

Swain, Carol M., ed. *Race Versus Class: The New Affirmative Action Debate*. Lanham, MD: University Press of America, 1996.

Takaki, Ronald, ed. *Debating Diversity: Clashing Perspectives on Race and Ethnicity in America*. New York: Oxford University Press, 2002.

————, ed. *From Different Shores: Perspectives on Race and Ethnicity in America.* 2nd ed. New York: Oxford University Press, 1994.

————. *Iron Cages: Race and Culture in 19th-Century America.* New York: Knopf, 1979. Reprint, New York: Oxford University Press, 1990.

————. *Strangers from a Different Shore: A History of Asian Americans.* Updated and rev. ed. Boston: Little, Brown, 1998.

Tatum, Beverly Daniel. *"Why Are All the Black Kids Sitting Together in the Cafeteria?" and Other Conversations about Race.* New York: Basic Books, 1997.

Thernstrom, Abigail, and Stephan Thernstrom. *America in Black and White: One Nation, Indivisible.* New York: Simon & Schuster, 1997.

————, eds. *Beyond the Color Line: New Perspectives on Race and Ethnicity in America.* Stanford, CA: Hoover Institution Press, 2002.

Thomas, Gail E., ed. *U.S. Race Relations in the 1980s and 1990s: Challenges and Alternatives.* New York: Hemisphere Publishing Corporation, 1990.

Tischauser, Leslie Vincent. *The Changing Nature of Racial and Ethnic Conflict in United States History: 1492 to the Present.* Lanham, MD: University Press of America, 2002.

Torres, Rodolfo D., Louis F. Mirón, and Jonathan Xavier Inda, eds. *Race, Identity, and Citizenship: A Reader.* Malden, MA: Blackwell Publishers, 1999.

Trager, Oliver, ed. *America's Minorities and the Multicultural Debate.* New York: Facts on File, 1992.

Utley, Robert M. *The Indian Frontier, 1846–1890.* Rev. ed. Albuquerque: University of New Mexico Press, 2003.

Van Sant, John E. *Pacific Pioneers: Japanese Journeys to America and Hawaii, 1850–80.* Urbana: University of Illinois Press, 2000.

Vaughan, Alden T. *Roots of American Racism: Essays on the Colonial Experience.* New York: Oxford University Press, 1995.

Venables, Robert W. *American Indian History: Five Centuries of Conflict and Coexistence.* 2 vols. Santa Fe, NM: Clear Light Publishers, 2004.

Viola, Herman J. *Trail to Wounded Knee: The Last Stand of the Plains Indians, 1860–1890.* Washington, DC: National Geographic, 2003.

Walker, Samuel, Cassia Spohn, and Miriam DeLone. *The Color of Justice: Race, Ethnicity, and Crime in America.* Belmont, CA: Wadsworth Publishing Company, 1996.

Wallace, Anthony F. C. *Jefferson and the Indians: The Tragic Fate of the First Americans.* Cambridge, MA: Harvard University Press, 1999.

Wallenstein, Peter. *Tell the Court I Love My Wife: Race, Marriage, and Law—an American History.* New York: Palgrave Macmillan, 2002.

Webster, Yehudi O. *The Racialization of America.* New York: St. Martin's Press, 1992.

West, Cornel. *Race Matters.* Boston: Beacon Press, 1993.

Wijeyesinghe, Charmaine L., and Bailey W. Jackson, eds. *New Perspectives on Racial Identity Development: A Theoretical and Practical Anthology.* New York: New York University Press, 2001.

Wilkinson, Charles F. *American Indians, Time, and the Law: Native Societies in a Modern Constitutional Democracy.* New Haven, CT: Yale University Press, 1987.

Williams, Juan. *Eyes on the Prize: America's Civil Rights Years, 1954–1965.* New York: Viking, 1987.

Williams, Patricia J. *The Alchemy of Race and Rights.* Cambridge, MA: Harvard University Press, 1991.

Williams, Vernon J., Jr. *Rethinking Race: Franz Boaz and His Contemporaries.* Lexington: University Press of Kentucky, 1996.

Wilson, William Julius. *The Declining Significance of Race: Blacks and Changing American Institutions.* 2nd ed. Chicago: University of Chicago Press, 1980.

————. *The Truly Disadvantaged: The Inner City, the Underclass, and Public Policy*. Chicago: University of Chicago Press, 1987.

Winters, Loretta I., and Herman L. DeBose, eds. *New Faces in a Changing America: Multiracial Identity in the 21st Century*. Thousand Oaks, CA: Sage Publications, 2003.

Winters, Paul A., ed. *Race Relations: Opposing Viewpoints*. San Diego, CA: Greenhaven Press, 1996.

Wood, Forrest G. *The Arrogance of Faith: Christianity and Race in America from the Colonial Era to the Twentieth Century*. New York: Knopf, 1990. Reprint, Boston: Northeastern University Press, 1991.

Wormser, Richard. *The Rise and Fall of Jim Crow*. New York: St. Martin's Press, 2003.

Yancey, George A. *Who Is White? Latinos, Asians, and the New Black/Nonblack Divide*. Boulder, CO: Lynne Rienner, 2003.

Zack, Naomi, ed. *American Mixed Race: The Culture of Microdiversity*. Lanham, MD: Rowman & Littlefield, 1995.

Index

About the Author

THOMAS J. DAVIS, Ph.D., J.D., teaches history and law at Arizona State University, Tempe. He is the author of *A Rumor of Revolt: "Great Negro Plot" in Colonial New York,* which the Gustavus Myers Center for the Study of Bigotry and Human Rights in North America prized as one of the outstanding books of 1985 on race relations. He is also author of numerous articles on race and law and co-author of *Africans in the Americas: A History of the Black Diaspora.*